WOMEN
AND
MATHEMATICS:
Balancing the Equation

WOMEN AND MATHEMATICS:
Balancing the Equation

Edited by
Susan F. Chipman
National Institute of Education
Lorelei R. Brush
Aurora Associates
and
Donna M. Wilson
National Institute of Education

LEA LAWRENCE ERLBAUM ASSOCIATES, PUBLISHERS
1985   Hillsdale, New Jersey   London

The opinions expressed herein are those of the authors alone and do not necessarily express the official policy of the National Institute of Education, the U.S. Department of Education, or any other government agency.

Lawrence Erlbaum Associates, Inc., Publishers
365 Broadway
Hillsdale, New Jersey 07642

Library of Congress Cataloging in Publication Data
Main entry under title:
Women and mathematics.

Includes bibliographies and indexes.
1. Women in mathematics. I. Chipman, Susan F.
II. Brush, Lorelei R., 1946–   . III. Wilson, Donna M.
QA27.5.W66 1985   510′.88042   84-18861
ISBN 0-89859-369-7

Printed in the United States of America
10 9 8 7 6 5 4 3 2 1

Contents

v

Foreword

In the mid-seventies, there was growing concern that early decisions not to study mathematics in high school might be limiting the occupational options available to women. A few dramatic reports, including that of Sells (1973), fired that concern. As part of a larger program on career development, the Career Awareness Division of the Education and Work Group, then one of the major organizational units of the National Institute of Education (NIE), initiated a special research grants program on women and mathematics. Research information that would sort out the competing explanations for women's lower rate of participation seemed a useful contribution to debates about possible remedial actions. Should there be, for example, widespread development and implementation of programs designed to reduce mathematics anxiety?

As an initial step in the research program, three review articles were commissioned to explore existing research and opinions about the major influences affecting women's choices in the study of mathematics and in the selection of occupations requiring mathematical competence: (1) social influences (Fox, 1977); (2) cognitive, affective, and educational influences (Fenema, 1977); and (3) biological influences (Sherman, 1977). These papers were presented to a 2-day long national working conference that brought together, in February 1977, a wide variety of persons concerned with the mathematical education of women. Later, additional presentations were made at the annual meeting of the American Educational Research Association (New York, 1977). The papers were published by the National Institute of Education and widely distributed. (They remain available through the ERIC system.) These papers, together with the resulting discussions and comments, contributed to specifications for research grants that were intended to provide "a better knowledge base for designing effective educational programs to encourage women to enroll in mathematics beyond the minimal school requirements." An intellectual consensus was developed that informed the design of the research studies that are discussed in this volume. The concise statements of the grants announcement (NIE, 1977), summarizing opinion at the time, provide a useful context for the reader of these research reports. For example, the opening statement describing the research requested was, "Women's lower enrollment in the study of advanced mathematics precludes them from entering a variety of occupations requiring mathematical competence."

The credit for the management of the activities mentioned, including the award and initial management of the resulting grants, belongs to Dr. Judith Shoemaker and Dr. Robert Wise. Without their efforts, this volume would not have been possible.

This volume represents the culmination of a research program to which many persons have contributed. Most of the studies which were funded through the NIE grants competition are reported by chapters in this volume. These research reports are supplemented by two integrative chapters. In chapter 1, information about the demographic facts of the women and mathematics problem is assembled. Chapters 2 and 3 present studies of two nationally representative student samples separated by nearly 20 years. Wise's analyses take advantage of the longitudinal data provided by Project TALENT, while Armstrong's study provides more current data about many questions specifically relevant to the issue of women and mathematics. The next group of chapters explores the factors that may influence mathematics enrollment and achievement. In chapters 4 and 5, Eccles and Brush provide quite comprehensive analyses relating many variables to mathematics enrollment. In chapter 6, Connor and Serbin examine in detail the relation of spatial abilities to mathematics performance. Chapter 7 by Boswell gives special attention to the sex stereotyping of mathematics within the framework of a study that explores many variables. Stallings, in chapter 8, particularly emphasizes school and classroom variables that may influence enrollment decisions. The next two chapters present studies of more highly selected populations of students: students selected for special accelerated programs of mathematics instruction (Fox, Brody, & Tobin) and students in regular school programs leading to and including Advanced Placement calculus courses (Casserly & Rock). Following the reports of the research studies, chapter 11 summarizes what has been learned of the "whys" of the problem, discussing practical implications, and identifying research questions that remain open. Chapter 11 discusses other major studies (Fennema & Sherman, 1977, 1978; Lantz & Smith, 1981; Sherman, 1979, 1980) that were done at about the same time, in addition to the studies reported in this volume. The authors of the integrative chapters 1 and 11, Chipman, Thomas, and Wilson, were staff members of the Learning and Development Division of the Program on Teaching and Learning, the organizational unit of NIE responsible for research on mathematics learning. Finally, there is a chapter that was commissioned to help realize the practical purposes of the research program. In chapter 12, Alma Lantz, who has contributed to research on women and mathematics and has evaluated intervention programs for women, discusses what this and other research suggests about the design of effective interventions.

Against the expectations that formed this research on women and mathematics, some of the simple statistical results were surprising. Armstrong (chapter 3) and others, found nearly equal participation of boys and girls in the standard sequence of high school mathematics courses. Wise's report (chapter 2) indicates that the large gap between male and female high school mathematics enrollments that existed in 1960—what most adult researchers had observed in their school experience—had started to close by 1972. Today, it is quite small, although women continue to be underrepresented among those receiving advanced degrees in mathematics (see chapter 1). One may speculate that the concerns behind this research program were part of a broad pattern of social change that was reducing the problem to which the research was addressed even before the research began.

The research results also modified the key initial assumption in the research program, the assumption that failure to study advanced mathematics excludes women from mathematics related careers. Appropriate educational preparation is vital, but some results suggest that an orientation towards or away from such careers preceeds and partially determines the decision to study advanced mathematics. In addition, the number of women well-prepared in mathematics has exceeded the number actually entering mathematics related careers. The problem of women's underrepresentation in such careers is more complex than the question of mathematics participation or avoidance.

Nevertheless, the emphasis of this research upon understanding the determinants of mathematics enrollment is of more urgent interest today than it was when the studies were initiated. Today the chief concern is that too few students, whether male or female, are pursuing these directions of study, that our appropriately educated human resources will be inadequate to meet the demands of a technological future. The results of the research are applicable to males as well as to females because the sex-specific influences upon enrollment such as the stereotyping of mathematics as a masculine subject or the availability of female role models proved to be rather unimportant, and because male students were included in the research samples. The results showing that women and girls are well-represented among those with mathematical knowledge required for post-secondary technical education and technical employment should help draw attention to the important resource represented by the abilities of our nation's majority group. Today many are concerned that efforts to encourage the participation of women in mathematics continue in order to sustain and improve upon the gains achieved. It is still uncertain whether the progress in high school enrollments will be followed by similar progress in more advanced education and careers.

In addition to its direct purpose, there are a number of other ways in which this volume may be of interest to readers. It provides the subject matter for a case study in social research. How did this research come about? How did attention come to focus upon secondary school preparation in mathematics, rather than upon the development of interests in mathematics related occupations, for example? How did it happen that some available data were not used in a preliminary study of the true national dimensions of the women and mathematics problem, even though considerable effort did go into preparation for the special research program? Perhaps everyone "knew" that it was a serious problem. One also could ask how the focus came to be so far-sighted. Mathematics and science education are of far greater national concern now than in 1973–1974, when the idea for the research program developed. Choices of research priorities to be both timely and timeless are not always so fortunate: What worked in this instance? There are probably lessons here for those who propose, plan, and manage social research.

These studies could provide the material for a graduate seminar in research methodology. It is unusual to be able to see so many researchers approaching the same problem at the same time in different ways. The complexity of this real social question clearly challenged the limits of available methodological resources. For those struggling to understand what multiple regression or path analysis can or cannot do, for example, these studies provide meaty examples.

Of course, this research was intended to provide mathematics supervisors, teachers, and others concerned with the education of young people with insights they can use to help students make more effective use of their school years in preparing for productive and successful working lives. For these readers, this volume provides an overview of the facts of women's participation in mathematics, a summary of research results concerning the factors that influence student participation in mathematics, and informed advice about strategies educators might use to improve mathematics participation. In the chapters reporting individual research studies, readers can explore particular aspects of the issue more deeply.

Lois-ellin Datta, Ph.D.
Associate Director for Teaching and Learning 1978–82
Assistant Director for Education and Work 1972–77
National Institute of Education

WOMEN
AND
MATHEMATICS:
Balancing the Equation

1 Women's Participation in Mathematics: Outlining the Problem

Susan F. Chipman
Veronica G. Thomas
National Institute of Education

Introduction

In recent years, there has been great public concern about women's capability and education in mathematics. Reading the newspapers and magazines, one might conclude that most women are paralyzed with mathematics anxiety. Often it is suggested that a major reason women are represented poorly in highly paid professional occupations is that they lack prerequisite mathematical knowledge. Therefore, it may come as a surprise to learn that in a recent 5 year period for which the data are available (1971–1976), women received 38% to 42% of all the bachelor's degrees in mathematics that were awarded, whereas they received only about 44% of all BA's. Throughout the 1950 to 1976 period, the average is clearly over 30% (United States Office of Education, 1976). In fact, mathematics is one of the least sex-typed college majors (see Fig. 1.1). If there were indeed serious psychological barriers preventing women from studying mathematics, it seems that we ought to see the effects of these barriers on the study of mathematics itself. We do not.

Of course, relatively few students of either sex major in mathematics. In 1964–65, 3.9% of BA's were awarded in mathematics and statistics, whereas by 1975–76 only 1.7% were in mathematics and statistics (National Science Foundation, 1980). Therefore, despite the relatively equitable representation of women in mathematics itself, there could be

The opinions expressed herein are those of the authors alone and do not necessarily express the official policy or position of the National Institute of Education or of any other government agency. Dr. Susan F. Chipman is now affiliated with the Personnel and Training Research Group, Psychological Sciences Division, United States Office of Naval Research in Arlington, Virginia. Dr. Veronica G. Thomas is now affiliated with the Institute for Urban Affairs and Research of Howard University in Washington, D.C.

1

substantial sex differences in knowledge of mathematics as it applies in other fields. It could be, though, that the concern about women and mathematics has been an expression of social stereotypes, representing a misidentification of the major barriers to the fulfillment of women's occupational and social aspirations. In this chapter, we examine data about women's participation in the study of mathematics and about women's achievement in mathematics in order to arrive at a better understanding of the problem to which the research reported in this volume was addressed.

THE HIGH SCHOOL YEARS

High School Participation in Mathematics Courses

At the time of the grants competition that resulted in the studies reported here, it was believed that women's low rate of enrollment in elective mathematics courses in high school precluded their entering a variety of college majors and occupations requiring mathematical competence. Lucy Sells (1973) had reported, based on a random sample of freshmen entering Berkeley in 1972, that 57% of the males had taken 4 years of high school mathematics, whereas 8% of the females had done so. In the paper she prepared for the National Institute of Education (NIE), Fennema (1977) reported course enrollment data obtained from the Wisconsin Department of Public Instruction for 1975–76. These data showed compara-

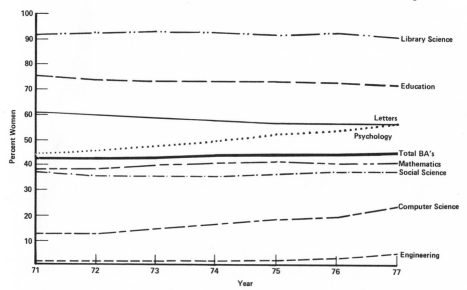

FIG. 1.1   Representation of women in selected college majors.

ble enrollments of males and females in algebra (about 41,000) and geometry (about 20,000) but substantial sex differences in advanced courses such as trigonometry (4,000 vs. 2,737), analytic geometry (1,752 vs. 970), precalculus (3,234 vs. 1,917) and calculus (611 vs. 262). Perhaps the most striking thing in these data is that so few students of either sex were continuing to study mathematics at the advanced level.

Samples drawn from particular schools and particular geographic locations at particular times may be influenced by idiosyncratic factors that are not representative of the situation nationwide. We have been able to locate several broadly representative samples that provide information about enrollment in high school courses in mathematics.

The 1979 report of the College Entrance Examination Board (ETS, 1979) states that 64% of males and 45% of females taking the Scholastic Aptitude Test (SAT) expected to have completed 4 or more years of mathematics. The mean number of years of mathematics was 3.62 for males and 3.27 for females. Over 900,000 individuals were included in this group although they are not, of course, a random sample of all students. Table 1.1 gives these data for 1973 through 1981. Note that twice as many males as females report *5 or more years* of mathematics study.

Another current report, Armstrong's 1978 National Assessment of Educational Progress (NAEP) women and mathematics survey (reported in this volume) of 1700 twelfth grade students indicated few sex differences in enrollment in lower level math courses. Females took more business and accounting math; males took more algebra II and probability/statistics. Nine other math courses showed no sex differences. Slightly more males had taken trigonometry (31% vs. 27%), pre-calculus (21% vs. 18%), and calculus (8% vs. 7%). Thirty-one percent of the males and 27% of the females had taken a variant of the typical 4 year mathematics sequence (usually algebra I, geometry, algebra II, and a fourth year that may include trigonometry, solid geometry, pre-calculus, etc.). In each type of high school program, this sample of twelfth graders indicated small sex differences in the percentages of students taking some version of the standard 4-year sequence (see Table 1.2).

In the 1977–78 NAEP math assessment of 17-year-olds, where there was a larger sample (24,000), sex differences in enrollment in advanced mathematics courses were found to be statistically significant. Although the percentages of both males and females who had taken advanced math courses were very small, 55% of those who had taken trigonometry were male as were 60% of those who had taken precalculus and about 60% of those who had taken calculus. Because most of the students in this NAEP sample were eleventh graders, this sample is not strictly comparable to Armstrong's special sample of twelfth graders. These figures could reflect sex differences in acceleration as well as in ultimate course participation.

TABLE 1.1
Number of Years of Study of Mathematics by SAT Applicants

Male

Year	'73 %	'74 %	'75 %	'76 %	'77 %	'78 %	'79 %	'80 %	'81 %
No Courses	0	0	0	0	0	0	0	0	0
One Year	2	1	2	2	2	2	2	2	2
Two Years	10	11	10	10	10	10	9	9	8
Three Years	28	29	28	27	26	25	24	23	23
Four Years	51	50	50	51	50	51	53	53	54
Five or more Years	9	9	9	10	11	12	12	13	13
Number Responding	387,692	403,094	402,850	383,441	397,998	433,079	439,862		
Mean Number of Years	3.54	3.53	3.55	3.57	3.57	3.60	3.62	3.65	3.68

Female

Year	'73 %	'74 %	'75 %	'76 %	'77 %	'78 %	'79 %	'80 %	'81 %
No Courses	0	0	0	0	0	0	1	0	0
One Year	3	3	3	3	3	3	3	3	2
Two Years	20	21	20	20	19	18	17	16	15
Three Years	40	40	39	37	36	35	34	33	32
Four Years	33	33	34	35	35	37	39	41	43
Five or more Years	4	4	4	5	5	6	6	7	8
Number Responding	402,988	427,454	428,264	415,116	436,145	477,981	490,020		
Mean Number of Years	3.14	3.13	3.15	3.17	3.19	3.22	3.27	3.32	3.38

Total

Year	'73 %	'74 %	'75 %	'76 %	'77 %	'78 %	'79 %	'80 %	'81 %
No Courses	0	0	0	0	0	0	0		
One Year	3	2	3	3	3	3	2		
Two Years	15	16	15	16	15	14	13		
Three Years	34	35	34	32	31	30	29		
Four Years	42	41	42	43	42	44	45		
Five or more Years	6	6	6	7	8	9	9		
Number Responding	790,680	830,548	831,114	798,557	834,142	911,060	929,882		
Mean Number of Years	3.34	3.32	3.34	3.36	3.37	3.40	3.44	3.47	3.52

Source: ETS National College-Board. Seniors (1973-1981)

5

TABLE 1.2
Students Taking Four or More Years of Mathematics:
Armstrong Study

	Total Group	College Prep.	Voc. Tech.	General
Males (N = 840)	31.3%	61.4%	4.7%	8.7%
Female (N = 936)	27.1%	55.8%	4.1%	6.6%

Source: Armstrong's Women and Mathematics Study (Unpublished Data).

Results of the National Civil Rights survey taken in 1976 (National Center for Education Statistics, 1979) are entirely consistent with the NAEP findings of little sex difference: In the highest level math courses available at each school, 48.9% were female as were 48.3% of the students enrolled in the most advanced available science courses. Many schools, of course, do not offer the most advanced mathematics courses in which some sex differences in enrollment do seem to be found. A still more recent survey of high school seniors in 1980 (National Center for Education Statistics, 1980) agrees with our other data sources in indicating that enrollment in advanced mathematics (trigonometry, calculus, 3 or more years cumulative enrollment) is about 60% male and 40% female.

In summary, current data on high school math course participation indicate that there continue to be substantial sex differences in math course participation but that the problem is not as severe as many people believe—

—about 40% of those who approach college with the standard level of mathematics preparation are women.

—about 40% of women entering college are well-prepared in mathematics, having taken the standard 4 years of high school mathematics.

Trends Over Time. There is considerable interest in knowing whether this represents a recent change. In the National Longitudinal Sample of persons who were twelfth graders in 1972, about 39% of the males and 22% of the females had taken 4 years of high school mathematics (Wise, personal communication).[1] In the 1960 Project TALENT sample, however, 9% of the girls and 33% of the boys were taking 4 years of high school mathematics. The distributions of levels of mathematics participation for boys and girls are shown in Fig. 1.2 (Wise, Steel, & MacDonald, 1979). The Educational Testing Service (ETS) data shown in Table 1.1

---

[1]The enrollment figures appearing in the original Wise final report on NIE-G-78-0001 are incorrect because students were asked how many semesters of mathematics they had taken in grades 10, 11, and 12 only.

also indicate a small increase in the math course participation of females over the 1973–79 period. It appears that a more significant change occurred between 1960 and 1972.

The sex differences found in the 1960 Project TALENT Sample are as extreme as the reports that caused so much concern about women's preparation in mathematics. However, an examination of the distribution shows that, even then, the difference is accentuated by looking only at the category of 4 or more years of study. Quite a few women had studied enough mathematics to provide a foundation for further work in college. Additional information from the Project TALENT sample does not support the view that poor mathematics preparation was functioning as a barrier to college major and career selection in 1960. Although only 9% of the girls had studied 4 years of high school mathematics, only 3% intended to enter math-related careers. Analyses of long term follow-up data from Project TALENT showed that only 20% of the males and 10% of the females who had originally planned to enter math-related careers actually were in such careers at age 29. Virtually no one who was not already planning a math-related career by twelfth grade later switched into a math-related career by 29 (Wise, Steel, & MacDonald, 1979). Thus, the early decision to enter a math-related career appears to be a critical and necessary, but very much not sufficient, step toward actual entry into

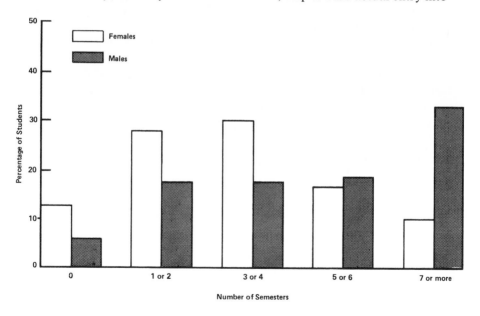

FIG. 1.2   Total semesters of high school math taken by 12th graders in the 1960 Project TALENT sample.

a math-related career. That decision may well contribute to participation in high school mathematics courses more than participation determines the career decision.

Mathematics Achievement in the High School Years

Sex differences in mathematics achievement frequently have been reported for students beyond the elementary school years (Maccoby & Jacklin, 1974). Earlier in the school years, such sex differences are not usually found. In Armstrong's 1978 Women and Mathematics National Survey, (Armstrong, 1979; this volume) 13-year-old females performed significantly better than males on a test of mathematical computation and performed equally as well as males on tests of problem-solving and algebra as well as overall mathematics achievement. Interestingly, females also performed significantly better than males on the test of spatial visualization at age 13. In the larger NAEP Second Mathematics Assessment (1977–78) also reported by Armstrong (1979; this volume), 13-year-old females performed better on computation items (53.4% vs. 49.9% correct) and males performed slightly better on problem-solving items (44.1% vs. 42.5% correct). The difference in algebra performance favored females (53% vs. 51%) but was not statistically significant. The Wise, Steel, and MacDonald (1979) analysis of the 1960 Project TALENT sample showed a very slight advantage for males among the ninth graders, statistically significant but less than .07 standard deviation. Practically speaking, this was no sex difference in mathematics achievement. A recent study (Dougherty, Herbert, Edenhurt-Pape, & Small, 1980) suggests that more refined and diverse measures of different aspects of mathematical performance might detect consistent sex differences in the elementary school years that are not evident in generalized measures of mathematics achievement. In a large curriculum evaluation study with a diverse student population, these investigators found evidence of such patterns: girls performing better than boys on measures of computation, boys performing better on other test scales such as estimation and a special set of word problems with low computational demands. The California Assessment Program has also reported a somewhat similar group of sex differences (Pandey, 1980; Marshall, 1982, 1983). However, Dougherty et al. (1980) who provided a good review of other work on the question, argue that there is no reason to regard some of these aspects of mathematical performance as "higher" or "lower" or more truly mathematical than others.

The exceptions to reports of equality of male and female mathematics achievement at the beginning of high school are the reports from the Johns Hopkins mathematical talent search (Astin, 1974b; Benbow & Stanley, 1980; Fox 1975b) that there are significant sex differences in the

SAT math scores obtained by gifted students as early as seventh grade. The procedures of the Hopkins talent search do not ensure representative samples. It is also true that because this group is a tiny minority of all students, such differences would not necessarily be evident in reports of the average performance of the total populations of males and females.

During the high school years, significant sex differences in mathematics achievement do seem to develop. In the 1978 Women and Mathematics study (Armstrong, 1979), twelfth grade males performed significantly better than females on problem-solving items (72% vs. 65% correct) but not on other aspects of mathematics achievement or spatial visualization. For 17-year-olds in the NAEP Second Mathematics Assessment (1977–78) (Armstrong, 1979), there were no significant sex differences in computation or algebra but there was again an advantage for males on problem-solving items (46% vs. 41% correct).

In the Wise, Steel, and MacDonald (1979) analysis of the 1960 Project TALENT sample, sex differences in average math achievement increased most sharply after the tenth grade, when mathematics courses usually become elective. Among the twelfth graders, the difference was about .6 standard deviation. Nearly the same result was found for the ninth grade students who were retested as twelfth graders in 1963 as for twelfth graders in 1960.

The ETS (1979) report on students taking the SAT examinations indicates that the average scores for males have typically been 40 to 50 points higher than the average scores for females. Again, this is about one-half of a standard deviation. ETS also reports that the difference is greater for students in the top tenth of their high school class: 67 points. Similarly, the number of males who receive very high scores on the SAT math is much larger than the number of females who do so (see Table 1.3 and Fig. 1.3). Despite its label as a test of aptitude, the SAT should not be regarded as a test of ability but more as a test of knowledge and skill that has less advanced particular mathematical content than the Level I and Level II examinations, which also differ from each other along the same dimension. Note that the numbers in these tables suggest that the same individuals probably account for the high scores in both the SAT and achievement groups, despite the huge differences in numbers of people participating in these examinations.

ETS data on mathematics achievement tests provide further evidence of sex differences in mathematics achievement, especially at the highest levels of achievement. In 1979, 74,219 males took the Mathematics Level I examination and 23,787 took the Mathematics Level II, whereas 71,353 females took Level I and only 10,726 took Level II. Thus, substantially fewer females chose the more advanced examination. Furthermore, there are large differences in the numbers of males and females who obtained high scores on these tests of mathematics achievement (Table 1.3). The

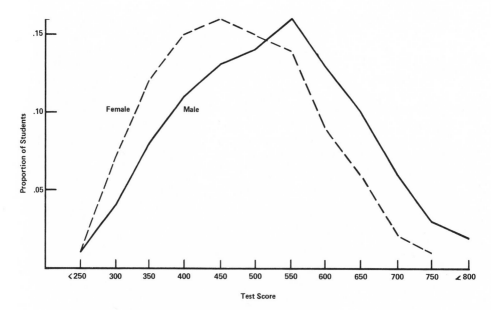

FIG. 1.3a   SAT math, 1979.

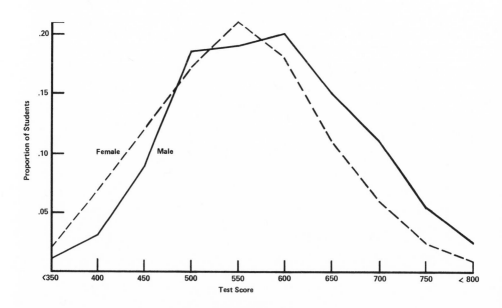

FIG. 1.3b   Mathematics level I, 1979.

10

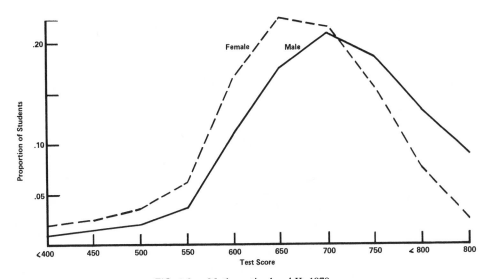

FIG. 1.3c   Mathematics level II, 1979.

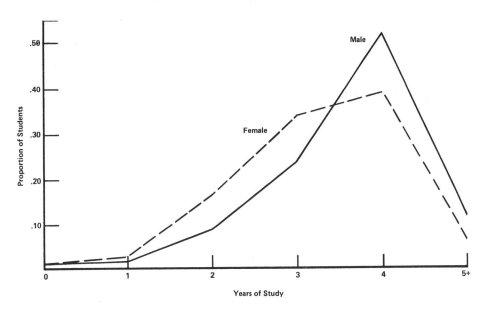

FIG. 1.3d   Years of math studied by 1979 SAT students.

11

TABLE 1.3
1979 Mathematics SAT and Achievement Test Performance

SAT		
Score	Males	Females
750 - 800	7,776	1,283
700 - 749	16,537	4,943
Total Participating:	479,099	512,306
Mathematics Level I		
Score	Males	Females
750 - 800	1,367	337
700 - 749	3,371	1,272
Total Participating:	74,219	71,353
Mathematics Level II		
Score	Males	Females
750 - 800	4,729	845
700 - 749	4,286	1,483
Total Participating:	23,787	10,726

figures in Table 1.3 provide a reasonable index of the relative number of males and females who are entering college with truly high levels of mathematical knowledge and skills. These individuals possess the degree of mathematical facility that eases the transition into the advanced study of scientific and technical subjects. This point is illustrated by Wise, Steel, and MacDonald's report (1979) that students selecting math-related careers averaged 80th percentile math achievement in twelfth grade, whereas those who were still in math-related careers at age 29 averaged 90th percentile mathematics achievement in twelfth grade. Undoubtedly, a more demanding career criterion (e.g., Ph.D. physicists) would reveal the importance of still more extreme levels of high school mathematics achievement. Clearly, male students are heavily over-represented in the group of students with extremely high mathematics achievement. Of course, it is quite possible that this degree of achievement already represents a degree of commitment to and investment in the preparation for such careers. In part, these sex differences in attainment very probably reflect the large sex differences in numbers of students reporting 5 or more years of mathematics study. At some point, the study of mathematics ceases to be generalized preparation for life and later education and becomes specific training for particular careers.

The most extreme available criterion of high school age mathematics achievement reveals still larger sex differences (Mientka, personal communication). Each year a group of mathematics professional organizations sponsors the High School Mathematics Contest. For the most part, information about the sex of students participating in this contest is not available. Of the 412,000 students competing in 1979–80, 254 were recognized on an honor roll for outstanding performance. Of these 254, 17 (less than 7%) have girls' first names and an additional 25 (10%) have names that Mientka cannot classify by sex (mostly because of Asian names). In the last 9 years, the top 120 scorers in this contest participated in the USA Mathematical Olympiad to select eight-member teams for the International Mathematical Olympiad. A total of 55 students have been on the eight member Olympic team (some more than once). All 55 students have been boys. In the 31 years of the Annual High School Mathematics Contest, 20 perfect examination papers have been written, only one of them by a girl. Participation in such contests is determined both by self-selection and by selective recruitment as well as by the factor of the school's participation in the contest. Therefore, such contests are not unbiased indicators of achievement. It is evident, nevertheless, that the mathematical elite of high school age remains a masculine domain—for whatever reason. This is consistent with Benbow and Stanley's report (1980) that extreme levels of mathematical performance are very rare among girls in seventh and eighth grades.

Returning to the issue of more typical student performance, another indicator of achievement in high school mathematics is the grades students receive in mathematics courses. Reported high school grades in mathematics (ETS, 1979) are nearly the same for males and females, 2.85 and 2.84, but across all subjects females generally report higher grades than males (3.13 vs. 3.01 overall). Grades in mathematics are substantially lower than grades in other subjects for both males and females. Because grades are an indicator of achievement in the courses actually taken, the equality of male and female grades is not inconsistent with differences on achievement test scores if there are differences in course enrollments. We now turn to a discussion of the relationship between course taking and achievement scores.

The Relation Between Mathematics Study and Mathematics Achievement

Fennema and Sherman (1977a) suggested that sex differences on measures of mathematics aptitude and achievement may result from differences in the number of math courses that males and females take. We have seen that there are some differences in math course enrollment, less dramatic than sometimes claimed but particularly evident for advanced mathematics courses. The question of the relationship between measured mathematics achievement and mathematics courses taken was addressed specifically by some of the studies reported here.

In their analysis of the 1960 Project TALENT data, Wise, Steel and

MacDonald (1979) found that virtually all of the sex difference in twelfth grade mathematics achievement could be accounted for by differences in the number of mathematics courses taken (see Fig. 2.3). However, they also found that females who studied advanced mathematics were a more select group than males who did so. That is, they had slightly higher mathematics achievement in grade nine. Further analysis showed that females with equal math participation and equal ninth grade achievement scores had twelfth grade math achievement scores one-tenth of a standard deviation lower than males. This difference was statistically significant, but it is extremely small. Only about one quarter (.29%) of 1% of the variation in twelfth grade math achievement remained to be explained by the unidentified variables that are associated with the sex of the student.

Armstrong (1979) also examined the relation between achievement and math course participation. In her study of twelfth graders sampled in 1978, students were classified according to the highest level mathematics course taken. For students who had taken calculus or precalculus, there were no sex differences in mathematics achievement. Among students who had taken Algebra II as their most advanced course, males scored significantly higher in overall math achievement and problem-solving. Problem-solving scores showed an advantage for males in several other groups with lower levels of math course participation. In the second NAEP assessment, males performed better in problem-solving at all levels of math course participation, but students of precalculus and calculus were not considered separately in this somewhat younger (age 17 rather than twelfth grade) sample. It appears from these data, therefore, that there are some small sex differences in mathematics achievement that are not accounted for by math course participation.

Comparable analyses of the ETS data are not available. The graphed distributions of reported years of study of mathematics for males and females (Fig. 1.3) show the same general relationship of the distributions as do the measures of mathematics achievement. Therefore, it appears that much, if not necessarily all, of the sex difference in achievement shown on ETS examinations would be accounted for by the sex difference in math course participation.

THE COLLEGE YEARS

Representation of Women in Mathematics-Related Majors

We have already noted the fact that women are relatively well represented among college mathematics majors. Table 1.4 illustrates that this has been so for many years. This fact seems to present a serious challenge to the notion that mathematics is a problematic subject for women. How-

TABLE 1.4
Bachelor's Degrees in Mathematics and all Fields
Awarded to Women, 1949-1977

| Year | BA in Mathematics[1] | | Total BA Degrees | |
	No. Women	%Women	No. Women	%Women
1949-1950	1,440	22.6%	103,915	24.0%
1951-1952	1,322	28.4%	104,895	31.6%
1953-1954	1,361	33.4%	105,380	35.9%
1955-1956	1,518	32.7%	111,727	32.8%
1957-1958	1,962	28.4%	112,800	30.8%
1959-1960	3,106	27.2%	139,385	35.3%
1961-1962	4,239	29.1%	154,377	40.3%
1963-1964	5,968	32.0%	197,346	42.9%
1965-1966	6,651	33.3%	221,052	42.5%
1967-1968	8,731	37.1%	274,653	43.5%
1969-1970	10,265	37.4%	341,276	43.1%
1970-1971	9,432	38.0%	304,136	43.4%
1971-1972	9,259	39.0%	386,683	43.6%
1972-1973	9,271	40.2%	404,171	43.8%
1973-1974	8,844	40.9%	418,463	44.2%
1974-1975	7,595	41.8%	418,092	45.3%
1975-1976	6,509	40.7%	420,821	45.5%
1976-1977	5,893	41.5%	424,044	46.1%

[1] Includes degrees conferred in Statistics.
Source: NCES, Series of Earned Degrees Conferred

ever, much of the concern about women and mathematics has focused on the notion that failure to study mathematics in high school restricts women from entering many college majors that require mathematics. In Table 1.5, we have rearranged the data on earned degrees for 1975–76 in relation to the math-relatedness of the college major. This classification is modeled on the one made by Wise, Steel and MacDonald (1979) and distinguishes three groups of subjects: those requiring substantial mathematical knowledge at the college level (physical sciences); those which may require a good high school training and statistics or similar quantitative skills at the college level (psychology or business); and those which clearly have no significant relation to mathematics. It appears to us that factors other than the math-relatedness of the major are important determinants of the sex ratio. In particular, we suggest that majors with direct vocational implications tend to reflect the sex-segregation of those occupations, whereas liberal arts subjects show a more balanced representation of the sexes. We also suggest that mathematics itself may be a liberal arts major that is selected primarily because of liking for the subject and that this helps explain why women are well represented in mathematics, in contrast to their low representation in most math-related majors.

TABLE 1.5
Participation of Women in Math-Related
College Majors (1975-76)

Subjects	% Women	Total Degrees
Mathematics	40.7%	16,085
Engineering	3.2%	46,717
Computer Science	19.8%	5,664
Physical Sciences	19.2%	21,559
Architecture	19.0%	9,169
Biological Sciences	34.8%	54,913
Agriculture	18.0%	19,460
Business & Management	19.8%	145,035
Education	72.8%	156,528
Health Professions	78.8%	54,339
Psychology	54.4%	50,363
Social Sciences	37.9%	127,936
Home Economics	95.9%	17,523
Area Studies	55.0%	3,111
Communications	41.5%	21,282
Fine & Applied Arts	60.9%	42,371
Foreign Languages	76.4%	15,587
Letters	56.9%	52,292
Public Affairs	43.7%	33,592
Theology	27.3%	5,537
Interdisciplinary Studies	45.0%	32,800
Law	18.8%	531
Library Science	93.1%	843
Military Science	.2%	1,206
All Degrees	45.6%	934,443

Source: NCES, Series of Earned Degrees Conferred.

The Relation Between Mathematics Preparation and College Major

Even though it is no simple matter to determine the direction of causality, there is considerable interest in the relationship between the college major and mathematics preparation in high school. Dunteman, Wisenbaker, and Taylor (1979) performed a secondary analysis of the 1972 National Longitudinal Sample and reported some relevant information. Females selecting mathematics and science majors had about the same level of mathematics preparation and achievement as did males (see Table 1.6). Wise, Steel and MacDonald (1979) reported that women in the 1960 Project TALENT sample who selected math-related college majors had higher levels of mathematics achievement than did males.

The Dunteman et al. (1979) study attempted to model the selection of a

TABLE 1.6

Mathematics Preparation by College Major, National Longitudinal Study

| | Mathematics | | Physical Science | | Life Sciences | | Social Sciences | |
	Females (N=35)	Males (N=38)	Females (N=34)	Males (N=124)	Females (N=179)	Males (N=274)	Females (N=284)	Males (N=278)
Achievement Score	63.98 ± 3.00	62.80 ± 5.92	60.74 ± 6.41	61.85 ± 6.34	58.67 ± 6.70	60.11 ± 6.06	55.41 ± 8.24	58.12 ± 7.47
Math Courses Taken*	5.98 ± .34	6.28 ± 1.39	5.99 ± 1.29	5.81 ± 1.23	5.02 ± 1.65	5.54 ± 1.72	4.24 ± 1.72	4.91 ± 1.80

*Students were asked how many semesters of math they had taken since a date corresponding to the end of 9th grade for most of them. Therefore, to convert to usual "years of math studied," divide by 2 and add 1.

Source: Table IV.8, Dunteman, Wisenbaker, and Taylor (1979).

17

science major. Consequently, they reported some analyses of interest. Their predictive model incorporated four major variables upon which females obtained lower average scores: (1) orientation toward things (⅔ s.d. lower) vs. orientation towards people; (2) reported mother's educational aspirations for child (³⁄₁₀ s.d. lower); (3) mathematics score (¼ s.d. lower); and (4) number of science courses (considerably lower). Even after these variables having a negative effect for females were taken into account, an unexplained direct negative effect of being female upon selection of college science remained, and it was about twice as important as the math score. In short, it seems unlikely that the underrepresentation of women in science fields can be attributed solely to lack of mathematics preparation in high school. According to Dunteman et al. black females were as likely as white females to select a major in the mathematical, physical, or biological sciences and were more likely to select a major in the social sciences.

Retention of Women in Math-Related Fields

It is sometimes suggested that women are more likely than men to drop out of mathematics-related fields of study. This may be selective perception of the fact that relatively few students of either sex carry out their initial aspiration for a science degree. Dunteman et al. (1979) also reported information concerning attrition. After 4 years, more female (28.7%) than male (15%) would-be math majors had actually completed a degree in the field. Females were somewhat less likely than males (13.5% vs. 17.8%) to have completed a physical science degree, but this was compensated for their greater propensity to shift into mathematics (8.1% vs. 1.3%). The number of female engineering majors (10) was too small to be meaningful, but they were, if anything, less likely to drop out. Black females' record of degree completion was about as good as white females in contrast to the record of black males. Again, we have an indication that mathematics itself is relatively more attractive to, or welcoming of, women than are the mathematics-related fields.

Levels of Mathematical Literacy in Other Fields

Tobias (1978) has suggested that women who are in fields that are not ordinarily considered to be math-related may be disadvantaged when confronting new developments or advanced work that does require mathematical knowledge. At present, we do not seem to have much information about the degree of mathematical knowledge or the amount of math course participation by students who are not in mathematical, scientific, or technical fields. Nor do we know how important mathematical knowledge is for people in those fields or for general citizenship. We do know, of course, that the average level of mathematical knowledge possessed by women is lower than the average level possessed by men. Data from Dunteman et al. (1979)—see Table 1.6—indicate that women in the life sciences and social sciences were somewhat less well prepared in mathematics than men in those fields. Additional data from this study indicated very little difference in the mathematics preparation of male and female humanities and arts majors, but a difference of one semester between male and female business majors. Oddly, female computer science majors had one semester more mathematics preparation, whereas female engineering majors had one full year less. Because of the small samples, these last may be chance results.

A recent dissertation (Pines, 1980) that examined math course enrollments of Hofstra University students suggests that sex differences in college math course participation are concentrated among students with the highest SAT math scores, scores over 680. Males with high SAT math scores but 3 or fewer years of high school math took more math courses in college than any other group of students (illustrating the fact that the failure to take 4 years of mathematics in high school does not preclude further participation in mathematics and math-related fields), whereas the comparable group of females took fewer math courses than any other group. Among students who had taken more than 3 years of math in high school and had SAT math scores over 680, there was also a substantial, but much less extreme, sex difference in math course participation. Presumably these differences in math course participation were related to the choice of college major, but these data were not presented by Pines. Nevertheless, this study provides further evidence that the level of mathematical knowledge at college entrance may not be the major factor causing sex differences in college course of study.

GRADUATE STUDY OF MATHEMATICS

Data concerning the participation of women in graduate education in mathematics must be interpreted against the background of information about women's participation in graduate and professional education in general. As Fig. 1.4 illustrates, there is a very severe drop-off in women's participation in education at these advanced levels, a situation that is improving only gradually. This education ceiling is also evident for women, as compared to men, within various ethnic minority groups. Even when this general effect is taken into account, however, it is evident

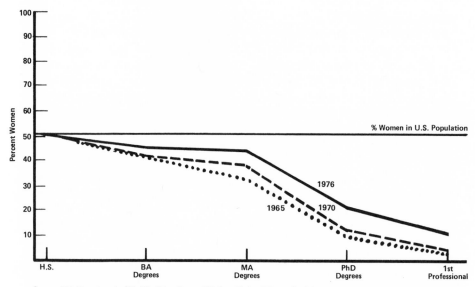

Source: U.S. Department of Health, Education and Welfare, National Center for Education Statistics, *The Condition of Education,* 1978 and *Digest of Education Statistics* 1977-1978, 1978.

FIG. 1.4   Percent degrees awarded to women by degree, 1965, 1970, 1976.

that women are progressively less well represented at more advanced levels of mathematics study. Thus, women received 43.9%, 44.4%, 45.4%, and 45.6% of all bachelor's degrees awarded in 1973, 1974, 1975, and 1976 while receiving 40.2%, 41.0%, 42.0%, and 40.7% of bachelor's degrees in mathematics in those years. Thus, women's share of bachelor's degrees in mathematics has been about .92 as large as their share of bachelor's degrees. In 1973, 1974, 1975, and 1976, women received 41.4%, 43.1%, 44.8%, and 46.4%, respectively, of all master's degrees awarded but only 29.9%, 31.0%, 32.9%, and 34.0% of master's degrees in mathematics. That is, women's share of master's degrees in mathematics was about .73 as large as their share of all master's degrees. For the years 1976, 1977, 1978, and 1979, women received 11.3%, 13.3%, 14.3%, and 15.4% of the doctorates awarded in mathematics as contrasted to 23.3%, 24.8%, 26.9%, and 28.6% of all doctoral degrees awarded in those years (National Research Council, 1979). That is, women's share of doctoral degrees in mathematics is only about .53 times as large as their share of all doctoral degrees. Therefore, there does seem to be some specific problem relating to women's transition to graduate study in mathematics.

Other sources of information suggest the same conclusion. Despite their good record of bachelor's degree completion, only 6.8% of female mathematics majors in the 1972 National Longitudinal Study were in graduate study in mathematics in 1976, whereas 87.3% were not in school in 1976. In contrast 49.1% of male mathematics majors were in graduate study of mathematics and only 23.6% were not in school. Interestingly, the record of female math majors also contrasts unfavorably with the 33.7% of female physical science majors who were in graduate school in physical science, plus 3.7% in graduate school in mathematics, and 52.4% not in school. Their record was closely comparable to male physical science majors: 39% in graduate school in physical science; none in graduate school in mathematics; and 52.8% not in school.

Casserly and Flaugher's (1977) analysis of the 1975–76 Graduate Record Examination (GRE) background questionnaire provides a similar view of approximately the same cohort of students. Nearly twice as many white male as white female math majors were registering for the GRE (4,098 vs. 2,355). In addition, 46.5% of the females were intending graduate study in mathematics while 58.8% of the males were. Twice as many females (19.7% vs. 9.1%) were intending graduate study in education. Again, the record of female physical science majors appears better: 55.8% were intending to continue in physical science and only 4.3% in education.

These data indicate that it may be important to take a closer look at the college programs of female mathematics majors. Perhaps their programs of study are directed at employment after college or at the teaching of mathematics in high school (though Casserly's data indicate that this is not as overwhelmingly common—only 20%—as one might have suspected). It would be interesting to know whether the females receiving beachelor's degrees in mathematics are as well prepared for graduate study as the males. The quantitative GRE scores of prospective graduate students in mathematics are very high, averaging about 675, as contrasted to 650 for engineering and physical science and 460 for education. These data are not available separately for males and females. Furthermore, people who take the GRE are self-selected in a way that prevents them from giving a balanced picture of educational outcomes.

As seems true for earlier stages of education, sex differences in participation in graduate education may reflect perception of or realities of employment opportunities for women with advanced degrees in mathematics. The fact that one-third of the recognized creative women mathematicians that Helson (1971) studied were unemployed indicates that these opportunities may have been extremely poor. Similarly, more general employment statistics indicate that advanced mathematical education is less beneficial for women than for men: in both 1975 and 1977, women with doctorates in mathematics were three times as likely as men to be unemployed (NRC, 1979). In the past, mathematical knowledge has not been the panacea for women's employment problems that it is sometimes suggested to be.

CONCLUSIONS AND OPEN QUESTIONS

Currently, the problem of girls' participation in high school mathematics courses persists but is not so severe as many people believe. This assessment of the situation nation-wide provides a standard that individual schools and colleges can use to gauge their progress in providing opportunity and encouragement to female students in mathematics. In some schools, girls continue to be severely underrepresented in mathematics courses. It is now obvious that such a situation is not inevitable and should not be viewed with complacency. Nationwide sex differences in course enrollment are largely confined to very advanced courses (calculus) not even offered by most high schools. These remaining differences, however, contribute to the problem most evident today: the large differences in the number of males and females who obtain very high scores on the ETS math achievement tests at the end of high school. Because these are the individuals with the best potential to enter the scientific elite, this is a phenomenon of some concern. The explanation of math course enrollments, especially of sex differences in math course enrollments, is the primary focus of the chapters in this volume.

It appears that most sex differences in mathematics achievement are accounted for by differences in math course enrollment. More sensitive measures of effort and time expended learning mathematics might well provide still better explanation, especially for the gifted minority. For example, Maines, Sugrue, and Hardesty (1981) have reported that females in their study entered graduate school in mathematics with their interests much less narrowly focused on mathematics and that they spent much less time working on mathematics than did male graduate students.

There is some evidence that girls perform less well on tests of mathematical problem-solving. However, problem-solving is not a purely mathematical operation. Good problem-solvers work with the content of the problem as much as with the mathematical form (Paige & Simon, 1966), and the content of existing SAT and achievement tests has been shown to favor males (Donlon, 1973; Donlon, Ekstrom, & Lockhead, 1976) in a way that can affect problem-solving performance (Graf & Ruddell, 1972). Without further investigation of this issue, apparent sex differences in problem-solving ability should not be presumed to be real. Consequently, understanding of the determinants of math course enrollments is critical to understanding currently evident sex differences in mathematics achievement.

Although women are well represented among college mathematics majors, our analyses indicate that there does seem to be a problem with their transition to graduate school in mathematics. This may warrant further investigation. Although women are underrepresented in many math-related fields, it is not obvious that mathematics requirements are the key to college major or career selection. The sex-typing of the eventual occupation and/or its relation to women's interests and values are major alternative explanations. There is some evidence that even women who enter college with good high school preparation and high SAT math scores do not often pursue their potential for success in math-related careers (Pines, 1980; Wise, Steel, & MacDonald, 1979).

The circular relation between career expectations and mathematical preparation, together with a massive social change, created a group of women for whom poor preparation mathematics may well be a severe problem. The high school girls of the 1950s and 1960s expected lives very different from the ones they are now leading, and most of them chose not to study mathematics. These women have raised many issues in mathematics education that are not fundamentally related to sex:

> What are the requirements for mathematical thinking in everyday life and in occupations that do not superficially require mathematical knowledge? Does mathematical training have a profound and valuable impact upon one's style of thinking? Are mathematical job requirements frequently unnecessary, acting as a means of selection for general intelligence? How high a level of high school mathematics achievement is sufficient for persistence and success in scientific careers? How extensive are current increases in the application of mathematics in additional occupations and fields of scholarship? Are today's students sufficiently aware of the mathematical requirements of the occupations they expect to enter? Do we know how to upgrade the mathematical skills of older individuals so that they can adapt to these changes? How can we teach mathematics, including problem-solving, more effectively to everyone?

Similarly, the understanding of students' decisions whether or not to study mathematics that has been achieved in the studies reported here should help us advise all students, male and female, majority and minority.

ACKNOWLEDGMENTS

We wish to thank all of the researchers and funding agencies whose work made this report possible. Special acknowledgment is due to Lauress Wise of the American Institutes for Research, Jane Armstrong of the Education Commission of the States, and Len Ramist of the Educational Testing Service for providing us with additional unpublished data.

2 Project TALENT: Mathematics Course Participation in the 1960s and its Career Consequences

Lauress L. Wise
American Institutes for Research

Introduction

The Project TALENT Women and Mathematics Study was designed to investigate questions concerning sex differences in the development of mathematical skills and the issue of entry into careers requiring mathematics. The primary goal of this study was to empirically examine the hypothesis that sex differences in high school mathematics in fact lead to sex differences in occupational attainment. The Project TALENT data are ideally suited for such an investigation because they include high school, college, and current employment information of a large and representative sample of young men and women just recently established in their careers. The Project TALENT data base also contains a special sample of cases with data collected in the ninth grade and again in the twelfth grade that provide a unique opportunity for analyzing sex differences in a second area—math achievement gains during these critical years. Because the TALENT data had not been previously analyzed to this end, such analyses were also planned for this study. Even though the world has changed considerably since the early 60s, basic relationships between aptitude, aspirations, coursework, and achievement are not likely to have disappeared.

The current investigation was organized into two separate substudies. The first substudy investigated origins of sex differences in high school math achievement and in participation in elective math courses. The second substudy investigated the importance of high school mathematics for persistence in math-related career plans. Although the two substudies used many of the same variables, they were based on different samples,

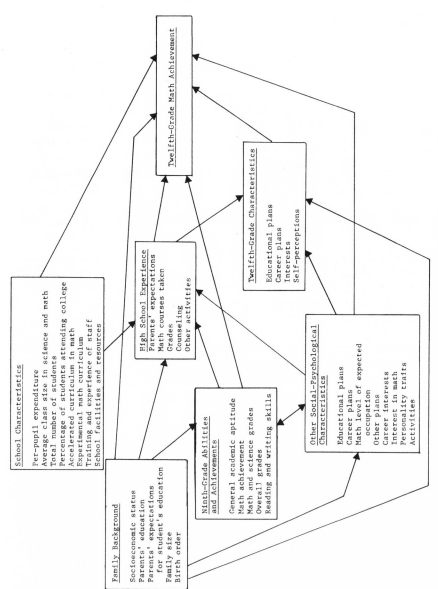

FIG. 2.1 Conceptual framework of study.

addressed different questions, and used data collected at different points in time. Because of the large degree of independence between the two substudies, each is discussed separately below.

ORIGINS OF SEX DIFFERENCES IN
MATH ACHIEVEMENT

Based on a review of existing research, mathematics achievement in high school may be said to result primarily from initial math aptitude and degree of participation in high school mathematics courses. Math participation, in turn, has been considered to be determined by students' family background, cognitive abilities, attitudes, and aspirations and by characteristics of the school environment. The relationships between these various factors are depicted in Fig. 2.1. In the first substudy it was hypothesized that:

1. Sex differences in high school math achievement will be explained primarily by sex differences in participation in elective high school mathematics courses; and
2. Sex differences in math participation will be explained primarily by sex differences in social-psychological characteristics (e.g. interests, aspirations, and plans).

Sample

The first substudy used data on a subset of the 1960 TALENT participants who were tested and surveyed as ninth graders in 1960 and again as twelfth graders in 1963 to examine factors influencing math gains during high school. The procedures used to select the original sample of TALENT participants and the selection of this special retest sample are described in detail by Wise, McLaughlin, and Steel (1979). Briefly, a cluster sampling approach was used with American public and private high schools as the primary sampling unit. High schools were stratified by geographic region, by public versus private control, by size, and by retention rate (the ratio of graduates to tenth graders). The initial sample included 5% of all U.S high schools with an oversampling of large schools and an under-sampling of small schools to increase data collection efficiency. Roughly 93% of the schools chosen agreed to participate. All of the students in these 987 schools were included in the TALENT probability sample, a total of over 375,000 students.

The analyses reported here were based on a special sample of approximately 7500 ninth graders who were retested as twelfth graders. In selecting the retest sample, the public schools in the 1960 sample were sorted by size, region, and "economic level" and a subsample of 118 schools were selected. All of the seniors in these schools were tested and surveyed. Roughly 75% of those tested were found to have been tested in 1960, the other 25% being accelerated students or transfers from non-TALENT schools.

In order to shorten the time required for testing in 1963, seven overlapping test batteries were used, each containing about half of the 1960 test material. In the current study, Battery D was of primary interest because it contained both student background information (including courses taken) and also the mathematics achievement tests. Roughly 1100 of the 1960 students completed Battery D in 1963. (For a more complete description of the 1963 study see Shaycoft, 1967).

Study Variables

As indicated in Fig. 2.1, the dependent variables of interest were mathematics achievement, measured in twelfth grade, and level of participation in high school math classes. These variables were measured as follows.

Math Achievement. The math achievement measure used in this study was the students' score on a 54-item test including 16 "word problem" items designed to measure arithmetic reasoning, 24 introductory math items primarily covering elementary algebra and number theory, and 14 advanced math items covering topics generally taught in grades 10 to 12 including plane and analytic geometry, trigonometry, and elementary calculus.

Math Participation. The measure of math participation used was the number of math courses marked in the 1963 Student Information Blank. The list included first-year algebra, plane geometry, second-year algebra, solid geometry, trigonometry, and analytic geometry or calculus. Scores on this measure ranged from 0 to 6.

As shown in Fig. 2.1 several variables besides sex were also hypothesized to influence high school math participation and/or achievement. These include students' family background, their cognitive and social-psychological attributes in ninth and twelfth grade, their experiences during high school, and several characteristics of the schools themselves. Most of these variables were assessed directly in the 1960 and/or 1963 questionnaires. However, three variables that were of considerable theoretical interest were not assessed directly but, rather, were derived from available data.

Math Level of Expected Occupation. Some initial analyses were done in defining the math level of students' planned careers. Three indicators of the amount of college and high school math typically taken by those in each career were developed. Table 2.1 shows these indicators and the resultant classification of careers into six math levels. Careers at levels four, five, and six mostly require some college math and so are grouped together and labeled "math-related" careers in many analyses. Careers at level 3 generally require college participation and may require some statistics but do not require calculus or other college math. They are used as the "intermediate" level in many analyses to provide a comparison group with a level of education somewhat comparable to the "math-related" careers. Levels 1 and 2 include careers labeled as "low math level" in most analyses.

Math Level of Expected College Majors. College majors were classified into the same six math levels used in classifying careers. The six levels were collapsed into three groups—math-related, intermediate and low math level, analogously to the career categories.

Interest in Math and Math-Related Careers. A 205-item interest inventory with 17 scales was administered in 1960 and 1963. The primary scales used in the present study were "Physical Science, Math and Engineering Interest" and "Interest in Office Work." In addition, four items relating specifically to mathematics were combined to form a new measure of interest in math itself.

Analytic Approach

Several analyses were performed to determine the antecedents of sex differences in high school math participation and achievement. First, the first-order relationships of each of the variables to the two primary dependent variables were examined. The results served to focus attention on the independent variables with the most significant relationships to math participation and achievement.

After the first-order analyses were completed, higher-order analyses, primarily regression analyses and analyses of covariance, were used to investigate the interactions between the study variables that were predictive of math participation and achievement. These higher-order analyses addressed the following specific questions:

1. To what extent were sex differences in math achievement evident during high school?

TABLE 2.1
The Math Level of Careers as Defined by Three Required
Math Education Indicators

| | Indicator | | |
| | College Math | | High School Math |
Career Plan (No. of cases) (1-year Follow-Up)	(Percent in first year math & earning high grades)	(Percent taking or planning to take college math)	(Percent taking more than 2 years)
Level 6:			
Mathematician (86)	88	92	92
Level 5:	*		
Engineer (682)	76	87	90
Physical Scientist (184)	75	90	92
Architect (73)	71	88	77
Pilot (13)	69	92	85
Level 4:	*		
Pharmacist (70)	65	87	80
Dentist (68)	63	79	87
Physician (264)	61	87	89
Biological Scientist (109)	59	86	75
Armed Forces Officer (38)	59	72	87
Level 3:	*		
Forester (38)	45	68	61
Lawyer (183)	43	67	84
College Professor (73)	48	62	77
Engineering Aide (15)	43	57	67
Medical/Dental Technician (145)	40	58	50
Accountant (402)	40	48	55
High School Teacher (1427)	30	57	62
Elementary Teacher (587)	40	57	54
Sociologist/Psychologist (97)	34	70	68
Political Scientist/Economist (80)	32	48	74
Businessman (398)	33	51	58
Librarian (22)	36	55	59
Clergyman (106)	34	49	55
Writer (94)	26	45	62
Social Worker (95)	25	46	47
Level 2:		*	
Nurse (490)	7	9	50
Salesperson (97)	22	31	51
Policeman/Fireman (58)	4	19	41
Armed Forces Enlistedman (73)	15	29	51
Artist/Entertainer (160)	6	23	41
Farmer (187)	18	31	34
Skilled Worker (418)	10	12	49
Structural Worker (82)	12	15	38
Level 1:			*
Secretary/Officer (972)	6	8	17
Barber/Beautician (173)	1	1	14

*Denotes gap in indicator values that were used in defining the 6 levels.

2. To what extent can differences in math achievement gains be attributed to different levels of math participation?
3. What other factors "predict" gains in math achievement?
4. What factors predict math participation and to what extent do sex differences in these factors account for sex differences in math participation?
5. Are there characteristics of schools and school environments that affect math participation after controlling for initial student characteristics?
6. What high school experiences and twelfth-grade characteristics typified students with higher than expected levels of math participation and achievement?

Based on the results obtained, structural equation models of the relationships between sex and math participation and achievement were estimated and tested.

First-Order Relationships to Math Participation and Achievement

The data analyses began with an examination of the direct relationship of each independent variable to the amount of math taken in high school (math participation) and to twelfth grade math achievement. Table 2.2, which lists the variables with correlations of .2 or more, provides a good overview of the main variables in these analyses. Most of the variables that were correlated strongly with math participation also tended to correlate strongly with twelfth grade math achievement. Moreover, with the exception of variables relating to sex stereotyping (e.g., participation in male- or female-stereotyped activities or interest in male- or female-stereotyped careers), the direction of the relationships was consistent for both sexes. However, some clear sex differences were evident in the strengths of these relationships.

These results provided an initial estimate of the relative importance of different factors in determining math participation and achievement, and they were used to guide the order in which potential predictors were further examined. However, it must be remembered that these relationships themselves do not imply causality, but rather serve as reference points that must be matched by underlying casual models.

Extent of Sex Differences in Math Achievement During the High School Years

Figure 2.2 shows the mean math achievement scores, based on the TALENT 1960 tests, for males and females in each high school grade. The

TABLE 2.2
Summary of the Significant First-Order Relationships
Between Study Variables and the Amount of
Math Participation and Achievement

| | Correlations With: | | | |
| | Math Taken | | Twelfth- Grade Achievement | |
	M	F	M	F
Background Variables				
Father's Level of Education	.21	.31	.23	.30
Mother's Level of Education	.18	.24	.21	.24
Socioeconomic Status	.31	.41	.35	.42
Birth Order	-.14	-.18	-.26	-.18
Father's Occupational Prestige	.07	.22	.01	.15
Math Level of Father's Occupation	.09	.21	.02	.14
Family Size	-.14	-.19	-.16	-.20
Ninth Grade Characteristics				
Ability Measures				
Math Achievement	.61	.63	.77	.79
General Academic Abilities	.60	.59	.78	.77
Ninth-Grade Math Grades	.33	.42	.39	.52
Ninth-Grade Science Grades	.38	.43	.38	.45
Ninth-Grade Grades, All Subjects	.41	.52	.44	.56
Self-Perception of Reading Skills	.27	.32	.29	.33
Self-Perception of Writing Skills	.23	.23	.21	.24
Educational Plans				
Amount of Education Expected	.50	.57	.45	.49
Type of High School Program	.44	.54	.43	.48
Parents' Expectations	.28	.48	.35	.40
Importance of Father's Expectations	.25	.38	.16	.28
Importance of Mother's Expectations	.26	.36	.15	.27
Importance of Teacher's Expectations	.20	.23	.07	.18
Importance of Friends Not Going to College	-.24	-.11	-.28	-.13
Discussed Plans with Father	.14	.29	.17	.23
Discussed Plans with Mother	.14	.22	.17	.18
Importance of College for Girls	-.04	-.22	-.12	-.21
Career Plans				
Importance of College for Career	.43	.37	.37	.31
Math Level of Expected Career	.25	.37	.27	.31
Math Level of Desired Career	.25	.35	.29	.33
Importance of Getting a Job as Soon as Possible	-.11	-.20	-.10	-.24
Importance of College for Learning About Careers	.21	.21	.14	.12
Importance of College Earnings	.31	.21	.21	.14
Other Plans				
Importance of Marriage over College	-.22	-.14	-.23	-.10
Expected Number of Children	.12	.24	.10	.23

TABLE 2.2 *cont'd.*

	Correlations With:			
	Math Taken		Twelfth-Grade Achievement	
	M	F	M	F
Interests				
Interest in Math	.44	.36	.43	.37
Interest in Physical Science, Engineering, and Math Careers	.36	.35	.35	.31
Interest in Office Work	-.04	-.26	-.09	-.23
Interest in Skilled Trades	-.23	-.05	-.26	-.06
Interest in Labor Careers	-.20	-.10	-.22	-.11
Activities				
Study Habits	.32	.34	.32	.36
Extracurricular Reading	.19	.24	.16	.30
Variety of Extracurricular Activities	-.03	.06	-.24	-.05
Participation in Female-Stereotyped Activities	-.08	.05	-.27	.07
Traits				
Mature Personality	.25	.25	.25	.26
Tidiness	.24	.14	.20	.13
Calmness	.22	.18	.22	.21
Self-Confidence	.20	.10	.22	.18
Enjoy Learning	.13	.31	.11	.24
High School Experiences				
Courses Taken				
Amount of Math Taken	1.00	1.00	.71	.74
Number of Business or Commercial Courses	-.35	-.47	-.28	-.32
Number of Science Courses Taken	.42	.40	.35	.28
High School Program*	.60	.67	.54	.57
Grades				
Math Grades	.28	.36	.38	.45
Science Grades	.28	.36	.33	.38
All Grades	.31	.38	.30	.40
Counseling				
Discussed Plans with Teachers or Counselors	.37	.45	.33	.39
Discussed Plans with Others	.24	.34	.23	.30
Activities				
Number of Leadership Roles	.14	.28	.11	.26
Hours Studied Each Week	.21	.20	.21	.20
Twelfth-Grade Characteristics				
Educational Plans				
Amount of Education Expected	.57	.60	.52	.54
Expect to Attend College	.57	.60	.51	.52

TABLE 2.2 *cont'd.*

	Correlations With:			
	Math Taken		Twelfth-Grade Achievement	
	M	F	M	F
Plan to Attend 4-Year, 2-Year, More	.51	.58	.50	.51
Plan to Attend Full-Time	.50	.53	.48	.46
Saving for College*	.48	.48	.45	.44
Plan to Attend Business or Commercial School	-.28	-.30	-.26	-.29
Plan to Attend Vocational School	-.28	-.16	-.30	-.23
Math Level of Expected Major	.51	.42	.50	.50
Type of College*	.57	.59	.59	.55
Major*	.53	.65	.52	.58
Expected College Costs	.15	.21	.09	.11
When College Expected*	.51	.61	.49	.55
Career Plans				
Math Level of Planned Career	.38	.34	.37	.30
Prestige of Planned Career	.36	.38	.35	.33
Number of Occupations Considered	.10	.10	.20	.12
Financial Aspirations	.21	.14	.23	.12
Interests				
Interest in Math	.40	.40	.44	.46
Interest in Physical Science, Engineering or Math Career	.35	.41	.40	.47
Interest in Biological Science or Medical Career	.24	.30	.27	.30
Interest in Office Work	.01	-.40	-.03	-.32
Interest in Skilled Trades	-.23	-.07	-.23	-.06
Interest in Female-Stereotyped Careers	.04	-.23	.02	-.19
Interest in Male-Stereotyped Careers	-.06	.17	-.03	.20
Predominance of Interest in Female-Stereotyped Careers	.08	-.30	.01	-.29
Self-Perceptions				
How Do You Compare on Intelligence?	.27	.32	.33	.33
Do You Have a Good Ideal of Your IQ?	.17	.24	.13	.18
School Characteristics				
Daily Percent Absenteeism	-.02	-.04	-.27	-.28
Percent in College Prep Program	.12	.05	.31	.24
Honors Courses in Math	.17	.17	.25	.22
Number of Full-Time Teachers	.01	.09	.24	.25
Number of Books in Library	-.10	.12	.11	.24
Number of Extracurricular Activities Available	.06	.15	.18	.21
Training and Experiences of Staff	.17	.17	.26	.20
Variety of Community Facilities Available	.01	.06	.15	.20

*Based on 643 females and 567 males in the 1963 retest sample for whom twelfth-grade questionnaire and math achievement data were both available.

*Eta is shown for categorical variables.

difference in male and female means among ninth graders, whereas statistically significant because of the very large sample size, was less than .07 standard deviations, too small to be of much practical significance. (The results in Fig. 2.2 were based on just under 5000 cases for each grade and sex.) The male gains in math achievement during high school were more than twice the female gains. Sex differences in math achievement increased most sharply after the tenth grade, the time at which mathematics courses became truly elective.

The Importance of Math Participation

The two strongest predictors of twelfth grade math achievement were ninth grade math achievement ($r = .78$) and the amount of math taken in high school ($r = .73$). Ninth grade math achievement is, indeed, a powerful predictor, as higher ninth grade scores were associated with higher raw gain scores, so that individual differences tended not just to remain constant, but to increase. (The opposite was true for other measures such as Reading Comprehension or English, where there was some tendency for students with lower scores to "catch up.")

The positive correlation between ninth grade achievement and raw gain scores is related to the fact that students with higher ninth grade scores took more math courses during the intervening years ($r = .62$). Nonetheless, for students who took the same amount of math, initial

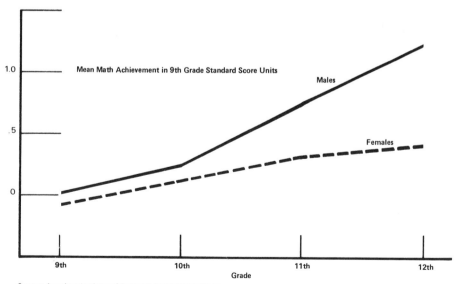

Source: American Institute of Research, Project Talent Data

FIG. 2.2   Mean mathematics achievement levels of high school boys and girls.

abilities were highly predictive of final level of achievement (the correlation pooled within level of math taken and sex was .55; the partial correlation controlling for amount of math taken was .60). On the other hand, the amount of math taken also had a strong effect on twelfth grade math achievement independent of initial abilities (a partial correlation of .44).

The amount of math taken and ninth grade math achievement together have a multiple correlation of .84 with twelfth grade math achievement, accounting for just over 70% of the variation. The multiple correlation begins to approach the reliability of the twelfth grade math achievement measure (an upper bound) estimated at .93 for males and .91 for females (Shaycoft, 1967). Nevertheless, there are a number of variables that account for significant amounts of the remaining variation, to be discussed next.

In order to assess the extent to which sex differences in twelfth grade achievement could be explained by differences in math participation, a two-way *ANOVA* with sex and amount of math taken as the independent factors was performed. Table 2.3 shows the results, which are further illustrated in Fig. 2.3. The sex differences were literally nonexistent after controlling for amount of math taken, although there was a small interaction effect with women scoring higher at moderate levels of math taken and males scoring higher at the extremes.

These results are, however, somewhat misleading, because they do not also include controls for initial abilities. Females who took advanced high school math were a more select group than males with the same level of participation. Table 2.3 shows another two-way analysis of variance with ninth grade achievement controlled as a covariate. The results indicate that females with math participation and math ability equal to males had scores that averaged .1 standard deviations lower than male scores. Although this difference is significant, it is not large. Math taken and ninth grade achievement account for 71.1% of the variation in twelfth grade

TABLE 2.3
Results of Two-Way Analyses of Variance and Covariance
of Twelfth-Grade Math Achievement

Type of Analysis	Source of Variation	df	F	p
Analysis of Variance ($R^2 = .548$)	Sex	1	.02	.99
	Amount of Math Taken	6	228.32	.001
	Sex x Amount	6	2.48	.02
Analysis of Covariance ($R^2 = .174$)	Sex	1	9.14	.003
	Amount of Math Taken	6	64.54	.001
	Ninth-Grade Math Ach't (Covariate)	1	639.92	.001
	Sex x Amount	6	.79	.99

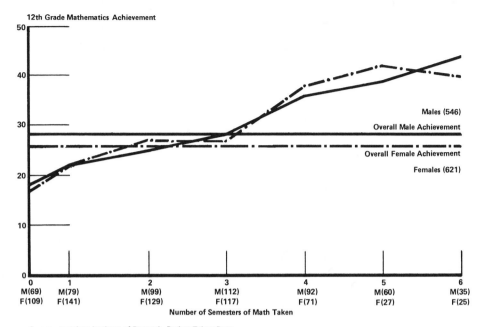

12th Grade Mathematics Achievement

Source: American Institute of Research, Project Talent Data

FIG. 2.3   Mean twelfth grade math achievement by amount of math taking and sex.

achievement. Sex can account for 1.6% of the variation in twelfth grade achievement when these factors are not controlled, but only 0.2% after controls are introduced. In this sense, roughly seven-eighths of the relationship between sex and twelfth grade math achievement an be attributed to math taken and ninth grade achievement differences.

Other Factors Predicting Gains in Math Achievement

Several exploratory regression analyses were performed on other background and ninth grade variables to identify additional predictors of math achievement gains. Three factors were identified as additional predictors:

1. General academic aptitude, which includes both math and non-math aptitude and ability measures;

2. Interests in mathematics and math-related occupations relative to office work;

3. Low levels of participation in extracurricular activities in ninth grade.

The above three variables together with math participation and ninth grade math achievement form a general model predicting math achievement in high school. The essential ingredients of this model are:

TABLE 2.4
Sex Difference in Math *Achievement* Predicted by Each Variable
in the General Regression Equation

Predictor Variable	Mean Sex Difference in Predictor Variable	Regression Coefficient	Predicted Sex Difference	Percent of Actual Sex Difference
Ninth-Grade Math Achievement	.376	.236	.089	3.5%
Amount of Math Taken	.602	2.041	1.299	47.8%
General Ninth-Grade Academic Aptitude	-23.303	.032	-.746	-29.0%
Math Level of Expected Occupation	1.574	.371	.584	22.7%
Interest in Math	4.585	.089	.408	15.9%
Interest in Office Work	-10.217	-.058	.593	23.1%
Degree of Extracurricular Activity	-2.144	-.038	.081	3.2%
Total Sex Predicted Difference			2.238	87.2%
Actual Sex Difference			2.569	
Amount Explained by Other Factors			.331	12.8%

Multiple Correlation = .86
Variance Accounted for = 74%

1. Ability—including a foundation of knowledge of basic math concepts and also general academic skills;

2. Participation—exposure to math curriculum in appropriate math courses and the lack of excessive extracurricular involvements that might detract from participation in courses taken; and

3. Motivation—interests in math and math-related careers relative to interests in other careers not requiring math.

Table 2.4 shows the regression coefficients for the specific variables included in the model and also the extent to which sex differences in math achievement are "predicted" by sex differences in these variables.

Whereas the general model applied to both males and females, a few significant sex differences were observed. Males who had higher levels of spatial visualization and those who scored higher on table reading tended to show larger than expected achievement gains. This is consistent with the suggestion that males use a spatial approach to math learning more than females. Scientific attitude (essentially a belief in lawfulness) and electricity and electronics knowledge were also significant predictors of math achievement for males.

For females, socioeconomic status and a number of related variables (low immediate concern with earning a living, high law, and sports knowledge) were significant predictors of math achievement. In addition, self-confidence was a much more significant predictor of math achievement for females than for males. This result is consistent with current widespread efforts to increase female math achievement through anxiety reduction (Tobias, 1976; Tobias & Donady, 1977).

While there were some significant sex differences in the residual factors that predict math achievement, it should be noted that none of these factors add even 1% to the percent of variation accounted for by the general model. Because sex differences in ninth grade aptitude and achievement measures are small to nonexistent, differences in the amount of math taken and in math interests are by far the most significant component of sex differences in twelfth grade math achievement. Any intervention that does not affect one or both of these factors is unlikely to have a very large effect in reducing sex differences in achievement levels.

Predictors of Math Participation

As with twelfth grade math achievement, the largest correlate of the amount of math taken was ninth grade math achievement ($r = .62$). For students with equal initial achievement, expected educational attainment was the most significant predictor of level of math participation (with a partial correlation of .39). The variable Educational Expectations accounts for an additional 9% beyond the variation accounted for by ninth grade math achievement. However, because sex differences in both ninth grade math achievement and educational expectations are relatively small, neither of these factors accounts for very much of the sex difference in math participation.

Several other variables that predict math participation after controlling for ninth grade achievement and educational expectations do predict the significant sex differences in math participation. These are measures of interest in math and interest in math-related careers relative to interest in office work.

The final regression equation for predicting math participation is shown in Table 2.5. Table 2.5 also shows that significant sex differences in the interest variables can account for most of the sex differences in participation.

Table 2.6 lists the variables for each sex that have significant correlations with math participation after controlling for the variables in the general regression equation shown in Table 2.5. For males, table reading, visualization in 3-dimensions, and information on foreign countries were significant predictors of math participation "gains." The first two of these variables appear to be related to mathematics ability (Fennema & Sherman, 1977a); the latter variable is most likely an indicator of general knowledge and ability levels. In addition, males who had discussed their plans with counselors more frequently in the ninth grade tended to end up with lower participation rates. This may be because they were planning a specific career that did not require math, because college-bound students would have been somewhat less likely to have discussed career plans with their counselors.

For females, much of the remaining variation in math participation was related to their fathers. The prestige and math level of father's occupation were significantly related to the amount of math taken by the daughter, as was the number of times in the ninth grade she discussed post-high school plans with her father and not with a school counselor. The factor of parental expectations regarding college was also a significant predictor of math participation "gains" for women.

Characteristics of Schools and School Environments

In order to analyze the relationship of school characteristics to student participation and achievement in math, the student data were aggregated at the school level. In all, there were 54 schools for which math achievement data were available and 44 schools for which math participation data were available. After discarding schools with fewer than 10 students re-tested, there were 44 schools with math achievement data and 40 schools with math participation data.

TABLE 2.5
Sex Differences in Math *Participation* by Each Variable
in the General Regression Equation

Predictor Variable	Mean Sex Difference in Predictor Variable	Regression Coefficient	Predicted Sex Difference	Percent of Actual Sex Difference
Ninth Grade Math Achievement	.376	.065	.024	4.0%
Expected Level of Education	.231	.264	.061	10.1%
College Preparatory Curriculum	.048	.475	.023	3.8%
Interest in Math	4.584	.022	.101	16.8%
Interest in Math-Related Careers	9.301	.015	.140	23.3%
Interest in Office Work	-10.217	-.015	.153	25.4%
Total Predicted Sex Difference			.502	83.4%
Actual Sex Difference			.602	
Difference Resulting from Other Factors			.100	16.6%

Multiple Correlation = .73
Variance Accounted for = .53%

TABLE 2.6
Partial Correlations of Background and Ninth-Grade Characteristic
Variables with the Amount of Math Taken by Sex

| | Partial Correlation[1] | |
Name of Variable	Females	Males
Variables Significant for Females		
Father's Characteristic		
Prestige of Father's Occupation	.14***	-.03
Math Level of Father's Occupation	.11*	-.03
Change in Head of Household	-.12*	.03
Discussed Plans with Father	.11*	-.08
Parents' Educational Expectation	.12*	-.08
Academic Program		
Academic Level of High School Coursework	.14***	.02
Number of Science Courses Taken	.13***	-.02
Interests and Plans		
Expected Number of Children	.11*	-.03
Cultural Activities	-.11**	-.05
Computational Interests	-.11*	-.01
Discussed Plans with Counselor	-.12**	-.13**
Variables Significant for Males		
Knowledge and abilities		
Visualization in 3-Dimensions	.06	.13**
Table Reading	.03	.14**
Information on Foreign Countries	.00	.15***
Career Interests and Plans		
Biological Science, Medicine Interest	-.11*	-.14**
Prestige of Expected Occupation	.02	-.13*
Guidance Received in High School	-.09	-.14**
Discussed Plans with Counselor	-.12**	-.13**

[1] Partial correlations after controlling for ninth-grade abilities, interests and plans.

$*p <$ .01
$**p <$ .005
$***p <$ .001

The "expected" math participation and twelfth grade math achievement levels of each student were computed based on the background and ninth-grade characteristics variables shown in Tables 2.4, 2.5, and 2.6. The difference between the actual and predicted levels, the "unexpected" gains, were computed for each student and then averaged over all students in each school. In addition, the "unexpected" mean gains for females in each school were computed. The mean unexpected gains (or losses) were then correlated with variables from the General School Characteristics Questionnaire. The most significant correlations are shown in Tables 2.7 and 2.8.

TABLE 2.7

Correlations of General School Characteristics with Math Participation

	Partial Correlation with Twelfth-Grade Math Achievement	Partial Correlation with Twelfth-Grade Math Achievement for Females Only	First Order Correlation with Twelfth-Grade Math Achievement
I. Variables correlated with "expected" twelfth-grade math achievement gains but not with "unexpected" gains.			
Honors Courses	0.03	0.09	0.48***
Number of Full-time Teachers	-0.03	0.13	0.30
Staff Experience/Training	0.02	0.10	0.40**
Percent Students Enrolled in College Prep Courses	0.06	-0.01	0.45**
Percent Males and Females Going on to College	0.08	0.12	0.51***
Per Pupil Expenditure	0.17	0.14	0.35*
II. Variables correlated with "unexpected" twelfth-grade math achievement gains.			
Percent Daily Absenteeism	-0.29	-0.36*	-0.39**
Current School Tax per $1000	0.41**	0.26	0.44**
III. Variables correlated with "unexpected" twelfth-grade math achievement gains for females.			
Accelerated Curriculum in Science	0.15	0.32*	0.22

*$p < .01$
**$p < .005$
***$p < .001$

TABLE 2.8
Correlations of General School Characteristics with
Math Participation

	Partial Correlation with Math Participation Level	Partial Correlation with Math Participation Level for Females Only	First Order Correlations with Math Participation Level
I. Variables correlated with "expected" math participation levels, but not with "unexpected" levels.			
Honors Courses	0.21	0.21	0.55***
Accelerated Math Curriculum	0.18	0.18	0.35*
Number of Full-time Teachers	0.03	0.04	0.30
Staff Experience/Training	0.04	0.07	0.35*
Percent Students Enrolled in College Prep Courses	0.18	-0.02	0.53***
Percent Males and Females Going on to College	-0.09	-0.23	0.48***
Per Pupil Expenditure	-0.10	-0.05	0.40**
Percent School Support from Local Sources	-0.00	-0.27	0.42**
II. Variables correlated with "unexpected" math participation levels.			
Count of School Facilities Available	-0.27	-0.22	0.03
III. Variables correlated with "unexpected" math participation levels for females.			
Percent Parents in PTA	0.14	0.27	0.11
Frequency of Standardized Testing	0.22	0.36*	0.19

*$p < .01$
**$p < .005$
***$p < .001$

A number of key school characteristics were found to be significantly correlated with twelfth grade achievement and participation levels, but not with the unexpected gains in these levels. For twelfth grade achievement (Table 2.7, Part I) this included financial data (per-pupil expenditure, percent support from local sources), a school descriptor (honors courses offered), teacher characteristics (training and experience), and characteristics of the student body (percent college bound and percent enrolled in college preparatory courses). These variables were all correlated with and hence confounded with "expected" participation and achievement gains. Although they do not show independent effects on the outcomes, they cannot be ruled out as contributors.

In examining achievement gains, two variables were found to predict gains independently of the students' ninth grade characteristics (Table 2.7, Part II). The observed relationship between high school absenteeism and achievement was not surprising, although the strength of the relationship may be. The relationship between tax rate and achievement gains was less obvious, particularly in light of the lower correlations for per-pupil expenditures. One explanation that warrants further investigation is that the tax rate is an indicator of community support for education which is in turn related to increased achievement.

One variable, the availability of accelerated science curriculum, was a significant predictor of "unexpected" achievement gains for girls but not for boys (Table 2.7, Part III). This finding was investigated further by correlating the availability of an accelerated science curriculum with the most significant predictors of math achievement. The results showed that there was a greater reduction in female interest in office work in schools with an accelerated science curriculum ($r = .12$, $p < .01$). The male interest levels were relatively unchanged ($r = .01$). The availability of an accelerated science curriculum seems to have encouraged females to widen their career interests.

Most of the same financial, school, teacher, and student body variables that predicted overall achievement gains were also found to predict math participation (Table 2.8). The availability of an accelerated curriculum in math and science showed marginally significant relationships to "unexpected" levels of participation as well as to the overall level. The variety of "facilities" available to students was related to lower than expected math participation (although this variable was not at all related to overall participation levels).

Two variables were found to predict higher than expected participation levels for females but not for males. The percent of parents in the PTA may indicate the kind of parental interest and support that encourages females to elect to pursue mathematics. The frequency of standardized testing was also found to be a much stronger predictor of math participation for females than for males. This may reflect the effects of a greater thoroughness in counseling and testing in some schools, or it may reflect the effect of increased confidence in females resulting from a greater awareness of their own abilities.

Summary Model of the Relationship of Sex to High School Mathematics Achievement

The final data analysis step in this substudy was to model the process by which sex and other independent variables relate to high school math participation and achievement. Structural models incorporating those independent and moderator variables found to have the strongest relationships to math participation and achievement were developed and tested using the LISREL IV program (see Joreskog, Sorbom, & Magidson, 1979 for a discussion of this technique). In the case to be discussed, the model presented in Fig. 2.4, the probability of obtaining a sample correlation matrix at least as discrepant from the predicted matrix as the one actually observed was .41. Thus, the observed data did not in any way reject this model despite the relatively large sample size.

The acceptable model reiterated the pattern of relationships discussed previously, and was especially effective in describing the relationship of sex to twelfth grade math achievement. In particular, the strongest direct predictors of twelfth grade math achievement were amount of mathematics taken in high school ($b = .36$), ninth grade math achievement ($b = .24$), and, in addition, overall ninth grade academic ability ($b = .27$). The other variables of significance—ninth grade interest in math, ninth grade interest in math-related careers, ninth grade math level of expected occupation, and ninth grade expected level of education—affected twelfth grade math achievement or participation. The effect of sex, in turn, was always indirect, operating through girls' lesser interest in math ($b = -.23$), lesser interest in math-related careers ($b = -.65$), and lower math level of planned careers ($b = -.24$).

Whereas both overall academic abilities and ninth grade math achievement strongly influenced participation in high school math courses, their modest relationships with sex suggest that these factors operate independently and do not account for much of the sex difference in math participation. The observed sex differences in math achievement by the end of high school can thus be explained by differences in career interests and plans which are evident at the beginning of high school and which strongly influence the number of high school math courses taken.

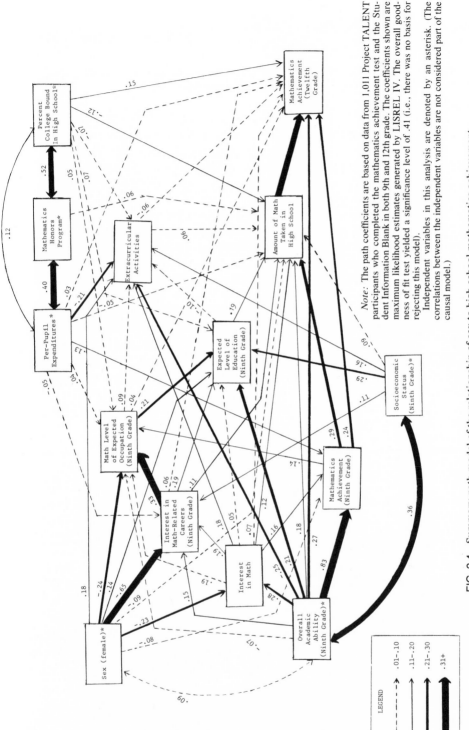

Note: The path coefficients are based on data from 1,011 Project TALENT participants who completed the mathematics achievement test and the Student Information Blank in both 9th and 12th grade. The coefficients shown are maximum likelihood estimates generated by LISREL IV. The overall goodness of fit test yielded a significance level of .41 (i.e., there was no basis for rejecting this model).

Independent variables in this analysis are denoted by an asterisk. (The correlations between the independent variables are not considered part of the causal model.)

FIG. 2.4   Summary path model of the relationship of sex to high school mathematics achievement.

46

CAREER CONSEQUENCES OF SEX DIFFERENCES IN MATH ACHIEVEMENT

The second substudy was organized around the following four questions:

1. To what extent were sex differences in the development of math-related careers reflected in sex differences along the educational paths leading to such careers?
2. How important and accurate were early career plans with respect to the development of math-related careers?
3. To what extent was high school math achievement predictive of success in the pursuit of math-related career goals?
4. To what extent can differences in the proportions of males and females entering math-related careers be explained by differences in our moderator variables?

Sample

The analyses performed in the second substudy were based on the twelfth grade "complete data" sample of Project TALENT. This sample consists of 12,759 of the twelfth grade participants—those who supplied data in all three follow-up surveys. This sample heavily overrepresents the most academically able students because they were significantly more likely to respond to the follow-up surveys. In one sense this oversampling is advantageous to the present study which concerns careers that require higher levels of academic skills. However, it is also essential that this sample be weighted so that estimates of national norms can be appropriately produced.

Several steps were taken to generate case weights that correct fully for potential nonresponse bias. Each of the follow-up surveys included an intensive follow-up sample of roughly 2500 participants from each grade cohort who failed to respond to the mail survey. These intensive sample cases were tracked down and interviewed by telephone. In general, over 90% of the intensive sample members were located, and interviews were obtained from over 90% of those located. When the intensive sample cases are weighted to represent all of the initial nonrespondents, an effective response rate of over 85% is achieved. The weights have been further adjusted to correct for the small amount of nonresponse in the intensive samples. The final weights have been shown to eliminate virtually all known bias (Wise, 1977).

Study Variables

The variables analyzed in the second phase of this study are questionnaire items and test scores selected from the following sources:

The 1960 student questionnaire and test battery;
The 1960 school characteristics questionnaire;
The 1 year follow-up questionnaire for the twelfth grade cohort;
The 5 year follow-up questionnaire for the twelfth grade cohort, and
The 11 year follow-up questionnaire for the twelfth grade cohort.

A description of each of the tests and reproductions of the full questionnaires may be found in *The Project TALENT Data Bank Handbook.*

The variables of primary interest in this substudy were twelfth grade math achievement (as defined above), high school math participation (also as earlier), twelfth grade career interests, math level of college majors, and math level of expected careers at ages 18, 19, 23, and actual occupation at age 29. The math levels of careers and college majors were coded into six categories as described by Table 2.1. In some analyses, these six levels were collapsed into three groups—math-related, intermediate level, and low math level.

Sex Differences in Educational Path Leading to Math-Related Careers

The second phase of the study examined factors that affected the development of math-related careers during the period from twelfth grade through age 29. Because the math-related careers studied were those that require some college-level math, the first step was to analyze sex differences in educational attainment and the relationship of these differences to sex differences in entry to math-related careers. Figure 2.5 shows the educational paths followed by females and males in the TALENT twelfth grade cohort. All percentages were calculated from the 12,759 "complete data" cases using case weights that provide unbiased estimates of national norms for all 1960 twelfth graders.

Overall, the proportion of males in college one year after high school was larger than the proportion of females (46% compared to 33%). By 5 years after high school, the proportion of females and males having completed college were similar (19% and 23% respectively), but roughly twice as many males as females had gone to graduate school. Between 5 and 11 years after high school, 16% of the males who had not previously completed college did so compared to only 3% of the females who had not previously completed college. By age 29 sex differences in educational attainment were quite significant. In addition, even controlling for sex differences in educational attainment, males were much more likely to have followed an educational course leading to a math-related career. Only 3% of the females with advanced degrees went into math-related careers compared to 23% of the males with advanced degrees.

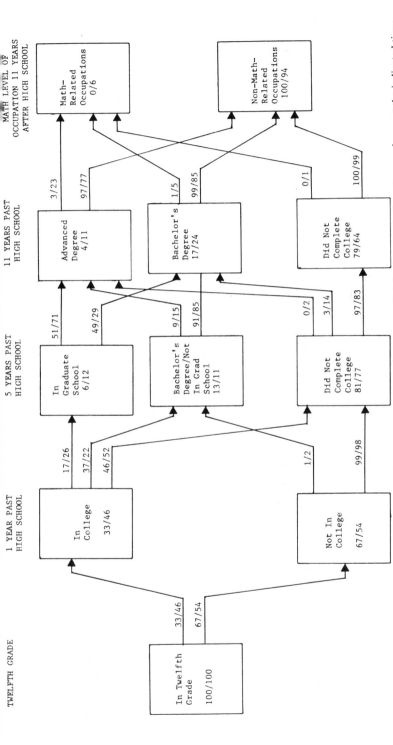

FIG. 2.5   Educational paths to math-related careers.

Note: The numbers in each box are the percentages of all females/males from the Class of 1960 who were in the category shown at the indicated time. The numbers along the lines are the percentages of females/males from the adjacent category who had moved to the indicated category by the time of the next follow-up survey. The percentages are based on 12,759 cases from the Project TALENT Class of 1960 sample. Case weights were used to eliminate bias in estimating national norms.

49

These findings indicate that sex differences in educational attainment, particularly in the proportions earning advanced degrees and in the proportions completing college after an interruption, can account for a proportion of the sex difference in the math level of occupation at age 29. Much more striking, however, are the very large sex differences within each level of education.

Importance and Accuracy of Early Career Plans

The second question concerning the development of math-related careers dealt with career planning. How essential was early career planning to eventual entry into math-related careers? How successful were those who planned, in high school, to enter a math-related career?

For these analyses, three levels of career plans were investigated: careers generally requiring college-level math; other careers generally requiring some college; and other careers that do not generally require college. Individuals with no specific career plan or no specific occupation at age 29 were excluded from the analysis as were those reporting no occupation outside the home, in order to make the remaining groups more comparable. Table 2.9 shows the relationship between career plans in twelfth grade, 1 year later, 5 years later, and occupation at age 29.

The results indicate that a relatively low proportion of those who planned to enter a math-related career actually did so. More than 80% of

TABLE 2.9
Occupational Outcome at Age 29 for
Each Level of Career Plan at Ages 18, 19, and 23

	Percent in Low Math-Level Careers		Percent in Intermediate Math-Level Careers		Percent in Math-Related Careers	
	Male	Female	Male	Female	Male	Female
Age 18 Career Plans						
Low Math Level	85	80	15	20	0.6	0.0
Intermediate Math Level	44	39	53	60	3.1	0.2
Math-Related	39	54	43	38	17.7	7.7
Age 19 Career Plans						
Low Math Level	82	81	16	19	1.9	0.0
Intermediate Math Level	34	31	63	69	3.4	0.3
Math Related	31	18	43	57	25.7	24.7
Age 23 Career Plans						
Low Math Level	87	87	13	13	0.5	0.0
Intermediate Math Level	30	22	67	78	3.0	0.7
Math-Related	26	16	26	47	48.0	37.2

the males and 90% of the females who planned math-related careers in twelfth grade were in other kinds of careers at age 29. From the date at age 19, when most of those planning science careers had completed a year of college, only a quarter of those who planned math-related careers, realized their plans by age 29. (The figure would be even lower had homemakers at age 29 been included.) And, only half of those planning math-related careers at age 23 persisted in those plans to age 29.

The second finding concerning math-related career plans was that virtually no one who was not already planning a math-related career by twelfth grade later switched into a math-related career by age 29. Even among those who were planning college-related but not math-related careers, only 3% of the males switched into math-related careers. This finding and the fact that over one-third of those planning math careers in twelfth grade had changed to other career plans 1 year later indicate that there are important early selection factors for math-related careers that both screen out a significant number of students initially planning math-related careers and make it difficult for others to change later into a math-related career path.

The Importance of High School Math Achievement for Persistency in Math-Related Career Plans

By twelfth grade, a strong relationship between math achievement and plans regarding math-related careers was evident. The third area of investigation concerned the relationship between high school math achievement and the realization of plans to enter math-related careers. The data presented in Table 2.9 show clearly that a significant proportion of those planning math-related careers are not working in math-related careers at age 29. The goal of these analyses was to determine the extent to which lack of success in meeting math-related career goals was predicted by failure to develop math skills while in high school.

Table 2.10 shows the mean math achievement scores of TALENT participants with various levels of math-related career plans in twelfth grade who did or did not enter a math-related career. Those who were successful in pursuit of a math-related career had had dramatically higher math achievement scores in twelfth grade. Those who were not planning math-related careers in twelfth grade but later entered a math-related career also had markedly higher twelfth grade achievement scores than their counterparts who did not switch into math-related careers, indicating the importance of math skills for keeping career options open even if a math-related career is not explicitly planned.

The same results were in fact true for career plans held at approximately age 23 (Table 2.11). These results are somewhat more surprising.

By this age nearly all of those who were planning math-related careers had completed their undergraduate education and either gone on to graduate school or entered the labor force. It would have been reasonable to suppose that skills developed during high school would be relatively unrelated to success in the development of math-related careers between age 23 and age 29. Yet those who were successful in entering math-related careers had average twelfth grade math scores roughly .3 standard deviations greater than those who switched into careers requiring only statistics and over .7 standard deviations higher than those who switched into careers requiring little or no college math at all. The relationship between high school math achievement and switching into a math-related career from an intermediate-level career at age 23 was even more dramatic. Those switching into math-related careers had twelfth grade math scores averaging .7 standard deviations greater than these remaining in inter-

TABLE 2.10
Mean Twelfth-Grade Math Achievement*
by Math Levels of Twelfth-Grade Career Plan and Occupation at Age 29

Math Level of Occupation at Age 29	Mathematics Level of Twelfth-Grade Career Plan			
	Some College-Level Math	May Require Some Statistics	High School Math Only	Plan Not Classified
Males				
Some College-Level Math	1.23±.08 (509)	.69±.22 (78)	.42±.49 (16)	.63±.35 (31)
May Require Some Statistics	.83±.06 (931)	.34±.06 (1118)	-.17±.14 (195)	-.06±.13 (239)
High School Math Only	.27±.08 (583)	-.11±.16 (149)	¬47±.07 (691)	-.46±.10 (373)
Not Classified	.70±.13 (242)	.29±.16 (149)	-.39±.23 (70)	-.17±.26 (58)
Total	.76±.04 (2265)	.21±.04 (1955)	-.39±.06 (972)	-.25±.07 (701)
Females				
Some College-Level Math	1.29±.42 (21)	1.02±.74 (7)	.48±1.39 (2)	1.25±.74 (7)
May Require Some Statistics	.96±.20 (97)	.25±.07 (820)	-.39± .12 (286)	-.06±.14 (194)
High School Math Only	-.05±.29 (46)	-.26±.11 (1244)	-.58± .05 (1692)	-.47±.07 (752)
Total	.66±.11 (315)	.05±.04 (2394)	-.57± .04 (1906)	-.41±.06 (1202)

*In standard score units (with numbers of cases in parentheses) with approximate 95% confidence bounds.

TABLE 2.11
Mean Twelfth-Grade Math Achievement
by Math Levels of Career Plan at Age 23 and Occupation at Age 29

Math Level of Occupation at Age 29	Mathematics Level of Career Plan at Age 23							
	Some College Level Math		May Require Some Statistics		High School Math Only		Plan Not Classified	
Math								
Some College-Level Math	1.18±.09	(523)	1.03±.23	(75)	.50±.54	(13)	.38±.41	(23)
May Require Some Statistics	.91±.13	(224)	.49±.05	(1776)	-.02±.12	(246)	.15±.13	(237)
High School Math Only	.45±.16	(158)	.10±.09	(174)	-.35±.06	(1185)	-.29±.10	(396)
Not Classified	.82±.19	(102)	.66±.15	(174)	-.16±.19	(104)	-.05±.17	(139)
Total	.97±.06	(1007)	.44±.04	(2543)	-.28±.05	(1584)	-.09±.07	(705)
Females								
Some College-Level Math	1.27±.38	(26)	1.05±.65	(9)	–	(1)	–	(1)
May Require Some Statistics	.87±.38	(27)	.21±.06	(1070)	-.37±.19	(105)	-.20±.14	(195)
High School Math Only	.89±.80	(6)	-.20±.14	(191)	-.50±.07	(757)	-.68±.08	(590)
Not Classified	1.18±.37	(28)	.16±.06	(1058)	-.42±07	(725)	-.57±.04	(2028)
Total	1.09±.11	(87)	.16±.04	(2328)	-.45±.05	(1588)	-.57±.04	(2814)

*In standard score units (with numbers of cases in parentheses) with approximate 95% confidence bounds.

mediate-level careers and .9 standard deviations greater than those ending up in non-mathematical careers.

One plausible explanation for the relationship of high school math achievement to career development after age 23 is that high school math achievement is related to events after high school that mediate the relationship of math achievement to later career development. Two potential mediators, educational attainment at age 23 and math level of college major were examined. For each of these variables, an analysis of variance was run to test the relationship of twelfth grade math achievement to math level of occupation at age 29, after these variables were controlled. Note that this procedure was not used to predict twelfth grade math scores. In particular, the question of main interest was whether students who planned careers at the same math level at age 23 and had completed the same level of education (or had completed majors at the same math level) but who ended up in occupations at different math levels had had different levels of twelfth grade math achievement.

Table 2.12 (top) shows the ANOVA results when educational attainment at age 23 is controlled. This analysis was inclusive in that students who were not planning careers outside the home at age 23 or were not working outside the home at age 29 were included in separate categories. The differences by outcome group were statistically significant, although modest in a practical sense. The inclusive nature of the analyses undoubtedly introduced some noise into the statistics, as decisions regarding

TABLE 2.12
Results of Three-Way Analyses of Variance of
Twelfth-Grade Math Achievement with Amount of Education
at Age 23, Separately for Males and Females

Source of Variation	df	Males F	p	Females F	p
Occupation at Age 29	3	14.14	.001	3.65	.01
Career Plan at Age 23	3	40.45	.001	33.93	.001
Amount of Education at Age 23	3	373.44	.001	410.89	.001
Occupation x Career Plan	9	2.00	.04	1.46	.16
Occupation x Education	9	1.35	.20	1.95	.05
Career Plan x Education	9	.72	.99	5.44	.001
Three-way Interaction	26	1.75	.01	1.39	.12
		$(R^2=.359)$		$(R^2=.310)$	

Variable + Category	Males N	Adjusted Mean	Females N	Adjusted Mean
Occupation at Age 29				
0. Unclassified	487	32.87	3680	26.04
1. Low Math Level	2132	31.16	1446	25.44
2. Intermediate Level	3272	31.77	1343	26.00
3. Math-Related	604	34.35	35	29.59
Career Plan at Age 23				
0. Unclassified	731	30.69	2697	25.10
1. Low Math Level	1467	30.53	1485	26.25
2. Intermediate Level	2446	31.73	2238	26.39
3. Math-Related	951	35.45	84	34.79
Amount of Education at Age 23				
1. No College	1472	24.57	3071	21.36
2. Some College	1873	31.37	1499	26.83
3. Bachelor's Only	1057	35.69	1275	31.78
4. Some Graduate Work	1193	38.50	659	33.85
GRAND MEAN		31.91		25.93
STANDARD DEVIATION		10.90		9.78

TABLE 2.13
Results of Three-Way Analysis of Variance of
Twelfth-Grade Math Achievement with Math Level of
College Major, Separately for Males and Females

Source of Variation	df	Males		Females	
		F	p	F	p
Occupation at Age 29	2	38.06	.001	5.08	.01
Career Plan at Age 23	2	9.67	.001	5.68	.004
Math Level of College Major	2	57.27	.001	21.16	.001
Occupation x Career Plan	5	.70	.99	.83	.99
Occupation x Math Level	4	.38	.99	1.66	.17
Career Plan x Math Level	4	.97	.99	1.35	.25
Three-way Interaction	7	.55	.99	1.50	.21
		$(R^2=.143)$		$(R^2=.092)$	

Variable + Category	Males		Females	
	N	Adjusted Mean	N	Adjusted Mean
Occupation at Age 29				
1. Low Math Level	686	33.43	299	30.10
2. Intermediate Level	1780	35.89	979	31.92
3. Math-Related	555	38.92	32	35.92
Career Plan at Age 23				
1. Low Math Level	377	33.92	216	30.69
2. Intermediate Level	1865	35.84	1044	31.54
3. Math-Related	799	36.97	50	36.75
Math Level of Major				
1. Low Math Level	484	34.53	422	32.48
2. Intermediate Level	1341	34.06	685	30.12
3. Math-Related	1196	38.49	203	34.78
GRAND MEAN		35.89		31.60
STANDARD DEVIATION		9.81		9.46

homemaking may be somewhat independent of ability. As shown on Table 2.12 (bottom), those who did end up in a math-related career had averaged .24 (for males) or .37 (for females) standard deviations higher on twelfth grade math achievement compared to those who ended up with careers at the intermediate level.

Table 2.13 shows the ANOVA results when the math level of college major is controlled (i.e., all students with careers with math level unclassified were excluded). For contrast, this analysis was also limited to college attenders who planned careers outside the home at age 23 and were working outside the home at age 29. Again, twelfth grade math achievement was significantly related to occupational outcome at age 29 even after career plan at age 23 and college major were controlled.

To What Extent Can Sex Differences in Math-Related Career Attainment be Explained by the Moderator Variables?

The tables and figures presented here indicate that students entering math-related careers were characterized by: early plans to enter math-related careers; high levels of educational attainment; the completion of math-related college majors; and high mathematics achievement scores in twelfth grade. The final question addressed in the study was related to the interaction among these characteristics and the processes leading to the tremendous differences between the proportions of males and females in math-related occupations. Specifically, the importance of sex differences in high school math achievement was examined in the context of other moderator variables.

As in the first substudy, the approach used was to construct a causal (path) model that hypothesized relationships between the variables in terms of a set of structural equations and then to examine the extent to which the correlations observed could be explained in terms of the hypothesized relationships. The main hypothesis tested with these models was that sex differences in occupational outcomes could be explained in terms of differences in the moderator variables so that no direct path between sex and the occupational outcome variable was included.

The variables selected for this summary model (Fig. 2.6) included career plans, educational expectations or attainment, and expected or actual college major, each assessed at three points in time (roughly ages 18, 19, and 23). This approach provides two advantages. First, it allows for the examination of effects of math achievement at different points in career development. It is thus possible to identify points at which interventions may be most effective. The second advantage is that it allows for the identification of variables relating to changes in plans. When career plan at age 19 is used as a predictor of career plan at age 23, the other predictors are in effect predicting career plan at age 23 above or below expectations based on career plan at age 19.

As before, the LISREL IV program was used to generate estimates of the path coefficients and a chi-square goodness-of-fit statistic. The probability level for the path model was .09, meaning that the model was not rejected by the data, even at the .05 level of significance.

Figure 2.6 shows the model finally adopted. In this model the path coefficients demonstrate that sex has the largest effects on the amount of math taken in high school ($b = -.25$), math achievement at the end of high school ($b = -.14$), and most of all on the math level of twelfth grade career expectations ($b = -.30$). The relationship of sex to the math level of high school career plans leads to large indirect effects on career plans at

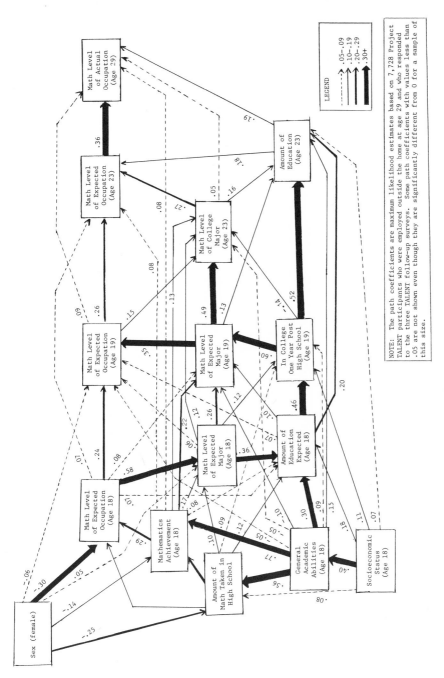

FIG. 2.6   Summary path model of the relationship of sex to math level of actual occupation at age 29.

NOTE: The path coefficients are maximum likelihood estimates based on 7,728 Project TALENT participants who were employed outside the home at age 29 and who responded to the three TALENT follow-up surveys.   Some path coefficients with values less than .05 are not shown even though they are significantly different from 0 for a sample of this size.

57

ages 19 and 23 and thus on occupation at age 29. High school career plans affect college major expectations (b = .58), which in turn affect later career plans.

High school math achievement has a large effect on the math levels of career plans (b = .29) and somewhat smaller effects on college major plans, and thus has a sizable indirect effect on later career plans. Math achievement also has a somewhat smaller, but very significant, direct effect on occupation at age 29 (b = .08). Amount of math taken in high school has direct effects on the amount of education expected (b = .12), on whether one is actually in college at age 19 (b = .09), and on the math level of expected college major (b = .10). These effects are all in addition to the substantial indirect effects of math participation through higher twelfth grade math achievement.

On the whole, the model shown in Fig. 2.6 suggests that career plans and math achievement in high school are especially important determinants of the math level of one's career at age 29. Sex differences in the outcome measures appear to develop almost entirely through differences in these two variables.

SUMMARY

For the cohort studied significant sex differences in math achievement did develop during the high school years. Sex differences in career interests and interest in math itself were already evident by ninth grade. These interest differences predicted the large sex differences in number of math courses taken during high school. The sex differences in the number of courses taken and the interest differences accounted for the sex differences in math achievement that emerged during the high school years.

In the second phase of this study, twelfth grade mathematics achievement was found to be highly predictive of persistence in plans to enter a math-related career and also of switching into a math-related career path. Sex differences in twelfth grade math achievement, together with the sex differences in career plans, accounted for most of the sex difference in career outcomes.

ACKNOWLEDGMENT

The research reported here was carried out with funds provided through Grant No. NIE-G-78-0001 from the National Institute of Education.

3 A National Assessment of Participation and Achievement of Women in Mathematics

Jane M. Armstrong
Education Commission of the States

Introduction

Among U.S. women who pursue a career outside the home, very few choose roles in science, engineering, or medicine.

Social, educational, and cultural barriers have prevented women from entering such technical fields. These barriers have existed for years, and despite hopeful rhetoric, they have changed little during the last half century. Only one-tenth of 1% of engineers are women; only 2% of physicists are women; only 5% of chemists are women.

Many factors work against women's entry into technical fields. For example, most technical pursuits require training in college-level mathematics. Without such training, women are barred. However, women's mathematics course-taking deficiency begins long before college and, by the time most women reach college, they do not have the mathematics background necessary for technical careers. According to a 1978 report from the College Entrance Examination Board, approximately 63% of college-bound males had taken 4 or more years of high school mathematics. Only 43% of females were similarly qualified. In most colleges and universities, 4 years of high school mathematics are required to take calculus—which is in turn required for virtually every technical or scientific major. Thus, without remedial work, more than half of all college-bound women are unable to major in the technical fields.

Why do women often avoid careers that require a foundation of mathematics? It is generally accepted that elementary school girls excel in arithmetic and science. However, the picture begins to change in junior high school as boys overtake and pass their female contemporaries in mathematics achievement. From the eighth grade on, female participation in mathematics declines steadily until, by high school graduation, male students outnumber women in mathematics classes.

Most of the large-scale research studies conducted in the last 20 years on sex differences in mathematics achievement and participation focused on these facts to support an underlying premise that because males traditionally take more mathematics they, therefore, tend to have higher achievement scores.

Traditional attempts to explain women's lack of participation in mathematics have viewed mathematics, a discipline characterized by abstract logic and deductive thought, as basically unfeminine. Through the ages mathematics has been regarded as a male domain. Women supposedly shy away from the logic and deductive thought required by mathematics in favor of aesthetic beauty and intuitive thought.

In fact, in earlier ages it was believed that women could not pursue mathematics because, for example, their heads were too small, their nervous systems too delicate, or their reasoning capacities insufficient. Such an eminent educational theorist as Rousseau believed that women were not qualified for research in abstract areas such as mathematics and science because their brains were unfit.

While such notions are clearly passé, they do have 20th century counterparts. For example, the possibility of a genetic effect favoring males in the area of spatial visualization is currently a topic under investigation. Is there a genetic barrier against female participation in mathematics? Or do society's preconceptions condition women against excelling in mathematics?

Preconceptions can be manifested in many factors in a young woman's environment. The interaction of these factors may work to help or hinder her in mathematical progress. Identifying and examining these factors and their interaction was one of the objectives that the National Institute of Education addressed with the Women and Mathematics grant program. Specifically, the program was designed to "identify and explain how selected cognitive, affective, educational, familial, or social factors influence achievement and participation of women . . . in their study of mathematics, their attitudes toward the study and usefulness of mathematics, and their preferences for occupations requiring mathematical competence."

This study was conducted by the Education Commission of the States (ECS) as a part of the Women and Mathematics program to identify the most important factors related to the problem of women's participation in mathematics and, further, to explore the relative importance of those factors in an effort to guide future research and to aid the development of strategies to remove the bias against women in the world of mathematics.

The survey approach used in this study is particularly appropriate for a complex problem such as women's participation in mathematics where the diversity of factors and their relationships may offer numerous plausible explanations. Previous studies reflect a clear lack of agreement regarding the effect of many of the variables on participation. Most of these studies looked at only a few of the possible affective factors at one time. Further, the sample sizes were small and the results frequently inconclusive due to a lack of statistical power. A national sample such as that used in the current study is one way to resolve the conflicts produced by previous limited samples. A large-scale survey can detect the small but stable influences overlooked by smaller, less sensitive studies. Thus, a major significance of the study reported here will be the determination for the relative importance of each of the possible factors affecting women's participation in mathematics based on national data.

RELATED RESEARCH

The findings of previous research on women's participation and achievement in mathematics were instrumental in defining the present study. Brief summaries of research findings are presented for each of the variables used in this study.

Mathematics Achievement

Most of the large-scale studies performed during the 1960s and 70s found significant sex differences in achievement beginning at puberty and continuing through adulthood, with males generally having superior scores (Fennema & Sherman, 1977b; National Assessment of Educational Progress, 1975, 1979a, b; Schonberger, 1976; Wilson, 1972).

Mathematics Participation

Unfortunately, mathematics course-taking or participation was not controlled in most of the previous studies on sex differences in achievement. However, several recent studies have focused on the question of sex-related differences in participation. Differential enrollment patterns in mathematics begin to appear at the level of algebra II, and increase thereafter (Fennema, 1977). One study performed at the University of California found that among entering freshmen, males who had taken 4 years of high school mathematics outnumbered females by more than 7 to 1 (Sells, 1973). Fennema (1977) found a 2 to 1 ratio in advanced mathematics classes.

Sex-Role Stereotyping

A number of studies have attempted to determine the relationship between sex-role stereotyping and mathematics participation by women. These studies suggest that many females regard careers for themselves as incompatible with family responsibilities. In general, it appears that if a woman anticipates a conflict between a career and the traditional role of homemaking, she is much more likely to choose the traditional role (Astin, 1974a; Rossi, 1965a). Additionally, Ory and Helfrich (1976) found that women seeking professional careers were less traditional in their views of women's sex-role identity than women choosing nonprofessional careers.

Mathematics as a Male Domain

Several studies have centered upon the sex-typing of mathematics as a "male domain"—a field of study and work appropriate only for males. In general, researchers have found that girls experience a strong conflict between academic achievement and popularity, in many cases choosing not to pursue mathematics because it might hamper their social relationships with boys (Coleman, 1961; Fennema & Sherman, 1977b; Hawley, 1971, 1972; Komarovsky, 1946; Lavach & Lanier, 1975; Sherman & Fennema, 1977).

Other research studies have focused upon the masculine identity hypothesis. That is, boys and girls who identify with their fathers or the male sex-role are better at mathematics. However, the results here are contradictory (Block, 1973; Heilbrun, 1974; Plank & Plank, 1954).

Career and Academic Plans

It appears that many college women may shun mathematics study because of a perceived conflict of roles (Smith, 1976). A science or mathematics career could interfere with raising a family and might conflict with the husband's career. Hawley (1971, 1972) and Astin (1974a) found that marriage was the primary goal of most women and, in choosing a career, the women based much of their decision on what they believed men could or would tolerate.

Attitude Toward Mathematics

A student's feelings toward mathematics can be a strong influence in his or her decision to continue with or begin to avoid mathematics. Enjoyment, confidence, and anxiety about mathematics combine to reflect the student's attitude toward mathematics.

In addition, the perceived usefulness of mathematics is an important factor in shaping the student's view of the subject. Several studies have found sex differences in student's perception of the usefulness of mathematics (Fennema & Sherman, 1976b; Fox, 1975a; Haven, 1971; Hilton & Berglund, 1974; Sherman & Fennema, 1977). In general these studies suggest that women who believe that mathematics would be useful in their future studies are much more likely to continue to take mathematics courses.

Parental Influence

Research suggests that parental influence strongly affects a student's course-taking, achievement in mathematics, and career aspirations through role modeling, direct encouragement, and expression of positive attitudes toward mathematics. Parental factors that have been found to mold the students' attitudes toward mathematics most strongly are the parents' enjoyment, confidence with, and use of mathematics. However, the exact nature of the parental influence is not clear from the research. Poffenberger and Norton (1956, 1959) found that male students were more prone to like mathematics if the father both liked mathematics and was good at it. This was not generally true for daughters, however.

Fennema (1977) noted that students' perception of their parents' attitudes were related to the students' course-taking intentions. Parental expectations seemed to influence students' success in mathematics, although parents appeared to have lower expectations for daughters than for sons (Casserly, 1975; Hill, 1967; Levine, 1976; Poffenberger & Norton, 1956). Fox (1976c) concluded that the expectations of the father, but not his attitude or occupation, influenced mathematics achievement for girls. Poffenberger and Norton (1956) found that, while the mother's expectations were important, her liking of mathematics was not. This was true for both sons and daughters (Burbank, 1968).

Influence of Other Significant People

A considerable amount of evidence indicates that the student's peers, counselors, and teachers exert a strong influence on the student's view of mathematics.

A considerable amount of evidence suggests that girls are seriously concerned about negative consequences of academic success, especially in mathematics. Even highly competent and achievement-motivated young women usually put their "femininity" before their academic success when conflict between the two images would arise (Horner, 1972).

Counselors appear to have a negative or neutral effect on girls who want to pursue mathematics or professional careers (Casserly, 1975, 1979). In some cases, counselors advised further counseling when girls wanted to pursue nontraditional careers and often discouraged girls from pursuing mathematics (Thomas & Stewart, 1971).

Many studies indicate that students' attitudes toward mathematics are strongly influenced by their experience with teachers. Students tend to be swayed by what they believe the teacher thinks of them and their ability in mathematics (Fennema & Sherman, 1976b). The seriousness of this influence on women's participation in mathematics is reflected by the fact that, in many cases, teachers tend to treat boys and girls differently (Bean, 1976; Parsons, Heller, & Kaczala, 1979).

On the other hand, at least two studies showed that teachers can have a tremendous positive influence on women's participation in mathematics. Casserly (1975) found that in high schools that had high female enrollment in advanced placement physics and mathematics, the teachers had actively recruited girls for their courses. Luchins (1976) found that many women successful in mathematics had at least one encouraging teacher during their education.

METHODOLOGY

Having reviewed previous work on the network of interrelated factors affecting achievement and participation in mathematics, the present study isolated and defined each factor for the development of measures to use in the subsequent survey.

Defining the Variables

Based on a thorough literature search, a tentative list of variables that might affect participation was developed. Relevant research articles and existing instruments were reviewed by staff and definitions of each variable were drafted. Following this review, a rough first draft of scales or individual items for each of the variables of interest was prepared by staff for consideration by a five-member advisory board. The board, comprised of three mathematics educators and two research psychologists, was formed to give its reaction to products and plans and to advise the project staff. The advisory board refined definitions of the variables and reviewed existing instruments for accuracy, completeness, item quality, and content validity.

In February, 1978 all items and scales were field tested on approximately 500 eighth grade and 500 twelfth grade students from Duluth, Minnesota, and Columbus, Georgia. These sites were selected to represent the national average based on the sampling plan developed by the National Assessment.

Following the two initial field tests, the advisory board reviewed the results and recommended those items that should be included in the final survey. Consultants then reviewed the selected items and filled in gaps where items had been deleted or refinements had been made in the definition of the variables. In April of 1978, the instruments were again field tested, this time on 900 eighth and eleventh grade students in Minnesota, Rhode Island, and Connecticut.

Following the April field tests, items were analyzed once again, and the weaker items (based on item-to-scale correlations and standard deviations) were rejected. Also at this stage, items were rejected if they were repetitious.

Sampling

The drawing of the survey sample and the administration of the questionnaire were performed under subcontract by the Research Triangle Institute (RTI). Research Triangle Park, North Carolina. The sample was drawn in the early spring of 1978 and the survey administered between October 9 and December 15, 1978.

An attempt was made to identify the most important factors affecting women's participation and achievement in mathematics by bracketing the time when changes occur. Thirteen-year-olds were one data base since most 13-year-olds are in the eighth grade, the point where required mathematics generally ends. Seniors in high school were selected as the other sample. Here, students will have completed or will be completing their high school mathematics careers. The survey was administered to these two groups to detect shifts or changes in attitudes and achievement in mathematics during the high school years.

The sample for the 13-year-old population included 82 schools, with group administration sizes ranging from 12 to 25 students; 1,452 13-year-olds were surveyed. For twelfth grade students, the sample consisted of 71 schools and 1,788 students. As many as 35 students per school were surveyed.

The larger sample size for high school seniors was a result of oversampling. It was feared that, in a national probability sample, there might be insufficient mathematically advanced females, and possibly advanced males, to form a group large enough for statistical comparisons. Thus, students who had taken trigonometry or higher-level mathematics courses were considered "advanced" and were oversampled. In the statistical analysis, weights were used to represent the occurrence of the various types of students in the nation.

Administration

Students were paced through the 90 minute survey by an audio tape to assure they would finish answering all questions and to put a time limit on the achievement items included in the survey.

Answer sheets were scanned by Westinghouse DataScore Systems and the results put on computer tapes. A weight for each respondent was computed by RTI and these data were merged onto the data tape. The weighted tape was then sent to ECS for analysis.

Survey Content

Achievement

Achievement in mathematics was assessed by tests in the following four areas:

- computation (items from the Stanford Achievement Test)
- algebra (items from the Cooperative Algebra I and Algebra II Tests)
- problem solving (items from the Metropolitan Achievement Tests)
- spatial visualization (items from the Revised Minnesota Paper Form Board)

Participation

For the purposes of the survey, participation was defined using the most advanced mathematics course a student took during high school. Four levels were used:

- general mathematics and/or algebra I
- algebra II and/or geometry
- trigonometry and/or probability and statistics
- precalculus and/or calculus

For the twelfth grade sample, mathematics participation was determined by asking respondents to indicate which of twelve mathematics courses they had taken. Courses ranged from general, business, or consumer mathematics to precalculus and calculus. Each student was categorized into one of the four participation levels listed above based upon the level at which he or she terminated his or her mathematics course work.

To measure *intended participation* for 13-year-olds, the survey asked 13-year-olds to indicate the number of years of mathematics they planned to take during 4 years of high school.

Students were also asked if they took (for the grade 12 sample) or if they were presently taking (for the 13-year-old sample) algebra while in eighth grade. This variable was included because algebra in the eighth grade could represent "fast tracking" in mathematics. A differential enrollment for the sexes at this early point in their mathematics careers might be a starting point for the disparity in course-taking for males and females.

Sex-Role Stereotyping

Sex-role stereotyping influences included three variables. The first, *general sex-role stereotyping,* addressed the effects of traditional sex-roles on a female's view of mathematics. Students with "traditional" views about sex-roles might be less likely to view mathematics as useful to their future. The second variable measured the student's perception of *mathematics as a male domain.* The third variable looked at *men's attitudes toward women who are successful in mathematics.* Scores on this item provided an indication of the level of women's concern for male attitudes and how that concern might affect mathematics course-taking for women.

Career and Academic Plans

Students were asked to choose *the career that they planned to have* from a list of eight groups of careers. They were then asked how *much mathematics was necessary for that career.* Finally, they were asked to rate the importance of a list of *factors that might have affected their decision* about pursuing a particular career.

Two items were included in *academic plans.* The first was *academic aspirations*—that is, the highest level of education the student expected to complete. The second variable measured the importance of nine different *factors affecting the students' course-taking decisions.*

Attitudes Toward Mathematics

The students' attitudes toward mathematics were divided into two categories:

- mathematics and oneself
- usefulness of mathematics

Mathematics and oneself included three variables:

- enjoyment of mathematics
- confidence in one's ability in mathematics
- anxiety in mathematical situations

Two components of usefulness were addressed—usefulness of mathematics in daily life and usefulness to career and educational plans.

Parental Influence

Parental influence can strongly affect a student's course-taking, achievement in mathematics and career aspirations through role modeling, direct encouragement, and expression of attitudes toward mathematics. Variables in the area of parental influence measured the student's perceptions of the attitudes, behaviors, and abilities of parents.

The first variable in this area was that of the *role model of the parents,* which measured the parents passive influence, or the results of the examples set by the parents. Next was *parents' encouragement in mathematics,* a measure of the active encouagement given by the mother and/or father. Even if a parent has very limited ability in mathematics, he or she could still have a strong positive influence through direct encouragement. *Parents' stereotyping of mathematics* measured whether or not the student believed his or her parents thought mathematics is "more for males than for females." The next variable determined *which parent helped with homework,* followed by the variable which measured *who used more mathematics,* mother or father.

Parents' educational expectations for offspring indicated the highest level of education that each parent expected the student to complete.

Influence of Others

The influence of significant other people in the students' life was gauged by seven scales or items. The first was that of *peer influence.* This variable dealt with what the students' friends think about people who are "good" in mathematics. The second, *peer stereotyping of mathematics,* measured whether or not the students' friends think that mathematics is more for males than for females. The next two variables measured *teacher encouragement in mathematics* and *counselor encouragement to take more mathematics.* The next two variables determined the extent of *teacher stereotyping of mathematics* and *teacher differential treatment* (does the teacher behave differently toward male and female students?). The last variable in this area, *sibling role models,* noted whether or not the student had an older brother or sister who was good in mathematics.

Background Variables

This group of influences was divided into four categories:

- age or grade of each student
- socioeconomic status
- parents' education
- parents' occupation

RESULTS

Three sets of results will be reported in this section: first, the results from the analysis of the mathematics achievement and participation data; second, the relationships (correlations) between students' attitudes and achievement or participation in mathematics; and finally, the results from a predictive model of students' achievement and participation in mathematics. The predictive model was produced by applying regression analyses to the survey data.

Sex Differences in Achievement

Figure 3.1 illustrates the achievement data for high school seniors and for 13-year-olds. The pattern of results found for the high school seniors and 13-year-olds on achievement subtests is similar to trends reported in previous surveys. Sex differences in achievement for the twelfth grade sample favored males on all four subtests, but the only statistically significant difference was the problem-solving test. Males scored approximately seven percentage points higher on the problem-solving test. There were no significant sex differences on the spatial visualization measure.

For the 13-year-olds, females outperformed males on the computation subtest, a finding that agrees with earlier research. Females were evenly matched with males on problem-solving ability, but surpassed their male counterparts on the spatial visualization test by five percentage points.

For comparison, Figure 3.2 shows the results from the second mathematics assessment, which was conducted in 1977–78 by the National Assessment of Education Progress (NAEP). This assessment used a large national sample of 9-, 13- and 17-year-olds. Summary results of exercise sets on computation, algebra, and application are reported for approximately 24,000 13-year-olds and 24,000 17-year-olds. Although these exercise sets were developed to measure the same mathematical skills, they are not the identical items that appeared in the standardized tests chosen for the Women in Mathematics study. Another difference is that students in the older group in the present Women in Mathematics study were in grade 12. Seventy-two percent of the 17-year-olds were in grade 11 and only about 14% in grade 12 in the NAEP study. Results from the NAEP second mathematics assessment are reported here because they are current, represent a very large national probability sample and substantiate the pattern of sex differences in achievement found in this study.

The results for 17-year-olds on comparable measures from the NAEP second mathematics assessment are similar to the results for the present study. No significant sex-related differences existed for computation or algebra, but a large and statistically significant difference of five percentage points favored males on the application (problem-solving) exercise

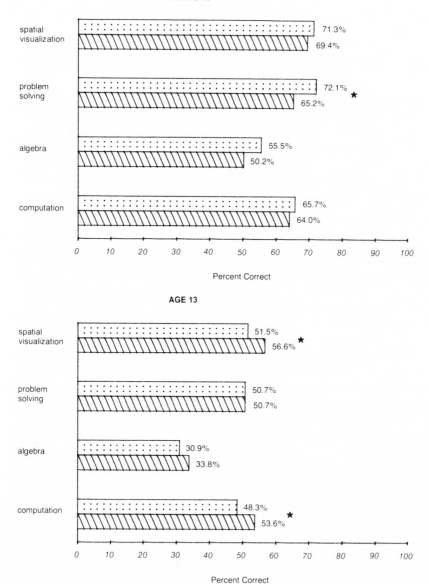

FIG. 3.1 Mathematics achievement from the Women in Mathematics Survey, Fall, 1978. Percentages of correct responses by age and sex.

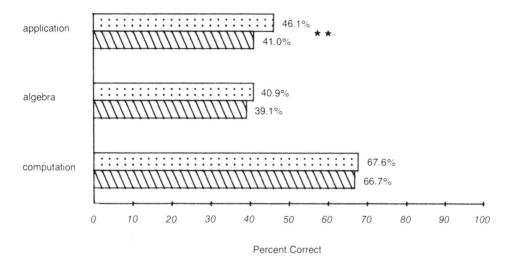

AGE 17

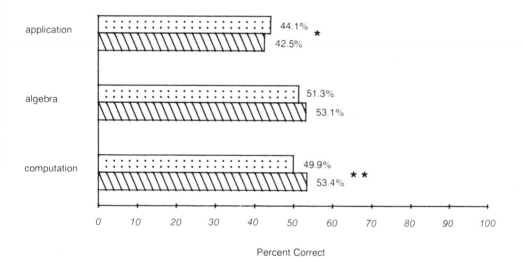

AGE 13

*difference is statistically significant at .05 level
**difference is statistically significant at .01 level

Key: Males
Females

FIG. 3.2 Mathematics achievement from the NAEP Second Mathematics Assessment, 1977–78. Percentages of correct responses by age and sex.

set. Again, 13-year-old females did significantly better than males on computation items. One difference in results between the two surveys is that 13-year-old males outscored females by one and a half percentage points on problem-solving skills in the larger NAEP assessment.

Results from the two surveys indicate the same general pattern of performance for the two sexes and two ages. Females enter high school with approximately the same mathematical understanding and skills as the males. Sometime during the high school years, males catch up with and then surpass the females in certain areas of mathematics achievement. Is this phenomenon easily explained by the notion that males take more mathematics while in high school and thus have higher achievement scores? Some insight into this hypothesis can be obtained by looking at high school mathematics participation for both males and females.

Sex Differences in Participation

Figure 3.3 shows percentages of students in grade 12 who indicated that they had completed, or were presently taking, each of 12 high school mathematics courses. Few sex differences in mathematics participation were found for the lower-level high school mathematics courses; in fact, only three of the twelve courses showed significant sex differences in enrollment. Significantly more females took business or accounting mathematics while significantly more males took algebra II and probability/statistics: Almost 4% more males took trigonometry; 5% more took computer programming and 3% more took calculus. None of these differences, however, were statistically significant.

Enrollment statistics for 17-year-olds are reported for the NAEP second mathematics assessment in Fig. 3.4. Because most of these students were in the eleventh grade, they had not had the opportunity to take as much mathematics as the students reported on in Fig. 3.3. Thus, the total percent for course enrollments is somewhat lower. The trends in participation are similar, but some interesting differences appear.

Significant sex-related differences in enrollments were found for the higher-level mathematics courses of trigonometry and precalculus/calculus. Although only 3.6% more males took trigonometry, this percentage difference represents a 55–45% male-female enrollment split in the classroom. Similarly, the fact that only 1.8% more men took either precalculus or calculus can be somewhat deceiving because this represents almost a 3:2 ratio of men to women in these higher-level courses. Fully 60% of the students in precalculus/calculus are men and only 40% are women, according to the NAEP survey. The finding that 3.5% more males than females took precalculus in the Women in Mathematics study

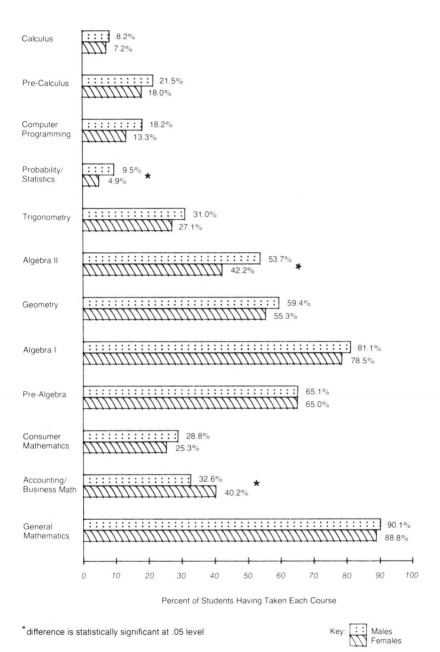

FIG. 3.3 Mathematics participation of grade 12 students from the Women in Mathematics Survey, Fall, 1978. Percentages of students by sex presently taking or having completed each course.

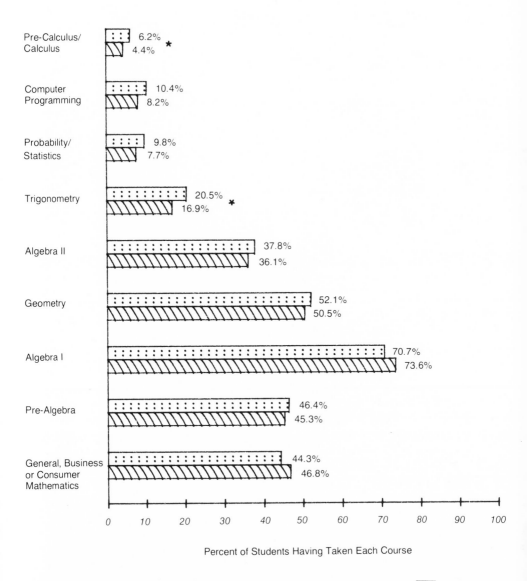

Pre-Calculus/
Calculus   6.2% *
    4.4%

Computer
Programming   10.4%
    8.2%

Probability/
Statistics   9.8%
    7.7%

Trigonometry   20.5% *
    16.9%

Algebra II   37.8%
    36.1%

Geometry   52.1%
    50.5%

Algebra I   70.7%
    73.6%

Pre-Algebra   46.4%
    45.3%

General, Business
or Consumer
Mathematics   44.3%
    46.8%

0   10   20   30   40   50   60   70   80   90   100

Percent of Students Having Taken Each Course

*difference is statistically significant at .05 level

Key: :: Males
     Females

FIG. 3.4 Mathematics participation of 17-year-old students from the NAEP Second Mathematics Assessment, Spring, 1978. Percentages of students by sex who have studied each course.

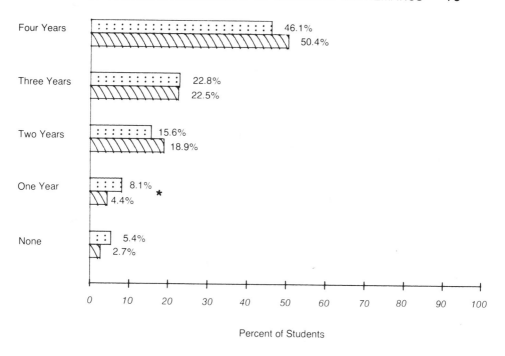

Key: Males / Females

FIG. 3.5   Intended mathematics participation for 13-year-old students from the Women in Mathematics National Survey, Fall, 1978. Precentages of students by sex who intend to take high school mathematics courses.

may reflect a reliable difference that might have been significant if a larger and statistically more powerful sample had been drawn.

For 13-year-olds, the reported number of years that they intended to take mathematics in high school is shown in Fig. 3.5. It is important to remember that the results are an intended rather than an actual participation measure; therefore, it may not be as valid a measure as that for the grade 12 sample. More males than females intended to take 1 year of high school mathematics, but approximately the same number of females as males intended to take 2, 3, or 4 years of high school mathematics. Thus, no significant sex differences were found among 13-year-olds for intended participation in higher-level mathematics courses.

The results suggest that the widely disparate sex differences in participation found in earlier small-scale studies (Ernest, 1976; Sells, 1973) are diminishing. The pattern for both the NAEP and the present survey indicate that participation for males and females is similar for the basic mathematics courses, whereas some differences in mathematics enrollment favor males at the higher-level courses.

TABLE 3.1

Mathematics Achievement Within Participation Level
for Grade 12 Students From the Women in Mathematics
National Survey, Fall, 1978. Percentages of Correct Response by Sex

Level of Participation		Male	Female	Difference	Male	Female	Difference
		Computation			Algebra		
General Math, Business	%	47.50	48.05	- .55	31.23	25.40	5.83
Math, Consumer Math,	S.E. †	1.97	2.53	3.20	1.51	2.68	3.08
Pre-Algebra	n §	116	119		95	109	
Algebra I	%	56.21	58.05	-1.84	32.39	35.73	-3.34
	S.E.	2.30	2.50	3.40	2.13	1.50	2.61
	n	114	145		108	142	
Geometry	%	60.59	63.09	-2.50	46.37	44.90	1.47
	S.E.	3.38	2.72	4.34	5.42	2.95	6.17
	n	55	101		54	99	
Algebra II	%	70.87	67.04	3.83	64.50	57.20	7.30
	S.E.	1.58	3.51	3.85	2.71	3.61	4.51
	n	113	122		133	121	
Trigonometry and/or	%	70.40	68.34	2.06	60.32	64.89	-4.57
Probability/Statistics	S.E.	2.89	2.58	3.87	2.87	2.54	3.83
	n	161	167		157	165	
Pre-Calculus	%	77.78	76.76	1.02	75.04	70.30	4.74
	S.E.	1.81	2.17	2.83	2.14	3.18	3.83
	n	192	175		191	175	
Calculus	%	80.59	86.21	-5.62	80.85	83.10	-2.25
	S.E.	2.57	1.68	3.07	2.72	2.34	3.59
	n	110	84·		109	83	
		Problem Solving			**Spatial Visualization**		
General Math, Business	%	58.49	51.20	7.29*	63.77	56.89	6.88*
Math, Consumer Math,	S.E.	2.16	2.58	3.36	2.55	1.50	2.96
Pre-Algebra	n	115	121		111	117	
Algebra I	%	66.11	60.10	6.01*	68.15	65.31	2.84
	S.E.	2.10	1.94	2.86	4.91	1.94	5.28
	n	115	145		109	142	
Geometry	%	68.36	66.15	2.21	66.08	73.71	-7.63
	S.E.	3.26	1.82	3.73	3.09	2.33	3.87
	n	55	102		51	99	
Algebra II	%	76.27	64.39	11.88*	72.56	69.90	2.66
	S.E.	2.01	2.88	3.51	2.63	2.77	3.82
	n	113	122		111	115	
Trigonometry and/or	%	73.52	67.23	6.29*	71.35	74.23	-2.88
Probability/Statistics	S.E.	1.91	1.77	2.60	2.46	1.78	3.04
	n	162	167		154	160	
Pre-Calculus	%	81.87	79.68	2.19	79.64	77.29	2.35
	S.E.	1.58	2.60	3.04	1.27	2.75	3.03
	n	190	175		186	166	
Calculus	%	86.49	85.52	.97	78.34	79.96	-1.62
	S.E.	2.79	1.98	3.42	2.42	2.15	3.24
	n	109	84		107	82	

* difference is statistically significant at .05 level
† S.E. is the standard error
§ n is the sample size

The participation results raise the question as to whether the few sex differences in mathematics participation are large enough to account for the observed sex differences in achievement. To investigate any possible effect of participation on achievement, achievement scores were tabulated within levels of participation.

Sex Differences in Achievement Within Participation Levels

Scores on the four achievement subtests are shown in Table 3.1 for males and females in grade 12 within seven different participation levels. These levels were defined by the highest mathematics course taken when in high school and can be thought of as the stopping point in a student's mathematics education. Achievement subtest scores, sample size, standard errors, the difference in scores between sexes, and the standard error of the difference are given for each level of participation.

No statistically significant sex-related differences existed on the computation or algebra achievement tests at any level of participation. Differences did appear in favor of males on the problem-solving measure in four of the seven participation levels. However, no significant difference in achievement appeared at the two highest levels of participation.

For spatial visualization, a significant sex difference was found only at the lowest level of participation where males scored higher than females on the spatial test.

The NAEP sample of 17-year-olds also showed sex differences in achievement within levels of mathematics participation. The results are presented in Table 3.2 and indicate persistent sex differences favoring males at every level of participation on the application (problem-solving) set of items. The increase in the size of the sex difference as the level of mathematics participation increases is striking.

Interpreting these results is difficult. Based on the achievement scores for 13-year-olds, women start out in high school mathematics on a par with men. For most participation groups, women do as well as men on tests measuring the skills of computation and algebra. But, even when differences in participation are taken into account, men at nearly every level of participation have an advantage in solving typical one- and two-step textbook word problems.

Figures 3.1–3.5 and Table 3.1 and Table 3.2 have presented data on the national picture of achievement and participation in mathematics for male and female 13-year-olds and high school seniors. Given that there are some significant sex differences in participation, what factors affect students' decisions to take more mathematics?

TABLE 3.2

Mathematics Achievement Within Participation Levels
for 17-Year-Old Students From the NAEP Second Mathematics
Assessment, Spring, 1978. Percentages of Correct Responses by Sex

Level of Participation		Computation (127 Items)			Objective Algebra (59 Items)			Application (136 Items)		
		Male	Female	Difference	Male	Female	Difference	Male	Female	Difference
General Mathematics	%	47.03	48.32	-1.29	22.79	21.96	.83	30.39	27.95	2.44**
	S.E. †	.82	.83	1.16	.36	.44	.57	.48	.37	.61
	n §	2,500	2,534		2,501	2,536		2,500	2,534	
Algebra I	%	62.25	61.51	.74	31.44	30.33	1.11	38.93	34.53	4.40**
	S.E.	.90	.76	1.17	.64	.55	.85	.72	.61	.94
	n	1,631	2,176		1,629	2,179		1,632	2,176	
Geometry	%	70.66	69.35	1.31	37.93	37.62	.31	48.07	43.53	4.54**
	S.E.	.78	.75	1.13	.75	.65	.99	.70	.52	.87
	n	1,588	1,920		1,588	1,920		1,587	1,919	
Algebra II	%	80.44	78.08	2.36**	52.83	52.18	.65	55.06	48.73	6.33**
	S.E.	.69	.59	.90	.81	.75	1.08	.74	.65	.97
	n	2,619	2,890		2,618	2,892		2,617	2,891	
Higher Course than Algebra II	%	88.27	86.41	1.86*	69.02	65.56	3.46*	67.69	60.29	7.40**
	S.E.	.55	.58	.80	1.05	1.19	1.58	.66	.94	1.15
	n	1,539	1,139		1,539	1,139		1,539	1,139	

* difference is statistically significant at .05 level
** difference is statistically significant at .01 level
† S.E. is the standard error
§ n is the sample size

Relative Importance of Certain Factors Affecting the Decision To Take More Mathematics

Students were directly asked to rate the importance of each of nine factors that might have affected their decision to take more mathematics. The results were rank ordered and are shown in Table 3.3.

In grade 12, males and females selected nearly the same factors as important in deciding whether or not to take more mathematics. Both sexes indicated that the usefulness of mathematics was the most important factor, followed by confidence in and enjoyment of mathematics. Although the influence of parents, teachers, and counselors was thought to be moderately important, peer influence was not.

Thirteen-year-old females ranked the importance of the nine factors in the same order as males. Like high school seniors, 13-year-olds considered usefulness of mathematics to be most important and peer influence to be least important. Parents and teachers, however, had a stronger influence on the 13-year-olds.

The results in Table 3.3 are useful in two respects. First, by rank-ordering the results, the relative importance of the factors affecting the decision to take more mathematics is determined. And, even more significantly, the results give the student's direct indications as to which

TABLE 3.3
Rank Ordered Results on the Relative Importance of Certain Factors
Affecting Students' Decisions To Take More Mathematics

Factors	Mean	Rank Order	Mean	Rank Order
	Grade 12 Females		Grade 12 Males	
1. How useful mathematics will be	80.91	1	79.27	1
2. How good or bad in mathematics	74.55	2	68.81	3
3. How much math is liked or disliked	72.43	3	69.20	2
4. What math teachers think	66.40	4	64.63	4
5. What mother thinks	65.73	5	63.03	6
6. What father thinks	62.51	6	64.19	5
7. What school counselor thinks	56.27	7	55.69	7
8. Whether friends take mathematics	25.12	8	31.83	8
9. Whether classmates approve	16.48	9	24.89	9
	Age 13 Females		Age 13 Males	
1. How useful mathematics will be	88.15	1	82.54	1
2. What mother thinks	79.40	2	77.12	2
3. What father thinks	77.41	3	76.45	3
4. What math teachers think	76.38	4	73.57	4
5. How good or bad in mathematics	72.87	5	69.47	5
6. How much math is liked or disliked	72.62	6	67.98	6
7. What school counselor thinks	63.86	7	62.06	7
8. Whether friends take mathematics	45.43	8	43.72	8
9. Whether classmates approve	35.05	9	42.21	9

factors have the most potential for inclusion in future programs to increase participation.

Correlations of Study Variables With Participation

Whereas reporting the sex differences for each variable included in the study would be interesting, it is more important to examine the correlation between each variable and participation or achievement. Correlations indicate the relationship between a variable and participation or achievement—sex differences, *per se,* do not.

Table 3.4 shows the correlations of the study variables with participation for both males and females in grade 12 and at age 13. Most correlations with participation are positive because all variables were scored in the direction of their contribution to a positive influence on participation (or achievement). For example, a high score on a stereotyping item indicated a "contemporary" attitude, that is, *no* stereotyping. Thus, a high correlation of mathematics as a male domain with participation indicated that those students who did *not* view mathematics as a subject only for males tended to take more mathematics. The same is true of the anxiety measures. A high score indicates *low* anxiety.

Grade 12 Sample

For high school seniors, career and education plans were positively related to mathematics participation. The chosen career, the student's perception of the necessity of using mathematics and the amount of mathematics required for a job were all highly correlated with course-taking. Students' education aspirations were significantly related to taking high school mathematics. Those students who planned to continue their education through college and graduate school were more likely to have taken more advanced mathematics than those students who had lower academic aspirations.

A second category of variables, positive feelings toward mathematics and one's ability in mathematics, showed a strong positive relationship with mathematics course-taking. A positive attitude toward mathematics, indicated by confidence in mathematics, low anxiety and enjoyment of

TABLE 3.4

Correlations Between Study Variables and Mathematics Participation
for Grade 12 Students and 13-Year-Olds
From the Women in Mathematics National Survey, Fall, 1978

Variables	Grade 12		Age 13	
	Male	Female	Male	Female
I. Sex-Role Stereotyping				
A. General Sex-Role Stereotyping	.074	.110	.182**	.060
B. Mathematics as a Male Domain	.099	.188**	.179**	.095
C. Men's Attitudes Toward Successful Women	.076	.081	.141*	.084
II. Career Plans				
A. Career Aspirations	.286**	.288**	.154*	.039
B. Mathematics Preparation Required for a Job	.499**	.400**	.193**	.103
C. Job Using Mathematics	.298**	.216**	-.116	-.142*
D. Job Done by Members of Opposite Sex	-.079	.014	.031	.008
III. Mathematics and Oneself				
A. Confidence in Mathematics	.466**	.423**	.280**	.194**
B. Anxiety in Mathematics	.348**	.325**	.285**	.192**
C. Anxiety in English	.109	.096	.015	.072
D. Anxiety in School	.212**	.225**	.272**	.092
E. Enjoyment of Mathematics	.472**	.375**	.284**	.264**
F. Locus of Control	.067	.046	.059	.097
IV. Usefulness of Mathematics	.341**	.301**	.378**	.256**
V. Academic Plans				
A. Educational Aspirations	.475**	.452**	.267**	.167**
VI. Parental Influences				
A. Father as a Role Model	.161**	.116**	.168**	.096
B. Mother as a Role Model	-.124*	-.032	.153*	.117
C. Father's Encouragement in Mathematics	.304**	.320**	.252**	.132
D. Mother's Encouragement in Mathematics	.340**	.305**	.276**	.177**
E. Father's Stereotyping of Mathematics	.050	.105	-.087	-.022
F. Mother's Stereotyping of Mathematics	.029	.100	-.083	-.065
G. Father's Educational Expectations	.466**	.386**	.207**	.104
H. Mother's Educational Expectations	.451**	.361**	.240**	.095

(This table is continued on the next page)

TABLE 3.4 (Cont.)

Variables	Grade 12		Age 13	
	Male	Female	Male	Female
VII. Influences of Significant Others				
A. Peer Influence	.209**	.207**	.243**	.137*
B. Boys' Stereotyping of Mathematics	-.121	.028	-.063	-.001
C. Girls' Stereotyping of Mathematics	-.004	.085	-.057	-.037
D. Counselor Encouragement	.279**	.238**	.118	.240**
E. Teacher Encouragement	.414**	.433**	.243**	.161*
F. Teacher Stereotyping of Mathematics	.102	.104	.054	.024
G. Teacher Differential Treatment	.196**	.089	.149*	.059
H. Brother as Role Model	.077	.147*	.025	-.021
I. Sister as Role Model	.114	.099	.071	.010
VIII. School Experience				
A. Grades in Mathematics	.453**	.440**	.223**	.246**
B. Taking Algebra in 8th Grade	.344**	.256**	.002	.084
IX. Achievement				
A. Computation	.451**	.440**	.232**	.112
B. Algebra	.610**	.648**	.154**	.102
C. Problem Solving	.397**	.447**	.205**	.091
D. Spatial Visualization	.217**	.306**	.099	.086
X. Background Variables				
A. Father's Education	.258**	.329**	-.003	-.049
B. Mother's Education	.167**	.237**	.032	-.016
C. Socioeconomic Status	.122	.181**	.136	.005
D. Father's Occupation	.149*	.257**	-.015	.016
E. Mother's Occupation	.153*	.136*	.023	.087

* difference is statistically significant at .01 level
** difference is statistically significant at .001 level

mathematics, was highly correlated with participation. Students who liked mathematics and believed they were good in it tended to take more mathematics while in high school than students with poorer attitudes.

The variables of parental, teacher, peer, and counselor encouragement, a third category of variables, also affected participation in mathematics. Fathers (but not mothers) as role models and the active encouragement of both mothers and fathers were significantly correlated with participation for both males and females. Another form of parental encouragement was parents having high academic expectations for their children. Those students, especially males, whose parents had high academic expectations for them took more mathematics.

Students who perceived their teachers as encouraging tended to take more mathematics. Teacher differential treatment was one of the few variables for high school seniors that was significantly correlated with course-taking for males, but not for females. Males who perceived mathematics teachers as treating males the same as females tended to take more mathematics.

Counselor encouragement seemed to have an effect on course-taking for most students. Only those students who indicated they had been counseled (59% of the grade 12 sample) were included in this correlational analysis. Both male and female students who indicated they had a counselor who encouraged them to take mathematics were more likely to have taken mathematics.

Approval, support, and encouragement of peers may contribute to mathematics participation. Although not as highly correlated as other variables, peer influence did have a low but significant correlation with taking high school mathematics.

For females, having an older brother who was good in mathematics was related to taking more mathematics. This was not true for either males or females having an older sister who was good in mathematics. This is not surprising because males have traditionally taken more mathematics so it would be more likely to have an older brother, rather than an older sister, who was good in mathematics.

Correlations of participation with achievement were among the highest correlations found. This is not an unexpected result, especially when the correlation with algebra is examined. This is the one subtest which was probably the most course-dependent. That is, a student would have had to have a course in algebra to do well on this subtest. This idea is substantiated by the highest correlation of algebra with participation of all the achievement subtests. In general, high correlations of achievement subtests with participation indicated that taking more mathematics was highly related to better performance on achievement measures.

Numerous background variables were related to mathematics participation for both males and females. A student's typical letter grade in mathematics was highly correlated with participation as was taking algebra I in the eighth grade. This latter variable is probably a surrogate for other factors such as high achievement in mathematics in the elementary school, size of the school and a well-developed mathematics program.

Socioeconomic status (SES) showed a low but significant correlation with participation for females but not for males. But, components of SES—parents' education and occupation—were significantly correlated with course-taking for both sexes.

Although these positive correlations of variables with participation are important, it is also significant that some of the "causal variables" identified in earlier studies were not correlated. In general, most of the stereotyping measures were not significantly correlated with participation (for example, stereotyping of sex-roles or parent, teacher and peer stereotyping of mathematics as a male domain).

One interesting exception to the lack of significant correlations with stereotyping measures is the result for twelfth grade women on the mathematics as a male domain scale. The women who did pursue advanced mathematics courses tended not to sex-type mathematics as a subject appropriate only for men.

13-Year-Old Sample

The basic categories of variables that correlated with participation for the high school seniors were similar, although not identical, to those for 13-year-olds. The participation variable for 13-year-olds was based on the item that asked how much mathematics they intended to take while in high school; it was not a measure of actual participation.

Educational aspirations, a positive feeling toward mathematics and the influence of parents, peers, and teachers were related to participation for 13-year-olds, as they were for high school seniors.

Thirteen-year-old males seemed to be influenced more by their fathers than their mothers; the reverse was true for 13-year-old females. Parents as role models and parental encouragement were related to intended mathematics participation for males, but the only similar significant parental influence for females was mothers' encouragement. Interestingly, fathers' and mothers' educational expectations were correlated with intended participation only for males and not females, even though 13-year-old females perceived their parents as having higher educational expectations for them than did 13-year-old males. As was found for twelfth grade students, peer influence and teacher encouragement were related to intended participation for 13-year-olds. Counselor encouragement was related only for females.

Fewer background variables were correlated with participation. Socioeconomic status and parents' occupation and education were not correlated for 13-year-olds as they were for seniors, probably because 13-year-olds were unsure of and, therefore not as accurate in reporting, the parents' education and occupation.

Grades in mathematics were related to intended course-taking for both sexes, but achievement scores in mathematics as measured by the subtests were correlated for males but not for females.

In summary, the information gained from the correlational analyses indicated that many of the variables may be "operating" in the same way for males and females, especially for the older group. The variables that correlated with participation were those related to career and future educational aspirations, perceived usefulness of mathematics, liking mathematics and being good in it, and the active approval and encouragement of taking more mathematics by parents, teachers, counselors, and to some degree, peers.

Correlations of Study Variables with Achievement

Table 3.5 shows the results of correlational analyses for mathematics achievement. Because participation is a likely predictor of achievement, it is not surprising that many of the variables that correlated with participation also correlated with achievement. Career plans, mathematics required for the chosen career, liking of mathematics, usefulness of mathematics, parental encouragement, parental educational expectations, peer and teacher influence, and socioeconomic status were significantly correlated with achievement for the grade 12 sample. Mathe-

TABLE 3.5
Correlations Between Study Variables and Mathematics Achievement
for Grade 12 Students and 13-Year-Olds
From the Women in Mathematics National Survey, Fall, 1978

Variables	Grade 12		Age 13	
	Male	Female	Male	Female
I. Sex-Role Stereotyping				
A. General Sex-Role Stereotyping	.068	.075	.198**	.329**
B. Mathematics as a Male Domain	.209**	.313**	.267**	.451**
C. Men's Attitudes Toward Successful Women	.115	.137*	.176**	.318**
II. Career Plans				
A. Career Aspirations	.298**	.194**	.168*	.186*
B. Mathematics Preparation Required for a Job	.405**	.323**	.049	-.056
C. Job Using Mathematics	.291**	.174**	-.103	-.034
D. Job Done by Members of Opposite Sex	-.095	-.122*	.094	-.057
III. Mathematics and Oneself				
A. Confidence in Mathematics	.479**	.424**	.360**	.338**
B. Anxiety in Mathematics	.354**	.321**	.313**	.270**
C. Anxiety in English	.102	.066	.078	239**
D. Anxiety in School	.283**	.198**	.256**	.273**
E. Enjoyment of Mathematics	.396**	.361**	.181**	.080
F. Locus of Control	.104.	.075	.102	.038
IV. Usefulness of Mathematics	.292**	.255**	.295**	.200**
V. Academic Plans				
A. Educational Aspirations	.462**	.395**	.237**	.238**
VI. Parental Influences				
A. Father as a Role Model	.183**	.099	.161*	.157*
B. Mother as a Role Model	-.104	-.041	.026	-.054
C. Father's Encouragement in Mathematics	.316**	.320**	.130	.095
D. Mother's Encouragement in Mathematics	.298**	.256**	.124	.095
E. Father's Stereotyping of Mathematics	.066	.055	-.062	-.121
F. Mother's Stereotyping of Mathematics	.026	.074	-.083	-.132
G. Father's Educational Expectations	.501**	.325**	216**	.198*
H. Mother's Educational Expectations	.505**	.228**	.190*	.161*

(This table is continued on the next page)

TABLE 3.5 (Cont.)

Variables	Grade 12 Male	Grade 12 Female	Age 13 Male	Age 13 Female
VII. Influences of Significant Others				
A. Peer Influence	.275**	.238**	.238**	.234**
B. Boys' Stereotyping of Mathematics	-.052	-.016	-.053	-.074
C. Girls' Stereotyping of Mathematics	.038	.127	-.196	-.219**
D. Counselor Encouragement	.202**	.258**	.256**	.195**
E. Teacher Encouragement	.380**	.360**	.238**	.188**
F. Teacher Stereotyping of Mathematics	.100	.084	.174*	.164*
G. Teacher Differential Treatment	.225**	.183**	.225**	.297**
H. Brother as Role Model	.131*	.158*	.095	.198*
I. Sister as Role Model	.237**	.110	.130	.125
VIII. School Experience				
A. Grades in Mathematics	.447**	.480**	.386**	.403**
B. Taking Algebra in 8th Grade	.160**	.216**	.309**	.373**
IX. Participation	.559**	.596**	.263**	.120
X. Background Variables				
A. Father's Education	.282**	.318**	-.060	-.073
B. Mother's Education	.272**	.286**	-.056	-.099
C. Socioeconomic Status	.167**	.258**	.150*	.186**
D. Father's Occupation	.237**	.197**	.030	.065
E. Mother's Occupation	.156*	.091	.002	.009

* difference is statistically significant at .01 level
** difference is statistically significant at .001 level

matics as a male domain was correlated with achievement for both males and females in grade 12. Absence of stereotyping women who are successful in mathematics was related to achievement only for women.

When 13-year-olds were compared with high school seniors, stereotyping proved to be a much bigger issue for the younger age group. Females who did not accept traditional sex-role stereotypes (e.g., they did not feel that mathematics is a male domain or did not think that men hold negative attitudes toward women who are successful in mathematics) tended to have higher achievement scores. Another interesting difference was that 13-year-olds who did well in mathematics did *not* perceive the parents (either father or mother) as being encouraging. Also, neither the mathematics preparation required for a job nor the fact that a job required mathematics correlated with achievement for the 13-year-olds, although they did for the seniors.

In summary, many of the variables that correlated with participation also correlated with achievement. After examining these correlations, it is easy to understand why so many previous studies looked at so many different variables that might affect participation and achievement. Many of the variables included in earlier studies were shown to be significantly related to course-taking by the present survey.

Given the correlations just discussed, the obvious question is: Which of the factors that correlated with participation or achievement are the best predictors? To address this question, the correlation matrix of selected variables was incorporated into a predictive model to gain more insight into the importance of individual factors in predicting participation or achievement in mathematics.

Predictive Analyses

For this study, a purely predictive model, rather than a causal model was used. Predictive models have the advantage of requiring few assumptions about the causal connections between predictors. Causal models, such as the technique of path analysis, require numerous *a priori* assumptions, resulting in many possible causal models. For these reasons, regression, a more conservative predictive technique, was used.

Factor analysis was used to reduce the study variables to a smaller set of relatively independent factors composed of scales. Even after the survey items were subjected to factor analysis, a fairly diffuse pattern of correlations between factors remained. This poses a problem in regression analysis because a step-wise hierarchical design is used. For example, if two or three variables are highly correlated with each other, the regression model might identify only the variable that is the strongest predictor of the three variables, leaving the other two unidentified.

To alleviate the problem of diffuse correlations, variables were sorted into one of three categories before they were entered into the regression analyses. First, they were classified as to whether they were "intervenable" through conventional means (e.g., through programs that may be initiated in the schools). Nonintervenable variables included school enrollment, availability of mathematics courses offered by the school, and socioeconomic status (SES). The remainder of the scales were categorized as either representing "self" or "others" characteristics. "Self" characteristics were scales related to student attitudes toward mathematics and stereotyping. The "others" category included effects of parents, teachers, and school counselors. Separate regression analyses were performed for each of the "self" and "others" variables. The nonintervenable variables were considered primary whenever achievement or participation were predicted by a confounded variation of intervenable and nonintervenable variables. Technically speaking, the predictive models were hierarchical designs that identified portions of residual variance in achievement or participation which were tied to variance in either "self" or "others" variables. Nonintervenable variables were entered simultaneously in the first step. The remainder of the variables were then entered in a step-wise fashion. In each step, the variable that was included was the one with the highest partial correlation with either achievement or participation. Although this method established an *a posteriori* sequence based upon the unique residual covariance in each step, the order of predictor variables should not be taken too literally because of the existence of some intercorrelations between variables. What should be noted is the increase in predicted variance over that which is possible from the nonintervenable factors.

Results of the regression analyses predicting achievement are presented in Table 3.6. Analyses were done separately for each age and sex. Looking at Table 3.6, it can be seen that parental encouragement, the passive influence of mother as a role model and the parents' educational expectations accounted for an additional 28% of the variance for the twelfth grade males when "others" were used to predict achievement. In a second model in which student characteristics were used, attitudes toward mathematics, educational, and career aspirations and the perceived amount of mathematics needed for a job accounted for a 31% increase in total variance after the nonintervenable variables were accounted for. In these two models, "self" and "others" variables explained about 30% of the variances, making these fairly powerful predictive models.

Similar results were found for females in grade 12. In terms of "others," influences of parents and teachers seemed to be the best predictors of achievement. Teacher encouragement, father's educational expectations, parental encouragement, mother as a role model, and counselor encouragement accounted for a 19% increase in explained variance. The second model predicting mathematics achievement for twelfth grade females considered student characteristics. A 26% increase in predicted variance was attributable to attitudes toward mathematics, educational aspirations, and the amount of mathematics preparation needed for a job.

Considerably less variance could be determined based on the characteristics of "others" or "self" for 13-year-old males. Only 10% of the variance could be predicted by teacher differential treatment, father's educational expectations, and counselor encouragement. Characteristics of the student predicted achievement better for 13-year-old males. Attitudes toward mathematics, the (lack of) stereotyping of women, educational aspirations and locus of control (the student perceiving himself as solely responsible for how well he does in mathematics) predicted an addition 16% of the variance.

Results on achievement regression analyses for 13-year-old females were similar to those for males. Again, teacher differential treatment, father's educational expectations and counselor encouragement were the variables related to "others" which best predicted achievement. Lack of stereotyping of women, attitudes toward mathematics, school anxiety, and educational aspirations were the student characteristics that best predicted achievement.

TABLE 3.6
Predictive Models for Mathematics Achievement Utilizing Student Attitudes or Parental and Teacher Characteristics*

Variable	Squared Multiple Correlation	"Intervenable" Variance R^2 Total—R^2 Nonintervenable
Grade 12 Males		
"Nonintervenable" Variables		
School Enrollment		
Socioeconomic Status		
Number of Mathematics Courses Offered		
Most Advanced Mathematics Course Offered	.06	.00
Predictive Model 1: Characteristics of Others		
Mothers Educational Expectations		
Teacher Encouragement		
Mother As a Role Model	.35	.28
Parental Encouragement		
Predictive Model 2: Characteristics of Self		
Attitudes Toward Mathematics		
Educational Aspirations		
Mathematics Preparation Required for Job	.38	.31
Career Aspirations		
Age 13 Males		
"Nonintervenable" Variables		
School Enrollment		
Socioeconomic Status	.03	.00
Predictive Model 1: Characteristics of Others		
Teacher Differential Treatment		
Fathers Educational Expectations		
Counselor Encouragement	.13	.10
Predictive Model 2: Characteristics of Self		
Attitudes Toward Mathematics		
Stereotyping of Women		
Educational Aspirations	.19	.16
Locus of Control		

Variable	Squared Multiple Correlation	"Intervenable" Variance R^2 Total—R^2 Nonintervenable
Grade 12 Females		
"Nonintervenable" Variables		
School Enrollment		
Number of Mathematics Courses Offered		
Socioeconomic Status		
Most Advanced Mathematics Course Offered	.12	.00
Predictive Model 1: Characteristics of Others		
Teacher Encouragement		
Fathers Educational Expectations		
Counselor Encouragement		
Parental Encouragement	.31	.19
Mother As a Role Model		
Predictive Model 2: Characteristics of Self		
Attitudes Toward Mathematics		
Educational Aspirations		
Mathematics Preparation Required for Job	.38	.26
Age 13 Females		
"Nonintervenable" Variables		
School Enrollment		
Socioeconomic Status	.03	.00
Predictive Model 1: Characteristics of Others		
Teacher Differential Treatment		
Counselor Encouragement		
Fathers Educational Expectations		
Mother As a Role Model	.23	.20
Predictive Model 2: Characteristics of Self		
Stereotyping of Women		
Attitudes Toward Mathematics		
School Anxiety	.26	.23
Educational Aspirations		

*Only variables adding at least 1% to predicted variance are included.

Table 3.7 presents results of the regression analyses for mathematics participation. As was done for the analyses predicting achievement, nonintervenable variables of school characteristics were entered first and taken into account in the subsequent analyses.

For twelfth grade males, father's educational expectations, counselor encouragement, mother as a role model, mother's educational expectations, and parental encouragement accounted for a 28% increase in explained variance. Attitudes toward mathematics and educational and career aspirations accounted for an additional 36% of the variance when only "self" variables were included in the analysis.

When the predictive models for achievement and participation are compared for males in grade 12, the results are remarkably similar. The identified variables for both predictive models were identical, but for achievement, teacher encouragement added to the predictive model of "others," and career aspirations added to the predictive model of "self."

For twelfth grade females, the variables related to "others" that were the best predictors of participation were father's educational expectations, teacher encouragement and (lack of) stereotyping. This variable accounted for an increase of 21% of the variance. The characteristics of "self" that were most predictive were educational aspirations, attitudes toward mathematics, and the mathematics preparation required for a job. These accounted for 30% of the variance in this model after the variance attributed to the nonintervenable variables was accounted for.

Differences do exist for "others" variables, that predict participation when grade 12 males and females are compared. Father's educational expectations predicted participation for both groups, but teacher variables seemed to play a more important role in predicting female participation. Influences of parents and counselors appeared to be better predictors for males.

The lack of validity of the participation measure for 13-year-olds made it very difficult to accurately predict intended participation. This is reflected in the low percentages of variance explained by either predictive model for both sexes.

Results of the predictive models for intended mathematics participation for 13-year-old males are also included in Table 3.7. The nonintervenable variables of school enrollment and SES were accounted for in both predictive models. Mother's educational expectations and parental encouragement accounted for a small increase of 8% in the variance in the model including the influences of "others." The usefulness of mathematics, attitudes toward mathematics, and educational aspirations accounted for a 17% increase in common variance in the "self" predictive model. For 13-year-olds, it is not surprising that the variable of usefulness is a better predictor of participation than the variable of mathematics preparation

TABLE 3.7
Predictive Models for Mathematics Participation Utilizing Student Attitudes or Parental and Teacher Characteristics*

Variable	Squared Multiple Correlation	"Intervenable" Variance R^2 Total—R^2 Nonintervenable	Variable	Squared Multiple Correlation	"Intervenable" Variance R_2 Total—R_2 Nonintervenable
Grade 12 Males			**Grade 12 Females**		
"Nonintervenable" Variables			"Nonintervenable" Variables		
School Enrollment			School Enrollment		
Socioeconomic Status	.03		Number of Mathematics Courses Offered		
Number of Mathematics Courses Offered			Socioeconomic Status	.07	
Most Advanced Mathematics Course Offered		.00	Most Advanced Course Offered		.00
Predictive Model 1: Characteristics of Others			**Predictive Model 1: Characteristics of Others**		
Fathers Educational Expectations			Fathers Educational Expectations		
Counselor Encouragement			Teacher Encouragement		
Mother As a Role Model			Teacher Stereotyping	.28	.21
Parental Encouragement	.31				
Mothers Educational Expectations		.28			
Predictive Model 2: Characteristics of Self			**Predictive Model 2: Characteristics of Self**		
Mathematics Preparation Required for a Job			Educational Aspirations		
Educational Aspirations			Attitudes Toward Mathematics		
Attitudes Toward Mathematics	.39	.36	Mathematics Preparation Required for Job	.37	.30
Age 13 Males			**Age 13 Females**		
"Nonintervenable" Variables			"Nonintervenable" Variables		
School Enrollment			School Enrollment		
Socioeconomic Status	.02	.00	Socioeconomic Status	.00	.00
Predictive Model 1: Characteristics of Others			**Predictive Model 1: Characteristics of Others**		
Mothers Educational Expectations			Counselor Encouragement		
Parental Encouragement	.10	.08	Fathers Educational Expectations	.07	.07
Predictive Model 2: Characteristics of Self			**Predictive Model 2: Characteristics of Self**		
Usefulness of Mathematics			Usefulness of Mathematics		
Attitudes Toward Mathematics			Attitudes Toward Mathematics		
Educational Aspirations	.19	.17	Educational Aspirations	.09	.09

*Only variables adding at least 1% to predicted variance are included.

required for a job, which was the better predictor for students in twelfth grade. Thirteen-year-olds seem to have a general notion that mathematics will be useful, but they are probably poorly informed regarding course work needed for career preparation.

For 13-year-old females, father's educational expectations, and counselor encouragement were the best predictors of intended participation, but these accounted for only a slight 7% increase of the explained variance. As was true for 13-year-old males, the best "self" predictors of intended participation were the perceived usefulness of mathematics, attitudes toward mathematics, and educational aspirations.

CONCLUSIONS

The purpose of this survey was to identify the factors affecting the mathematics participation of male and female students and to assess the relative importance of those factors. The analysis of the survey results suggests certain areas for possible intervention and change. A summary of those results and suggestions follows.

Achievement

Achievement data from the present study as well as data from the second NAEP mathematics assessment suggest that 13-year-old females start their high school mathematics program with at least the same mathematical abilities as males. Thirteen-year-old females are better at computation and spatial visualization than their male counterparts. At this age, the problem-solving skills of females and males are nearly equal.

By the end of high school the situation has changed. Twelfth-grade males show superior scores on problem-solving measures, and females have lost their advantage in computation and spatial visualization. However, the hypothesis that males' superior achievement in mathematics is due to a superior ability in spatial visualization is not supported by the results of this study. Although males were found to be better problem-solvers by the end of high school, no sex differences were found in spatial visualization ability.

Participation

The large sex differences found in participation in earlier studies were not found in this national survey. The results from both the NAEP data and this survey on course-taking indicate that no sex differences in participation exist for general mathematics courses or for algebra I and geometry.

The NAEP assessment found statistically significant differences favoring males for the advanced course of trigonometry and precalculus/calculus. The Women in Mathematics survey found significant differences favoring males for algebra II and probability/statistics, but not for the higher-level courses of trigonometry, precalculus and calculus. However, the nonstatistically significant differences found in course-taking for these advanced courses always favored males.

Thirteen-year-old men and women were equally optimistic about how much mathematics they planned to take while in high school. In fact, although the difference was not significant, 4% more women intended to take 4 years of high school mathematics. When this result is combined with the data indicating 13-year-old women achieve as well as or better than their male counterparts at this age, it seems that they start their high school mathematics experience on equal footing with men. That is, they start high school with the same ability and willingness to take mathematics. These results suggest that intervention strategies should focus on nurturing the skills and maintaining the attitudes that 13-year-olds exhibit throughout the high school years.

Attitudes and Participation

The results of both the correlation analyses and regression analyses suggest that three groups of variables have the greatest effect upon participation:

- positive attitudes toward mathematics
- perceived need for and usefulness of mathematics
- positive influences of significant other people (parents, teachers, counselors)

Future intervention strategies should emphasize the positive effects of these variables.

Intervention Strategies: Suggestions

Positive Attitudes Toward Mathematics

In the area of attitudes toward mathematics, teachers need to help instill mathematical confidence and enjoyment in their students. Students' feelings toward mathematics are largely a reaction to mathematics teaching, the mathematics program, and classroom activities. Methods and programs that will increase students' liking of mathematics need to be developed and evaluated.

Career Awareness and the Usefulness of Mathematics

Career awareness programs in junior high and senior high schools are an obvious area for intervention. Students who know they will need mathematics in their future career or to complete their education are more likely to take mathematics. Three or four years of academic mathematics in high school are required for most college mathematics, at least 2 years are needed for vocational or technical schools.

As an example of the type of intervention proposed, the Math/Science Network in the San Francisco Bay area has pioneered intervention programs to widen options and improve the career awareness of students. Articulate women in nontraditional fields attend conferences for high school girls and discuss aspects of their careers and the training required. Classroom activities encourage students to consider as many career options as possible, to learn about careers related to their interests and to determine and take the necessary mathematics and science courses that these careers will require.

Teachers are not the only change agents in terms of career awareness and educational aspirations. Students' educational aspirations are frequently a reflection of their parents' aspirations for them. Because of this, parents should encourage their children to set their educational goals as high as is realistic and to help them realize that taking mathematics is a necessity for getting into college or technical school as well as to prepare them for further studies. Increasingly, college majors, especially in the social sciences, require a background in mathematics.

School counselors can play an important role in making students more aware of career options and the requisite courses they need to take while in high school. Counselors need to become aware of career possibilities for women, because over 90% of the women they counsel will work for a significant portion of their lives. It is hoped that Title IX, which requires nonbiased counseling for women, has prompted counselors to give more attention to career opportunities for women.

Parents, Teachers, Counselors

Parents, teachers, and school counselors are in ideal positions to encourage both men and women to take more mathematics. When scales measuring the effects of significant others were entered into regression equations, parental encouragement, parental education expectations, and counselor encouragement were the best predictors of participation for twelfth grade men. For women, father's educational expectations and teacher encouragement were the best predictors of course-taking.

It is the active encouragement of parents, teachers, and counselors that seems to affect participation. The measure of parents' influence as role models, a passive influence, did not correlate with participation. Evidently parents don't need to set good examples regarding mathematics for their children to take mathematics in school. But, they can stress the importance of mathematics and encourage their children to take it by discussing high school course selections and future career options.

A point needs to be made regarding the effects of stereotyping of mathematics on women's participation. Although an absence of teacher stereotyping of mathematics was one of the predictors for participation of senior women, most of the stereotyping measures showed a low or insignificant correlation with participation. Stereotyping may not be one of the dominant factors affecting participation, but it does deserve some attention in terms of intervention. For senior women, the "mathematics as a male domain" scale had a significant correlation with participation. Women who saw mathematics as a field of study equally appropriate for women and men were more likely to take advanced mathematics courses. Areas for intervention could include programs that help women realize the appropriateness of pursuing a career in a mathematical or technical field.

Summary

The factors affecting participation are both numerous and complex. Results reported in this study indicate that the large differences in participation between men and women have diminished considerably in the past few years. It was also found that many of the factors that affect participation are the same for males and females.

Simply because large sex differences in participation were not found, the issue of mathematics participation should not be forgotten or ignored. The importance of taking high school mathematics cannot be overemphasized. Of the 42% of all students who indicated they were in a college preparatory program, only 25% had taken the 4 years of high school mathematics necessary for the college mathematics they would need for many majors.

Participation in mathematics is mostly an issue of awareness. If parents, teachers, and counselors understand and transmit to students the necessity of taking mathematics to keep their options open and if they have the same high expectations for women as they have for men, then a basis for equal opportunity in scientific and technical fields will exist—for *men* and *women*.

ACKNOWLEDGMENT

This research was funded by the National Institute of Education under Grant No. NIE-G-77-0061.

4

Self-Perceptions, Task Perceptions, Socializing Influences, and the Decision to Enroll in Mathematics

Jacquelynne Eccles (Parsons)
University of Michigan

Terry F. Adler
Robert Futterman
Susan B. Goff
Caroline M. Kaczala
Judith L. Meece
Carol Midgley

Introduction

Competence in mathematics has long been identified as a critical skill directly related to educational and occupational choices. Mathematical skills are important for admission to many college majors, for a number of professional occupations, and increasingly for computerized technical occupations. Yet compared to male students, fewer female students elect to take mathematics beyond the minimal requirements. Although females may receive less encouragement from parents and teachers, it is not the case that they are being systematically excluded through discriminatory course availability. On the contrary, all too frequently females *choose* not to take more advanced mathematics courses (Meece, Parsons, Kaczala, Goff, & Futterman, 1982; Sells, 1980; Sherman & Fennema, 1977).

The purpose of this research project is to investigate determinants of students' course selection in mathematics. In most schools students have the choice of whether or not to continue in math after 1 year of high school math. Although some of the factors influencing this decision are difficult to change, such as parents' education or their careers, other factors are modifiable. Identification of these modifiable factors will lay the foundation for the design of appropriate intervention programs aimed at increasing the likelihood of students continuing to take mathematics.

To date, there has been extensive research on the possible causes of sex differences in math achievement and course selection. This research has yielded four basic explanations for this problem:

1. Males outperform females on spatial problem-solving tasks and on other mathematics aptitude measures. Consequently, they are more able

to continue in math (Aiken, 1971; Astin, 1974b; Maccoby & Jacklin, 1974; Wittig & Petersen, 1979).

2. Males receive more encouragement than females from parents, teachers, and counselors to enroll in advanced mathematics courses or to pursue math-oriented careers (Casserly, 1975; Fox, Tobin, & Brody, 1979; Haven, 1971; Luchins, 1976).

3. Mathematics is commonly perceived as a male achievement domain. Consequently, because of its potential conflict with their sex-role identity, females are more likely to avoid mathematics (Armstrong & Kahl, 1979; Ernest, 1976; Fennema & Sherman, 1977a, b; Fox, 1975a; Nash, 1979; Sherman & Fennema, 1977; Stein & Smithells, 1969).

4. Males perceive themselves as more competent and report greater confidence in learning mathematics than females (Ernest, 1976; Fennema & Sherman, 1977a, b; Fox, Tobin, & Brody, 1979; Robitaille, 1977).

Each of these bodies of research has provided insights into the mechanisms contributing to students' math achievement behaviors. However, researchers have approached this area of study from a variety of theoretical perspectives, focusing their research on a subset of possible causes. Consequently, there has been no general model linking together the findings. What is needed is a theoretical framework that acknowledges the complex interplay of these factors, takes into account the sociocultural context in which mathematics learning takes place, and provides a more comprehensive approach to the problem. An integrative model of math achievement and course choice can aid in the identification of the determinants of individual differences on these variables and the specification of the relation of these differences to course plans.

Decision, achievement, and attribution theorists (e.g., Atkinson, 1964; Edwards, 1954; Weiner, 1974) have all addressed the issue of choice behavior. Applying these theories of behavior to students' decisions to continue taking mathematics, we have proposed a model of achievement behavior that links students' enrollment decisions to their expectations for their performance in a particular math course and to students' perceptions of the importance or incentive value of taking mathematics (Eccles–Parsons, Adler, Futterman, Goff, Kaczala, Meece, & Midgley, 1983). Figure 4.1 presents this model. According to this model, choice is influenced most directly by the students' values (both the utility value of math for attaining future goals and the attainment or interest value of ongoing math activities) and the students' expectancies for success at math. These variables, in turn, are assumed to be influenced by students' goals, and their concepts of both their own academic abilities and the task demands. Individual differences on these attitudinal variables are assumed to result from students' perceptions of the beliefs of major socializers, the students' interpretation of their own history of academic

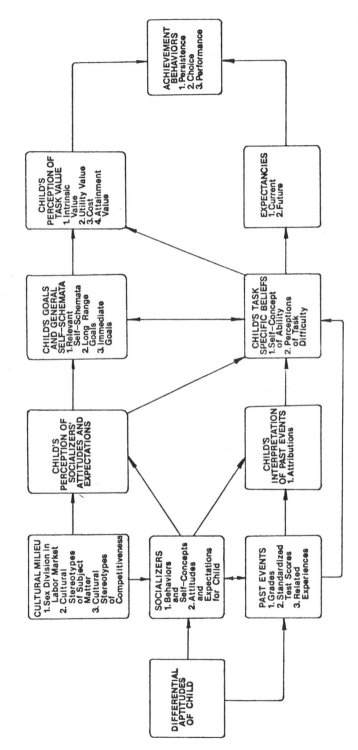

FIG. 4.1 General model of academic choice. (Adapted from Parsons, J. E., Adler, T. F., Futterman, R., Goff, S. B., Kaczala, C. M., Meece, J. L., & Midgley, C. Expectancies, values, and academic behaviors. In J. T. Spence (Ed.) *Perspectives on achievement and achievement motivation.* San Francisco, CA: Freeman, 1983).

97

performance, and the students' perception of appropriate behaviors and goals.

This theoretical model seems particularly relevant to the problem of sex differences in students' course selection in mathematics. The model assumes that the effects of experience, namely past history of grades in math, are mediated by the individual's interpretation of the events rather than the events themselves. For example, doing well in math is presumed to influence one's future expectations to the extent that doing well is attributed to one's ability. Past research has shown that girls do as well in math as boys throughout their formative years, yet they do not expect to do as well in the future nor are they as likely to go on in math. This apparent paradox is less puzzling if we acknowledge that it is the subjective meaning and interpretation of success and failure that determine an individual's perceptions of the task and not the objective outcomes themselves. The extent to which boys and girls differ in their interpretation of outcomes and the extent to which they receive different information relevant to their expectations of success and to the value of various achievement options might account, in part, for the observed sex differences in students' enrollment in math courses.

The model also assumes that the decision to take mathematics is made in the context of a variety of choices and is guided by core values such as achievement needs, competency needs, and sex-role values, and by more utilitarian values such as the importance of math achievement for future goals. Thus, if a girl likes math but feels that the amount of effort it will take to do well is not worthwhile because it decreases the time she will have available for more preferred activities (i.e., activities more consistent with her personal values), then she will be less likely to continue taking math. If a girl stereotypes mathematics or careers involving competency in mathematics as masculine and not consistent with her own sex-role values, then she will be less likely to value mathematics learning and less likely to continue her mathematical studies, especially if she does not expect to do well.

To test these hypotheses, a 2-year cross-sectional/longitudinal project was designed with the following specific goals:

1. The plotting of the developmental emergence of individual differences on the various psychological factors selected for study in the cross-sectional samples of fifth- through twelfth-grade students;

2. The assessment of the relative importance of these factors in mediating differential participation in mathematics; and

3. The identification of the developmental origins of individual differences on these variables.

The selection of specific variables for study was guided by this theoretical model.

RESEARCH DESIGN AND METHODOLOGY

The project used both longitudinal and cross-sectional methods. In year one, a cross section of 339 students in grades 5–11 were selected as the main sample. Their parents and their math teachers were included in this wave of testing. In year two, these same children were re-tested. These data comprised the longitudinal portion of this study.

Data were collected in several forms: student record data, a student questionnaire, a parent questionnaire, a teacher questionnaire, and classroom observations. Information taken from each student's school record included final grades in mathematics for the 4 years between 1975 and 1979 and standardized achievement test scores.

The student questionnaire included measures of expectancies for success, incentive values, perceived ability, perceived task difficulty, sex-role identity, sex steryotyping of math as a male domain, perceived cost of success, and causal attributional patterns, as well as measures of the children's perceptions of their parents' and teachers' beliefs regarding the children's abilities and the importance of math. The major attitudinal scales were factor analyzed using a maximum likelihood factor analytic procedure developed by Jöreskog, Sorbom, and Magidson (1979). These factor scales were used primarily as summary variables for the path analyses. Several additional composite scores based on only two or three items were formed for specific analyses. These are discussed where appropriate in the presentation of our findings.

Parents completed a similar battery assessing attitude regarding both themselves and their children. Teachers completed a brief questionnaire assessing their beliefs about the causes of the sex-differentiated participation rates and their judgments of each child's math ability and performance.

Using an observational system based on the systems developed by Brophy and Good (1974) and Dweck, Davidson, Nelson, and Enna (1978), observers coded interactions between teachers and individual students during 10 classroom sessions. These data were then used to describe both variations in the general social milieu across math classrooms and variations in the specific teacher-student interaction patterns across children.

During the first year of the study the measures were administered to a sample of students in grades 5–11. Because junior high school has been suggested as a particularly critical period for the formation of high school course plans and because many of the analyses of the observational data were to be based on the classroom as the unit of analysis, particular attention was paid to seventh and ninth grades. Thus, the 18 mathematics classes observed included two fifth-grade classes, one sixth-grade class, eight seventh-grade classes, and seven ninth-grade classes.

During the second year, 94% of the first-year sample was relocated. Slightly modified questionnaires were administered to the relocated students, and their current mathematics teachers. There were no classroom observations in Year 2.

During the second year, an additional control group of 329 students was drawn from the schools sampled during the first year of the study. This sample included students in grades 5–12. Selection of this sample allowed for comparisons suggested by Nesselroade and Baltes (1974) and Schaie (1965). In particular, we used this sample to assess test-retest effects and to rule out the possibility that our longitudinal findings reflect the impact of unique historical effects rather than general developmental processes. These analyses indicated that the control sample and the Year 2 main sample did not differ. Thus, we can safely conclude that test-retest effects were minimal. The control sample and the Year 1 sample also did not differ; therefore, changes in the students' attitudes from Year 1 to Year 2 do not reflect the impact of unique historical events. Based on these results and on the fact that the questionnaire had been modified slightly from Year 1 to Year 2, the control and Year 2 sample were merged making a total Year 2 sample of 668 children; Year 1 and Year 2 data were analyzed separately, except for the longitudinal analyses.

FINDINGS

Student Attitudes and Course Plans

Descriptive Analyses

To assess the effects of grade and sex on the student variables, analyses of variance using grade and sex as the independent variables were performed on each of the student scales. Table 4.1 and Table 4.2 summarize the results.

Descriptive Analyses: Sex. Relatively few sex differences emerged but they formed a fairly consistent pattern. Across both years, boys, compared to girls, rated their math ability higher, felt they had to exert less effort to do well in math, and held higher expectancies for future successes in math, even though there had been no difference between the past math performances (both standardized test scores and course grades) of these same boys and girls. In addition, boys in Year 1 rated both their current math courses and advanced math courses as easier than did the girls; boys in Year 2 had higher expectancies for success in current (as well as future) math courses; and boys in Year 2 rated math as more useful than the girls. Thus, to the extent that there are sex differences on

TABLE 4.1
Summary of Significant Sex Differences from Analyses
of Variance: Years 1 and 2

Variables yielding significant sex effects	Direction of Effect	P
	Year 1	
Future expectancies for success in math	M > F	.01
Difficulty of current math course	F > M	.01
Anticipated difficulty of future math	F > M	.01
Effort to do well in math	F > M	.01
Task difficulty of math for self*	F > M	.05
Self-concept of math ability*	M > F	.05
Femininity score	F > M	.0001
Masculinity score	M > F	.0001
Perceived math utility for females	M > F	.01
Stereotyping of math as male domain	F > M	.05
Parents' perceived importance of math*	M > F	.01
Father's perception of task difficulty*	F > M	.01
Mother's perception of task difficulty*	F > M	.01
	Year 2	
Math ability (subjective estimate)	M > F	.01
Current expectancies for success in math	M > F	.04
Future expectancies for success in math	M > F	.01
Effort to do well in math	F > M	.01
Self-concept of math ability*	M > F	.05
Utility of mathematics	M > F	.01
Utility of advanced math	M > F	.001
Femininity score	F > M	.0001
Masculinity score	M > F	.0001
Perceived math utility for females	F > M	.05
Sex stereotyping of math ability	M > F	.05

*These scales are composites developed through factor analyses.

these self and task perception variables, boys have a more positive view of both themselves as math learners and of math itself.

Boys and girls also differed in the causal attributions they made for previous successes and failures in math. Chi-square tests of sex by attributions in both years indicated that boys attributed failure less to ability than did girls (Year 1: $X^2 = 9.76, p < .05$; Year 2: $X^2 = 9.77, p < .05$); the boys also attributed success more to ability than the girls (Year 1: $X^2 = 7.99, p < .05$; Year 2: $X^2 = 16.0, p < .05$). In contrast, the girls attributed success more to consistent effort than did the boys (Year 1: $X^2 = 8.80, p < .05$; Year 2: $X^2 = 5.73, p < .016$). When we divided the Year 1 sample into expectancy groups (low, medium, or high), we found that these attributional differences were characteristic only of high expectancy students. It was the high expectancy girls who attributed their

TABLE 4.2
Summary of Significant Age Effects

Variables yielding significant age effects	Direction of Effect	P
Year 1		
Math aptitude[1]	$O > Y$[2]	.01
Math ability (subjective estimate)	$Y > O$[3]	.01
Performance in math (subjective estimate)	$Y > O$	.01
Current expectancies for success in math	$Y > O$	.01
Difficulty of current math course	$O > Y$	.001
Task difficulty of math for self*	$O > Y$	.0001
Self-concept of math ability*	$Y > O$[3]	.001
Importance of math	$Y > O$	.01
Utility of advanced math	$Y > O$	.001
Interest in math	$Y > O$	.01
Subjective math value*	CURV. U[4]	.01
Liking of teacher	$Y > O$	.01
Perceived math utility for males	CURV. U	.01
Sex stereotyping of math ability	CURV. ∩	.05
Student perception of socializers' perception of math difficulty*	$O > Y$	.01
Student perception of socializers' perception of math ability*	$Y > O$	.0001
Student perception of others' expectancies for math	$Y > O$	.01
Mother's perception of task difficulty*	$O > Y$	.05
Teacher's rating of child's math ability	$Y > O$	.0001
Year 2		
Math ability (subjective estimate)	$Y > O$	.01
Performance in math (subjective estimate)	$Y > O$	.0001
Current expectancies for success in math	$Y > O$	.001
Difficulty of current math course	$O > Y$	.001
Anticipated difficulty in future math	$O > Y$	.0001
Self-concept of math ability*	$Y > O$	.0001
Utility of advanced math	$Y > O$	.001
Interest in math	$Y > O$	.01
Liking of teacher	$Y > O$	.0001
Masculinity score	CURV. U	.0001
Perceived math utility for females	$Y > O$	.0001
Perceived math utility for males	$Y > O$	.0001
Sex stereotyping of math ability	$O > Y$	.001
Student perception of socializers' perception of math difficulty*	$O > Y$	.0001
Student perception of socializers' perception of math ability*	$Y > O$	.0001
Student perception of others' expectancies for math	$Y > O$	.0001

[1]Tested only in Year 1.

[2]$O > Y$ = linear trend increasing with age

[3]$Y > O$ = linear trend decreasing with age

[4]CURV. U-curvilinear relationship with age, decreasing and then increasing

math failures more to lack of ability and their math success less to ability than the high expectancy boys ($X^2 = 6.95$, $p < .05$). It was also high expectancy girls who attributed their math successes more to consistent effort than the boys ($X^2 = 11.03$, $p < .05$). The boys and girls in the other two expectancy groups did not differ in their attributional pattern.

These differences in attributional patterns and attitudes toward mathematics reflect very different perceptions of both the task demands inherent in math and the potential value and cost of enrolling in advanced math courses. The girl who attributes her math success to consistent effort rather than ability may have low future expectancies precisely because she thinks future courses will be more difficult, demanding even more effort than her current math course. The amount of effort she can, or is willing to, expend on math has limits. Consequently, perceptions of the need for even greater effort may lower her expectancies for future success in math and predispose her against continuing to take math, especially if she feels that math is not very useful for her long range goals. The same dynamics would not apply to a boy who views his ability rather than his efforts as the more important cause of his successes in math. He may well assume that his ability will allow him to continue performing well with little or no additional effort. Combining these results with the fact that boys also rate math as more useful than girls leads us to predict that more boys than girls in this sample will enroll in difficult advanced math courses. In fact, our longitudinal follow-up data indicate that they do ($p < .05$). But the difference is quite small, as are the differences associated with most of the relevant attitudinal variables. (More details on the attributional data can be found in Eccles-Parsons, Meece, Adler, & Kaczala, 1982.)

Descriptive Analyses: Grade.   Grade effects were both more numerous and, in general, stronger than sex effects. What emerges from an inspection of Table 4.2 is a sense that children become more pessimistic and negative about math as they grow older. The older children had lower expectancies for their current math performance, rated both their math ability and math performance lower, saw both their present and future math courses as more difficult, thought their parents shared these pessimistic views of their abilities and performance potential, were less interested in math activities in general, liked their math teachers less, and rated the utility of advanced math courses as lower than the younger children. For most of these variables, there was a consistent downward linear trend as a function of grade with the girls preceding the boys. No consistent grade by sex interactions emerged.

Descriptive Analyses: General.   Several additional findings emerged that are of interest. Each is discussed in this section.

All students rated math as more useful for males (Year 1, $\bar{X}$ = 5.60; Year 2, $\bar{X}$ = 5.03) than for females (Year 1, $\bar{X}$ = 2.98; Year 2, $\bar{X}$ = 4.22; $p < .0001$ in each year). Students in general, however, did not rate males as having more math ability than females. The stereotyping of math as more useful for males than for females (calculated by subtracting the usefulness for women score from the usefulness for men score; hereafter referred to as the stereotyping of math as a male domain) dropped from Year 1 to Year 2. This drop was due largely to the increase in the rating of the usefulness of math for women from Year 1 to Year 2. Neither grade nor sex influenced these results.

We had the tenth to twelfth grade, Year 2 students rate the amount of encouragement to continue in math they had received from each of the following sources (listed in descending order of the mean encouragement score): father, mother, last year's teacher, guidance counselor, older friends, siblings, and peers. Of these, only fathers, mothers, and previous math teacher were perceived as having provided any encouragement. The other individuals were perceived as having neither encouraged nor discouraged the students. Peers were *not* seen as having discouraged the students' decision. One sex difference emerged: boys, in comparison to girls, felt that their counselor had provided them with more encouragement ($p < .05$). Counselor encouragement did not, however, predict future course plans.

The students also rated the importance of various reasons in influencing their decision to take math. Three reasons emerged as the most influential: preparation for either a college major or career, gaining admission to a prestigious college, and the importance of math in a well rounded education. Intrinsic properties of math, such as its challenge, ease, or interest value were clearly seen as less important. One sex difference emerged: boys rated the importance of future plans (college or career) in their decision higher than did girls ($p < .01$).

Relational Analyses

Relational Analyses: Sex-Role Measures.   Several researchers have suggested that the stereotype of math as a male domain inhibits female participation. To evaluate this hypothesis and its many variations, we correlated the students' rating of the usefulness of advanced math for both males and females, their perception of math as being more useful to males, their sex stereotyping of math ability, and their ratings of themselves on a simplified version of the PAQ (Spence, Helmreich, & Stapp, 1975) with the other student measures.

Femininity as measured by the PAQ related to very few student measures in either year; no relationship was consistent across years. Masculinity, however, usually related significantly and positively to measures of expectancy and self-concept of math ability for both boys and girls (see Eccles–Parsons et al., 1983 for more details). The fact that masculinity was so consistently related to self-concept of math ability in both boys and girls could be because the character traits of rationality and an analytical approach to life commonly ascribed to males are also characteristic of individuals who are able in mathematics. Or, "masculinity" may actually be a measure of a form of self-confidence, instrumentality, or self-esteem rather than sex-role typing. This latter conclusion, which is in line with recent suggestions of several other researchers in the field of androgyny, for example, Locksley and Colten (1979) and Spence and Helmreich (1979), makes the use of the PAQ or other personality inventories as measures of sex-role identity suspect. In fact, Spence and Helmreich (1979) now advise against using the PAQ as a measure of sex-role identity.

Further support for the latter conclusion comes from our analyses of the multivariate contingency tables. The variables used in these analyses included the sex-role typing of the individual (neuter, feminine, masculine, or androgynous, formed using the median-split procedures outlined by Spence, Helmreich, & Stapp, 1974), the stereotyping of math as a male domain (neuter, moderately or highly masculine, formed using a composite score of the sex-stereotyping of math's usefulness and of math ability), sex of student, and each of the following student attitudinal variables: self-concept of math ability, concept of task difficulty, concept of the value of math, estimates of the utility of math for future goals, current expectancies, and interest. A student's sex-role classification had no significant influence on any of the dependent measures (see Eccles–Parsons et al., 1983 for more details). This finding, in conjunction with the correlational findings reported earlier, suggests that it is *only* the responses to the "masculine" items that are related to the attitudinal measures. Sex-role typing as conceptualized by researchers on androgyny is not a critical factor. This finding does not, however, invalidate the significance of a student's sex-role identity as an influence in his/her course selection. What it does suggest is that the masculine scale of the PAQ items is best interpreted as a measure of instrumentality rather than "masculinity."

Responses to the usefulness items yielded several interesting findings. First, whereas math was seen as more useful to men, the magnitude of this stereotype decreased over the 2 years of our study. Given this decrease and the difficulty in its interpretation, we correlated the Year 1 stereotyping measures with both Year 1 and Year 2 attitudinal measures; the Year 2 stereotyping measures were correlated only with the Year 2 student measures.

In Year 1 the usefulness of math for females was generally *not* related to other variables. It was, however, negatively related to two measures of the value of math for both boys and girls. Seeing math as useful for women did not increase its value for girls as one might expect. Instead it was the usefulness of math for males that predicted positively its value for both boys and girls as measured by interest in math ($r = .38$), importance of doing well in math ($r = .44$), and the utility of advanced math ($r = .38$) (see Eccles et al., 1983 for more details). One could conclude from these data that the stereotype of math as a male domain has a positive effect for everyone and ought to be encouraged; but results from other studies and the Year 2 data suggest that this conclusion is oversimplified. Instead, what it does suggest is that perceiving math as very useful for males does not necessarily have a negative consequence for girls, perhaps especially when the stereotype reflects an awareness of the high status jobs that are both male-dominated and math-related. In this case, it may be the status of the job rather than its male domination that elevates the perceived usefulness of advanced math courses for both high ability boys and girls.

What is striking about the Year 2 results is that, for both boys and girls, the stereotyping of math as useful for *either* men or women yielded identical patterns of relations: the higher the rating of usefulness, the higher the students' ratings of future expectancies, current expectancies, interest, utility, self-concept of ability, and concept of the value of math. Further, the stereotyping of math as a male domain was not related to anything. Recall that stereotyping of math as a male domain had dropped from Year 1 to Year 2. These data, taken together, suggest that math is either becoming less sex-typed or that students are less willing to report sex-typed attitudes.

To test whether the effects of stereotyping math as a male domain had disappeared, we correlated Year 1 sex-typing questions with Year 2 attitudes. What we found was quite interesting. Year 1 sex-typing measures correlated in exactly the same pattern with Year 2 measures of the value of math as they had with Year 1 measures of the value of math. Past sex-typing of the usefulness of math was still influencing attitudes even if the current sex-typing was not. Further, the Year 1 and Year 2 measures of the stereotyping of math as a male domain did not correlate with each other and the correlation of the perceived usefulness of math for women in Year 1 correlated negatively with Year 2 measures of the perceived usefulness of math for both women ($r = -.38$) and men ($r = -.23$). This shift in the use of the scales was not apparent in the correlations of the Year 1 measure of the perceived usefulness of math for men with Year 2 variables.

This strange set of findings led us to question the validity of the responses of the Year 2 sample on our sex-stereotyped questions and left us with one major conclusion: stereotyping math as a masculine domain does not necessarily have an adverse effect on girls' math attitudes or course plans. Results from our multivariate contingency table analyses provided further support for this conclusion. Neither sex, nor personal sex-typing (neutral, feminine, masculine, or androgynous) had any consistent effect on the dependent measures tested. The stereotyping of math as a male domain did; people who stereotyped math as a male domain saw it as having higher future utility, being more enjoyable, and in general being more valuable.

Nash (1979) and others, ourselves included, have suggested that one must take account of the sex of the individual, the sex-role identity of the individual, and the sex stereotype of math in order to explain math achievement behaviors. Admittedly, the PAQ does not appear to be a good measure of sex-role identity and thus may not allow for a truly adequate test of this hypothesis. Nonetheless, using our measures, we found little evidence for the need of an interactive model to explain relations among these variables in our sample. Three-way interactive effects emerged only in the analysis of the concept of the value of math. In this case, only one cell of the multivariate contingency table had a higher frequency than one would expect by chance: girls who valued math highly perceived themselves as neutrally sex-typed and saw math as moderately male stereotyped. The other cells, which one would expect to support commonly predicted relations, did not have unusually high or low frequencies.

Relational Analyses: Students' Attitudinal Items. We assessed the relations among the student attitudinal variables using correlational and multivariate analyses. The zero order correlation matrices of selected variables for each year are presented in Table 4.3. As predicted for both boys and girls, in each year self-concept items correlated positively with each other, and in most cases with intent to continue in math; they correlated negatively with ratings of task difficulty. Self-concept items also correlated positively with the value of math items and negatively with the cost of math participation items.

To assess the origin of these attitudes we correlated the student attitudinal measures to teacher behavior, parents' attitudes and beliefs, and to a composite standardized score reflecting both past math grades and performance on either the CAT or MEAP. The analyses relating the student measures to the socializer measures are discussed in later sections. The relation of the math aptitude score to the other student measures varied depending on the sex of the student. Boys' past math aptitude was consistently related to their self-concept measures; girls' past math aptitude scores were not (see Eccles, Adler, & Meece, 1984, for more details).

Relational Analyses: Path Analyses. Path analyses were done separately for the Year 1 and Year 2 samples. Because the Year 2 sample included over 90% of the Year 1 students, and because the questionnaire had been improved based on Year 1 data, only the Year 2 data are dis-

TABLE 4.3
Correlation Matrix of Selected Student Attitudinal Variables

	1	2	3	4	5	6	7	8
1. Intention to take	–	.26	.29	.45	-.06	.41	.47	.04
more math	–	.19	.42	.53	-.08	.43	.36	-.01
2. Math aptitude	-.11	–	.34	.12	-.22	.01	[.28	.05
	.14	–	.49	.19	-.36	.03	.49]	-.08
3. Self-concept of	.30	.18	–	[.40	-.65	.32	.82	.06
math ability	.36	.30	–	.60]	-.57	.40	.86	-.10
4. Subjective value	.43	-.06	.51	–	-.05	.77	.57	-.10
of math	.44	.13	.58	–	-.08	.81	.69	-.19
5. Task difficulty	-.15	-.15	-.68	-.13	–	-.09	-.38	.00
of math for self	-.16	-.26	-.60	-.17	–	-.10	-.39	-.02
6. Utility of advanced	.23	-.13	.32	.77	-.09	–	.41	-.17
math	.26	-.01	.39	.80	-.13	–	.53	-.14
7. Future expectancies	.44	.15	.77	.63	-.37	.46	–	.00
for success in math	.41	.31	.80	.64	-.39	.47	–	-.10
8. Sex stereotyping of	-.03	-.02	[-.19	-.11	.07	[-.11	[-.16	–
math ability	.09	.02	.21]	.16	-.14	.21]	.24]	–

*Upper half of matrix contains correlations for Year 1; lower half of the matrix contains correlations for Year 2. Females are top correlation, males are bottom correlation in each pair.

$r > .19$ is significant at $p < .05$; $r > .27$ is significant at $p < .01$.

[ ] indicates significant ($p < .05$) sex difference in the magnitude of the correlation.

cussed here (Fig. 4.2). In addition, because the measure of stereotyping math as a male domain appeared to be reactive in Year 2, the Year 1 measure was used to provide the maximal likelihood of sex-typing effects emerging if they were in fact influencing students' math attitudes.

Path coefficients were calculated using a series of regression equations with each variable regressed on the set of variables to its left (those theorized to have had a causal effect on it). The standardized beta weights derived from the appropriate regression analyses are the path coefficients and reflect the relative strength of the relations specified by each path. Figure 4.2 represents a reduced path model depicting only those path coefficients significant at the $p < .01$ level or better. Less significant paths were omitted for clarity of presentation.

As predicted, intentions to continue taking math were most directly influenced by the perceived value of math and combined expectancies (current and future). These concepts, in turn, were related to students' estimates of both their own math ability, and of their parents' and teachers' beliefs regarding their math ability. Past history of math grades and performance on math achievement tests (Past Math Performance) did not have a direct effect on students' intention to take more math, on their expectancies for current or future performance, or on their subjective

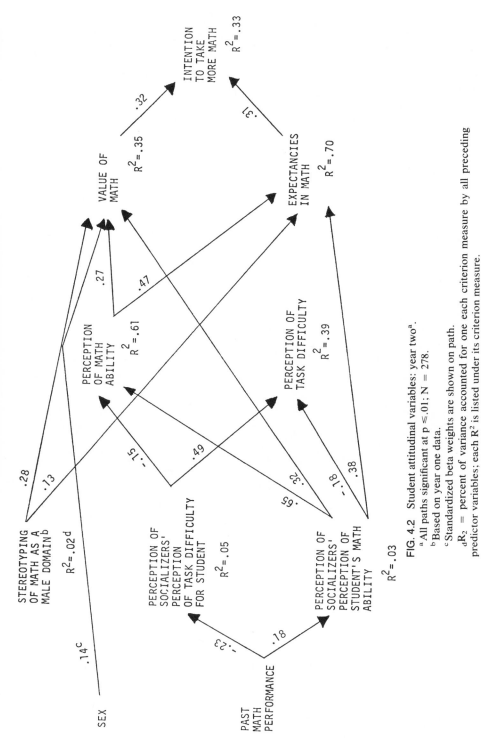

FIG. 4.2 Student attitudinal variables: year two[a].

[a] All paths significant at p ≤.01; N = 278.

[b] Based on year one data.

[c] Standardized beta weights are shown on path.

[d] R_2 = percent of variance accounted for one each criterion measure by all preceding predictor variables; each R^2 is listed under its criterion measure.

109

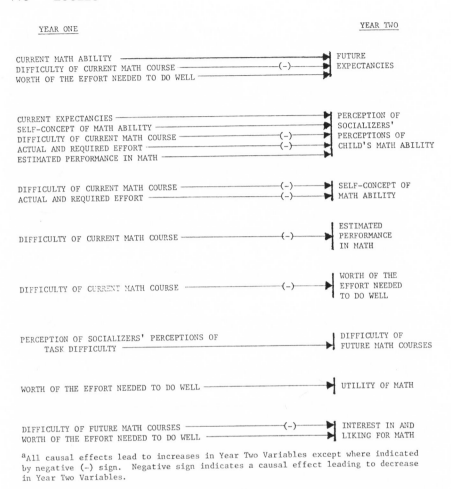

FIG. 4.3   Causal effects from cross-lagged panel analyses.[a]

estimates of either their own math ability or the difficulty of math. In addition, as predicted, stereotyping of math as a male domain increased the value of math, and, to a lesser extent, expectancies. Thus, it is clear that students' perceptions of themselves as math learners and of math itself are more important mediators of math course plans than are past performance and course grades.

Relational Analyses: Longitudinal Analyses.   Our relational analyses culminated in a series of cross-lagged panel longitudinal analyses. This statistical technique makes use of longitudinal data to test causal inferences from correlational data. Cross-lagged panel analyses consist of the examination of the correlations between pairs of variables both within and between data collection points.

Our results are illustrated in Figure 4.3. All causal effects leading to increases in Year 2 variables are represented by a unidirectional arrow. A negative sign on this arrow indicates a causal effect leading to a decrease in a Year 2 variable. Interpreting these arrows, then, we see that shifts in future expectancies are caused by one's self-concept of math ability, by one's beliefs about the difficulty of current math courses, and the value of the effort needed to do well. Shifts in one's self-concept of math ability in turn are caused by one's beliefs about the difficulty of current math courses, and by one's perception of the actual and required effort to do well. Both estimated performance in math and the worth of the effort needed to do well are also influenced by the perceived difficulty of the current math course. Student perceptions of socializers' attitudes enter the figure as important particularly in the prediction of the difficulty of future math courses, a variable which in turn predicts an interest in and a liking for math.

Summary. In summary, the proposed model provides an adequate explanation of these data. The variables included in the model explain 32% to 36% of the variance in intentions to take math. The path diagram graphically illustrates that intentions to continue in math are indeed affected by expectancies for success and assessment of the personal value of math. These, in turn, are mediated by perceptions of one's own math ability. This pattern suggests that to be effective, an intervention program designed to promote higher math participation should focus on the following goals: (1) heightening girls' expectancies for success in math achievement situations, (2) providing the girls with accurate information regarding the utility of math for their futures, and (3) working to increase the intrinsic interest value of math. Because sex-typing math as a male domain did not appear to have detrimental effects on girls' plans or attitudes toward math, our data suggest that programs aimed at decreasing the stereotyping of math as a male domain without also pointing out its potential value for the individual will not be effective in increasing girls' participation in advanced math.

DEVELOPMENTAL ORIGINS

Teacher Effects

The effects of teachers' expectancies on their students' performance have been studied extensively since the publication of Rosenthal and Jacobson's *Pygmalion in the Classroom* (1968). While their results have been difficult to replicate, research by Brophy and Good (1974) has shown that teachers' naturally occurring expectancies for the students in their class-rooms affect the kinds of interactions teachers have with their students and that these interactions can affect the children's achievement. Of particular importance is the finding that some teachers treat girls for whom they have high expectancies in ways that are less facilitative of achievement than the way they treat comparable groups of boys.

Another mechanism that might explain girls' lower expectancies for success in math has been proposed by Dweck and her colleagues (Dweck et al., 1978). Their model emphasizes the importance of the relative proportion of praise and criticism allocated by the teacher to academic work versus the form of the work and the student's conduct. They argue that boys receive frequent criticism for non-academic as well as academic behaviors and consequently can discount these negative evaluations as indicators of their own abilities. Girls, in contrast, receive less criticism than boys, and when it occurs, it is directed specifically to the quality of their academic work. Because of its very specific use, these authors suggest that criticism cannot be discounted as easily by the girls. They propose a similar though reversed pattern for praise. In addition, they suggest that teachers are more likely to attribute boys' failures to lack of effort than to lack of ability, thus further reinforcing the boys' sense of control and confidence.

Based on these studies, we tested the following hypotheses: (a) teachers' behaviors would influence students' expectancies for success; (b) students who received positive feedback would have higher expectancies for success than those who received negative feedback; (c) boys would receive more indiscriminate criticism (criticism toward both the quality and form of their academic work and toward their conduct) than girls; (d) girls would receive more discriminate criticism (criticism directly only to the quality of their work) and more indiscriminate praise than boys; and (e) teachers' attributions to effort would influence students' expectancies positively.

A Sex X Grade X Expectancy group (High, Low) analysis of variance (using the classroom as the unit of analysis and using scores standardized within each classroom) was done on each of our 51 classroom variables. Of the 51 variables, significant effects ($p < .01$) were found on only three, each of which was a main effect due to sex. Girls received less criticism than did boys during dyadic interactions, received less criticism for work, and a lower percentage of girls' dyadic interactions were criticized.

Contrary to our predictions, then, teachers did not give more positive feedback to students in the high expectancy group, and boys and girls did not differ in the amount of discriminate and indiscriminate praise and criticism they received for the quality or form of their work, or their conduct (see Heller & Parsons, 1981 and Eccles-Parsons, Kaczala &

Meece, 1982 for details). No support was found for the suggestions of Dweck et al. (1978). The only significant main effect of sex on evaluative feedback was the amount of criticism from the teacher directed toward the work and toward the quality and form of the work combined; girls received less work-related criticism than did boys, and less criticism to the quality plus form of their work. Surprisingly, boys and girls did not differ in the amount of criticism directed to their conduct or on any of the forms of praise. Further, in a series of stepwise regression analyses, classroom interactional measures did not emerge as significant predictors of student attitudinal variables. However, teachers' expectancies, measured by the teacher questionnaire, were predictive of student expectancies (see Heller & Parsons, 1981 for details). Thus, while the proposed relations between teachers' expectancies and students' expectancies were supported, the mediating effects of classroom behavior on expectancies were not demonstrated.

The analyses reported thus far were performed on the entire sample. It is possible that the effects of classroom behaviors are dependent on teacher style. For example, some teachers may treat boys and girls differently, whereas others may not. By collapsing across all of our teachers, these effects would have been masked. To explore this possibility, we selected from the sample the five classrooms with the largest sex differences in the students' self-reported expectancies and the five classrooms with no significant sex differences in expectancies and reanalyzed the data using raw frequency scores to allow for classroom comparisons.

As was true for the previous analyses, most variables did not yield significant differences. None of the variables predicted by Dweck's model yielded classroom-type effects. Those effects that were significant were divided into three types: behaviors characteristic of teacher style (teacher behaviors under primary control of the teacher, e.g., use of praise following a correct answer), behaviors characteristic of student style (behaviors under primary control of the student, e.g., student-initiated dyadic interactions), and behaviors dependent on both teacher and student style (behaviors requiring interactive responses of both the teacher and the student, e.g., total dyadics). Clearly, these classroom types differed in the dynamics we observed. Teachers in high sex-differentiated classrooms were more critical, were more likely to use a public teaching type (asking open questions, giving opportunities for responses, receiving answers) and less likely to rely on more private dyadic interactions, and gave more praise ($p < .01$) (see Eccles-Parsons, Kaczala, & Meece, 1982 for details).

Several interesting sex differences ($p < .01$) also emerged in these analyses. In the low-difference classrooms girls interacted more than boys (gave more responses, asked more questions, initiated more interactions) and they received more praise for work and criticism for form. In high-difference classrooms, boys interacted more (having more response opportunities, asking more questions and giving more answers) and received more praise for work and criticism for form. Boys' expectancies did not differ across the two classrooms while the girls' did; in fact, the girls' expectancies in high-difference classrooms were significantly lower than the expectancies of any other group.

To test whether teacher behavior accounted for this sex difference in expectancy, we correlated the teacher-style variables that discriminated the low from the high sex-differentiated classrooms with the students' attitudinal variables. Unfortunately, none of these correlations were significant. As we had found earlier, however, teacher's expectancies as reported on the questionnaire were strongly related to both boys' and girls' current and future expectancies and their perceptions of the current difficulty of math and their math ability (see Eccles-Parsons, Kaczala, & Meece, 1982).

Next we divided the sample into two additional groups: those students for whom the teacher had high expectancies ("bright" students) and those students for whom the teacher had low expectancies. In general, we found that both "bright" males and "bright" females were treated quite differently in each of the two classroom types ($p < .01$; see Eccles-Parsons, Kaczala, & Meece, 1982). "Bright" girls interacted the most, answered more questions, received more work and form praise and less criticism in the low sex-differentiated classrooms. In contrast, "bright" boys were accorded the most praise and interacted the most in the high sex-differentiated classrooms. "Bright" girls were accorded the *least* amount of praise of *any* of the eight factorial groups in the high sex-differentiated classrooms. But whether this differential use of praise was "causing" the "bright" girls to have lower expectancies in some classrooms and how such an effect might have been mediated cannot be determined from our data.

In concluding, these additional points are important to stress: first, the frequency rates of all these interaction variables are quite low. Second, interaction variables are not as predictive of students' expectancies as are other variables we measured, for example, students' sex and teachers' expectancies. Third, the effect of classroom type may be mediated by the general social climate in the classroom rather than by the direct effects of one-to-one teacher-student interactions. Social climate is a function of both the teacher and the set of students in each particular class. Consequently, whereas classroom interactions may be having an effect on children's expectancies, the effects are not large and may be as much a function of the children as the teacher. Finally, we did not see teachers actively discouraging girls' attitudes toward math; nor, however, did we see them making any special effort to encourage the girls. Instead, teachers appeared to be playing a rather passive role in the process of socializing boys' and girls' attitudes towards math. Other studies clearly suggest that teachers can play a very active role in this socialization process. Thus, to the extent that teachers can be induced to cooperate, classrooms could be a very powerful target for intervention programs.

Parent Effects

It has been suggested by many achievement theorists that parents influence their children's achievement behaviors through their roles as models and through their more direct role as expectancy and value socializers. Both of these hypotheses are discussed in this section.

The importance of role models in socialization is a recurring theme throughout the sex difference literature. According to this hypothesis, important models, in particular parents, exhibit behaviors that children imitate and later adopt as part of their own behavioral repertoire. If mothers exhibit different behavior patterns than fathers, then, girls and boys should acquire sex-differentiated behavior patterns. With regard to math expectancies in particular, it has been hypothesized that girls exhibit more math avoidance and have lower math expectancies than boys because mothers are more likely than fathers to exhibit math avoidance behaviors. To test this hypothesis, we compared the mathematics relevant self-concepts of the mothers and fathers in our sample. (These data are presented in more detail in Eccles-Parsons, Adler, & Kaczala, 1982.)

In comparison to mothers' responses, fathers said that they were and have always been better at math, that math was and always has been easier for them, that they needed to expend less effort to do well at math, that they have always enjoyed math more, and that math has always been more useful and important to them ($p < .01$). In sum, fathers were more positive toward math and have a more positive self-concept regarding their math abilities. What is more, we found that these sex-differentiated beliefs were specific to math. Consistent with the fact that girls on the average outperform boys in school, mothers rated their general high school peformance higher than fathers did.

In line with the modeling hypothesis, one might conclude at this point that we have identified a major source of sex-differentiated math self-concept in today's school children. Boys and girls differ because their parents' behavior is sex-differentiated. But one needs to demonstrate a relation between parents' behaviors and children's beliefs before this conclusion is justified. To test the modeling hypothesis more directly, we correlated the parent self-concept variables with the children's responses to the student questionnaire and to their math aptitude score. None of the more than 100 correlations were significant at a psychologically meaningful level ($r = .25$ or greater). Thus, while parents' self-concepts did differ in the predicted direction, the influence of these differences on children's math self-concept was minimal.

The second source of influence is the parents' beliefs about the math abilities of their children and the importance of math for their children. To test these influences, we compared the parents' of boys perceptions of their sons' math ability, interest and effort, their expectancies for their sons' future performance in math, and their perceptions of the relative importance of a variety of courses for their sons to similar beliefs of the parents of girls.

The sex of the child had a definite effect ($p < .01$) on parents' perceptions of their child's math ability and on the parents' perceptions of the relative importance of various high school courses. Whereas parents did not rate their daughters' math abilities significantly lower than they rated their sons', they did think that math was harder for their daughters and that their daughters had to work harder to do well in math. Further, fathers exhibited more frequent sex-differentiated responses.

That parents feel their daughters have to try harder to do well in math is of particular interest. It suggests that both parents and their daughters share the perception of how hard girls need to try in order to do well. We do not know whether this reflects parents' echoing comments they have heard their daughters make or whether it demonstrates the parents' strength as teachers of good or bad attitudes towards math. But it seems likely that it could lead parents to support their daughters' decisions to drop out of math, especially when they don't believe math is that important for their daughters' futures. Similarly, as math is seen as relatively easier and more important for sons than for daughters, parents should be less tolerant of a son's decision to drop math.

Are these parental beliefs about their children's abilities and plans predictive of future math expectancies and future course plans? To answer this question, we correlated the major parent and child variables from Year 1 with each other. The children's current and future expectancies were related consistently ($p < .01$) in the predicted direction to variables tapping perceptions of their parents' beliefs and expectancies and to the parents' actual estimates of their children's abilities (See Eccles-Parsons, Adler, & Kaczala, 1982 for details). Thus, parents do appear to have an effect on children's expectancies, and we have found another intervention route.

Socializers: General Findings

As hypothesized, we found that parents' and teachers' beliefs are related to children's expectancies and plans. The zero order correlation matrices

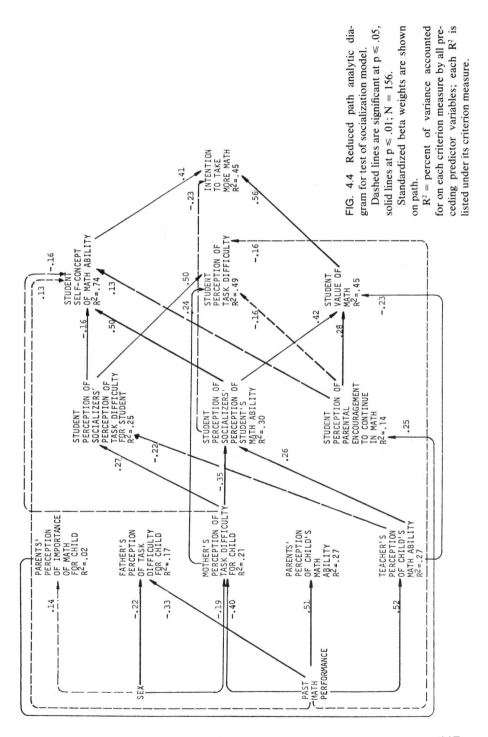

FIG. 4.4 Reduced path analytic diagram for test of socialization model.

Dashed lines are significant at p ≤ .05, solid lines at p ≤ .01; N = 156.

Standardized beta weights are shown on path.

R^2 = percent of variance accounted for on each criterion measure by all preceding predictor variables; each R^2 is listed under its criterion measure.

TABLE 4.4

Correlation Matrix of Selected Student, Parent, and Teacher Variables:
Year One Variables Only

	Child's self-concept of math ability	Child's perception of task difficulty	Child's rating of the value of math	Child's intention to take more math	Math aptitude	Child's future expectancies for math
1. Math aptitude	.34 .48	-.21 -.36	.12 .19	.26 .19	— —	[.28 .49]
2. Parents' perception of importance of math for child	.11 .25	.00 -.13	.21 .18	.09 .02	-.06 .12	.17 .21
3. Mother's perception of task difficulty for child	-.57 -.60	.49 .46	-.27 -.28	-.28 -.34	-.37 -.50	-.48 -.43
4. Father's perception of task difficulty for child	-.49 -.54	.46 .42	-.26 -.28	-.18 -.22	-.27 -.45	-.37 -.44
5. Parents' perception of child's math ability	.31 .35	-.20 -.16	.23 .28	.24 .08	.49 .42	.31 .35
6. Teacher's perception of child's math ability	.44 .59	-.36 -.44	-.08 .12	.21 .20	.50 .57	[.29 .52]
7. Child's perception of socializers' perception of child's math ability	.72 .78	-.41 -.34	[.31 .51]	.14 .28	.21 .33	.60 .70
8. Child's perception of parental encouragement to continue taking math	.30 .37	-.09 -.20	.42 .30	.09 .15	-.11 .05	.36 .43
9. Child's perception of socializers' perception of task difficulty for child	-.52 -.56	.58 .58	[-.08 -.27]	-.06 -.19	-.13 -.23	-.32 -.40

Correlation for female is the upper figure, correlation for males is the lower figure.
$r > .19$ significant at $p < .05$; $r > .27$ significant at $p < .01$.
[ ] = Correlation is significantly different for girls and boys.

118

of selected variables for each year are presented in Table 4.4. We predicted that this link would be mediated by children's perceptions of their parents' and teachers' beliefs rather than affected directly by the socializers' beliefs or by the shared knowledge of the children's math aptitude. To assess these hypotheses, we performed a series of recursive path analyses on the teacher, parent, and child factor scale scores. Figure 4.4 depicts the relations between Year 1 socializer scores and Year 1 student scores. A second analysis, testing the long-range effects of Year 1 variables on the Year 2 measures of student attitudes, yielded similar results.

In support of our predictions, expectancies and goals of socializers were related (mostly indirectly) to children's math self-concept and directly to the children's perceptions of their parents' and teachers' beliefs about their math aptitude and potential. Thus, student perceptions acted as mediators between socializers' attitudes and children's self-concepts of ability (including expectancies), task difficulty, and the value of math. In addition, the child's previous math performances were only indirectly related to intent to study math. That is, measures of children's self-concept and expectancies were more directly related to course plans than either past objective measures of the children's performance or parents' actual attitudes. Much of the effect that these past objective measures have on the children's self-concept is mediated by their impact on the perceptions of teachers and parents.

In conclusion, parents had sex-differentiated perceptions of their children's math aptitude despite the similarity of the actual performance of boys and girls. This difference was most marked for parents' estimates of how hard their children have to try to do well in math. Parents also thought advanced math was more important for their sons than for their daughters. Parents' perceptions of and expectations for their children were related to both the children's perception of socializers' beliefs and to the children's self-concept, future expectations, and plans. Further, parents' beliefs and children's perceptions of these beliefs were more directly related to children's self-concepts, expectancies, and plans than were the children's own past performance in math. Finally, parents as role models of sex-differentiated math behaviors did *not* have a direct effect on their children's self-concepts, expectations, and course plans.

Socializers: Summary and Implications

Because parents' responses were predictive of student attitudes, it would seem that intervening with the parents would have significant impact. Unfortunately, parents are not an easy target group for intervention. Given the number of people and the diversity of opinions and values represented in parent groups, such interventions would be costly and high risk. Consequently, whereas the gain might be great, the cost-benefit ratio is probably low. Nevertheless, were such interventions designed, they should include the following components:

1. Both parents should be provided with information about the value of math for future jobs; stress should be placed on the opening fields of computer science and on the importance of math for careers in social sciences.

2. Parents should be made aware of the detrimental effects of feedback to their children that conveys the sense that math is a hard subject. Because their perceptions of the difficulty of math for their children are influential, parents should be cautioned about the effects of communicating these beliefs to their children.

3. Although seemingly benign, reinforcing girls' opinion that their successes are due to hard work appears to have a long range debilitating effect on girls' self-concept of ability and on their course enrollment plans. Parents should be made aware of this effect and cautioned against attributing their children's, especially their daughters', successes to hard work. Children's success and hard work should be attributed instead to their ability and interests.

One additional point should be made about parental influences. Parents do not have much influence as role models, thus, we do not have to worry about inducing major changes in parents' views about their own math abilities. Instead, we have to stress to them the importance of not projecting these beliefs, if negative, onto their children. Admittedly, this is not an easy task, yet it is certainly easier than convincing them that their own self-concepts of math ability are inaccurate.

Turning now to the school system, our data suggest that teachers also have some impact on students' math attitudes. They are a convenient target group and there are ameliorative behaviors available to them that were observed very infrequently in our classrooms. For example, teachers made few attributions. Teachers could use classroom interactions as an opportunity to model and reinforce beneficial attributional patterns for high ability girls. Similarly, we observed few incidences of the discussion of the importance of math for later careers; teachers could be giving this information to students at all grade levels. Finally, we observed few incidences of encouragement to continue taking math courses or to consider math-related careers. Whereas the variation in existing levels of encouragement was not predictive of plans, increasing the overall level of encouragement given to girls might have beneficial effects. In addition, given the importance of parental attitudes, teachers could work with parents in encouraging math-able girls to consider math-related careers. A well timed phone call letting parents know that their daughter is math-able and should consider one of the many lucrative fields involving her math skills could do wonders. Providing teachers with information regarding the importance of each of these behavior clusters would be an inexpensive intervention. And, because most teachers we talked to wanted to do a good job, our intuition is that they would make use of such information as best they were able.

With regard to classroom interaction patterns, two effects emerged. Both democratic teaching styles and increased opportunity for interaction coupled with appropriate evaluative feedback were associated with high expectancies in "bright" girls. Consequently, teachers should be encouraged both to call on specific students rather than relying on student volunteers for answers and to provide these students with appropriate work praise and criticism.

One additional intervention strategy is suggested indirectly by our data. We found that interest and enjoyment of math was significantly related to other attitudinal variables, that boys and girls did not differ on these variables, and that interest in and enjoyment of math decreased with age. These data suggest that positive attitudes toward math might be maintained by activities designed to capitalize on the enjoyment of math expressed by the younger children. Further, because boys and girls did not differ in their enjoyment of math, it should be possible to design activities that appeal to both boys and girls. Involving children in such activities might maintain their interest and increase participation in advanced math courses.

ACKNOWLEDGMENT

This research was supported in part by Grant No. NIE-G-78-0022 from the National Institute of Education.

5 Cognitive and Affective Determinants of Course Preferences and Plans

Lorelei R. Brush
Aurora Associates, Inc.

Introduction

From this study's conception in 1976, its goals have been to trace the development of students' desire to participate in mathematics or to avoid it, and to closely examine the differences between boys' and girls' reasons for enrollment or avoidance. The motivation for the study is the conviction that too many students, particularly girls, are dropping mathematics in high school as soon as they can. They do not realize that their lack of mathematical preparation will restrict their job opportunities, keeping them out of many of the higher-paying jobs and seriously limiting their opportunities for growth and advancement in other jobs. We need to know why students decide to quit taking mathematics in order to reverse the process.

To trace this decision-making process, information was collected from nearly 2000 students in three New England school systems. In the 1976–77 school year these students were enrolled in the sixth, ninth, and twelfth grades, and the younger two groups were followed through the 1977–78 and 1978–79 school years.

A wide variety of topics were broached with students in the search for the reasons they used to decide about taking more courses in mathematics: the background factors of socioeconomic status and ability; students' attitudes toward mathematics as an easy, creative, enjoyable, and useful field, and their interpretation of the clues they were given by their social milieu concerning the appropriateness of their studying mathematics. This latter topic included asking about the degree of encouragement they felt they were receiving from teachers, parents, and peers; the degree to which they felt it was appropriate for females as well as males to study mathematics; and the degree to which they felt they shared any personality characteristics with mathematicians. All students were given a yearly questionnaire on these topics, and in addition, a number of girls were asked to talk at length about them in interviews.

SUMMARY OF LITERATURE

The research literature repeatedly demonstrates that women participate in mathematical activities less often than men, beginning with optional high school mathematics courses and continuing through college courses and majors, graduate school programs, and jobs in quantitative areas (Admissions Testing Program, 1977; American Mathematical Society, 1975; Centra, 1974; Kreinberg, 1979; McCarthy & Wolfe, 1975; National Assessment of Educational Progress, 1979; Sells, 1974).

Possible explanations for differential participation include each of these topics as reasons for exploration. For each factor there is some evidence that boys and girls differ and that the factor is related to participation in mathematics. For example, a group of researchers have examined student attitudes about the usefulness of mathematics (Aiken, 1974; Armstrong, 1979; Fennema & Sherman, 1977; Haven, 1971; Hilton & Berglund, 1974; Husen, 1967; Sherman & Fennema, 1977; Wise, 1978). Most found sex differences, but these differences were not always replicated in every site or school in each study. In the Fennema and Sherman work, for instance, sex differences were only apparent in two of their four high schools. But each of the researchers investigating the relationship between students' attitudes toward the usefulness of mathematics and enrollment in optional mathematics courses found significant positive correlations (Armstrong, 1979; Haven, 1971; Sherman & Fennema, 1977).

In the present project the explanatory factors proposed in other studies were examined simultaneously so that each factor could be compared to the next to determine what variables differentiated boys and girls and which were the most powerful predictors of participation. Results from the study lead to suggestions for school systems about ways to encourage more girls to study optional mathematics. (See Brush, 1980, for an expanded discussion of the study.)

METHODOLOGY

This 3-year study began with students in the sixth, ninth, and twelfth grades. The sixth graders were followed through seventh and eighth grades, and the ninth graders through tenth and eleventh grades. At the end of the study, then, complete information was available on students in the entire range of grades from the sixth grade through the end of high school.

Sample. Students were enrolled in three New England school systems. One is located in a rural area, one is in a suburb of a large city, and one encompasses a small city. In the first year of the study, about 100 children from each of the three selected grades from each school system were tested. These students comprise the primary sample for the study and were followed for the maximum amount of time possible. In the second year of the study, all of the remaining children in the appropriate grades (seventh and tenth) in these systems who were not in the primary sample were also tested. They comprise a comparison sample for the study.

Table 5.1 summarizes descriptive data on the samples. A total of 816 children comprise the primary sample, and we have a full 3 years of data on 275 middle school students and 239 high school students. About 8% are members of ethnic minority groups, whereas 46% of the eighth and eleventh graders in the primary sample and 29% of the twelfth graders are from working-class families. Both percentages are below the national averages of 17% of children under 15 years of age who belong to minority groups and 60% who are from working-class families (Women's Bureau, *1975 Handbook on Women Workers*). On the other hand, the number of working mothers is close to the national average: among the eighth and eleventh graders, 60% of the mothers are working and among the twelfth graders, 50%, whereas the national average is 56%.

Procedure

In the fall of each year of the study, all students in the appropriate grades in the three school system answered an extensive questionnaire covering the areas of potential interest: family background, course preferences, and enrollment plans; expected liking of future courses; career plans; attitudes toward coursework; and distance between students' self-perceptions and their perceptions of mathematicians and writers. Attitude questions were asked about English and mathematics, so that the mathematics results could be placed in perspective. On the second year questionnaire there were also several essay questions so students could express their opinions about mathematics in their own words. In each year, students took from 25 to 40 minutes (about one class period) to fill out the questionnaire.

In the spring of the second and third years of the study, 48 girls were interviewed about their views of mathematics. Each was selected because her plans to study mathematics changed considerably from the past year

TABLE 5.1
Description of Final Sample Composition after Attrition

Primary Sample (Eighth and Eleventh Graders)

Grade Level (1978-79)[a]		Eighth			Eleventh		Total
School District[b]	A	B	C	A	B	C	
Number	91	95	89	90	70	79	514
Mean Age (Years)	13.07	13.25	13.23	16.08	16.26	16.19	
Sex (Male/Female)	41/50	63/32	43/46	35/55	26/44	31/48	239/275
Percent Minority	0	12	8	2	17	9	8
Percent Working Class	67	57	15	66	68	6	46
Percent Mothers Employed	60	66	50	71	60	51	60
Percent College-Bound	85	65	94	72	67	96	80

Comparison Sample

Grade Level (1978-79)		Eighth			Eleventh		Total
School District	A	B	C	A	B	C	
Number	76	87	78	26	62	55	384
Mean Age (Years)	13.12	13.06	13.17	16.12	16.19	16.22	
Sex (Male/Female)	38/38	44/43	34/44	15/11	28/34	34/21	193/191
Percent Minority	0	14	10	0	8	11	8
Percent Working Class	49	56	6	52	67	7	39
Percent Mothers Employed	65	71	45	62	72	53	61
Percent College-Bound	68	68	97	89	63	95	78

Primary Sample (Twelfth Graders)

Grade Level (1976-77)		Twelfth		Total
School District	A	B	C	
Number	98	102	102	302
Mean Age (Years)	16.96	17.04	17.24	17.15
Sex (Male/Female)	60/38	43/59	40/62	143/159
Percent Minority		—not assessed—		—
Percent Working Class	46	42	3	29
Percent Mothers Employed	55	60	35	50
Percent College-Bound	66	79	98	82

[a] Background data were collected in all three years of the study. The most recent data are presented here because they apply to the sample in its final form—that is, after attrition had taken place.

[b] A is a rural school district, B a small city, C a suburb of a large city, all in New England.

to the present one; half wanted to take more mathematics, the other half less. Findings from the interviews supplement the questionnaire results.

With parental permission, we collected students' IQ test scores, mathematical and verbal achievement scores, and, for high school students, space relations scores. All three systems gave the Differential Aptitudes Test (DAT) to eighth graders, so scores from this instrument sufficed for high school students. IQ scores for the middle school students came from a wide variety of IQ tests, achievement scores from the Stanford Achievement Tests or the Iowa Test of Basic Skills (mathematics and verbal scores); no space relations scores were available.

Questionnaire Measures

Family Background. These questions concerned age, sex, ethnic background, school, father's and mother's employment and education, and number and order of siblings. For analysis purposes, all non-Caucasian children were classed as "minority," and father's occupation was used in rating the socioeconomic status of the family unless no father was present.

Course Preferences or Plans. Questions about this key criterion variable differed for middle school and high school students. The younger students were asked to circle the course they would prefer to take in each of nine pairs of courses. In each pair, one course was mathematics, physics, or chemistry, and the other English, social studies, or a foreign language. *Course Preferences,* the criterion variable for these students, was scored from 0 to 3 depending on the frequency of selection of mathematics. For the older group, students were asked to write down the number of courses they intended to take in each of the school's departments by the time of graduation. *Course Plans* was scored as number of years beyond the two required in each high school that the student planned to take or had taken, ranging from 0 to 3.

Liking of Courses. All students were asked to rate a list of courses from 1 to 5 according to how well they thought they would like future courses in that area. They were told to pretend that they didn't know who the teacher would be, only that the course was in a particular subject. On this scale 1 represented "I expect to dislike it very much"; 2 represented "I expect to dislike it somewhat"; 3 represented "I am indifferent"; 4 represented "I expect to like it somewhat"; and 5 represented "I expect to like it very much." All students rated biology, chemistry, English, history, languages, mathematics, and physics.

Career Plans. Students were asked to list their first three choices for a career. Each choice was then rated for the level of education required—0 represented a high school diploma, 1 represented a college degree, and 2 represented an advanced degree—and for its subject area—physical science, natural science, or other.

Attitude and Anxiety Scales. Items from four pairs of attitude scales were meshed to form an attitude inventory in the first year of testing, and items from two additional scales were included in the second and third years. In Year 1, the scales described mathematics and English as easy/difficult, creative/dull, useful/not useful, and enjoyable/anxiety-provoking. In Years 2 and 3 additional scales probed the degree of sex-typing of each discipline and perceived encouragement for each discipline from parents, teachers, and peers.

On each item a student was requested to strongly agree, agree, express uncertainty, disagree, or strongly disagree with the statement. A strongly negative feeling toward a subject (whether this was expressed by strong agreement or strong disagreement with the statement at hand) was coded as 1; a somewhat negative feeling ("agree" or "disagree") was coded as 2; indifference ("uncertain") was coded as 3; a somewhat positive feeling (again, "agree" or "disagree") was coded as 4; and a strongly positive feeling (again, "strongly agree" or "strongly disagree") was coded as 5. The scores for each item were then summed to provide a measure of the student's attitude toward mathematics or English.

The first three pairs of scales were primarily derived from those of Husen (1967) and Fennema and Sherman (1976a). One pair of attitude scales (Math is Easy/Difficult, English is Easy/Difficult) contained items about the difficulty or accessibility of mathematics and English. A second pair (Math is Creative/Dull, English is Creative/Dull) dealt with the degree to which students see mathematics or English as challenging, interesting, and fun, as well as the degree to which they feel they can contribute their own ideas as opposed to memorizing what others already know. A third pair of attitude scales (Math is Useful/Useless, English is Useful/Useless) dealt with the usefulness of the two subjects for everyday life outside of school and for future job and life plans. In each pair the mathematics scale contained 10 items (five negative, five positive), and the English scale eight items (four negative, four positive).

The fourth pair of scales (Math is Enjoyable/Anxiety-Provoking, English is Enjoyable/Anxiety-Provoking) were simplified forms of items on the Mathematics Anxiety Rating Scale (Richardson & Suinn, 1972; Suinn, Edie, Nicoletti, & Spinelli, 1972) and on the Fennema and Sherman Math Anxiety Scale (Fennema & Sherman, 1976a), with parallel items constructed about English. Twelve statements (six positive, six negative) comprised each scale.

The four pairs of scales just described were used in all three years of testing; two other pairs were used only in the second and third years. One of these examined the sex-typing of mathematics and English, and included the Fennema and Sherman (1976a) Math as a Male Domain Scale (renamed Math is Open to All/A Male Domain) as well as a comparable measure of English constructed for this study. The point was to determine the degree to which students felt each subject was more appropriate for one sex to study than the other. The other pair (Support/No Support from Others—Math, Support/No Support from Others—English) was designed to assess students' perceived support from parents, teachers, and peers. The items followed a pattern: My (parents, teachers, peers) (expect, do not expect) me to do well in (math, English); My (parents, teachers, peers) (encourage, do not encourage) me in my study of (math, English). Each of these last four scales contained 12 questions.

All 12 attitude scales had high split-half reliabilities, ranging from a low of .59 on Math is Creative/Dull for sixth graders to a high of .92 on Math is Useful/Useless for eleventh graders. Most reliabilities were between .7 and .9, indicating a great deal of consistency in student responses.

Stereotypes Versus Self-Image. The last set of questionnaire items, given only to tenth through twelfth graders, asked students to describe their perceptions of a mathematician and a writer, and then to describe themselves on a series of 21 bipolar items first used by Beardslee and O'Dowd (1961). For each item we computed two distance scores, one between the student's self-rating and his/her rating of a writer, the other between this same self-rating and the student's rating of a mathematician. Finally, for each occupation, these distances were totalled across all 21 items. Thus, a smaller total implies a greater identification with a member of that profession.

RESULTS

Two sets of results are reported in this section. First, we present the results from the analysis of the Course Preferences/Plans variables and the attitude variables, concentrating on grade and sex differences on these measures. Because students were tested each year over a 3 year period, multiple analyses were necessary. Means for boys and girls in each of the grades tested in a given year are compared through two-way analyses of variance, and means for the same children tested over the 3 year span of the study are compared using analyses of variance with repeated measures for the grade factor.

Second, we discuss the prediction of students' Course Preferences/Plans from the variables of socioeconomic status, gender, ability, attitudes surrounding liking of mathematics, the usefulness of the field, and the social factors that impinge on students' work in the field. These predictions were made from multiple regression analyses conducted separately for the sixth through eighth graders and the ninth through eleventh graders.

Students' Course Preferences/Plans and Attitudes

- Students have reasonably ambitious plans to continue their study of mathematics.

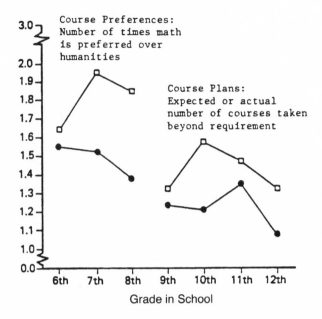

FIG. 5.1   Course preferences/plans in mathematics.

Figure 5.1 reports the results for the Course Preferences/Plans variables. Students in the sixth through eighth grades state that they would prefer to take mathematics courses over humanities courses half of the time or somewhat more often; high school students plan to take a bit more than one course in mathematics beyond the 2 years of mathematics that is required.

- There appear to be some grade differences in Course Preferences/ Plans with older students scoring lower than younger students. However, those may well be due to the differences in measures for middle and high school students, rather than to legitimate differences in coursework plans in mathematics.

Table 5.2 and Table 5.3 present the results for the cross-sectional and longitudinal analyses of Course Preferences/Plans. The former analyses examine differences in the means of the three grades tested in the first year of the study (sixth, ninth, and twelfth graders), and the two grades tested in the second year (seventh and tenth graders), and the third year (eighth and eleventh graders). The longitudinal analyses are concerned with changes in students from the sixth to the eighth grade and from the ninth to the eleventh grade.

TABLE 5.2
F-Ratios for Main Effects and Interactions for Cross-Sectional Analyses

| | Grade Comparisons | | | | | | | | |
| Scale | Sixth/Ninth/Twelfth | | | Seventh/Tenth | | | Eighth/Eleventh | | |
	Sex	Grade	SxG	Sex	Grade	SxG	Sex	Grade	SxG
Course Preferences/Plans	5.43*	6.29**	.62	17.48***	12.38***	.10	12.31***	4.85*	3.59
Like/Dislike	.07	9.55***	.46	.04	6.28**	.52	3.51	2.07	.04
Easy/Difficult	18.21***	14.71***	1.17	15.90***	2.98	.05	13.67***	9.62**	.14
Enjoyable/Anxiety-Provoking	18.05***	12.61***	1.47	20.38***	.69	.27	16.48***	4.45*	.52
Creative/Dull	3.00	28.86***	2.18	.27	18.66***	1.11	.84	12.72***	3.81
Useful/Useless	8.06**	13.37***	2.10	3.92*	5.99*	.05	1.61	19.16***	2.21
Support/No Support from Others		NA		7.13**	.32	.08	.73	10.40**	.07
Math as Open to All/A Male Domain		NA		59.57***	1.54	1.06	82.28***	.27	.16

*p≤.05
**p≤.01
***p≤.001

TABLE 5.3
F-Ratios for Main Effects and Interactions for Longitudinal Analyses

Attitude Scale	Sex	Grade (linear)	Grade (quadratic)	Sex x Grade$_L$	Sex x Grade$_Q$
Sixth-Eighth Grade:					
Course Preferences	11.19***	.03	3.74	4.55*	.08
Like/Dislike	.53	3.93*	.30	1.81	.02
Easy/Difficult	7.85**	1.76	2.86	.66	2.68
Enjoyable/Anxiety-					
Producing	9.14**	13.28***	3.59	.01	.29
Creative/Dull	.36	11.31***	.04	.08	.08
Useful/Useless	1.47	.15	.00	2.23	.36
Seventh-Eighth Grade:					
Support/No Support					
from Others	2.65	.64	NA	1.59	NA
Math as Open to All/					
A Male Domain	38.85***	5.45*	NA	1.02	NA
Ninth-Eleventh Grade:					
Course Plans	9.43**	3.38	.06	3.20	.74
Like/Dislike	.46	1.32	.00	.00	4.24*
Easy/Difficult	12.69***	.62	1.58	.49	.53
Enjoyable/Anxiety-					
Producing	18.72***	6.49*	2.40	.16	.02
Creative/Dull	5.06*	7.98**	.43	.01	2.18
Useful/Useless	7.39**	17.61***	.75	.99	1.46
Tenth-Eleventh Grade:					
Support/No Support					
from Others	1.32	7.75*	NA	1.26	NA
Math as Open to All/					
A Male Domain	51.24***	.02	NA	1.78	NA
Distance of Self-					
Mathematician	.46	11.40***	NA	.15	NA

$*p \leqslant .05$
$**p \leqslant .01$
$***p \leqslant .001$

The only significant grade differences in Course Preferences/Plans appear on Table 5.2 in the cross-sectional analyses; none are evident on Table 5.3. The sixth graders do not change in Course Preferences across seventh and eighth grades, nor do the ninth graders change in Course Plans across their first 3 years in high school. This suggests that the Course Preferences measure used in middle school and the Course Plans measure used in high school are not genuinely comparable so that the significant cross-sectional comparisons on Table 5.2 may simply be due to the use of different measures.

• Boys plan to study more mathematics than do girls; even as early as the seventh grade they show a greater preference for math courses.

The sex differences in Course Preferences/Plans are consistently significant in all of the cross-sectional and longitudinal analyses of variance displayed in Table 5.2 and Table 5.3. In each case girls plan to take fewer mathematics courses than boys. Figure 5.1 shows the means for Course Preferences/Plans, and these suggest that girls find mathematics a relatively less attractive option as early as seventh grade.

- Most students are neutral or slightly positive in their attitudes toward the pleasure and enjoyment of the study of mathematics.

Most of the means on the measures Like/Dislike, Easy/Difficult, Enjoyable/Anxiety-Provoking, and Creative/Dull are in the neutral to slightly positive range (see Fig. 5.2 and Fig. 5.3). Students say that they like mathematics somewhat, that the subject tends to be easy or at least not overwhelmingly difficult, that they often enjoy classes and only infrequently experience anxiety in quantitative situations, and that they sometimes find it challenging, fun, and an opportunity to be creative.

- There is a clear decline in students' liking and enjoyment of mathematics over time.

This decline is obvious on the four graphs shown in Fig. 5.2 and Fig. 5.3, and is supported by the analyses of variance. First, if you look for consistency in grade differences in these analyses, you can see that the Creative/Dull scale shows clear regular differences. In Table 5.2 there are highly significant grade differences in all three cross-sectional comparisons and in Table 5.3 the pattern is continued with two significant linear grade effects on the longitudinal comparisons. Thus, there is a continual and significant decline in students' attitudes toward the nature of mathematical work. As they grow older, students feel more and more that their role in mathematics is to memorize what other people tell them rather than to think things through on their own and contribute their own ideas. Concommitantly, mathematics seems less interesting, challenging, and fun the further students get in its study.

Second, in each of the other instances of a significant grade effect, the direction of the effect is consistent: students like mathematics less and less as they grow older; students find mathematics more difficult and more anxiety-provoking with increasing age. So, whereas the findings are not completely consistent for grade differences in Like/Dislike, Easy/ Difficult, and Enjoyable/Anxiety-Provoking, the trends are clear:

1. There is a decrease in students' liking of mathematics with age on the straightforward index of degree of like or dislike of the field.

2. With increasing age students are most likely to say that mathematics

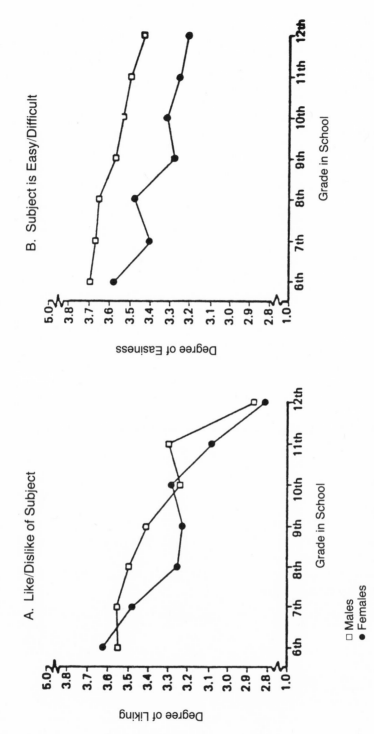

FIG. 5.2   The attitude factors of like/dislike and easy/difficult.

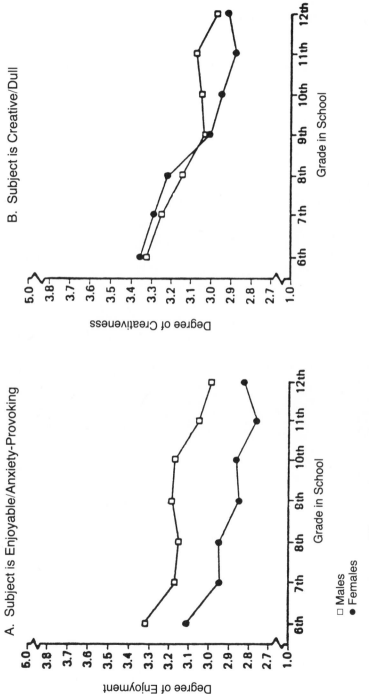

FIG. 5.3   The attitude factors of enjoyable/anxiety-provoking and creative/dull.

135

tends to be difficult and that they may not be able to do advanced work in the field.

3. As time goes on, more and more students admit to being uncomfortable and even anxious in quantitative situations. More agree that tests are unpleasant, and that it is problematic to find enjoyable lessons in mathematics.

- The decline in attitudes over time that characterizes mathematics does not characterize English. That is, the decline does not reflect a growing dislike of *school,* but is particular to mathematics (and possibly other subjects).

For each of the scales about mathematics, students were given a parallel scale about English. The trends for English were just the opposite from those for mathematics. Particularly in high school, pleasure in the study of English increased over time; students claimed to like it more, find it easier, more enjoyable, and more creative the farther they went. Thus, the findings about mathematics do not reflect an increasingly negative attitude toward school in general, but rather are specific to certain subjects—one of which is mathematics.

In the question about Like/Dislike of school subjects, we asked students to rate the degree of their liking for a whole set of school subjects: biology, chemistry, English, history or social studies, languages, mathematics, and physics. The relative rankings of each of the subjects is presented in Table 5.4. In the sixth grade, students placed mathematics high on their list of favorite courses, second only to "science," which for children of this age probably means biology. In the seventh grade, students ranked mathematics second only to chemistry, and in the eighth grade it followed languages and biology. By the ninth grade, however, mathematics lagged behind both English and history/social studies and it never recovered its position of prestige above the major humanities. Hence, students' growing dislike of mathematics accompanies a growing dislike of the physical sciences and stands in opposition to the trend of increasing liking of history and English.

- Girls claim that mathematics is more difficult than boys do and girls rate themselves as more anxious in quantitative situations.

These results might seem to suggest that girls do not have as high mathematical ability as boys and so do experience more difficulty with the subject. In fact, such a difference was not the case in this sample. The middle school girls had a lower mean percentile score on the standardized mathematics achievement test ($\bar{X} = 41.49$) than the boys ($\bar{X} = 48.03$), but

TABLE 5.4
Relative Rankings of Liking of School Subjects

Sixth	Seventh	Eighth	Ninth	Tenth	Eleventh	Twelfth
Science[a]	Chemistry	Languages	Biology	English	English	English
Mathematics	Mathematics	Biology	English	Biology	History	Biology
Languages	Languages	Mathematics	History	History	Biology	History
English	Biology	English	Mathematics	Mathematics	Mathematics	Mathematics
HIstory	English	Chemistry	Languages	Languages	Languages	Languages
	History	History	Science[a]	Chemistry	Chemistry	Science[a]
	Physics	Physics		Physics	Physics	

[a] In Year 1 of the study, "Science" was used to encompass biology, chemistry, and physics for the sixth graders. "Science" was a combination of the ratings of chemistry and physics only for the ninth and twelfth graders.

the high school girls' mean ($\bar{X} = 65.25$) was approximately equal to the high school boys' ($\bar{X} = 65.19$), and the main effect for sex in a two-way analysis of variance was not significant.[1]

Another possibility is that girls are more willing to admit they are having trouble or are anxious than boys when in fact the sexes do not differ. For example, boys may be denying the anxiety they feel because it wouldn't be "masculine" to acknowledge it. Similarly, they may be mustering some bravado and stating they find nothing difficult, rather than admitting that sometimes they too find mathematics to be hard.

A third possibility is that girls are more conscious of the image they present in class, and therefore less likely than boys to ask a question that might appear "stupid." This could easily result in their finding the material more difficult and in their being more anxious in class.

- The findings on students' perceptions of the Useful/Useless nature of mathematics are similar to their attitudes about the pleasure of studying the field. That is, the overall means on this scale show that students of all ages think mathematics is a fairly useful subject to know, but the means decrease over time, and girls see mathematics as less useful than boys.

Figure 5.4 and Table 5.2 and Table 5.3 summarize the results for the Usefulness variable. The means for both sexes and all seven grades are

---

[1] The large grade difference is due to the fact that the tests given the middle school students in the sixth grade (those used in this study) had many problems about fractions, and one of the three school systems did not introduce fractions until sixth grade, after the administration of this standardized test. The means reported here are thus accurate reflections of students' achievement levels, but deflated from those that would result from retesting in the spring of the year. Unfortunately, such a testing was not possible within this project.

well above the neutral score of 3.0, implying that all students see mathematical knowledge as fairly useful to know. The consistently significant grade differences shown on the tables support a decline in perceptions of Usefulness over time, though the graph indicates that the decline is not monotonic. Girls increase slightly in middle school; boys increase slightly at the beginning of high school. In addition, sex differences only appear in two of the cross-sectional analyses and in the longitudinal analysis of high school students. Hence, we may conclude that the degree to which students think mathematics is useful tends to decrease with age, particularly in high school, and that high school girls see mathematics as less useful than do high school boys.

The girls who were interviewed in the third year of the study provided some insight into the reasons for the decline in the perceived usefulness of mathematics over time. They were almost unanimous in their feeling that mathematics would be useful for some aspects of their lives outside of school, and when asked to mention these aspects, they suggested figuring out family budgets, balancing check books, filling out income tax forms, and doing the weekly shopping. All of the examples required only the skills of *arithmetic,* none the more advanced knowledge provided in high school mathematics. As one might expect, a very small percentage of students wished to pursue professional careers related to mathematics, so that mathematics was not seen as useful for specific career plans. In fact, high school algebra and geometry were only seen as useful for the further pursuit of school mathematics.

- Boys and girls alike feel they are receiving some positive support from parents, teachers and peers for their study of mathematics but the amount of perceived support seems to be less in high school than in middle school.

Figure 5.5A displays the means for the social factor of perceived support from others for work in mathematics. All means are above the neutral score of 3.0. The analyses of variance summarized on Table 5.2 and Table 5.3 indicate significant grade differences in the cross-sectional analysis of eighth versus eleventh graders and in the longitudinal analysis of tenth and eleventh graders, suggesting a decrease in support across the high school years. And there was only one sex difference—in the cross-sectional analysis of the seventh and tenth grade scores. In this case females felt they had less support than males felt they had. Thus, there is little evidence from this measure of the social milieu that boys and girls are encouraged differentially in mathematics, and little evidence that encouragement differs for the grades below eleventh. This does not mean that the sexes actually receive identical treatment, but it does imply that

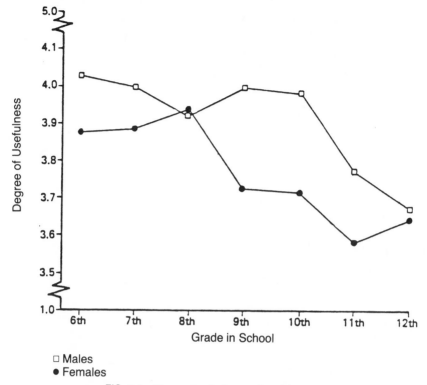

□ Males
● Females

FIG. 5.4   The pragmatic factor of usefulness.

boys and girls do not believe that the significant people in their environment are treating them very differently.

- Most students feel that mathematics is an appropriate subject for both sexes to study, though females are much more adamant in this opinion than males.

The means plotted on Figure 5.5B indicate that all students think mathematics is appropriate for both sexes. The tests of significance summarized in Table 5.2 and Table 5.3 show that there are no grade differences in thoughts about appropriateness of mathematics for both sexes, as is apparent on the graph, but there are huge and consistent sex differences. Girls are always more certain that mathematics is appropriate for everyone.

The reasons for the strong sex differences and the lack of grade differences may be that this scale is tapping an opinion that all of our society knows is required—you are supposed to say that women and men are equally competent in all fields, whatever your age and actual beliefs,

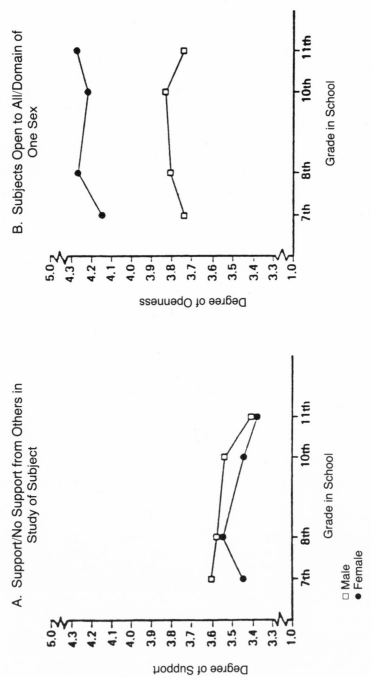

FIG. 5.5 The social factors of encouragement from others and sex-typing of mathematics.

whatever your behavior would seem to imply. Girls, in particular, may be responding to the questions on this scale with what they feel are appropriate "liberated" answers.

It may also be that these students firmly hold the belief that mathematics *should* be appropriate for both sexes, and that women *can* be as good at mathematics as men. At the same time, they may recognize that fewer women are known as geniuses in mathematics and fewer and fewer women will be in their mathematics classes as they get older. Girls' conclusion for their own behavior from these conflicting messages may logically be that they, of course, *could* choose to study more mathematics, but won't. Thus, this measure may not be tapping a central reason for participating in or avoiding mathematics, but only a belief peripheral to the issue.

- Students feel fairly close to mathematicians in a series of personality characteristics, but, as is the case with the Math as Open to All/A Male Domain scale, the meaning of this finding is not clear.

The means on Fig. 5.6 (1.4 to 1.9) imply that students feel they share some qualities with mathematicians. A O score would have meant equivalence with their stereotype of a mathematician, a 6 vast differences. Because the grade and sex differences are inconsistent, however, it is difficult to interpret these data further. Students become closer to their images of mathematicians from tenth to eleventh grade (Table 5.3), but the trend reverses at the twelfth grade, according to the means on Fig. 5.6. There are no sex differences in the tenth/eleventh grade comparison (Table 5.3), but the sexes do differ in twelfth grade ($t(298) = -4.63$, $p < .001$). This feature of the social milieu as well as the other two do not show as consistent and illuminating effects as the earlier indices of pleasure/displeasure and usefulness.

Prediction

Many variables were potentially available for multiple regression analyses of Course Preferences/Plans, but two forms of redundancy needed to be eliminated before such analyses could be done. First, the indicators of ability were highly correlated, as were several of the attitude measures given each year. In order to reduce the redundancy among measures, we constructed a single index of Ability by summing the standardized scores of IQ and mathematics achievement for middle school students, and these two scores plus the Space Relations score for the high school students. Among the attitude measures, we eliminated the single question of Like/ Dislike because this sentiment was described in more detail on items in

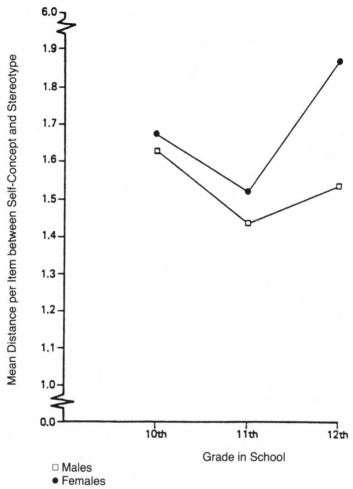

FIG. 5.6   Distance between self-concept and stereotype of a mathematician.

other scales, and factor-analyzed the remaining attitude scales using a series of principal components analyses with varimax rotations, one for each grade of students. One central factor contained items from three scales: Easy/Difficult, Enjoyable/Anxiety-Provoking and Creative/Dull. Items that consistently loaded on this factor were summed to create a conglomerate variable called *Feelings*. A high score indicates a student thinks that mathematics is easy, creative, and not anxiety-provoking. Usefulness items loaded on a factor by themselves as did items on the Math as Open to All/A Male Domain scale and the Distance of Self/ Mathematician score. The teacher items from the Support/No Support from Others scale clustered in a fifth factor that was titled Support/No Support from *Teachers;* the remaining items from this scale were scattered and so were dropped from further analyses. Thus, for each year of testing we defined five attitude variables that could be used with Gender, SES, and Ability to predict Course Preferences/Plans.

The second form of redundancy was caused by the repeated measurement of students in the 3 years of the study. Because the attitude scales and the Course Preferences/Plans measures were given each year, some combinations of variables had to be defined in order to use the maximal amount of information in the prediction equations. This was accomplished by redefining each variable measured in all 3 years into three new component parts. The first was an indicator of *Level* and was defined as the mean for the variable across the 3 years of testing. The second represented *Linear Changes* and was the difference between the Year 3 and Year 1 scores. The third represented *Quadratic Change* and was calculated as the Year 1 score plus the Year 3 score minus 2 times the Year 2 score. Level, linear and quadratic change scores were defined for Course Preferences/Plans, Feelings, and Usefulness, whereas only level and linear change scores were defined for the social milieu variables because they were only measured in Years 2 and 3 of the study.

The findings from the ordinary least-squares regression analyses appear in Table 5.5 and Table 5.6. Table 5.5 summarizes the analyses using only Years 2 and 3 of the data in order to include the maximal set of variables; Table 5.6 summarizes the analyses using 3 years of data from all available sources. Additional analyses were done for each sex separately; the results, where important, are presented in the text, though they do not appear on any table. The presentation is organized to discuss the results for middle school students first, then for high school students.

Middle School Students.   In the 2-year analyses (Table 5.5) the level of Course Preferences is explained primarily by the level of Feelings one has about mathematics and by one's Gender.

- The first major predictor of the level of students' Course Preferences or, for this age of students, choice of many courses in mathematics over courses in the humanities, is the student's general level of Feelings about mathematics. Students who are more positive about the field more frequently prefer mathematics courses to humanities courses.

- A student's Gender is the other major predictor of level of Course Preferences. Males in middle school have a stronger preference for mathematics courses over humanities courses than do females, even

TABLE 5.5
Prediction Results Using Two Years of Data

| | Seventh/Eighth | | Tenth/Eleventh | |
	Level of Course Pref.	Linear Change in Pref.	Level of Course Plans	Linear Change in Plans
Level of Feelings	.29***			
Change in Feelings		.32***		
Level of Usefulness				
Change in Usefulness				
Level of Teacher Support				
Change in Teacher Support				
Level of Math as Male Domain				
Change in Math as Male Domain				
Level of Self/Mathematician	n.a.	n.a.		
Change in Self/Mathematician	n.a.	n.a.		
Ability			.30***	
Gender	.28***		.34**	
SES			.10***	
R^2	.42	.26	.45	.07
Number of Students in Analysis	271	271	187	187

** $p \leqslant .01$
*** $p \leqslant .001$

after accounting for differences in Feelings, Usefulness, Teacher Support, Math as a Male Domain, Ability, and SES. The number on Table 5.5 implies that middle school boys who are equivalent to their female classmates on all other predictors score .28 higher on Course Preferences than their female classmates. Because this Course Preferences variable only ranges from 0 to 3, this difference of slightly more than one quarter of a course is relatively large.

• None of the other predictors in this equation account for a large portion of variance in Course Preferences. Usefulness, Teacher Support, Math as a Male Domain, Ability, and SES are not major predictors of level of Course Preferences for middle school students. In particular, relatively low-ability students and students from working-class homes have not ruled out mathematics as a subject to study.

The next analyses are the predictions of change in Course Preferences for the seventh/eighth graders (Table 5.5). With the sexes together in the equation, only one predictor is significant: changes in Feelings toward mathematics.

TABLE 5.6
Prediction Results Using Three Years of Data

	Sixth/Seventh/Eighth			Ninth/Tenth/Eleventh		
	Level of Course Pref.	Linear Change in Pref	Curved Change in Pref	Level of Course Plans	Linear Change in Plans	Curved Change in Plans
Level of Feelings	.26**					
Linear Feelings		.26***				
Curve of Feelings			.34***			
Level of Usefulness						
Linear Usefulness						
Curve of Usefulness						
Ability				.33***		
Gender						
SES				.10***		
R^2	.42	.27	.30	.41	.06	.06
Number of Students in Analysis	271	272[a]	271	187	187	187

$**p \leqslant .01.$
$***p \leqslant .001.$
[a] One child lacked Year 2 data on Course Preferences, so was not included in the level or curve analyses, but could be included in the linear change analysis.

- The more a child increases in his/her Feelings about mathematics, the more that child increases in preference for taking mathematics courses. This suggests that an intervention program aimed at increasing participation in mathematics could try to change students' feelings about the difficulty of mathematics or the degree to which it is fun and creative, and expect that changes in preferences for courses would follow along. In addition, because boys' and girls' preferences change in the same way over time, the same method could be used for both sexes.

The separate-sex analyses of linear change in Course Preferences over this 2 year period show again that change in Feelings is the primary predictor of change in Course Preferences, but in addition to this variable, the regression for girls demonstrates that a change in Usefulness predicts a change in Course Preferences. Thus,

- An intervention program for girls might try to alter their notions of how useful mathematics can be, because this study suggests that girls whose ideas of the usefulness of mathematics expand tend to want to take more mathematics courses.

The 3 year analyses generally support the conclusions from the 2 year analyses (Table 5.6). The single deviation in the prediction of level of Course Preferences is in the role of Gender.

- Gender was a significant predictor of level of Course Preferences in the 2 year analysis, but was not significant when the sixth grade scores were included. The reason for this may be that Gender has no predictive role in the sixth grade, but only becomes important in the seventh grade. When you add the sixth grade scores to the data set, they mitigate the role of gender for all three grades.

In addition, these analyses extend the findings about change in Course Preferences in that they contain analyses of quadratic as well as linear change.

- Quadratic change in Feelings is a strong predictor of quadratic change in Course Preferences, so that changes in Feelings completely track changes in Course Preferences. Thus, intervention programs aimed at affecting students' feelings about mathematics may be expected to succeed at changing their preference for mathematics courses.

High School Students. In the analysis of level of Course Plans for the tenth/eleventh graders (Table 5.5), the significant predictors are a different set than for the younger children. The measure of feelings is irrelevant to Course Plans, but Ability, SES, and Gender are very significant.

- The Feelings factor does not have the same role for the older students as for the younger. The reason for this may be the differences in the measures of Course Preferences/Plans. In any event, these attitudes toward the subject matter of mathematics do not predict the number of courses high school students say they will take in mathematics departments, whereas they do predict younger students' preferences for mathematics courses over humanities courses.

- Usefulness and the three measures of the social milieu (Teacher Support, Math as a Male Domain, Distance between Self and Mathematician) are unimportant to the prediction of Course Plans for high school students, as they were to the prediction of Course Preferences for middle school students. At least as they are measured here, these indices of the social milieu do not seem to affect Course Plans.

- Two significant predictors for the older group are Ability and SES. Everything else being equal, high-ability students plan to take more mathematics courses, as do students in higher socioeconomic classes. This is very different from the results for the younger students.

- Gender also predicts level of Course Plans for high school students. The number in the table implies that boys and girls of equal ability and SES with equivalent attitudes toward mathematics do not enroll in the same number of high school mathematics courses. Boys take .34 more courses than girls. In a possible range of 0 to 3 courses, this is a considerable difference.

The only difference between the separate-sex analyses and the combined-sex analysis is that the SES finding for the group as a whole is only repeated for girls. The general SES finding as stated earlier needs to be modified.

- Girls from higher SES groups are more likely to want to take a large number of high school mathematics courses, but boys' choice of courses is not as strongly affected by SES. One reason for this difference may be that low-SES girls have decided that a business or secretarial track is more desirable and have stopped taking mathematics when it became optional. Low-SES boys may not have stopped mathematics for lack of clear options or because the available options (e.g., carpentry, drafting) require an additional year or two.

None of the variables proved to be significant in the prediction of *change* in Course Plans for high school students.

- For those people interested in intervention programs for high school students, we can offer little advice. Students seem to have typed themselves as "in" or "out" of mathematics according to their ability and SES. Changing their Feelings toward the subject, their knowledge of its Usefulness, or even their social milieu cannot be expected to change their Course Plans.

The 3 year analyses of Course Plans deviated in only two ways from the 2 year. First, Gender was not a significant predictor of level of Course Plans in the 3 year analysis for the high school students, although it was significant in the 2 year test. Second, Feelings did not enter the 2 year analyses in any significant way, but did enter for boys in the 3 year analysis of level of Course Plans. Thus,

- The lack of significance of Gender in the 3 year analysis is puzzling. The effect is quite large when only the tenth and eleventh grade scores are in the equation, but is not significant when the ninth grade scores are added. With the middle school students we appealed to a lack of sex differences in the criterion variable, Course Preferences, and most predictors for the sixth graders, but that is not the case with ninth graders, for whom many sex differences exist. We can offer the suggestion that the ninth graders (tested in the fall) had little idea of high school requirements for mathematics and were random in their answers, whereas the older students were knowledgeable and consistent.
- The Feelings variable has a much weaker role for high school students than it did for middle school students. It has no role for girls, but does have a small predictive role for boys in the analysis of level of Course Plans.

The analyses of the quadratic change scores indicated that none of the variables was successful at predicting significant quadratic changes in Course Plans. As we found with the linear change analyses of high school students, nothing predicts the changes they make in their number of planned courses in mathematics.

CONCLUSIONS

The final step in a project such as this is to translate the results into workable solutions that can encourage students to enroll in optional mathematics courses. We need to convince students that mathematics can be enjoyable (a change in many students' present attitudes) and increase their participation in mathematical endeavors.

Five strategies may be proposed from this project:

Relax the Atmosphere in Mathematics Classrooms. This is another way of saying: change students' Feelings about mathematics, but aim at the core of these feelings, their reaction to the mathematics classroom. For middle school students this strategy may be expected, if successful, to change students' Feelings and also to change their Course Preferences. For high school students we cannot expect that it will change Course Plans, but it will certainly improve the quality of the day-to-day lives of the students.

Present Information to Students on Mathematical Careers. Our evidence relevant to such an effort suggests that if it succeeds in changing middle school girls' notion of the usefulness of mathematics, it will also change their Course Preferences. Although we have no similar evidence of this effect for sixth to eighth grade boys and high school students, we can argue that such an effort would still have benefits. For example, few of the students tested had any knowledge of the uses of advanced mathematics outside the classroom. That is, we were not comparing students with such knowledge to those without in our statistical tests. Perhaps such a comparison—which would be possible after an exploration of career options—would show that knowledge of concrete uses for mathematics does influence Course Preferences/Plans.

Devise Special Programs for Parents, Teachers, and Guidance Counselors on the Usefulness of Mathematics. Our results showed that parents and teachers generally encourage students in their study of mathematics. Though we cannot talk from our results about how this encouragement works, we can at least suggest that if all the significant people in a student's world tell him/her that mathematics is a necessary subject to study, the pressure will be clearly placed on that student to keep trying.

Introduce New Non-Remedial Mathematics Courses into the Curriculum. For many students in the middle school, making the mathematics class less formal should be sufficient to encourage students in their continued pursuit of mathematics. But for some sixth to eighth graders and for high school students, it may be productive to develop new courses in addition to changing the regular classes' atmosphere. These new courses could aim at teaching a similar curriculum to the traditional courses, but with a different twist. For example, a teacher could try teaching algebra through the medium of social science experiments and statistics or the use of computers. Or perhaps it would be useful to introduce students to non-traditional areas of mathematics such as non-Euclidean geometry or group theory in interesting ways. The idea is that the success students would experience in these new courses might change their notions of their own ability, actually increase their mathematical knowledge, and thus motivate them to re-enter the regular mathematics curriculum or take more courses in mathematics than originally planned.

Require Four Years of High School Mathematics.   In the introduction of this chapter, the vital importance of mathematics was discussed. This study has shown that there are relationships between some attitudes and Course Preferences/Plans. Earlier strategies for increasing participation have been based on one interpretation of the results: that changes in attitudes will lead to changes in Course Preferences/Plans. This strategy is based on the opposite interpretation: that changes in Course Preferences/ Plans will change attitudes, and presumably, better prepare students for the world they will enter after graduation. Quite apart from the results, this strategy can be seen as solving the issue in one blow without recourse to any psychological research.

For a particular school system one strategy may be more appropriate than another or more feasible than another. Whatever the choice, educators need to implement some strategy or strategies to encourage students to take more mathematics. This research suggests that girls have a more serious need for such programs than boys, but that the same sort of programs will succeed with both sexes. Choices of strategies need to be made now so that students in the 1980s will enroll in the mathematics they need for their future lives.

ACKNOWLEDGMENTS

The first year of this three-year study was supported by a grant from the Spencer Foundation, the second and third years by Contract No. 400-77-0099 from the National Institute of Education to Abt Associates, Inc.

6 Visual-Spatial Skill: Is it Important for Mathematics? Can it be Taught?

Jane M. Connor
State University of New York at Binghamton

Lisa A. Serbin
Concordia University
Montreal, Quebec

Introduction

The fact that large numbers of women avoid mathematics in the latter years of high school and to a certain degree do not achieve as well as males even when they continue with mathematics (Fennema & Sherman, 1977a) has been of increasing concern to educators, psychologists, sociologists, and other students of human behavior. This deficit in mathematics education has serious implications for the career options available to both women who attend 4 year colleges and to those who choose to enroll in more vocationally oriented programs (Sells, 1973).

A variety of potential sources for this deficit have been examined by researchers working under the recent NIE program on Women and Mathematics and by others. These include the role played by mathematics anxiety (Tobias & Donady, 1977), sexist wording of mathematics problems and text books (Carey, 1958; Graf & Ruddell, 1972), lack of parental encouragement (Fox, 1975b), teacher influences (Ernest, 1976; Fennema, 1977; Pederson, Shihedling, & Johnson, 1975), and attitudes toward mathematics (Fennema & Sherman, 1977a).

The present research was directed towards examining the influence of cognitive factors on sex-related differences in mathematics achievement. More specifically, two lines of research were pursued examining: (1) the relationship between different types of visual spatial skill and mathematics achievement; and (2) the trainability of visual-spatial skill in junior high school students.

151

THE RELATIONSHIP BETWEEN VISUAL-SPATIAL
SKILL AND MATHEMATICS ACHIEVEMENT

Several types of evidence suggest an important role of visual-spatial skill in mathematics achievement and for understanding sex-related differences in mathematics achievement. Developmentally, sex-related differences in visual-spatial test performance and mathematics achievement appear to emerge at roughly the same age, 12–14 years (Maccoby & Jacklin, 1974). In correlational studies visual-spatial skill is frequently found to be a significant predictor of mathematics achievement. Fennema and Sherman (1977a), for example, obtained significant correlations between math achievement and a spatial-visualization measure in four secondary schools. These correlations tended to be higher than correlations between math achievement and general intelligence (verbal) measures. Further evidence is furnished by I. Macfarlane Smith (1964) in his book *Spatial Ability: Its Educational and Social Significance,* in which he describes a great many studies that demonstrate the importance of spatial ability for success in mathematics.

Lastly, a logical analysis of the nature of visual-spatial ability and of mathematics achievement indicates that they should bear an important relationship to one another. Visual-spatial ability is a cognitive skill involving the ability to perceive spatial relationships and to manipulate visual material mentally. According to several mathematicians, the nature of mathematical thinking is highly dependent on such a cognitive skill. Hamley, a mathematician and psychologist, states (in Smith, 1964) that, "Mathematical ability is probably a compound of general intelligence, visual imagery, ability to perceive number and space configurations and to retain such configurations as mental patterns" (p. 104). Another mathematician, Meserve, notes (in Fennema, 1977) the extensive use of geometrical models in all areas of mathematics and says that ". . . geometrical thinking must retain some link . . . with spatial intuition" (p. 90).

Despite the findings relating visual-spatial skill to mathematical achievement, research in this area is complicated by the fact that neither the domain of skills represented by the term "visual-spatial" nor the domain represented by the term "mathematics achievement" is unidimensional. Potentially certain types of visual-spatial skills may be related to certain types of mathematics problems, whereas other types of visual-spatial skills may be totally unrelated to any aspect of mathematics achievement.

The two studies that follow were designed to examine the relationship between mathematics achievement (including computation, algebra, and geometry) and visual-spatial skill. The visual-spatial tests that were used included tests from the subdivision of skills referred to as "spatial orientation-visualization" and from the subdivision referred to as "closure" (Ekstrom, French, Harman, & Dermen, 1976). In this way mathematics achievement could be related to specific types of visual-spatial skills.

STUDY 1

Subjects

Research participants were the entire seventh and tenth grades of a suburban-rural school district, almost all of whom were white. This included 134 seventh graders (71 male, 63 female) and 205 tenth graders (108 male, 97 female).

Testing Materials

Three sets of measures were obtained from each grade level. These included: (a) six measures of visual-spatial skill and a measure of verbal skill; (b) a mathematics achievement test formulated for this project; and (c) various standardized test scores and school grades obtained from school records. Each of these sets of measures is now discussed in detail.

The Visual-Spatial Tests. Five visual-spatial tests were selected from the Educational Testing Service Kit of Factor Referenced Tests (Ekstrom, et al., 1976). The Cube Comparisons test consists of 21 problems each one of which is a picture of two cubes with letters on the three visible faces of the cubes. The subject must decide which of the two pictures represents images of the same three-dimensional cube. This test is thought to be a measure of the skill of Spatial Orientation. The Card Rotations Test is thought to be a measure of the same skill. This test consists of 80 problems for each of which the subject must decide if a given symbol can be rotated in a two-dimensional plane to match another symbol. For the Hidden Patterns test, a measure of flexibility of closure, the subject must decide if a shape that looks somewhat like an upside-down Y with an extra line attached is or is not embedded in each of 200 line drawings. The Gestalt Completion Test, a measure of speed of closure, consists of 10 incomplete black and white drawings. The subject tries to determine what each is a picture of. The Paper Folding Test, a measure of visualization skill, contains ten problems, each one depicting how a piece of paper is folded in a specific way and then a hole punched in the folded paper. The task is to decide how the holes would appear on the paper if it were unfolded. The vocabulary test that was used was also taken from the ETS kit and consisted of 18 vocabulary items. The sixth visual-spatial test that was used was an abbreviated version (only 10 items) from the Space Relations part of the Differential Aptitude Test or DAT (Bennett, Seashore, & Wesman, 1973). Each item consists of a drawing of a two-dimensional shape which, if folded along indicated lines, could make a three-dimensional shape. The subject must choose from four alternatives which shape this would be. The test involves the skills of both spatial orientation and visualization.

The Mathematics Test. This test consisted of 48 problems adapted from a number of standardized mathematics tests. The purpose of the adaptation was to construct a test that included 16 problems each from the areas of arithmetic, algebra, and geometry. The classification of problems was determined by agreement of at least four out of five mathematics majors as to the content area of each problem used. Separate tests appropriate for seventh and tenth graders were so constructed.

Standardized Scores and School Grades. With the use of coded subject numbers to ensure confidentiality, the following information from subjects' permanent school records was obtained:

Seventh Graders

   a. Sixth-grade results on the Stanford Achievement Tests (SAT)—Vocabulary, Reading Comprehension, Word Studies, Math Concepts, Math Computation, Math Applications, Spelling, Language, Social Science, and Science.
   b. Sixth-grade I.Q., New York State Reading, and New York State Mathematics scores.
   c. Sixth-grade English and mathematics grades, first-quarter seventh-grade English and mathematics grades.

Tenth Graders

   a. Sixth-grade results on the Stanford Achievement Tests—Word Meaning, Paragraph Meaning, Spelling, Language, Arithmetic Computation, Arithmetic Concepts, Arithmetic Applications, Social Studies, and Science.
   b. Sixth-grade I.Q., third-grade New York State Reading, and sixth-grade New York State mathematics scores.
   c. Ninth-grade English and mathematics grades, first-quarter tenth-grade English and mathematics grades.

Results

Sex Differences in Mean Performance. The means, standard deviations, sample sizes, and F-ratios for all measures for seventh and tenth graders are shown in Table 6.1 and Table 6.2.

Among the seventh graders females performed significantly better than males on the SAT Word Studies section, on the SAT Language section, and in sixth- and seventh-grade English class (p < .01). They also tended (p < .10) to do better on the SAT Spelling section, the SAT Math Concepts section, and in sixth-grade math class. Seventh-grade males tended to do better than females on the DAT Space Relations Test. There were

TABLE 6.1
Means and Standard Deviations for All Measures:
Seventh-Grade Students

Test	Males			Females			F-Ratio
	X	S.D.	N	X	S.D.	N	
Mathematics Achievement Tests							
Geometry	6.89	2.47	71	6.79	2.35	63	< 1
Algebra	7.56	2.66	71	7.90	2.81	63	< 1
Arithmetic	8.77	3.11	71	9.62	2.93	63	1.73
ETS Tests							
Cube comparisons	2.98	3.97	64	2.87	4.18	55	< 1
Hidden patterns	62.28	29.37	64	62.91	28.20	55	< 1
Gestalt completion	4.78	1.88	64	5.09	1.91	55	< 1
Paper folding	3.45	2.65	64	3.46	2.57	55	< 1
Vocabulary	3.88	3.12	64	3.62	2.53	55	< 1
Card rotations	38.06	18.19	64	37.40	16.39	55	< 1
DAT Test							
Space relations	5.63	2.50	64	4.81	2.40	55	3.31*
SAT Tests							
Vocabulary	57.74	24.75	57	60.04	21.65	53	< 1
Reading comprehension	60.12	26.56	57	63.81	22.31	53	1.1
Word study	62.30	28.41	56	72.29	19.41	52	4.48**
Math concepts	66.30	23.75	56	72.62	18.63	53	2.36
Math computation	63.89	22.39	56	68.91	21.06	53	1.78
Math application	65.75	22.38	56	61.66	21.27	53	< 1
Spelling	52.46	29.65	57	59.77	23.86	53	2.43
Language	56.46	24.56	57	66.28	21.26	53	5.70**
Social studies	62.75	25.19	57	68.13	18.56	53	1.93
Science	67.39	24.70	57	66.96	20.46	53	< 1
Intelligence Quotient	108.27	13.91	55	111.00	10.15	52	< 1
New York State Tests							
Reading	57.09	23.54	54	61.60	19.18	53	< 1
Mathematics	54.89	23.23	54	53.77	17.15	53	< 1
School Grades							
English - 6th grade	81.18	8.78	55	85.22	5.41	51	7.54**
Mathematics - 6th grade	78.36	10.96	55	81.37	8.88	51	2.49
English - 7th grade	74.12	11.65	60	84.43	8.93	56	25.83**
Mathematics - 7th grade	78.02	12.00	60	82.63	8.99	56	3.42*

* p < .10.
** p < .05.

no significant differences between seventh-grade males and females on any of the ETS factor-referenced cognitive tests.

Among the tenth graders, males performed significantly better than females on the geometry subscale of the math achievement test (p < .05) and on the following Stanford Achievement Tests: Arithmetic Applications, Social Studies, and Science. Males also tended to perform better on

TABLE 6.2
Means and Standard Deviations for All Measures:
Tenth-Grade Students

Test	Males			Females			F-Ratio
	X	S.D.	N	X	S.D.	N	
Mathematics Achievement Tests							
Geometry	7.15	5.74	108	5.46	2.81	97	5.52**
Algebra	5.63	2.63	108	5.05	2.48	97	1.29
Arithmetic	8.19	3.48	108	8.09	2.70	97	<1
ETS Tests							
Cube comparisons	6.52	5.91	102	6.48	5.77	89	<1
Hidden patterns	70.94	37.54	102	69.04	35.71	89	<1
Gestalt completion	7.19	1.68	102	7.18	1.74	89	<1
Paper folding	4.15	2.58	102	4.39	2.58	89	<1
Vocabulary	7.30	3.73	102	7.06	4.42	89	<1
Card rotations	49.64	20.91	102	47.78	21.43	89	<1
DAT Test							
Space relations	7.47	2.08	102	6.83	2.95	89	3.13*
Sixth-grade Stanford Achievement							
Word meaning	50.23	26.49	91	44.68	28.83	71	1.30
Paragraph meaning	49.58	27.84	91	44.68	28.83	71	< 1
Spelling	37.96	26.33	91	46.34	25.97	70	4.06**
Language	36.48	23.50	91	42.59	24.14	70	2.60
Arithmetic computation	23.34	19.01	91	20.72	14.31	71	< 1
Arithmetic concepts	49.89	27.02	91	42.99	21.76	70	3.05*
Arithmetic application	48.60	28.45	91	30.14	23.43	70	19.37**
Social studies	46.79	27.91	91	37.63	25.64	71	4.09**
Science	49.76	29.18	91	40.01	24.15	71	4.66**
TOTAL	57.02	13.70	91	56.23	11.40	70	< 1
Intelligence Quotient	109.02	14.69	93	107.97	12.27	71	< 1
New York State Tests							
Reading	51.78	22.34	81	56.97	25.08	63	1.99
Mathematics	48.10	25.67	91	39.37	22.05	71	1.89
School Grades							
English - 9th grade	77.35	10.94	98	78.98	11.42	83	1.54
Mathematics - 9th grade	78.09	11.42	96	78.46	10.55	82	< 1
English - 10th grade	77.71	14.26	97	78.53	11.96	83	1.24
Mathematics - 10th grade	81.07	13.05	69	77.92	12.79	52	1.50

*p <.10.
**p <.05.

the abridged DAT Space Relations Test, on the SAT Arithmetic section, and on the New York State Mathematics Test.

Females performed significantly better than males on the Spelling section of the SAT ($p < .05$) and tended to do better on the SAT Language section and the New York State Reading Test ($p < .10$). There were no significant differences between tenth-grade males and females on any of the ETS factor-referenced tests.

Factor Analysis. Separate factor analyses (principal components type) were performed on the seventh- and tenth-grade data. The results of these analyses showed a clear separation between those measures that were primarily verbal in content (the ETS Vocabulary Test, the SAT verbal tests, and the New York State Reading Test), those which had substantial mathematical content (the Geometry, Algebra, and Arithmetic subscales, the SAT Arithmetic tests, and the New York State Reading Test), and the visual-spatial tests. In addition, among the tenth graders the distinction between a "spatial-visualization" skill and a "closure" skill was supported by the pattern of factor loadings. The Cube Comparison Test, the Paper Folding Test, the Card Rotations Test and the DAT Space Relations Test all had substantial loadings on the spatial-visualization factor, whereas the Hidden Patterns Test, the Gestalt Completion Test, and the Card Rotations Test were heavily loaded on the closure factor. (Further details about these analyses are available in Connor & Serbin, 1980.)

Correlations. In order to determine the extent to which the specific skills measured by the cognitive tests were related to mathematics achievement, univariate correlations between each of the ETS tests and each of the mathematics measures were calculated separately for boys and girls at each grade level (see Table 6.3 and Table 6.4).

Seventh Graders. For the boys the Card Rotations Test and the Space Relations Test were significantly correlated with almost every measure of mathematics achievement. For the girls only one of the 14 comparable correlation coefficients was significant. In addition, tests of the difference in correlation coefficients for boys and girls yielded six pairs in which the correlation between a visual-spatial measure and a mathematics measure was higher for boys. In one instance, a significantly higher correlation between vocabulary and mathematics was found for girls than for boys. The Hidden Patterns Test and Gestalt Completion Test tended to be poor predictors of mathematics achievement. For girls the Paper Folding Test and The Vocabulary Test were the best overall predictors of mathematics achievement.

Tenth Graders. Among the tenth graders the Cube Comparisons Test, the Paper Folding Test, the Vocabulary Test, and the Card Rotations Test

TABLE 6.3

Correlations Between Cognitive Measures and Mathematics
Achievement Measures: Seventh Grade

	Mathematics Achievement			SAT Tests			
Test	Geometry	Algebra	Arithmetic	Math Concepts	Math Computation	Math Application	New York State Mathematics
			BOYS				
ETS Tests							
Cube comparison	0.31*	0.18	0.25*	0.25	0.17	0.30*	0.21
Hidden patterns	0.16	0.39*	0.10	0.31*	0.19	0.24	0.19
Gestalt completion	0.17	0.15	0.09	0.24	0.13	0.23	0.07
Paper folding	0.37*	0.18	-0.01	0.11	0.06	0.20	0.01
Vocabulary	0.23	0.35*	0.10	0.28*	0.21	0.35*	0.25
Card rotations	0.36*	0.46*	0.39*	0.55*	0.39*	0.62*	0.40*
DAT Test							
Space relations	0.39*	0.42*	0.23	0.57*	0.31*	0.63*	0.55*
			GIRLS				
ETS Tests							
Cube comparison	0.05	0.04	0.09	0.15	0.06	0.22	0.04
Hidden patterns	0.01	0.13	0.20	0.31*	0.17	0.21	0.19
Gestalt completion	-0.06	0.04	0.00	0.17	-0.08	0.12	-0.25
Paper folding	0.35*	0.34*	0.24	0.16	0.13	0.32*	0.29*
Vocabulary	0.16	0.24	0.43*	0.40*	0.04	0.24	0.10
Card rotations	0.09	0.22	0.21	0.20	0.11	0.11	-0.15
DAT Test							
Space relations	0.22	0.31*	0.22	0.12	0.17	0.26	0.15

*Correlation significantly different from 0, $p < .05$.

TABLE 6.4

Correlations Between Cognitive Measures and Mathematics Achievement Measures: Tenth Grade

Test	Geometry	Algebra	Arithmetic	Arithmetic Computation	Arithmetic Concepts	Arithmetic Application	New York State Mathematics
				BOYS			
ETS Tests							
Cube comparison	0.24*	0.40*	0.31*	0.13	0.39*	0.46*	0.47*
Hidden patterns	0.19	0.38*	0.27*	0.16	0.19	0.22*	0.27*
Gestalt completion	0.07	-0.04	0.10	0.05	0.04	0.03	0.02
Paper folding	0.23*	0.35*	0.31*	0.15	0.41*	0.35*	0.41*
Vocabulary	0.14	0.29*	0.26*	0.16	0.29*	0.33*	0.37*
Card rotations	0.14	0.30*	0.36*	0.21	0.32*	0.29*	0.31*
DAT Test							
Space relations	0.12	0.10	0.14	0.09	0.27*	0.17	0.21
				GIRLS			
ETS Tests							
Cube comparison	0.30*	0.23*	0.36*	0.15	0.25*	0.38*	0.40*
Hidden patterns	0.13	0.26*	0.18	0.32*	0.33*	0.11	0.36*
Gestalt completion	0.10	0.18	0.25*	0.14	0.18	0.19	0.16
Paper folding	0.25*	0.24*	0.31*	0.26*	0.14	0.22	0.33*
Vocabulary	0.24*	0.23*	0.23*	0.32*	0.33*	0.45*	0.49*
Card rotations	0.22*	0.31*	0.36*	0.39*	0.24	0.30*	0.39*
DAT Test							
Space relations	0.14	0.21*	0.19	0.27*	0.24	0.38*	0.39*

*Correlation significantly different from 0, $p < .05$.

yielded a number of significant correlations with the mathematics measures for both boys and girls. The Gestalt Completion Test was generally unrelated to mathematics achievement. Only one statistically significant difference was found in the correlation coefficients for boys and girls; the correlation between performance on the Paper Folding Test and Arithmetic Concepts was higher for boys.

Canonical Correlations. In order to determine the relationship between the set of mathematics measures as a whole and the specific skill measured by the cognitive tests (the visual-spatial and vocabulary tests), canonical correlations between these two sets of measures were calculated separately for boys and girls and for seventh and tenth graders (see Table 6.5).

The canonical correlation between the two sets of measures for seventh-grade boys was .78, statistically significant at the .05 level. The largest canonical weights for this case were on the DAT Space Relations Test with a loading of − .71 and the SAT Mathematics Applications Test with a loading of − .79. The canonical correlation for seventh-grade girls was .61, which was not statistically significant.

The canonical correlation for tenth-grade boys was .73, statistically significant at the .01 level. The largest canonical weights for this case were on the Paper Folding and Card Rotations Test (loadings of − .48 and − .47 respectively) and the New York State Mathematics Test (loading of − .49). The canonical correlation for tenth-grade girls was .67, statistically significant at the .05 level. The largest canonical weights were on the ETS Vocabulary Test with a loading of .64 and the New York State Mathematics Test with a loading of .63.

Discussion

The results of the analyses of variance indicate that males tended to perform better than females on mathematics measures, whereas females tended to perform better on verbal measures. The male advantage in mathematics did not emerge until tenth grade. Females tended to do better on the verbal measures in both seventh and tenth grades. Although sex differences in mathematics achievement and verbal skill are not found in all studies, when they are obtained, they are almost invariably in the direction observed in this study (Maccoby & Jacklin, 1974).

Although males performed consistently better on the DAT Space Relations Test, there were no sex differences for either grade on any of the ETS visual-spatial tests. These results indicate that the discovery of a sex difference in visual-spatial skill is highly dependent on the type of visual-spatial measure used.

TABLE 6.5
Coefficients for the Canonical Correlation Between
Cognitive Measures and Mathematics Achievement

Group	Coefficients for the First Set		Coefficients for the Second Set	
Seventh-grade boys	Mathematics Achievement Tests		ETS Tests	
	Geometry	-0.11	Cube comparisons	0.01
	Algebra	-0.31	Hidden patterns	-0.10
	Arithmetic	0.36	Gestalt completion	-0.10
	SAT Tests		Paper folding	-0.04
	Math concepts	-0.37	Vocabulary	-0.24
	Math computation	0.33	Card rotations	-0.23
	Math application	-0.79	DAT Test	
	New York State Mathematics	-0.04	Space relations	-0.71
Seventh-grade girls	No significant (p <.05) canonical correlation was obtained.			
Tenth-grade boys	Mathematics Achievement Tests		ETS Tests	
	Geometry	0.24	Cube comparisons	-0.22
	Algebra	-0.37	Hidden patterns	-0.17
	Arithmetic	-0.43	Gestalt completion	0.24
	Sixth-grade Stanford Achievement		Paper folding	-0.48
	Arithmetic computation	0.21	Vocabulary	-0.20
	Arithmetic concepts	-0.20	Card rotations	-0.47
	Arithmetic application	-0.06	DAT Test	
	New York State Mathematics	-0.49	Space relations	0.10
Tenth-grade girls	Mathematics Achievement Tests		ETS Tests	
	Geometry	-0.24	Cube comparisons	0.00
	Algebra	0.15	Hidden patterns	-0.02
	Arithmetic	-0.16	Gestalt completion	0.28
	Sixth-grade Stanford Achievement		Paper folding	0.11
	Arithmetic computation	0.10	Vocabulary	0.64
	Arithmetic concepts	-0.15	Card rotations	0.23
	Arithmetic application	0.59	DAT Test	
	New York State Mathematics	0.63	Space relations	0.31

The results of the bivariate correlations showed that for boys, various types of visual-spatial skills were highly correlated with math achievement. Generally those tests with high loadings in the "spatial-visualization" factor were good predictors, whereas those tests with high loadings in the "closure" factor were poor predictors. The Gestalt Completion Test was especially poor as a predictor of mathematics achievement for boys. The conclusion that visual-spatial ability and mathematics achievement were closely related for boys was supported by the results of the canonical correlations. Strong statistically significant canonical correlations were obtained between the cognitive tests and the mathematics measures with the major weights on the DAT Space Relations Test for the seventh-grade boys and the Paper Folding and Card Rotations Tests for the tenth-grade boys.

In general, the relationship between visual-spatial skill and mathematics achievement was markedly less for girls. The bivariate correlations showed that some math measures were more highly correlated with scores on the visual-spatial tests than scores on the vocabulary tests, whereas for other math measures the reverse was true. It should be noted that those visual-spatial tests that *were* good predictors of math achievement among girls were all from the "spatial-visualization" subdivision of visual-spatial ability. For girls as for boys, these tests from the "closure" subdivision of visual-spatial ability were poor predictors of math achievement.

The canonical correlations for the girls yielded markedly different results than the parallel analysis for the boys. For the seventh-grade girls, no significant correlates were found, whereas for the tenth-grade girls the only cognitive test with a substantial weight on the canonical variable was the Vocabulary Test. These results suggest that for girls verbal skills may play a more important role than visual-spatial skills in mathematics achievement. However, because these results have not been reported in the literature previously, and because it is not possible to make a statistical test of the difference in canonical weights, this conclusion must be considered tentative at this time, pending replication.

STUDY 2

Study 2 was planned as a replication of Study 1. The purpose was to evaluate the generalizability of the results obtained in the first study by collecting additional data from other schools. Because the tests measuring the visual-spatial skills of flexibility and speed of closure (the Hidden Patterns and Gestalt Completion Tests) appeared to contribute relatively little to predicting mathematics achievement, these were dropped from the test battery. Instead, two tests of visualization were included (the ETS Form Board Test and the ETS Surface Development Test described below). By employing three tests of visualization, two tests of spatial orientation and one test involving both skills (the DAT Space Relations Test), we hoped to find empirical support for the distinction between these two skills and an evaluation of the relative importance of each skill for mathematics achievement.

Subjects

Subjects were 374 seventh graders (189 boys, 185 girls) enrolled in two junior high schools in a small city in upstate New York and 560 tenth graders (277 boys, 283 girls) enrolled in various mathematics courses in neighboring high schools.

Testing Materials

The mathematics achievement measures used in this study were the seventh- and tenth-grade math tests described in Study 1. Because the analysis of the algebra, geometry, and arithmetic scales added relatively little to the findings of Study 1, only a combined score was used.

The ETS Cube Comparisons Test, Vocabulary Test, Card Rotations Test, Paper Folding Test, and DAT Space Relations Test, described in Study 1, were included in the battery of cognitive tests given to the students. (Due to time constraints several of the tenth-grade classes were unable to do the Paper Folding Test.) The Hidden Patterns Test and the Gestalt Completion Test were replaced by the ETS Form Board and Surface Development Test. The Form Board Test contains 24 items, each one of which shows a geometric shape followed by five smaller geometric shapes. The subjects' task is to indicate which ones of the smaller shapes could together be arranged to form the larger shape. The Surface Development Test is similar to the DAT Space Relations Test. Ekstrom et al. (1976) describe it, "In this test, drawings are presented of solid forms that could be made with paper or sheet metal. With each drawing there is a diagram showing how a piece of paper might be cut and folded so as to make the solid form. Dotted lines show where the paper is folded. One part of the diagram is marked to correspond to a marked surface in the drawing. The subject is to indicate which lettered edges in the drawing correspond to numbered edges or dotted lines in the diagram" (p. 174). The test consists of five items in each of six drawings.

Procedure

Testing was carried out on two consecutive days in individual math classes in all schools except one, in which the entire seventh-grade student body was tested as a group. On the first day, five tests were administered in a 30-minute session, in the order listed: the Surface Development, Form Board, Cube Comparisons, Vocabulary, Card Rotations, and Spatial Relations Tests. On the second day, the appropriate mathematics achievement test was administered along with the Paper Folding Test. The math test took 30 minutes to administer and the Paper Folding, 8 minutes. For test administration in individual math classes ranging in size from 19 to 31 students, two experimenters were continuously present, whereas in the mass testing session, 10 proctors supervised administration of the tests to 126 students.

Results

Among the seventh graders, boys obtained a higher mean score on the Form Board Test ($p < .05$); no other reliable sex differences were obtained. Among the tenth graders the males had higher mean scores than the females on three of the visual-spatial tests: the Surface Development Test, the Form Board Test, and the Paper Folding Test. There was a trend for boys to do better on the DAT Space Relations Test. Girls tended to perform better than boys on the Vocabulary Test (see Table 6.6).

Correlations between the set of six visual-spatial measures and the vocabulary test with the mathematics achievement test are shown separately for boys and girls in Table 6.7. All of the correlations were positive, and with two exceptions, statistically significant. In four instances, the correlation of visual-spatial performance with mathematics achievement was significantly higher for boys than for girls. (This was seen for seventh graders on the Surface Development and Space Relations Tests and for tenth graders on the Form Board and Card Rotations Tests.) In most other instances the correlation coefficient was higher for boys but not significantly so. There was no sex difference in the strength of the association between performance on the Vocabulary Test and Mathematics Achievement.

TABLE 6.6
Means, Standard Deviations, Sample Sizes, F-Ratios for
Boys and Girls, Seventh and Tenth Grades

| | Seventh Grade | | | | | | |
| | Boys | | | Girls | | | |
	X	S	n	X	S	n	F-ratio
Vocabulary	3.26	2.86	174	3.55	2.77	182	< 1
Surface Development	4.16	2.90	174	4.00	2.77	180	< 1
Form Board	2.64	2.07	173	2.19	1.90	180	4.43**
Paper Folding	2.10	2.42	179	2.33	2.25	181	< 1
Cube Comparisons	3.26	3.50	176	3.30	3.93	181	< 1
Card Rotations	34.99	21.09	177	37.56	20.0	177	1.38
DAT Space Relations	5.35	2.65	170	5.22	2.85	177	< 1
Mathematics Test	12.18	8.07	182	12.70	6.85	184	< 1
	Boys		Tenth Grade	Girls			
	X	S	n	X	S	n	F-ratio
Vocabulary	6.84	3.89	260	7.47	3.81	264	3.51*
Surface Development	9.00	5.56	259	8.09	4.84	261	3.96*
Form Board	4.20	2.63	259	3.48	2.31	261	10.99**
Paper Folding	4.77	2.63	188	4.15	2.44	218	6.00**
Cube Comparisons	6.10	4.65	260	5.76	4.37	262	< 1
Card Rotations	47.18	20.21	261	49.20	18.35	264	1.41
DAT Space Relations	6.62	2.37	252	6.25	2.43	256	3.02*
Mathematics Test	9.04	6.55	256	9.04	5.70	218	< 1

*$p < .10$
**$p < .05$

TABLE 6.7
Correlations Between
Cognitive Measures and Mathematics Achievement

	Seventh Graders		Tenth Graders	
	Boys	Girls	Boys	Girls
Vocabulary	.40	.44	.48	.40
(n)	(172)	(177)	(240)	(248)
Surface Development	.40	$.12^{a,b}$	.30	.29
(n)	(171)	(175)	(239)	(248)
Form Board	.44	.34	.40	$.25^{b}$
(n)	(170)	(175)	(239)	(246)
Paper Folding	.51	.48	.39	.32
(n)	(178)	(181)	(187)	(218)
Cube Comparisons	.46	.33	.24	.19
(n)	(173)	(177)	(239)	(247)
Card Rotations	.38	.35	.32	$.12^{a,b}$
(n)	(174)	(178)	(240)	(248)
DAT Space Relations	.42	$.17^{b}$	.19	.30
(n)	(167)	(172)	(232)	(241)

[a] Correlation *not* significant at .05 level.
[b] Difference in correlation coefficient for boys and girls is satistically significant ($z > 1.96$, $p < .05$).

In order to examine the predictability of performance on the Mathematics Test from the set of cognitive measures as a whole, a step-wise multiple regression procedure was used. The results of this procedure for the two grades and for boys and girls separately are shown in Table 6.8. Greater predictability as indicated by the magnitude of the multiple correlation coefficient (R^2) appeared to be obtained for the seventh graders than for the tenth graders. A substantial beta weight was obtained for the Vocabulary Test in all of the analyses; it was the second variable entered into the regression equation for all of the groups except the tenth-grade girls, for whom it was the first variable entered.

For three of the groups the regression analysis yielded only three variables with significant beta weights. Interestingly, in each case one test from the spatial orientation domain (Form Board, Paper Folding, Space Relations, Surface Development), in addition to the Vocabulary Test, was always indicated in the final set of predictor variables.

Discussion

The results of Study 1 and Study 2 together show some consistency in patterns, as well as certain inconsistencies. With respect to sex differences in performance on visual-spatial tests, all of the differences that were significant favored males. There were many comparisons, however,

TABLE 6.8
Results of Step-Wise Regression Analysis,
Dependent Variable: Performance on Mathematics Test

Group	Variable	Beta weight	Standard error	F-ratio	p value
Seventh	Form board	1.90	.27	3.61	.05
grade	Cube comparisons	1.96	.16	3.83	.05
boys	Vocabulary	3.65	.19	13.31	.001
	DAT Space relations	2.06	.21	23.10	.001
R^2=.466	Paper folding	4.82	.22	23.10	.001
Seventh	Cube comparisons	1.77	.11	3.09	.08
grade	Vocabulary	4.24	.16	17.94	.001
girls	Paper folding	6.13	.19	37.51	.001
R^2=.362					
Tenth	Form board	3.46	.14	11.99	.001
grade	Vocabulary	2.74	.10	7.44	.01
boys	Card rotations	3.37	.02	11.36	.001
R^2=.262					
Tenth	Surface development	2.45	.06	5.99	.05
grade	Cube comparisons	2.16	.07	4.65	.05
girls	Vocabulary	3.42	.08	11.82	.001
R^2=.220					

on visual-spatial test performance that were not significant, despite the relatively large sample sizes that were employed. Differences favoring males were more noticeable among tenth graders than seventh graders, but even among the tenth graders no significant male advantage was found on six of the visual-spatial measures of Study 1 and two of the visual-spatial measures of Study 2. The tests that most consistently differentiated the sexes were the DAT Space Relations Test and the Form Board Test, both measures of visualization and with a very similar content. Nevertheless, even on these tests statistical significances at the .05 level were only obtained in two of the four relevant comparisons. In sum, it seems fair to conclude that junior and senior high school males will peform better than females on some visual-spatial measures, some of the time.

Sex differences in performance on the mathematics and verbal measures, when observed, were always in the direction of superior male performance on mathematics measures and superior female performance on verbal measures. As with the visual-spatial measures, however, there were many instances in which the relevant comparisons were not even close to approaching a level of statistical significance. Although the reliability of the different measures used in the two studies may be one factor in explaining these inconsistencies (the lower the reliability of a test, the less sensitive it is to "true" group differences), this one factor does not appear to be sufficient to explain some of the different results that emerged from the two studies when sex differences in performance on the same test were compared. An alternative interpretation is that sex differences in visual-spatial skill, verbal skill, and quantitative skill may be very greatly influenced by the measures used, the conditions of testing, and the learning experiences that boys and girls bring with them to the testing situation. We are unable to say, at this time, exactly how all of these variables interact to result in a significant or non-significant sex difference in performance. What is clear is that it is seriously misleading to simply summarize the state of knowledge at this time by saying boys do better in mathematics and the visual-spatial domain, whereas girls do better in the verbal area.

The analyses that examined the nature of the relationship between visual-spatial skill and mathematics achievement yielded some additional sex differences of interest. (The analyses were not exactly parallel in the two studies because of differences in the data sets available.) The results of the canonical correlations on the tenth-grade data in Study 1 and the bivariate correlations in Study 2 suggested that there may be a closer association between mathematics achievement and visual-spatial skill for boys than for girls. Again, we note that sex differences in strength of association were found in only a minority of the correlations calculated, but when obtained were in the direction just stated. One possible interpretation is that girls rely more upon verbal approaches to the solution of mathematics problems. However, this interpretation is questionable given the lack of a finding of a stronger relationship between the verbal measures and mathematics achievement for girls than for boys (except in the canonical correlation for tenth graders in Study 1). At this point we can only tentatively conclude that certain visual-spatial skills do not appear to be as relevant to mathematics achievement for girls as for boys.

The results of the factor analysis and the bivariate correlations in Study 1 showed that the visual-spatial skill of closure was not as closely related to mathematics achievement as the skills of visualization and spatial orientation. The results of the two studies suggest that visualization skill and spatial orientation skill are somewhat distinct and both contribute to predicting mathematics achievement. Further research examining the development and trainability of these skills, the focus of the second part of this project, thus appears warranted.

TRAINING VISUAL-SPATIAL SKILLS

In the psychological literature a number of reports indicating the trainability of visual-spatial skill at various ages have been published. Beneficial effects of training have been found in elementary school children (Connor, Serbin, & Schackman, 1977; Connor, Schackman, & Serbin, 1978), junior high school students (Brinkmann, 1966; Ciganko, 1973; Rennels, 1970), and college students (Blade & Watson, 1955; Goldstein & Chance, 1965; Myers, 1953). Such procedures have been found effective with students relatively high in visual-spatial ability (Connor, Serbin, & Freeman, 1978; Rennels, 1970). Three studies have found that training and/or practice effects are relatively stronger for females than for males (Connor et al., 1977; Connor et al., 1978; Goldstein & Chance, 1965).

The present study extends earlier work by: (1) examining the trainability of two visual-spatial skills, that is, spatial orientation and visualization; and (b) evaluating the effectiveness of five different sets of training materials designed to teach the skills most related to five different tests of spatial orientation and/or visualization. The materials were designed for eighth-grade students because students generally do not elect different types of mathematics courses at this grade level, and sex differences in visual-spatial performance are rarely observed prior to the high school years.

METHOD

Subjects

Subjects were 231 boys and 203 girls from eighth-grade mathematics classes in two suburban junior high schools in upstate New York.

Materials

Five sets of training materials for visual-spatial skills were evaluated. Each set was designed to progress from simple, more concrete tasks to more complex, demanding tasks over the course of a half-hour training session. Each set emphasizes training a specific type of visual-spatial skill measured by a particular test of visual-spatial skill. The relevant test was administered immediately following the training session.

Materials Training Spatial Orientation and Visualization as Measured by the Differential Aptitude Test. This set of materials was divided into two sections. In the first section, a set of 10 three-dimensional geometrical objects and 13 two-dimensional patterns were presented to the students. The students were asked to match each three-dimensional object with the two-dimensional patterns that could be folded to make it. Although the sides of the objects were painted different colors, the students were asked to ignore the colors and make their matches on the basis of shape only. Students could then fold the two-dimensional patterns to confirm their decisions.

In the second part, a page of drawings of three-dimensional structures having features such as windows, doors, and so forth, and a page of drawings of two-dimensional featureless patterns that corresponded to "unfoldings" of the solid structures on the first page were presented to the students. Students were asked to match drawn structures to the drawn pattern that could be folded to construct it, and then to draw the features of the structure in the appropriate positions on the unfolded blank pattern. Cut-outs of the patterns were provided so the students could confirm their matches by actually constructing in three dimensions the structure, originally pictured in two dimensions, from the two-dimensional pattern.

Materials Training Spatial Orientation as Measured by the Cube Comparisons Test. This set consisted of two sections. The first group of tasks involved constructing three-dimensional lattices or "trellises" using four wooden popsicle sticks or six strips of paper. Six different model lattices of increasing complexity were shown to the students, who had to construct each of the same lattices as viewed from the back. Then the students had to choose which one of eight drawings of lattices represented a picture of a model lattice seen from the back.

A series of exercises in which students were asked to visualize a single die being rotated completed the training session. These exercises progressed from simply determining where each number pattern of dots would end up on the die after a single rotation in a specific direction, to drawing on a blank picture of a die the pattern of dots that would be visible on each face following a sequence of three rotations in specified directions from a given original position.

Materials Training Visualization as Measured by the Form Board Test. This set of materials made use of Tangrams, a set of plastic geometrical pieces including one large triangle, two medium right-angle triangles, an acute angle triangle, a medium square, and a parallelogram. Students were given these pieces and a set of 10 worksheets with drawings of complex geometrical shapes that could be made from combinations of the Tangram pieces combined in as many different ways as possible. As training progressed, the student was asked simply to draw lines on the figures indicating where the Tangram shapes could be placed and to use the actual pieces only to confirm their decisions. Again, they also had to come up with as many different arrangements of the different pieces as were possible to make the worksheet figure.

Materials Training Visualization as Measured by the Paper Folding Test. One part of this set of materials consisted of paper-and-pencil exercises in which the student was asked to determine lines of symmetry in drawings of a wide variety of objects differing in visual complexity. The second task required the student to draw the mirror image of a figure about a given axis. There were eight different figures of varying levels of complexity. The final training item in this set of materials was a square divided into 36 smaller squares, each containing a number from 1 through 36. Arrows were drawn along the vertical midline, horizontal midline, and the diagonal. Students were given problems of the form:

$$2 \rightarrow \; ? \qquad \rightarrow$$

with the arrows indicating independent folding operations performed on the large square about the line indicated by the arrow. Starting with the square number indicated (in this example, 2), the child was to perform mentally the folding operations represented by the arrows and then respond as to which square number was now covered by the original square number (in this case, 2). Problems containing up to five arrows, that is, five independent operations, were included.

Materials Training Spatial Orientation as Measured by the Card Rotations Test. The first part of this group of materials consisted of drawing tasks in which the students had to imagine rotating letters of the alphabet through different degrees of rotation and then to draw them in their final positions. Actual rotation of the pages themselves could be used to confirm the student's answers. The second and most difficult part of this set consisted of a series of small squares containing a dot grid-work. Some of the dots were connected together to create a line figure. The student's task was to imagine the entire square rotated 180° and to draw in the physically unrotated square exactly where the line figure would end after the rotation. Transparent overlays of the square and line figure, which could actually be rotated on top of the original, were used to confirm the student's answers.

Procedure

Training sessions were carried out in individual mathematics classes ranging in size from 18 to 27 students. Groups of two or three students worked directly with one trainer. Half of each class was assigned to the control group; the other half of the class received training on one set of the visual-spatial training materials. After the half-hour training session, all members of the class were administered the appropriate visual-spatial skills test.

During the training session, trainers were directed to encourage participation and to maintain the motivation and interest of the students in the training materials. They were also instructed to use the training materials actively to try to teach students to accomplish the required tasks. Students were always encouraged to solve the problems in their heads. The use of physical manipulation was restricted to confirming or correcting the students' answers, or to instructing students having difficulty with the task as to what was required. Trainers were instructed to limit the amount of physical manipulation of the materials by the student as much and as early in the training session as was feasible, depending on the ability of the individual student and the amount of coaching he or she required.

Results

The score of each student was corrected for guessing. Two-factor analyses of variance were then conducted for each of the five sets of training materials-test groupings with sex of subject and experimental condition (training or control) as between-subjects factors. The significant effects obtained in these analyses, as well as the means, standard deviations, and sample sizes for each sub-group are shown in Table 6.9.

Significant training effects were found for the materials teaching the skills of spatial-orientation and visualization as measured by the Differential Aptitude Test and the skill of spatial orientation as measured by the Card Rotations Test. There were no significant training effects for the other three sets of materials. The interaction of sex of subject and experimental condition was significant on the Card Rotations Test. The training effect in this case was due to a marked training effect for boys and none for girls. Among the children in the control group, females tended to receive higher scores on the Card Rotations Test than males ($p < .10$). The opposite was true for the children in the training group.

Discussion

Thirty minutes of exposure to visual-spatial training materials resulted in significant increases in performance on a visual-spatial test for two of the five sets of materials developed. These results support the conclusion that visual-spatial skills are teachable in a classroom setting with junior high school students. The negative aspects of the results (i.e., that three of the sets of materials were not demonstrated to be effective) point to the difficulty of designing effective materials as well as the difficulty in having an impact on skills in brief training periods.

An examination of the tests on which an effect was demonstrated and the tests on which no effect was discernible suggests that visualization

TABLE 6.9
Means, Standard Deviations, and Sample Sizes
for Training and Control Groups

Test	Males		Females		Significance Effects (p <.05)
	Training	Control	Training	Control	
Differential Aptitude					
$\overline{X}$	6.67	3.74	4.73	3.02	TREATMENT,
s	2.85	3.14	2.63	2.01	SEX
n	21	33	20	15	
Cube Comparisons					
$\overline{X}$	6.52	5.93	7.28	6.00	--
s	4.19	4.26	4.65	4.28	
n	21	28	18	22	
Paper Folding					
$\overline{X}$	3.19	3.79	4.00	3.74	--
s	2.30	2.14	2.52	2.24	
n	22	25	19	17	
Card Rotations					
$\overline{X}$	54.75	34.40	44.05	44.58	TREATMENT,
s	14.87	20.70	15.29	17.03	INTERACTION
n	20	15	19	31	
Form Board					
$\overline{X}$	3.69	3.60	2.94	4.04	--
s	2.26	1.88	1.82	2.01	
n	26	20	17	25	

may be a more difficult skill to teach then spatial orientation. The two tests that have been defined as visualization tests (Form Board and Paper Folding) showed no training effect. Of the two tests defined as measures of spatial orientation (Cube Comparisons and Card Rotations) one showed a training effect and the results for the other were in the appropriate direction for each sex, though not statistically significant. Lastly, the Differential Aptitude Test, which is thought to be a measure of both spatial orientation and visualization, showed a training effect. The training results with the other tests suggest the possibility that scores on this test were elevated as a result of students' improvement in spatial orientation rather than visualization skill.

There was no indication in this study (as opposed to the findings of Connor et al., 1977; Connor et al., 1978) that females profited more from training than males. In fact, the only treatment by sex interaction that was obtained was in the opposite direction; that is, on the Card Rotations Test the males profited from the training, whereas the females did not. It is interesting to note, however, that in this case the males in the control group were performing less well than the females in the control group. What these findings suggest is that the sex that is performing less well without training is likely to benefit more from training.

The results of this training study are consistent with those of the correlational studies in the patterns of sex-related differences in overall scores. That is, the Differential Aptitude Test is a relatively consistent discriminator of male and female performance, but other measures do not yield sex-related differences consistently at all. This does not appear to be a function of the reliability of the tests, as the reliability for the ETS tests appears to be quite similar to that for the Differential Aptitude Test (Bennett et al., 1973; Ekstrom et al., 1976). The Space Relations section of the Differential Aptitude Test, however, is the visual-spatial test most widely used for vocational guidance to high school students and for admission selection of students to technical programs such as engineering and dentistry. This implies that the use of this visual-spatial test may be having a more negative effect on females' pursuing careers in technical fields than would be the case if a different visual-spatial test (or several visual-spatial tests) were used more widely.

CONCLUSIONS

The results of this research lead to the following conclusions:

1. It is noted that among junior and senior high school students the appearance and magnitude of sex-related differences in visual-spatial skill are quite variable. Although we have always found these differences to favor males when they appear, with many groups they did not appear at all. In the psychological and educational literature, references to sex-related differences in visual-spatial skill frequently imply that such differences are both more universal and more substantial than we find them to be. It would be appropriate for such references to be qualified by modifiers such as "On some tests . . ." or "As sometimes found . . ."

2. The skills of "flexibility of closure" (disembedding) and "speed of closure" appear to have little relationship to mathematics achievement. The skills of "spatial orientation" and "visualization" do appear to contribute meaningfully to predicting mathematics achievement. We recommend that researchers interested in examining visual-spatial skills related to mathematics achievement or educators concerned with the development of these skills concentrate their efforts on the latter two skills rather than the former two.

3. There was some indication from the results of this project that the

association between visual-spatial skills and mathematics achievement is stronger for males than for females. To the extent that mathematics problems are solvable in different ways, the implication is that females may be less likely to use a visual-spatial approach than males. The implications of such choices are unknown, nor is it clear that a difference in approach represents a deficit on the part of either sex rather than a preference. Further research on the use of different approaches to mathematics problem-solving appears to be a fruitful area to pursue.

4. The results of the training studies showed that junior high school students can improve their visual-spatial skills with brief training sessions. However, effective materials are not easy to design and cannot be assumed to be effective on the basis of content or face validity alone. It also appears that it may be easier to teach the skill of spatial orientation than the skill of visualization.

5. There was no consistent pattern of sex-related differences in response to training. The hypothesis that students who perform relatively poorly on visual-spatial tests may improve more as a result of training than students who perform well received some support from the results on the Card Rotations Test. (In this case, however, it was the males in the control group who performed somewhat less well than the females.)

ACKNOWLEDGMENT

This research was supported in part by NIE Grant No. NIE-G-77-0051.

7 The Influence of Sex-Role Stereotyping on Women's Attitudes and Achievement in Mathematics

Sally L. Boswell
Institute for Research on Social Problems

Introduction

Women are seriously underrepresented in fields involving mathematics. For example, fewer than 2% of the nation's engineers are women, and only 2.5% of those with doctorates in physics, and 10% of those with doctorates in mathematics in 1977 were women (U.S. Department of Labor, 1977).

This underrepresentation has been of concern to many, including educators, psychologists, and mathematicians. Most researchers who have dealt with this problem agree that women's lower participation in mathematics and mathematics-related fields is a result of many factors, including cognitive, social, and cultural, which interact in complex patterns and are extremely difficult to unravel. No common agreement exists, however, as to which factors are most salient at which developmental level, nor are there any existing conceptual models that deal with this issue, specifically with regard to mathematics.

The research described herein focuses upon the role of sociocultural factors in a developmental context. The basic assumptions underlying our research program are: (1) that sociocultural factors are transmitted primarily through parents, peers, and the educational settings; (2) that these factors profoundly shape women's attitudes toward mathematics; and (3) that attitudes subsequently affect women's performance in mathematics. This type of model is consistent with the views of current constructive theorists (e.g., Harvey, Hunt, & Schroder, 1961) who assert that individuals construct their experience in accordance with their beliefs about reality. Many of these beliefs relate to what American society tradi-

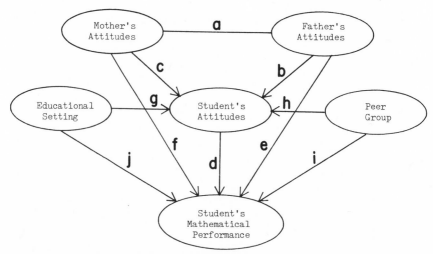

FIG. 7.1   Model reflecting relationship between parents, peers, educational setting, and students' attitudes and performances in mathematics.

LEGEND: a = agreement between mother's and father's attitudes toward mathematics
b = influence of father's attitudes upon student's attitudes toward mathematics
c = influence of mother's attitudes upon student's attitudes toward mathematics
d = influence of student's attitudes upon performance in mathematics
e = influence of father's attitudes upon student's performance in mathematics
f = influence of mother's attitudes upon student's performance in mathematics
g = influence of educational setting upon student's attitudes
h = influence of peer group on student's attitudes
i = influence of peer group upon student's performance in mathematics
j = influence of educational setting upon student's performance in mathematics

tionally has deemed appropriate (or inappropriate) as roles for women. These cultural mores and dictums are transmitted in the form of sex-role stereotypes. As a consequence of accepting these stereotypes, women are directed away from mathematical pursuits. The pathways along which this transmission may occur are depicted in Fig. 7.1.

Women are precluded from entering math-related fields because of three very different kinds of factors. The first includes *external structural barriers,* such as overt sex discrimination against women in educational, scientific, and business institutions. The second involves *social pressures* from significant others such as parents and peers. Negative attitudes and feelings may be expressed either overtly or subtly, but their effect is the same. A final inhibiting source is women's *internal barriers,* that is, their internalized negative attitudes and beliefs about mathematics. The present study focuses on these latter two factors.

In a review of the literature, Fox (1977) provides a persuasive case for the belief that women's lack of participation may be related to general sex-role stereotyping. The existence of specific stereotypes about women in mathematics has been documented, although not extensively. Levine (1976) reported that girls do not perceive themselves as competent in mathematics even when they earn good grades in that subject. Similarly, Fennema (1974a) noted that females rank themselves lower than males in mathematical ability even when they are outperforming males in math classes. Girls' self-concepts about their math ability, moreover, tend to become less positive with age. Sex differences on self-confidence measures of math ability appear as early as the eighth grade (Kaminski, Erickson, Ross, & Bradfield, 1976). Additionally, an example of the social pressures involved is seen in Levine's finding (1976) that boys behave negatively towards girls who demonstrate high levels of math proficiency.

There is also a suggestion in the literature that mathematicians are either masculine or perceived as masculine (Plank & Plank, 1954; Elton & Rose, 1967). The pattern here is far from clear-cut, however, because Jacobs (1974) and Lambert (1960) reported that high mathematics achievement in women is associated with a high level of femininity. These latter findings are puzzling and in conflict with the results of Rossi (1965b) and Luchins (1976), which showed that one of the primary reasons women do not pursue mathematics is fear of appearing unfeminine.

One problem with many earlier studies on sex-typing and mathematics is that they are based on older (and perhaps outdated) conceptions of masculinity and femininity, which considered these terms to be bipolar dimensions on a single continuum. Newer views hold that people can be more accurately described in terms of *both* masculinity and femininity (e.g., Bakan, 1966; Bem, 1974; Constantinople, 1976; Spence & Helmreich, 1979), and measures have been developed that have separate masculinity and femininity scales. Persons obtaining high scores on one and low on the other would not be dissimilar from those characterized as masculine or feminine in earlier studies. Separate measures, however, allow for two other possibilities: high scores on both scales (referred to as psychologically androgynous), or low on both (referred to as undifferentiated). These classifications have led to differential predictions. Bem and Lenney (1976) found, for example, that androgynous individuals have no difficulty in engaging in either traditionally masculine or traditionally feminine activities, whereas those classified as masculine or feminine could not switch easily. Use of this newer conceptualization may help clarify some of the conflicting results obtained earlier. Consequently, the degree to which competence in mathematics is related to psychological androgyny was investigated in the present research program.

In spite of recent changes in the sex role attitudes in contemporary society, the goal of raising a family still retains the highest priority among American women. A study by Parelius (1975) found, for example, that only 28% of college women would forego having children for the sake of occupational success. Thus, even in a group of women described as liberal by the author of the study, family life was a more potent motivating force than career aspiration. To this end, women are usually encouraged to develop social skills in order to "catch" a husband, raise a family, and so on. Qualities such as attractiveness, skill in personal interactions, and serving others are culturally valued in women, and these qualities may well be instrumental for successful familial pursuits. However, so many women are now entering the labor market that the majority of high school and college females consider a dual career a definite possibility. Hawley (1971, 1972) and Astin (1974a) concluded that since marriage is the *primary* goal of most women even when they do elect a career, their choice is limited by what they feel men can tolerate.

The literature suggests that there are a number of beliefs about women and mathematics that seem to be culturally pervasive. Among these beliefs are the notions that mathematics is not useful for women, that women who pursue careers in mathematics are masculine, that women are naturally incompetent in mathematics, and that women are more interested in social areas than theoretical areas. However, these beliefs may not be equally salient at all points in the developmental cycle. Various components of mathematical stereotyping may well be introduced at different times and by different agents. To date, there have been no studies that have investigated these relationships. Data indicate that males and females obtain approximately equal math achievement scores in elementary school (Maccoby & Jacklin, 1974). When students begin secondary school, males surpass females on mathematics achievement scores, and this male superiority increases with age (Mullis, 1975). The development of specific stereotypes regarding mathematics may be related to these differential achievement patterns.

One of the primary purposes of the present research study was to document the existence and content of stereotypes associated with women and mathematics and to specify the ages at which specific stereotypes exert maximal influence on female participation and achievement in mathematics. The basic rationale underlying the research program is that the sex-typing of the field of mathematics as masculine, combined with the negative stereotyping of women in the field, function as significant deterrents to increasing female participation in this area. The research strategy was as follows: first, to document the existence and content of stereotypes associated with mathematics; second, to determine the extent to which children and adolescents of various ages have sex-role stereotypes about mathematics; third, to investigate the sources of these stereotypes; and finally, to examine the effects of these stereotypes on mathematics achievement. In order to accomplish these aims, the research program was comprised of three separate studies: a study of female mathematicians, a study of children in elementary school, and a study of students in secondary school.

STUDY 1: FEMALE MATHEMATICIANS

In assessing the factors related to women's lack of participation in mathematics, a logical starting place is with female mathematicians themselves, since these women have managed to overcome the cultural and psychological barriers that seem to prevent so many others from entering the field. Thus, an investigation was undertaken to provide data concerning the specific personality and experiential characteristics that led these women to persevere in mathematics towards successful careers. Particular emphasis was placed on the influences of peers, parents, and educational settings during primary and secondary school. Although there have been several previous investigations of women who have obtained Ph.D.'s in mathematics, the present study is unique in its focus on newer conceptions of masculinity and femininity as well as in its emphasis on the development of stereotypic beliefs.

After a review of the pertinent literature and available instruments, a number of variables were selected for assessment. In those cases where no adequate instruments were available, items were developed and piloted. Particular care was taken to develop a meaningful measure of the stereotyping of women in mathematics. The pilot questionnaire was mailed to female students and faculty in the Mathematics Department and the School of Education at the University of Colorado and revised on the basis of their comments and responses. The final battery included background information (employment status, place of employment, number of siblings, influence of parents, peers, and teachers in math, perceived ability of parents in math) and personality measures including the Bem Sex Role Inventory (Bem, 1974), the Spence Attitudes Toward Women Scale (Spence, Helmreich, & Stapp, 1974), and questions about stereotyping in the respondents' fields.

Questionnaires were mailed in May 1978, to women throughout the country who had obtained Ph.D.'s in mathematics, English, and psychology during the past 10 years. Names of women who obtained Ph.D.'s were obtained from departmental chairpersons of universities in 48 states. Names were selected randomly from these lists. Based on the numbers of students who obtained Bachelor of Arts degrees in various fields in 1974, English was chosen as a representative of a traditionally "feminine" field (many more women than men obtained B.A.'s in English), and psychology was chosen as a representative of a field traditionally typed as neither "masculine" nor "feminine" (approximately equal numbers of males and females obtained B.A.'s in psychology in 1976). Because our primary goal was to investigate mathematicians, we oversampled women in this field. From 999 questionnaires mailed, we received a total of 460 completed questionnaires: 279 from mathematicians, 90 from English Ph.D's, and 91 from psychologists. Response rates were similar for the three groups, ranging from 49% to 52%.

Results

All three groups of women indicated a high frequency of stereotyping in their fields: 82.8% of the mathematicians responded that women are stereotyped in their field, whereas 73.9% of the English Ph.D.'s and 64.8% of the psychologists indicated that women in their field are stereotyped. Differences in these response patterns were highly significant (p < .01) as tested by Chi square. Thus, the respondents in all three fields perceived that society stereotypes women in their fields; however, there were differences in the extent of stereotyping depending on the field.

Another item asked respondents if society characterized their fields as masculine, feminine, or neutral. The majority of the mathematicians indicated that society considers their field to be "decidedly masculine," whereas the English Ph.D.'s indicated that society considers their field "somewhat feminine." Most of the psychologists indicated that society considers their field neither masculine nor feminine. An analysis of variance indicated that differences among the groups were highly significant (F = 294.30, p < .01). Note that mathematics was the field considered by the women to be most masculine and also the field associated with the highest degree of stereotyping.

When the respondents were asked (in an open-ended item) to list the *specific* stereotypes associated with women in their fields, there was a similarity of responses within each field. These attributes were then tallied according to the frequency with which each was specifically named. If these attributes had been grouped according to conceptual similarity, there would have been much more agreement on the stereotypes associated with each field. For example, the words "masculine" and "unfeminine" were placed in separate categories. The 10 most frequently named stereotypes for each field are shown in Table 7.1. An inspection of these lists indicates that stereotypes associated with women in psychology do not appear to be as negative as the stereotypes in the other two fields. Notice also that the stereotypes "masculine" and "unfeminine" are ranked higher for the mathematicians. The stereotype "masculine" is

TABLE 7.1
Stereotypes Perceived by Female Ph.D.'s in Three Areas*

	Mathematics	English Ph.D.'s	Psychologists
1.	Unattractive (23.3%)	Overly-Intellectual (23.3%)	Aggressive (17.8%)
2.	Masculine (22.6%)	Unattractive (21.1%)	Not as Competent as Men (16.5%)
3.	Cold/Distant (21.5%)	Old Maid (20.0%)	Interested in Children (13.2%)
4.	Unfeminine (18.6%)	Out of Touch With Reality (20%)	Interested in Helping People (13.2%)
5.	Intelligent (16.8%)	Aggressive (17.8%)	Masculine (12.1%)
6.	Overly-Intellectual (15.4%)	Obsessed With Proper Grammar (17.8%)	Analytical (12.1%)
7.	Incompetent Compared With Males (15.4%)	Not Serious (10%)	Cold/Distant (9.9%)
8.	Aggressive (12.9%)	Picky (10%)	Intelligent (9.9%)
9.	Socially Awkward (12.9%)	Non-Domestic (10%)	Many Personal Problems (8.8%)
10.	Analytical (9.7%)	Non-Sexual (8.9%)	Can Read Your Mind (7.7%)

*Percent of women *specifically* mentioning each attribute.

ranked fifth for the psychologists and does not appear in the top 10 list for the English Ph.D.'s. The word "unfeminine" only appears in the list of the mathematicians.

Interestingly, the respondents indicated that the stereotypes they had listed were generally *inaccurate* characterizations of women in their fields and, importantly, that these stereotypes were becoming somewhat weaker. It will be of interest to examine figures on the percentages of women entering mathematics and math-related fields during the next few years.

To assess psychological androgyny in the women in the three subject areas, we included in the battery the Bem Sex Role Inventory (Bem, 1974). When the women in the three groups were compared on their actual scores on the masculinity, femininity, and social desirability scales separately, Chi-squares indicated that the mathematicians were the least masculine, followed by the psychologists, and English Ph.D.'s ($p < .01$). There were no differences among the three groups on the femininity or social desirability scales.

In a further analysis, the masculinity and femininity scores were considered simultaneously using the median-split technique described by Spence et al. (1975). Each subject was placed into one of four categories: masculine, feminine, androgynous, or undifferentiated. Differences in the frequencies of women in the three fields who fell into the four categories were highly significant ($p < .01$) as tested by Chi-square. More of the mathematicians fell into either the masculine or feminine category, 52% as compared to the 46% of the English Ph.D.'s and 47% of the psychologists. The psychologists were classified less frequently as masculine, and the English Ph.D.'s were more frequently classified as androgynous.

A measure of traditional or liberal attitudes toward the roles of women in society was assessed by means of the Attitudes Toward Women Scale (Spence, Helmreich, & Stapp, 1975). The results indicated that the mathematicians responded in a slightly more traditional direction than the women in the other groups (p < .01). The responses of the women in all three groups were notably more liberal than responses obtained in other samples (e.g., Spence et al., 1975).

The women were asked to indicate the *source* of stereotyped information, that is, who in their environment first provided knowledge about the content of stereotypes about women in their professions. The results were similar for the three groups. The respondents felt that their *peer groups* were the primary source of stereotypes, particularly the male peer group. Family members were less often named as a source of stereotypes than either the media or peer groups. (Only 5% of the mathematicians indicated that their fathers were sources of stereotypes, whereas 14% of the English Ph.D.'s, and 11% of the psychologists indicated that their fathers were sources of stereotypes.) When asked at what age they became aware of these stereotypes, most of the respondents indicated that it was in junior or senior high school.

The respondents were asked to specify the age at which they decided to pursue careers in their fields. The responses of the women in the three groups indicated that the mathematicians became interested in pursuing careers in mathematics at a relatively early age. By their senior year in high school, 40% of the mathematicians had decided on careers in mathematics, whereas only 27% of the English Ph.D.'s, and 23% of the psychologists indicated that they had reached career decisions (p < .01). This finding is consistent with other literature that indicates that women who pursue careers in mathematics show an early and intense interest in the subject matter (e.g., Jacobs, 1974).

In an effort to identify factors that influenced women's decisions to pursue careers in mathematics, several items assessed the contributions of significant others, including parents, teachers, friends, and siblings.

In regard to parental influence, the responses to several items indicated that fathers of mathematicians were more encouraging and more influential than fathers of women in the other two groups. The English Ph.D.'s described their mothers as a career influence more often than the women in the other groups. Other than parents, there were no striking differences between the groups on the perceived degree of influence for other significant others. In general, respondents indicated "little" to "moderate" influence on the part of others.

In order to explore the issues related to female participation in mathematics in greater depth, we included two open-ended items in the test packet sent to the female mathematicians: "Indicate what factors led you to become a mathematician" and "What do you think could be done to encourage more women to pursue careers in mathematics?" Responses were lengthy and enthusiastic. The mathematicians indicated that the one factor that had the greatest bearing on their pursuit of a career in mathematics was a pronounced and early interest in the subject area. They frequently mentioned that this intense interest, together with a level of achievement in mathematics, led them to persevere in spite of negative environmental factors such as hostility or discouragement on the part of others. Although many respondents indicated that they encountered negative reactions from teachers, others mentioned positive experiences with educators. Almost 45% of the respondents spontaneously mentioned that they encountered at least one teacher or counselor who specifically encouraged them in mathematics. Almost 20% of the mathematicians noted the encouragement they received from both parents to pursue careers in mathematics; 11% mentioned that their fathers were encouraging; 5% indicated encouragement by their mothers.

The question "What do you think could be done to encourage more women to pursue careers in mathematics?" produced a wide variety of responses. The most frequent reply (34%) was that female students should be exposed to more positive female role modes in mathematics. Next in frequency (23%) was the response that female students should be informed about the importance and usefulness of mathematics. Other mathematicians suggested that the quality of mathematics education should be improved (22%), that female students should be encouraged by their teachers and counselors (21%), that sex-role stereotyping needed to be changed in society in general (19%) and in the educational setting (14%), and that special programs should be developed and implemented that will encourage females to pursue mathematics (12%).

In conclusion, the reasons why women pursue careers in mathematics are complex. A personality "type" that may characterize female mathematicians did not emerge from these data. There did appear to be a set of background factors common to many female mathematicians, including early interest in mathematics and, in some cases, the encouragement of fathers. As for sex-role ideologies, female mathematicians showed more varied patterns than women in the other groups.

In contrast, the results from the stereotyping portion of the questionnaire show striking within-group agreement and clearly differentiated women in the three groups. When the respondents were asked to list the stereotypes that society holds about women in their fields, the respondents showed a high degree of agreement regarding these stereotypes. They also indicated that these stereotypes were first conveyed to them by their male peer group in secondary school.

The mathematicians were the group that most consistently and emphatically asserted that society stereotypes women in their field. However, women in all three fields indicated that stereotypes were becoming weaker. They attributed this lessening of stereotypes to: (1) a decline in stereotyping in all segments of society, (2) more women entering male-dominated fields, (3) affirmative action programs, and (4) career awareness programs.

STUDY 2: ELEMENTARY SCHOOL

The results from the first study clearly indicate that female mathematicians perceive a number of negative stereotypes associated with women in their fields. At what ages do boys and girls become aware of these stereotypes and at what ages do they begin labeling mathematics as a subject in the male domain? To what extent do children's attitudes toward mathematics affect their achievement levels in mathematics? Are these patterns affected by their sex-role attitudes? In other words, are girls who adhere to more feminine sex-role orientations less likely to demonstrate interest and ability in mathematics than girls who show more balanced or flexible sex-role orientations?

In order to investigate these issues, a questionnaire was developed and administered to boys and girls in grades three through six. The questionnaire contained a number of measures. An assessment of sex-role orientation was developed on Bem's (1974) conception of psychological androgyny. Instead of using personality traits as measures, however, it was decided that preferences for toys and activities would be more appropriate for children (e.g., Rosenberg & Sutton-Smith, 1964). Based on the results of pilot testing, a list of 20 toys and activities was compiled that represented approximately equal numbers of "boy-preferred" and "girl-preferred" toys and activities. For the final sample there were two measures: the Toys Classification Test, based on the child's response when asked who usually prefers each toy or activity (boys or girls, or both boys and girls) and the Toys Preference Test, based on the child's response on a three-point scale indicating how much he or she liked the toy or activity ("a lot," "a little," "not at all"). The data from the latter measure were factor-analyzed in order to ensure discriminative or factorial validity for the masculinity and femininity scales. Three factors emerged from the factor analysis. The items that emerged in Factor 1 included sewing kit, working in the kitchen, flute, knitting, dolls, balls and jacks, ice skating, go shopping, gardening, and jump rope. This last item was subsequently discarded from analysis because of large between-school variability apparently resulting from one school's development of a jump rope program for both boys and girls.

The items that clustered on the second factor included skate board, boxing, go-cart, football, baseball, and drums. A third factor included model airplane, chess, woodworking, and train set. Because the children rated both the Factor 2 items and the Factor 3 items as preferred by boys, we combined these items for the masculinity scale. A Chi square procedure indicated that boys preferred the masculine toys and activities, and girls preferred the feminine toys (p < .01).

Because previous studies suggested that mathematical achievement may be related to spatial ability (e.g., Fennema & Sherman, 1977a), the test battery included the Hidden Patterns Test (French, Ekstrom, & Price, 1963).

The major portion of the test battery was comprised of items that were written to assess children's attitudes and beliefs about mathematics/arithmetic. Items involved the child's own attitudes toward math (e.g., "How often is math fun for you?"(percepton of peer math attitudes (e.g., "How much do your friends like math?"), and the stereotyping of adults (e.g., "Who can work with numbers best, Mr. or Mrs. Hill?"). Most items used a Likert format. The scales that were created from these items have both logical and discriminative validity, as well as adequate levels of reliability as assessed using Cronbach's alpha (at least .70).

The final sample was comprised of 562 males and females attending two elementary schools in Boulder. A pilot sample was obtained from a third elementary school. Boulder has a predominantly white, middle class population. Parent permission was obtained for all children in the sample.

Results

Achievement and Aptitude in Mathematics. Achievement and aptitude scores in mathematics were taken from the McGraw-Hill Test of Basic Skills. This test is routinely administered to students in Boulder each year. The mathematics portion of the McGraw-Hill test includes both aptitude and achievement scores. The achievement total score is comprised of three subscales: computation, concepts, and applications.

An analysis of variance on the raw scores indicated that there were no sex differences on the total mathematics achievement score (p > .10). There were sex differences on the subscales: the males outperformed the females on the concepts subtest (p < .01), and the females outperformed the males in the computation (p < .01).

Sex-Role Orientation. To investigate sex-role orientation and flexibility of boys and girls the toy preference masculinity and femininity scores were combined by the median-split technique (Spence et al., 1975) and each child classified as masculine, feminine, androgynous, or undifferentiated. As expected, the majority (67%) of boys fell into the masculine category, and the majority of girls (67%) fell into the feminine category. With age, greater numbers of both boys and girls were classified as masculine and smaller numbers as feminine; there were no increases in the number of children classified as androgynous. By this measure, there was no difference in girls and boys in terms of sex-role flexibility.

A second measure of sex-role flexibility was based on the selection of the "both boys and girls" category in indicating who prefers various toys or activities. On this measure girls were likelier than boys to categorize "masculine" toys as preferred by both boys and girls, a tendency that increased with grade. Thus, on this measure girls seemed more flexible in their sex-role orientation than boys, and this flexibility appeared to increase with age.

Attitudes Toward Mathematics. According to the results of analyses of variance, boys and girls in the third and fourth grade like math to a similar degree. The fifth and sixth grade boys continued to show the same degree of liking of math, whereas girls declined somewhat ($p < .03$).

There were no significant sex or grade differences in students' perception of how much their friends liked math (Factor 2: Peer Math Attitudes). However, there was a suggestion that with grade girls decreasingly perceived their friends as liking math ($p < .09$).

Mathematics in the Male Domain. Do elementary school children consider math to be in the male domain? When addressing this question, a distinction must be made between children's stereotyping of math *among adults* and their stereotyping of math *among their peers.* When children were asked about the math abilities of their peers, girls generally responded that girls are better in math, and boys typically responded that boys are better. By grades 5 and 6, however, the girls began to shift toward judgments of math ability favoring the boys. By comparison, girls' perception of peers' reading ability only shifted slightly towards favoring boys; their shift towards judging boys superior in math was far more dramatic.

Questions about mathematics in the adult world elicited a different pattern of responses from children. On two items about adult math competence, children of both sexes believed men to be more competent. Boys were stronger in the belief that men could work with numbers better than women ($p < .01$). There were no significant changes in these perceptions by grade.

Attitudes and Math Achievement in Elementary School. One of the primary purposes of this study was to determine the extent to which math attitudes are related to math achievement scores among elementary school children. A number of analyses are relevant to this issue.

First, several hierarchical regression analyses were conducted using the math attitude scales as independent measures and math achievement as a dependent measure. In order to control for aptitude effects, subjects' math aptitude scores were entered into the regression analysis as the first step. The aptitude score was a strong predictor of achievement scores for both sexes, but math achievement scores were also predicted to a small but significant degree by a number of the personality variables. Attitudes toward math were more predictive of achievement for boys than for girls ($p < .01$).

There are some indications that *sex-role flexibility* is related to higher math scores for females. The masculinity and femininity scores by themselves did not predict female math scores. However, the relative scores of the two measures (using MxF scores, as suggested by Spence & Helmreich, 1979) significantly predicted the math applications subscore ($p < .07$).

The correlations between math achievement and *stereotyping* were found to be dependent on the sex of the child. For girls, the more rigid their sex-role stereotypes of adults in mathematics, the lower was their math achievement level ($p < .05$). For boys there were no significant correlations between stereotyping of math at the adult level and math achievement scores.

The results of the study provide some evidence that: (1) attitudes toward mathematics are related to students' math achievement scores in elementary school; (2) sex differences emerge in children's attitudes toward mathematics in the later elementary years, although there were no overall sex differences in math achievement scores; and (3) by the third grade, children perceive math as in the male domain in the adult world.

In summary, it is clear that considerable stereotyping is associated with mathematics among elementary school children and that this stereotyping begins at relatively early developmental levels.

STUDY 3: JUNIOR AND SENIOR HIGH SCHOOL

In order to investigate attitudes and achievement in mathematics at the junior and senior high school level, we collected both attitude and achievement scores data from 279 males and 314 females in grades 7, 9, and 11 in two junior and two senior high schools in the Boulder Valley School District. The sample included 593 subjects: 109 males and 110 females in the seventh grade ($\overline{X}$ = 12 years, 0 months), 133 males and 153 females in the ninth grade ($\bar{X}$ = 15 years, 4 months), and 37 males and 51 females in the eleventh grade ($\bar{X}$ = 17 years, 1 month.) The overall participation rate of 34.7% was largely attributable to the low participation rate for the eleventh grade. School officials subsequently informed us that students of this age in Boulder Valley are reluctant to participate in volunteer testing programs. Thus, results with regard to the eleventh graders should be viewed with caution.

The methodology for the junior and senior high school study was similar to that for the elementary school study. A questionnaire was developed to assess attitudes toward mathematics, stereotyping in mathematics, perceived usefulness of mathematics, peer influences, degree of independence, background in mathematics, occupational preferences, family aspirations, and general personality traits (expressiveness, physical bravery, intellectual achievement, and negative self-concept). The questionnaire was balanced so that there were equal numbers of positively and negatively phrased items. Reliability on the various scales for this sample ranged from .62 to .85, with all but two scales having reliabilities above .70.

After parental permission was obtained, questionnaires were administered to students in small groups during school hours.

As in the elementary school study, achievement scores and aptitude scores were taken from the McGraw-Hill Test of Basic Skills, which is administered to a random sample of students each year as part of Boulder Valley's annual testing and evaluation program. We obtained achievement data for 91.2% of the students who completed questionnaires. Each student's mathematics achievement score was represented by a scale score (a normalized raw score) and a percentile based on national norms.

An analysis of variance on the achievement scores in mathematics yielded no significant sex differences. To compare students in the three age groups on math performance, it was necessary to use percentile scores as a dependent measure. The entire sample was well above average on national norms. However, there was a main effect for grade ($p < .01$) due to lower percentile means for the eleventh grade students (65%, as compared with 77% for the seventh graders and 75% for the ninth graders). This difference raises the possibility that the eleventh grade sample is not representative of students in their age group.

Each of the personality scales was developed by first reviewing the relevant literature and selecting items from existing scales with high reliability and/or face validity. New items were written and included if necessary. The entire test battery was then administered to a pilot sample of seventh and ninth graders. These data were factor-analyzed using varimax rotated factors (after rotation with Kaiser normalization) to determine those items that formed independent scales. Only those items that factored together to form discrete scales were included in the final questionnaire. After the data were collected from the final sample, they were again entered into a factor analysis. In general, the same factors emerged as with the pilot sample. Thus, these scales have been validated factorially using two separate samples.

Math Attitude Scale. The Math Attitude Scale was comprised of 12 items of two conceptually distinct sets: items related to math anxiety and items related to task competence motivation. Task competence motivation is defined as a student's motivation to achieve the demands of the task (Veroff, McClelland, & Ruhland, 1975). Math anxiety is defined as uneasiness or fear associated with situations involving mathematics. Although the items did not split into two separate scales on a series of factor analyses, the logical distinction between the two measures made it advisable to carry out several separate analyses on the data from the two subscales.

There was a general decline in task competence motivation across grades for both sexes ($p < .03$), though boys showed an increase from ninth to eleventh grade. Males had a higher level of task competence motivation than females at all grades ($p < .05$).

Math anxiety declined by grade for both sexes ($p < .03$), but was consistently at higher levels for females ($p < .05$).

Because factor analyses of the data did not reveal a factorial distinction between task competence motivation and math anxiety, these two subscales were combined to form the Math Attitudes Scale.

Stereotyping in Mathematics. Sex-role typing of math was tapped in the Math Stereotyping Scale, which was comprised of 11 items (e.g., "most girls are not good at algebra"). An analysis of variance indicated significant grade ($p < .01$) and sex differences ($p < .01$), with males showing higher levels of stereotyping than females. Stereotyping for both males and females was lowest for ninth graders and highest for eleventh graders. The curvilinear relationship obtained on the measure should be treated as tentative because, as mentioned previously, the samples from the three grades may not be directly comparable.

Occupations. Another index of students' conceptions of sex roles was devised by giving a pilot sample of seventh and ninth graders a list of occupations and asking them to indicate those that are usually performed by men, those by women, and those by both men and women. Students were also asked to rate their degree of interest in each occupation on a five-point Likert scale. Factor analysis yielded one factor comprised of occupations perceived as usually performed by men and another factor of occupations perceived as usually performed by women. The items on the Male Occupation Scale included engineer, bus driver, police officer, real estate salesperson, accountant, mathematician, and plumber. The Female Occupation Scale was comprised of social worker, dancer, head nurse, English professor, writer, secretary, and bookkeeper. Scores from the items on the two factors were scaled for each student and became measures of student's interest in male and female occupations.

Males were significantly more interested than females in the jobs on the Male Occupations Scale ($F = 12.15$, $p < .01$) and females were more interested than males in the jobs on the Female Occupations Scale ($F = 234.5$, $p < .01$). As they advanced in grade, students became more interested in the occupations on the Male Occupations Scale ($F = 3.71$, $p < .03$).

Personality and Aspirations. An adjective checklist made up of "masculine," "feminine," and "neutral" adjectives was given to students to rate on a five-point scale as a measure of self-reported personality. The adjectives were taken primarily from Williams and Bennett (1975), the Bem Sex Role Inventory (1974), and Silvern (1977). A factor analysis (using varimax rotated factors) of these data yielded four distinct scales:

1. Nurturance (affectionate, tender, emotional, gentle, sensitive, softhearted, mild)
2. Bravery (adventurous, aggressive, courageous, daring, forceful, tough)
3. Intellectual Achievement (independent, logical, realistic, smart, ambitious)
4. Negative Self (careless, complaining, moody, nagging).

Each of the items on the Nurturance Scale has been documented as related to femininity in previous studies. An analysis of variance using grade and sex as independent measures revealed significant main effects for sex ($p < .01$) and grade ($p < .01$). The females scored higher on this scale than the males, and both the males and females increased in nurturance with grade. Each of the items on the Bravery Scale has been documented as related to masculinity in previous studies. An analysis of variance revealed a significant sex effect ($p < .01$) and indicated that students obtained higher scores on this scale with increasing grade ($p < .01$). On items from the Negative Self Scale, not generally related to either masculinity or femininity in previous research, an analysis of variance yielded no significant effects.

Three other dependent variables involving students' self-report of personality, work style, and aspirations did not yield significant results on the analyses of variance (with sex and grade as independent variables). The first of these was the *Family Aspiration Scale,* included to assess student commitment to future family life. Four items comprised the final scale, for example, "I want to have a family more than I want a job or career." The second was the *Peer Influence Scale* consisting of three items assessing student perceptions of peers' reactions to academic success in mathematics and English (e.g., "It bothers me when other students know that I got good grades in mathematics.") The third was the *Independence Scale,* on which three items assessed students' independence of work style. Students indicated on a five-point rating scale ranging from "strongly agree" to "strongly disagree" their reactions to items, such as, "I enjoy working alone."

Math Usefulness. The Math Usefulness Scale was comprised of two subscales tapping perception of the usefulness of math for men and for women (e.g., "It is useful for a man/woman to have a good mathematics background."). On the Math Usefulness for Women Scale, male students rated math as less important for women to a greater extent than female students did ($p < .01$). Males remained relatively constant in this response level, whereas females declined in their perception of math as useful ($p < .03$ for the interaction).

On the Math Usefulness for Men Scale, both men and women increased in their perception of math as useful for men ($p < .05$).

Correlates of Math Achievement. A central aspect of the study was to examine the relationship of students' scores on the attitudinal and personality scales and their achievement test scores in mathematics. The correlation coefficients calculated for this purpose are presented in Table 7.2.

A number of variables were positively correlated with Math Achievement for both the male sample and for the female sample (combining each across grade): *Math Attitudes* ($p < .01$ for both sexes); *Usefulness* ($p < .04$ and $p < .01$); *Interest in Male Occupations* ($p < .01$ and $p < .03$); and *Intellectual Achievement* ($p < .01$ for both sexes). For both males and females, achievement scores were negatively correlated with *stereotyping* ($p < .02$ and $p < .01$).

For males only, there was a positive correlation between Math Achievement and the scale for Negative Self ($p < .03$). *Independence* showed a positive correlation with achievement scores for females ($p < .01$).

A more detailed picture is provided by the correlations that were computed by grade and sex separately. In general, the strength of the relationship between attitudes and achievement increased with grade level. Math Attitudes (Task Competence Motivation and low Math Anxiety, both

TABLE 7.2
Correlation Between Student Measures and Math Achievement
Scores (scale scores) by Grade and Sex

	7th Grade		9th Grade		11th Grade	
	Male	*Female*	*Male*	*Female*	*Male*	*Female*
Task Competence						
Motivation (A)	.40**	.20*	.32**	.33**	.53**	.40**
Math Anxiety (B)	-.38**	-.27**	-.34**	-.37**	-.50**	-.40**
Math Attitude (A & B)	.44**	.24**	.35**	.38**	.55**	.43**
Stereotyping	-.22*	-.28**	-.12	-.38**	-.07	-.47**
Usefulness	.04	.10	.15*	.29**	.35*	.16
Women	.02	.08	.12	.30**	.26	.23*
Men	.13	00	.17	.26**	.37	.01
Peer Influence	-.18	-.19*	.08	-.08	-.27	-.46**
Independence	.32**	.26*	-.16	.14	.12	.28
Family Aspiration	.09	.04	-.04	.13	-.44*	.10
Male Occupations	.26*	-.07	.31**	.09	.50**	.55**
Female Occupations	-.08	.11	.09	.04	.03	-.11
Nurturance	.05	-.10	.13	-.02	.07	.10
Bravery	-.14	-.33**	-.28**	.19*	.23	.04
Intellectual	.43**	-.35*	.14	.54**	.16	.26*
Achievement						
Negative Self	-.05	-.01	.30**	-.10	.11	.01

*$p < .05$
**$p < .01$

separately and combined) were highly correlated with math achievement for male and female students at all grade levels.

Math Usefulness increased in importance with grade as a predictor of math achievement. Specifically, females' math achievement was correlated with their perception of Math Usefulness for Women in the ninth and eleventh grade samples. Likewise, males' math achievement was correlated with their view of Math Usefulness for Men for the eleventh-grade sample.

Peer Influence was inversely correlated with math achievement scores for seventh and eleventh grade females. This finding was consistent with the expectation that for females lowered math scores are related to social influences. It is not clear why this relationship did not hold for the ninth grade females.

Interest in Male Occupations was positively correlated with math achievement for males at all grade levels and for females in the eleventh grade. This finding may indicate that both males and females associate future career interests with increased proficiency in mathematics. This association seems to occur at an earlier developmental level for males. Math achievement was unrelated to interest in Female Occupations, which indicates that students do not perceive any relationship between mathematics and the fields on this scale.

Several interesting results emerged from the correlations of math achievement with some of the self-reported Personality Adjective Scales. Scores on the Bravery Scale were inversely correlated with math achievement for ninth grade males and for seventh and ninth grade females. That is, as interest in physical prowess and courage increased, math scores decreased. Scores on the Intellectual Achievement Scale were positively related to math achievement scores at all grade levels for girls and at the seventh grade level for males.

Course Taking.   Males and females did not differ statistically in the number of math courses they had taken nor in the number they intended to take in the future. There were some sex by grade interactions, with seventh grade females intending to take more future math courses than their male counterparts, whereas among ninth graders, the males planned to take more math than the females did.

There was a strong relationship between students' intentions to enroll in future mathematics courses and their math achievement scores (for all groups except seventh grade boys). Achievement was also significantly correlated with courses taken for both males and females in the eleventh grade.

There were additional correlations that were only significant for the oldest group of females: scores for the Stereotyping Scale were inversely related to both the number of courses taken ($p < .01$) and the number of courses students intended to take in the future ($p < .01$).

Parent Measures.   A short questionnaire was mailed to the parents of students in the study. It contained items tapping attitudes toward mathematics and sex-role stereotypes. Among the parents who completed questionnaires (94 mothers and 76 fathers), fathers were found to have more positive attitudes toward math. Their responses also indicated more sex-role stereotyping in mathematics.

We were interested in determining the extent to which parent attitudes related to their children's math attitudes and achievement. Males' scores on the Math Attitude Scale were correlated with fathers' attitudes toward math ($p < .01$), whereas females' scores were correlated with mothers' attitudes toward math ($p < .01$).

Fathers' and mothers' scores on the parent stereotyping measure were significantly correlated ($p < .05$) and fathers' stereotyping scores were significantly correlated with the scores of the Stereotyping Scale for both sons ($p < .05$) and daughters ($p < .05$).

Prediction of Math Achievement Scales: Regression Analyses.   Several regression analyses were performed using mathematics achievement scores (percentiles) as dependent variables and attitude and aptitude scores as independent measures. When predicting math achievement using a stepwise regression model, the strongest predictor for both males and females was the nonlanguage aptitude score (from the McGraw-Hill Comprehensive Test of Basic Skills).

For males, additional variables accounting for a significant proportion of the variance were Math Attitudes and Interest in Male Occupations. The former predicted a significant proportion of the variance in all grades, whereas the latter was only a significant predictor for eleventh grade males.

For females, there were also several variables in addition to aptitude that accounted for a significant proportion of the variance. The Stereotyping Scale and the Intellectual Achievement Scale were predictors at all three grade levels. Scores on the Math Attitude Scale were predictive for females from ninth grade on, and the Math Occupations Scale was predictive for the oldest group.

Math Underachievement. Students who do not perform at their ability level in mathematics have been the focus of a number of studies attempting to identify contributing factors. In the present study, an estimate of student underachievement in mathematics was obtained by subtracting each student's math aptitude score from his or her achievement score. Thus, when a student's aptitude score is higher than the achievement score, the result is a negative *discrepancy score,* which is taken to indicate underachievement.

Analyses of variance performed on the students' discrepancy scores yielded no grade or sex effects. However, when discrepancy scores were correlated with attitudinal and other personality measures, an interesting pattern of results emerged. Three variables were significantly correlated with discrepancy scores for both males and females: Math Attitudes, Interest in Male Occupations, and father's attitude toward mathematics (in all cases, p < .01 for males and for females). Thus, achievement scores were closer to aptitude scores for students who had positive math attitudes and interest in the occupations traditionally viewed as male. Father's attitude toward math apparently facilitated student achievement relative to the student's ability level. For females, two additional correlations were found for math underachievement. Discrepancy scores were correlated with females' stereotyping of mathematics (p < .01) and with their fathers' stereotyping (p < .06).

Math Attitudes in Grades 3–11. Developmental differences necessitated the use of two different questionnaires for elementary and secondary school children, so few direct comparisons could be made. There were several items that appeared on both questionnaires, however, including four that assessed students' perception of the extent to which mathematics was liked by friends, mothers, fathers, and by the students themselves.

In response to an item about how much they themselves liked math, students showed a general decline with age. Eleventh-grade males showed a slight increase in liking of math, whereas females' liking of math continued to decline.

The older girls showed a sharper decline than the boys in perceptions of their mothers' liking of math, whereas age did not affect their perceptions of how much their fathers liked math.

Both males and females see their friends as liking math less than they themselves do. One explanation of this difference is that students may be more likely to give what they perceive as socially desirable responses when reporting their own liking of math. Another possibility is that with their peers students expressed more negativity about math than they felt because this was the "acceptable" way of behaving. There was, nonetheless, a highly significant correlation between students' own liking of math and their perception of their friends' liking of it.

To summarize the findings of the secondary school study, results indicated that:

1. Males were more positive than females in their attitudes toward math;

2. Math attitudes declined with grade for the females; males' math attitudes showed an upturn between the ninth and eleventh grades;

3. Female math attitudes were significantly related to their mothers' math attitudes, whereas male math attitudes were related to their fathers' attitudes;

4. Males at all grade levels held more stereotyped beliefs than females; and

5. Attitudes toward math were predictive of math achievement scores for both males and females. For the females, math achievement was predicted by perceived usefulness of math achievement, by interest in traditionally male occupations, and by less stereotyped beliefs about math as a male domain.

CONCLUSIONS

The results of this research clearly indicate that there are a number of stereotyped attitudes about women and mathematics that are culturally pervasive. The hypothesis that mathematics achievement is inversely related to these negative beliefs was supported. There was evidence that stereotypes associated with mathematics are learned by children at a very young age, and that this knowledge affects their participation and performance in mathematics.

There are two categories of stereotypes associated with mathematics. The first is a characterization of the field itself, namely, that mathematics has been traditionally considered a very *masculine* subject, a domain in which men typically have greater interest and ability. The second category includes more specific stereotypes pertaining to women who venture into this supposedly masculine domain.

It is important to note, however, that these beliefs are not equally salient at all points in the developmental cycle. The various components of mathematical stereotyping are introduced at different times and by different agents. For example, the notion that adult women are generally inferior to adult men in mathematics was present in our sample of elementary school children. Mathematics is apparently put forth as a male domain from an early point in development. However, at first children perceived this stereotype as a characteristic associated only with the adult world. They apparently did not identify closely with these sex differences, and their mathematics achievement scores were not affected.

These findings may well have implications for the general self-esteem for both males and females. For females, because development brings an increasing perception of themselves as incompetent in math relative to males, there may be a decline in general self-esteem. For males, however, there were few changes in their perceptions of their own abilities and involvement in mathematics, and thus their self-esteem may not be adversely affected.

The particular socialization agents transmitting stereotyped information are dependent on the grade level of the student. Peer groups appear to play increasingly potent roles as students advance in grade. The female mathematicians who completed our questionnaire indicated that they first became aware of negative perceptions and beliefs about women's involvement in mathematics during secondary school, primarily from their male peers. Of course, the fact that these women typically had a strong interest in mathematics may have increased their sensitivity to math-related stereotypes on the part of their peers.

The relevance of mathematics to career choice apparently becomes particularly significant at the high school level. In the present study, females' math achievement scores were related to interest in traditionally masculine occupations. This relationship increased with grade level. Furthermore, math was perceived as more or less useful, depending on its relevance for career choice. We may speculate that it is not until college that women begin to fully experience the stereotype that a career in mathematics is in conflict with family goals.

One of the hypotheses was that women internalize negative stereotypes into their belief systems. The results indicate that although women do indeed hold stereotyped beliefs, males hold them even more strongly. Many female mathematicians in our sample indicated that they had witnessed discrimination in their fields. Although women's beliefs and attitudes serve as deterrents to their pursuit of careers in mathematics, there are also external barriers in the form of discrimination and negative stereotyping on the part of males that still keep many women from pursuing interests in mathematics.

The implications of these results are particularly relevant for parents and educators. Because the data indicate that children reveal stereotyped beliefs about mathematics as early as the third grade (and no doubt, even younger), it is apparent that parents and educators need to project non-stereotyped attitudes and expectations when dealing with children. It is not so much a matter of encouraging females to enroll in math courses as of expecting them to take math. Textbooks and course curricula should be free of any suggestion that women are not proficient or are not equal participants in the mathematics realm. The importance of appropriate role models, both in teaching materials and teachers, cannot be overestimated. Psychologists have argued for some time about whether it is more effective to change the attitude before the behavior or vice versa. It may well be the case for women in mathematics that behavioral changes must come first.

On the basis of this study, it may be concluded that: (1) attitudes toward mathematics are related to students' mathematics achievement scores in elementary school; (2) sex differences emerge in children's attitudes toward mathematics in the later elementary school years, although there were no overall sex differences in math achievement scores; and (3) even third-grade children perceive math to be in the male domain.

In summary, the results of this study support the thesis that women's underrepresentation in mathematics is related to the larger issue of sexism in society. Not until women are encouraged to pursue their own interests and fulfill their own potentials without artificially imposed restraints will equity in the field of mathematics be attained.

ACKNOWLEDGMENTS

The information contained in this chapter is based on a project supported by the National Institute of Education under Grant No. NIE-G-78-0023.

8 School, Classroom, and Home Influences on Women's Decisions to Enroll in Advanced Mathematics Courses

Jane Stallings
Peabody Center for Effective Teaching

Introduction

Recognizing that women historically have been underenrolled in advanced occupations, SRI International has carried out a study to examine factors that influence women's decisions to take advanced math classes. The primary focus of this Women and Math study was to identify those factors that promote higher enrollment and encourage more positive attitudes toward mathematics among high school women. Specifically, the study was designed to: (1) identify major personal, social, and school-related factors that influence students' decisions to enroll in advanced math courses; and (2) to identify math programs or career education programs that promote high enrollment of women in math courses.

Data were collected from 11 schools (four urban and seven suburban) with high, medium, or low enrollments of women in advanced math classes. Over 2100 math students, 76 teachers in 91 classrooms, and 53 counselors in the San Francisco Bay Area participated in the study. Through the technique of classroom observations, instructional processes that are used with men and women were examined for differences. Through questionnaires and interviews, the influence of peers, parents, teachers, and counselors upon women's decisions regarding enrollment in math classes was examined. In addition, the study detailed the differences found in men's and women's attitudes toward mathematics and the differences in their demonstrated abilities and experiences in math classes.

STATEMENT OF THE PROBLEM

There is widespread concern in the United States about the underrepresentation of women in advanced math courses and mathematical careers. Especially in the context of occupational data, the facts pertaining to women's nonelection of advanced math courses take on broad significance. Women represent about 47% of the U.S. labor force and account for 42% of those engaged in professional occupations, but they account for only 12% of those in scientific or technical careers.[1] If one assumes that the nonelection of advanced math courses greatly reduces the possibility of entering certain scientific or technical programs of study at the undergraduate and graduate level, then one may also assume that underrepresentation of women in advanced math courses is related to the number of women in scientific or technical careers. Simply stated, career options for women may be severely limited by their decision not to pursue the study of mathematics beyond that which is required to earn a high school diploma.

Though statistics may suggest the scope and nature of the problem, they cannot account for the reasons that precipitated it. It may be that the field of mathematics has become sex-stereotyped and stereotypic values are being transmitted to women during their early interactions with school and other cultural institutions. The socialization process experienced by most women may convey the message that careers requiring an extensive background in mathematics are "masculine domains." The nature of such sex bias, the way in which it is transmitted, and the manner in which it impinges on women's decisions to take advanced courses in mathematics are issues addressed by this study.

Within the American cultural ethos there are numerous possible sources of sex bias which, singly or in combination, may account for this phenomenon. Schools, parental interactions, and peer relationships all possess the inherent capability for transmitting sex bias. Because all of these influences are interactive and may operate within a framework of shared values and goals, it is likely that sexist values are transmitted and reinforced.

If schools are considered as primary socializing institutions where key cultural values are transmitted to students, it follows that sexist beliefs may also be conveyed to students. Within the school these sex-stereotypic values in relation to mathematics and careers may be transmitted in several ways.

Teachers, both in the area of mathematics and other subjects, may

---

[1] Bureau of Labor Statistics (1977 data).

transmit sex bias in their instructional behavior. Whether through explicit statements or implicit behavioral cues, whether consciously or unconsciously, teachers may instruct male and female students differently. In the conscious and explicit mode, for example, teachers may use different criteria for assessing the progress of men and women students; or they may make statements that convey the belief that "mathematics is not a suitable subject for women." In the unconscious and implicit mode, teachers may respond differently to questions posed by male students than they do to questions raised by female students; they may be more willing to spend time "rapping" after class with men students than with women; or they may advise men and women differently on whether to take more advanced math courses.

Counselors may be critical influences in students' selection of courses. Male and female guidance counselors may provide advice on the basis of the sex of the students with whom they are interacting. It is possible, for example, that counselors perceive mathematics and careers related to mathematics in a sex-stereotypic manner and that they advise men and women students on the selection of advanced math courses accordingly.

School administrators, whereas they do not as a rule interact with students on a frequent basis, may hold sexist attitudes regarding mathematics that they transmit in shaping school-related instructional policies. Biases could be reflected in career education programs that expose women to a wide range of nonmath-related careers while exposing men to math-related careers. Professional women invited to speak on career days may or may not be from math-related occupations. To the extent that administrative sanction is required for extracurricular activities within the school, administrators may discourage activities intended to remediate sex bias, such as clubs for women students or consciousness-raising groups. They may or may not invite women professionals to address school assemblies or to speak with students during a school activity. Finally, administrators may act in implicitly sexist ways by hiring only male math teachers or assigning male teachers or counselors to more responsible positions.

This brief description of potential sources of sex bias in the school setting suggests that many of women's decisions regarding the pursuit of advanced math courses may be explained by school-related factors. The relationship of high school students to their parents can also influence students' decisions relating to course selection and career options. Parents may serve implicitly as sex-role models and as the transmitters of explicit values that indicate to daughters that they should or should not pursue various courses of study. Such related factors as the occupations of the father and mother and parental socioeconomic status most likely convey strong messages about "acceptable" courses and careers.

Sex bias transmitted by school and parents may be reinforced or coun-teracted by peer influence. If, for example, in a given school, the percent-age of girls enrolled in advanced math courses is fairly high, women students facing the critical decisions as to whether to take advanced courses may feel comfortable in electing to take them. Conversely, in a school with low female enrollment in such courses, or in cases in which friends elect not to take such courses, women students may elect not to undertake additional work in mathematics. Peer groups can exert more subtle influences as well. It is possible that the interaction of women students with each other is characterized by the same sex-role behavior as that promulgated by the school and parents. The interaction of men and women students may further serve to reinforce sexist values relating to the study of mathematics and selection of careers.

The ethos of American culture must also be considered as a potential source of sexist values that have a significant impact on women's deci-sions in relation to participation in advanced mathematics. The transmis-sion of sexist values may have a cumulative effect on women which, when considered in the context of other influences converging upon them, may further discourage them from electing to pursue courses in mathematics beyond those required. For example, the "woman-as-homemaker" image portrayed by television cannot help but affect the self-perception of young women as objects to be cherished and protected, not as individuals who question and probe.

The problem of women's underrepresentation in advanced math courses and scientific or technical careers no doubt has multiple antece-dents, all of which interact. It is the intent of this study to define and describe the several influences impinging on women's decisions regarding whether to pursue advanced courses in mathematics. The study analyzes the interrelationships among these forces and identifies ways in which each of these forces contributes to a decision concerning the further study of mathematics.

REVIEW OF RELATED RESEARCH

The most serious problem facing those concerned with equity in math education is ensuring that women continue their study of mathematics (Fennema & Sherman, 1976b). Recent studies have attempted to identify factors influencing the decision of women to continue their math educa-tion. The results of most of these studies, which are primarily cross-sectional, are inconclusive due to failure to control for relevant variables or inadequate research design and analysis. In a review of 36 studies on the sex-related differences in math education, Fennema (1974a) argues that those studies should have controlled for two confounding effects. First, more lower ability men than women students drop out of high school, resulting in a more homogeneous sample of men. Second, the women students who do elect math courses appear brighter than those who do not, thus creating a lower ability sample of women students not taking mathematics.

Clearly, a carefully designed, systematic study of women's participation in mathematics at the secondary level is needed to determine why fewer women than men enroll in math courses. Factors that are considered in this chapter include:

> Sex-stereotyping of mathematics as a male domain.
> Perceived utility of math courses.
> Peer influence.
> Parental influence.
> Sex differences in math aptitude and achievement.
> Math-related school programs and counselor advice.
> Sex-related attitudes and behaviors of math teachers
>   toward male and female students in classrooms.

Sex Stereotyping of Mathematics as a Male Domain

In the high school years, both men and women have been found more likely to perceive mathematics as a male domain (Ernest, 1976; Fennema & Sherman, 1977b). This stereotyping may well result in or accompany low math self-concept in many women. Maccoby and Jacklin (1974) argue that women tend to underestimate their intellectual abilities. Kagan (1964) found that they feel inadequate in many kinds of problem-solving activities. Fennema (1974b) even found low self-concepts among women who were achieving better than men. Some authors argue further that this lack of self-confidence often results in mathematical anxiety (Donady & Tobias, 1977; Ernest, 1976; Fennema & Sherman, 1977b; Levine, 1976; Tobias, 1976). Through many paths, then, a stereotyping of math as a male domain would be expected to decrease female participation in math courses.

Perceived Utility of Math Courses

A woman's perception of the usefulness of mathematics to her future activities is also likely to affect her participation in math courses. Much of the literature suggests that women in high school feel that their future roles as wife and mother preclude involvement in a traditionally male-dominated occupation. Hawley (1971) found marriage to be one of the primary goals for most high school women. Astin (1974a) concluded that if a woman anticipated a conflict between her roles as homemaker and career woman, she would give up her career. Fennema and Sherman (1977b) hypothesized that women do not see mathematics as an appropriate activity and do not recognize its usefulness in their career plans. In a study of secondary school students, Hilton and Berglund (1974) found that men perceived mathematics as more likely to be helpful in earning a living than did women. However, the Fennema and Sherman study did not find as great a difference between men's and women's beliefs as was found in the Hilton–Berglund study. It is suggested by Fennema and Sherman that this discrepancy in findings may indicate that the beliefs of women are becoming more similar to men in this respect. Fox (1976d) attributes the sex difference in the perceived usefulness of mathematics to women's lack of orientation to careers other than homemaking, to their interests in fields other than mathematics and science, and to their lack of awareness of the relevance of mathematics and science to many professions.

Peer Influence

Numerous studies show that peers exert a strong influence on adolescent attitudes and behavior (Coleman, 1961; Cusick, 1973; Hauser, Sewell, & Alwyn, 1976; Rigsby & McDill, 1972). Little research, however, has specifically examined the influence of peers on the decision of women to study mathematics. The few studies that do exist point to students' stereotypes about appropriate sex-linked behavior as an important agent of peer pressure. Matthews and Tiedeman (1964) reported that a decline in career commitment by women of high school age was related to perceptions of male classmates and disapproval of the use of female intelligence. Many researchers have reported that women are reluctant to continue with mathematics due to fear of social recrimination (Casserly, 1975; Fennema & Sherman, 1977b; Fox, 1976b; Levine, 1976; Solano, 1976). In an effort to encourage higher enrollment of women in math classes, all-women math classes have been introduced as an intervention strategy with varying degrees of success (Fox, 1974a; Hawley, 1971). A more acceptable alternative, early tracking of women in academic programs, has been recommended (Casserly, 1975; Fox, 1976a; Haven, 1971; Sells, 1978).

Parental Influence

Students may also be influenced by parents who hold sex-stereotypic views of women in mathematics. Fennema and Sherman (1976b, 1977a) showed that student reports of parental perceptions of the child as a learner of mathematics reflected sex differences. Researchers argue that parental encouragement of women to enroll in advanced mathematics is a crucial but often absent influence (Aiken, 1972a; Fennema & Sherman, 1977a; Haven, 1971; Poffenberger & Norton, 1956). Block (1973) found that parents stress interpersonal relations and affection with their daughters, whereas they emphasize achievement, competition, and control of feelings with their sons. Similarly, parents report buying more scientific games and toys for sons (Hilton & Berglund, 1974; Maccoby & Jacklin, 1974) and offering more rewards and reinforcements to their sons to learn mathematics than to their daughters (Astin, 1974a).

Fathers have been found to help more in mathematics homework in the higher grades than did mothers (Ernest, 1976). The mothers' low math self-concepts may explain their reluctance to help with math homework; Levine (1976) reported that mothers accepted low math achievement from their daughters because of their own lack of ability in mathematics.

The literature also suggests that parents hold lower educational and vocational aspirations for their daughters than for their sons. Fox (1975b) found that more men than women perceived their parents as favoring acceleration in mathematics. Casserly (1975) found that parents do not expect their daughters to achieve as much as their sons. It has also been found that daughters who identify with their fathers, or who have working mothers, tend to enroll in higher level math courses (Astin, 1974b; Astin, Harway, & McNamara, 1976).

Sex Differences in Math Aptitude and Achievement

It has been generally accepted that there are sex differences on math achievement tests for high school students (Aiken, 1976; Astin, 1974b; Fox, 1975a; Maccoby & Jacklin, 1974). Fennema and Sherman (1977a) have found minimal sex-related differences in math achievement in grades six through nine, but in half of the high schools they studied, men achieved at higher levels than women. Their research has also indicated trends for men to perform better on higher level cognitive tasks (Fennema & Sherman, 1977a). Stafford (1972) goes so far as to suggest the hypothesis that a sex-linked recessive gene is the cause for this difference.

An area of intellectual development theoretically related to math learning is spatial-visualization, and here again, women have been reported to perform less well than men (Fennema, 1974a; Maccoby & Jacklin, 1974). However, as with math achievement, Sherman and Fennema (1977) have found that men are not invariably superior in spatial-visualization. They suggest that sociocultural factors are highly important concomitants of sex-related differences.

Specifically, their explanation of the inconsistent findings of sex differences in math achievement and spatial-visualization is that differences are due to the failure of researchers to control for differential course-taking (Fennema & Sherman, 1976b, 1977a, b). It is hypothesized that the best predictors of success in mathematics are the same amount of mathematics studied and intelligence test scores.

The number of women who have the same capability as men for learning high school mathematics may well be larger than the number of women who elect to study mathematics. The results of the two national studies that claim higher achievement for men, Project TALENT (Flanagan, 1976) and the National Assessment of Educational Progress (Mullis, 1975) do not deal with this problem in that they failed to control for educational or mathematical background. On the one hand, then, sex differences in these students' achievement may be explained by differential participation. On the other hand, researchers such as Fox (1975b) and Astin (1974b) have found large sex differences in favor of men among gifted students as early as grade seven—before differences in course-taking existed. Further research on this relationship of achievement and course-taking needs to be done.

Math-Related School Programs and Counselor Advice

Few studies can be located that focus to any extent on the overall setting in which secondary school instruction in mathematics takes place. Little reference is found in the literature to such potentially significant factors as administrative support for increasing women's enrollment in mathematics, organizing school programs to facilitate increased enrollment by women in math courses, or provisions of informational materials to increase awareness of the potential value of math courses.

Occasional references to the value of role models in stimulating interest in quantitative fields appear in the literature. In a review of National Science Foundation projects, Lantz, West, and Elliott (1976) reported that role models were the most significant factor affecting women's enrollment in mathematics in some of the projects studied. Prediger, McLure, and Noeth (1976) found role models in mathematics to be more successful than those in other informational careers in science and technology.

Two highly visible role models in the school setting are the teacher and the counselor. The influence of the teacher will be discussed in the next section. Fox (1976d) reported that counselors are seen as the least potent influence upon the child. Still, women are more likely to seek advice from counselors than are men (Harway, Astin, Suhr, & Whiteley, 1976), particularly regarding advanced math courses (Haven, 1971).

A few counselors have actually admitted discouraging women students from taking advanced math courses (Casserly, 1975; Luchins, 1976). This discouragement, or lack of encouragement, may be a reflection of the counselor's biases. Schlossberg and Pietrofessa (1973) found that one of the major determinants of a counselor's advice concerns the opinion of what behavior is appropriate for women in society. In their observations of interactions between counselors and women students concerning the decision to major in engineering, they discovered that more than three-fourths of the statements made by counselors of both sexes were biased against the choice of the engineering major. More generally, Thomas and Stewart (1971) showed that both men and women counselors rated traditionally feminine career goals of women students as more appropriate than traditionally masculine career goals.

The counselors' stereotypical attitudes are reported to be decreasing during the present decade (Englehard, Jones, & Stiggens, 1976). Mac-Donald (1978) and Ernest (1976) have recommended that counselors increase math awareness by beginning career education programs early, upgrading existing career education programs, and counseling students to continue their math training. In the present study, we look at counselor attitudes and school offerings to see how they are related to mathematics participation by women students.

The Math Teacher: Sex-Related Attitudes and Treatment of Male and Female Students in the Classroom

The literature on teacher expectations for pupil behavior suggests that differential expectations for men and women may be a factor in the low enrollment of women in math courses. Many of the more recent studies on teacher attitudes toward mathematics involved prospective teachers for the elementary level. Ernest (1976) reported that 41% of the teachers he studied felt men did better in mathematics, whereas none felt women did better. Teachers also appear to have more negative perceptions of mathematically gifted women (Solano, 1976) and, in fact, can be hostile to them (Fox, 1974a, 1975a).

Although teacher/student interaction is believed to be an important factor in the decision of women to enroll in math courses, few classroom interaction studies focusing on differential treatment and response by sex can be found. Sears and Feldman (1966) found that in 76 studies reporting classroom observation in the *Handbook of Research on Teaching* (Gage, 1963), not one indicated to whom—man or women—the teacher behavior was directed. In the *Second Handbook of Research on Teaching* (Travers, 1973) we noted this same missing treatment in the reported observational studies. These authors did recognize, however, the need for future research studies to allow for individual differences.

Those studies that have looked at the sex of the student have suggestive results. Aiken (1972b) reported on the importance of verbal cues in the learning of mathematics. In one of the few classroom interaction studies at the secondary level, Bean (1976) showed that teachers initiated more contacts with male students than with female students, although no corresponding sex differences were found in the number of student-initiated contacts with the teacher. Other researchers have supported these findings (Good, Sikes, & Brophy, 1973). A study by Dweck and Reppucci (1973) suggests that math teachers provide different feedback to men than to women when the students give a wrong answer. Men are told to try harder; women are praised for even trying. Future research is needed to determine specifically whether secondary school teachers tend to expect higher achievement in mathematics by men than women and whether teachers differentiate between the sexes in rewarding math achievement.

STUDY DESIGN AND METHODOLOGY

The study was carried out in 11 San Francisco Bay Area Schools. These schools were selected from telephone survey information collected from 130 public and private high schools. Selection criteria were based upon the initial sample design, which required two urban schools with a high percentage of women enrolled in advanced math classes and two urban schools with a low percentage of women enrolled in these classes. From a suburban population we also selected two high schools with high women's enrollment in advanced math and two schools with low enrollment. In addition to these eight schools, three other suburban schools were included when the superintendent of a neighboring district requested participation for their three high schools at their district's expense. They were each judged to have a medium level of enrollment of women in mathematics.

The final sample included 91 classrooms in the 11 high schools. The classrooms were sorted into three types:

> Type I—General Math and Pre-algebra, courses
>   required for high school graduation.
> Type II—Algebra I and Geometry, courses required
>   for entry into the California university system.
> Type III—Algebra II, Trigonometry, Precalculus,
>   Calculus, Computer Science, Probability and
>   Statistics, courses required for entry into some
>   university science and math programs.

Within these 91 classes, approximately 2100 students were given questionnaires, interviews, instructor rating scales, an achievement test, and special ability tests. Seventy-six teachers were observed and given questionnaires. To study the broader school program, counselors were given questionnaires, and administrators and career personnel were interviewed.

The focus of the study was upon the 489 students in the 22 geometry classes in the 11 schools because these students are at the point of making a decision to pursue non-required advanced mathematics. We found the numbers of men and women enrolled in these Type II classes were approximately equal. Table 8.1 shows that of those enrolled, 82% of the women (189 of 231) were planning to elect the next semester's advanced math class in comparison to 89% of the men (230 of 258). Thus, the interesting questions became why fewer women than men decided to continue their studies in mathematics and what differentiated those women who were continuing from those who were not.

Five hypotheses were generated:

1. Factors (parents, peers, teachers, counselors, programs, potential careers, or college plans) identified by students as most influential in their decision to enroll or not to enroll in an elective math class can be identified and will vary by school, location, and by traditional degree of involvement of women in the schools' advanced math classes.

2. A positive relationship will be found between math aptitude and ability and decisions to continue in advanced math classes; further, men and women enrolled in advanced math classes will have similar achievement scores.

3. Particular combinations of classroom processes will be related to high enrollment of women in math classes.

4. Differential treatment of men and women students will be observed in math classrooms, and this difference will be related to enrollment in advanced math classes.

5. Schools in which women students are exposed to math-related programs or career education programs will have a higher enrollment of women in math classes than will schools without such interventions.

Instruments

To collect data that would allow an examination of the many factors that might influence women's decisions to enroll in advanced math classes, a variety of instruments were used. These included: survey reports, questionnaires, interview guides, tests, rating scales, and observation instruments.

TABLE 8.1
Percentage of Men and Women Continuing
With Advanced Mathematics

	Number Presently Enrolled	Continuing in Math	Not Continuing
Women	231	189	42
Men	258	230	28

A telephone survey report was used to select the sample of schools with high and low enrollment of women in advanced math classes and to identify schools with high and low intensity math-related career information programs. Information on students was collected by four instruments: a student questionnaire (including a student Rating Scale of Instructors), a student interview guide, a space relationships test to assess math aptitude, and a math criterion-referenced achievement test. The student questionnaire and interview protocols were used to assess students' decisions to enroll in math classes. Additional teacher and classroom data were obtained from two sources: a teacher questionnaire, and the SRI Secondary Observation system. Data on counselors and school programs was solicited through counselor questionnaires and interviews with administrators.

The testing instruments and the Student Rating Scale of Instructors have been used in previous studies in secondary schools and required no adaptation for this study. The SRI Classroom Observation Instrument required slight modifications. The survey report, the questionnaires, and the interview protocols were developed and pilot-tested within this study.

Student Questionnaires

Seven domains were assessed by the major student questionnaire. They were: students' attitudes toward mathematics (liking for math, difficulty of the subject, self-confidence in math ability, factors affecting decision to enroll in the next math course); prior experience in mathematics; perception of parent attitudes; opinions about teachers, counselors, and school programs in regard to mathematics; and estimates of peer influence. An additional questionnaire solicited specific opinions about the teacher's style of instruction. This Student Rating Scale of Instructors allowed us to examine students' subjective viewpoints of certain aspects of classroom processes. The scale was developed in 1973 by the staff of the Sequoia High School District in California and has been used in secondary classrooms in that district. The rating scale allows the student to select on a five-point scale a rating number that, in the student's opinion, best describes an instructor in areas such as clearness of course objectives, clearness of assignments, fairness in grading, classroom control or discipline, preparation for the class, communication, friendliness, course content, helpfulness, participation, and encouragement of independent ideas.

Student Interviews

The chief advantages of using questionnaires are that they are easy to administer and provide data that can be analyzed reasonably quickly. The primary disadvantage is that their format precludes the possibility of in-depth probing. To overcome this inherent drawback, student interviews were conducted with a stratified subsample of students, both men and women. The interview subsamples were stratified by sex and by the students' decisions to pursue or not to pursue additional math courses. The intent of the interviews was to collect comprehensive data regarding why students decided to pursue or not to pursue advanced courses in mathematics. Within the context of the interview, data were collected regarding students' perceptions of those factors that influenced their decisions.

The interview protocols call for probing into areas such as how well students like school, how they like math classes, and how they feel about what they are learning in math classes. If they did not like mathematics, we asked when they started to feel that way. Most of the probes were based on the answers students had given on the questionnaire. Although the interviews were highly structured, the protocols permitted interviewers ample opportunity to probe for responses in areas of interest to this study. For the most part, the interview protocol was close-ended, permitting the interviews to last no more than 30 minutes.

Space Relations Test

To examine math aptitude, a Space Relations subtest was used. This subtest (from the Differential Aptitude Tests, developed by George K. Bennett, Harold G. Seashore, and Alexander G. Wesman, published by the Psychological Corporation, 1973), has been described by past reviewers as the best available instrument of its kind. Significant for this study, separate norms are available for males and females.

Math Criterion Tests

It is quite possible that math achievement and/or math ability, real or perceived, will have a strong impact on whether a student enrolls in advanced math courses. In order to examine this area, math criterion tests were administered to all students participating in the study.

Rather than developing math criterion tests for all levels of classes involved in this study, SRI used an established battery of tests recommended by math department chairpersons at several local schools: the Cooperative Mathematics Tests developed by Educational Testing Service and published by Addison-Wesley. Separate tests were given at the following levels: general math (arithmetic), first-year algebra, geometry, second-year algebra, trigonometry, analytical geometry, and calculus.

Teacher Questionnaire

The teacher questionnaire was designed to collect data around three foci: teachers' stereotyping of the subject of mathematics; teachers' beliefs about sex bias in their own teaching; and teachers' perceptions of the problem of female underrepresentation in advanced mathematics.

SRI Secondary Observation Instrument

In order to examine classroom processes that might enter into the decision-making process, the SRI Secondary Observation Instrument (SOI) was used. This instrument was based on an observation system developed at SRI for use in secondary reading classrooms. Modifications were made that would allow observers to record events that occur in senior high math classes and to identify whether a teacher was interacting with a male or female student.

The SOI contains three sections. The first section, Identification Information, identifies the schools, teachers, classes, the number of adults, and male and female students present in the classroom.

The second section is the Classroom Snapshot. The Snapshot is a matrix that yields data about the activities of each adult and student in the classroom, the size of the group, and the materials being used. From this record information is obtained on how the teacher spends his or her time and with whom, how the aides spend their time and with whom, and how often the students operate independently and in what activities. This record is made five times during a class period. Three days of observation produced 15 snapshots of each class observed.

The third section, the Five Minute Interaction (FMI), is used to record the teacher's verbal interactions or nonverbal behaviors. It consists of a series of frames in which each behavior/interaction is recorded in the four categories provided: Who, To Whom, What, and How. Consecutive frames can record 72 continuous interactions during a 5 minute period. Five of these 5 minute interactions are recorded during one class period. Over the 3 days of observation, this provided 15 5 minute interactions and approximately 900 interaction frames for each class. This is a very complex system, and it requires 7 days to train observers. Only those observers who are able to record a criterion videotape at 80% reliability are allowed to collect data.

Adaptations in the coding system allowed us to answer questions such as:

> When the teacher asks questions of the entire class,
> who volunteers answers more often—male or
> female students?
> When the teacher calls on a specific student, is it
> more often—a male or female student?

Counselor Questionnaire

This short questionnaire probed the background and experience of the counselor, frequency and reasons for contact with students, decision-making about advising men and women students to take more math and science, and beliefs about the factors influencing students' course choices.

Administrator Interview Guide

The administrator interview guide gathered information on categorical aid programs, per pupil expenditures, and special career education programs. Several questions were asked regarding the importance placed by the school on math education and increasing students'—particularly women's—interest in mathematics.

ANALYSIS AND RESULTS

Several analyses were conducted to examine the five hypotheses posed in the study. The results from the analysis for each hypothesis are described in the following sections.

Hypothesis #1: Factors Influencing the Choice to Continue in Mathematics

Hypothesis #1 was tested by conducting discriminant function analyses and analyses of variance that first compared the student questionnaire responses of men and women who were continuing in mathematics and then compared women choosing to take advanced mathematics with those choosing not to take advanced mathematics. Variables were used from the student questionnaire, the space relationships test, and the geometry achievement test. Student interviews were used to document possible school influences in more detail.

Men Continuing Compared to Women Continuing

Through a discriminant function analysis substantiated by analyses of variance, significant differences were found in several factors influencing the continuation of women and men (see Table 8.2). First, men who were continuing reported more parental support of taking advanced mathematics. In their interview responses, they also noted their parents had higher expectations for their educational attainment. Second, they reported speaking more often to their math teachers and feeling more anxiety about mathematics than did women. Further, they scored higher on the spatial ability test but did not score higher on the geometry achievement test than did women continuing. These findings of more parental support, more teacher interaction, and higher spatial ability in males follow the trends in the literature, whereas the finding of higher math anxiety does not.

Women Continuing Compared with Women Not Continuing

When women who were continuing in math studies were compared with women who were not, four principal factors emerged: opinions about teachers, attitudes toward mathematics, spatial ability, and parental support (see Table 8.3). Those continuing in mathematics studies tended to rate their teachers higher on being professional, to feel less strongly that they needed to like a teacher to take a math class with him or her, and to care less about whether the teacher was male or female. Their decision about taking the math classes seemed to be more related to the subject

TABLE 8.2
A Comparison of Women and Men Geometry Students
Who are Continuing in Mathematics[1]

Variable of Interest[2]	Women Continuing N = 189		Men Continuing N = 230		Contrast p Value
	$\bar{x}$	S.D.	$\bar{x}$	S.D.	
Father Support for Taking Mathematics	.94	.18	.98	.04	.10
Talk to Math Teacher	1.42	2.13	3.39	6.20	.06
Spatial Ability	21.10	5.60	22.45	5.52	.06
Math Anxiety	.46	.40	.50	.43	.04

[1] All contrasts significant a $\alpha \leqslant .10$ are reported. These are contrasts *of interest*; they are not to be reported as significant at .1 as we are doing multiple tests.

[2] These variables comprised the discriminant function that identified factors which differentiated between continuation and no continuation. This is an analysis of variance on those factors.

TABLE 8.3
Comparison of Women Who Are Continuing Math Studies
With Those Who Are Not
(For All Geometry Classes Across All Eleven Schools)[1]

Variable of Interest[2]	Women Continuing N = 189		Women Not Continuing N = 42		Contrast p Value
	$\bar{x}$	S.D.	$\bar{x}$	S.D.	
Rate teacher as professional.	32.80	4.80	30.60	5.90	.03
Would not take a mathematics class from a teacher they didn't like.	1.60	.49	1.75	.43	.06
No preference regarding sex of teacher	.29	.43	.15	.50	.07
Difficulty with mathematics.	.58	.48	.77	.41	.02
Mathematics anxiety.	.46	.40	.73	.44	.001
Space relationships test.	21.10	5.60	19.10	5.60	.03
Father support for taking taking mathematics.	.94	.18	.88	.33	.04
Mother support for taking mathematics.	.98	.13	.93	.26	.04

[1] All contrasts significant at $\alpha \leqslant .10$ are reported. These are contrasts *of interest*; they are not to be reported as significant at .1 as we are doing multiple tests.

[2] The variables comprised the discriminant function that identified factors that differentiated between continuation and no continuation. This is an analysis of variance on those factors.

matter than to the teacher. This conclusion is substantiated by their statements in interviews that they didn't talk to their math teachers very often and that they took mathematics courses because such courses were needed to complete career or educational plans.

Women who were continuing in math studies had more spatial ability, more positive feelings about the difficulty of mathematics, and less anxiety than women who were not continuing. From the student interviews, it was also clear that the perceived utility of mathematics was more important to women who were continuing. They frequently cited their need for mathematics for their future careers (e.g., architecture, psychology, law). Thus, we may conclude that some attitude and aptitude measures are factors in students' continuing in math studies. Note that actual achievement in the geometry test was not related to the decision to continue or not continue, nor was a perception of math as a male domain. Thus, this population of women responded differently from those described by Ernest (1976) and Fennema and Sherman (1977b).

Women who were continuing in math studies received more support from their father and mothers to take math courses, and these parents had higher expectations for them regarding college. In fact, the factor most often found to differentiate the students continuing in mathematics from those who were not, identified from the student questionnaire, student ratings, and test data, is parental expectations and support in taking advanced mathematics. Men were more influenced by fathers, whereas women were influenced by mothers and fathers. Prior research suggests that parental encouragement of women to enroll in advanced math classes is crucial but often absent (Aiken, 1972a; Fennema & Sherman, 1977a; Haven, 1971). Our data suggest that parents are perhaps the most important factor for women as well as men in continuing math studies.

Teacher influences were not among the highly rated influences on students' decisions to take more mathematics. Women continuing rated their math teachers as being more professional than did those not continuing. They also said they would take a class from a teacher they did not like. Special treatment and good interactions did not seem as important. Nor did men and women students credit peers, counselors, or school programs as important in affecting their math enrollment decisions.

Hypothesis #2: Math Aptitude and Achievement

The second hypothesis stated that a positive relationship would be found between math aptitude (as measured by spatial ability) and math achievement, and that men and women enrolled in advanced math classes would have similar math aptitude and achievement scores.

To examine the relationship between spatial ability and math achievement, Pearson product moment correlations were computed for each level of math test and the space relationships test. The results of these computations are presented in Table 8.4. There are significant correlations for men and women between spatial ability and math achievement above the level of arithmetic. There are significant correlations for women at all levels but curiously not for men in either algebra II or calculus.

With regard to sex differences, similar to the findings of Fennema

TABLE 8.4
Correlation of Space Relationships and Achievement Tests

Tests	N	Overall		Men		Women	
		r	p	r	p	r	p
Calculus	81	.20	—	.17	—	.57	.01
Analytic Geometry	69	.68	.001	.70	.001	.60	.001
Trigonometry	206	.38	.001	.27	.01	.50	.001
Algebra II	275	.15	.01	.05	—	.24	.01
Geometry	471	.53	.001	.49	.001	.52	.001
Algebra I	281	.49	.001	.50	.001	.45	.001
Arithmetic	153	.11	—	.20	—	.03	—

TABLE 8.5
Means and Standard Deviations of Men's and Women's Achievement
Test Scores and Space Relationships Scores By Course Level

Course	N	Achievement Test		Space Relationships Test	
		$\bar{x}$	S.D.	$\bar{x}$	S.D.
Calculus					
Men	58	10.76*	3.28	26.06	3.59
Women	23	8.78	3.94	24.26	4.75
Analytical Geometry					
Men	37	11.51*	3.66	23.70	5.69
Women	32	9.25	3.94	19.96	6.37
Trigonometry					
Men	106	7.94	3.57	23.72	5.47
Women	100	7.78	3.51	22.58	5.93
Algebra II					
Men	149	12.95	5.49	24.25*	4.98
Women	126	12.71	5.53	21.91	5.21
Geometry					
Men	248	15.99*	3.08	23.03*	5.52
Women	223	14.75	3.74	20.65	5.76
Algebra I					
Men	136	12.81*	3.86	20.32*	5.95
Women	146	11.88	3.97	17.42	6.34
Arithmetic					
Men	70	4.00*	1.69	14.48	5.54
Women	83	4.53*	1.64	13.72	4.57

*p .01

(1974b) and Maccoby and Jacklin (1974), we found that men sometimes, but not always, score higher on the space relationships test (see Table 8.5). In our case men enrolled in algebra I, geometry, and algebra II scored higher than women enrolled in those courses. We also found that women continuing in math studies scored higher on the space relationships test than women who did not continue.

With regard to the subject matter tests, women taking an arithmetic course scored *higher* than men on the arithmetic test; women in algebra II and trigonometry did as well as men; but men in algebra I, geometry, analytic geometry, and calculus scored higher than women. Thus, these results could be viewed as supporting the findings of Sherman and Fennema (1977) that men are not *invariably* superior in math achievement or spatial-visualization when the number of math courses and the nature of the courses taken are considered. However, when sex differences are found in higher mathematical skills, men do score higher than women.

The second hypothesis was confirmed in part. There are relationships between spatial ability and math achievement. From our analysis of hypothesis #1, we may recall that women who enroll in more advanced courses do have higher spatial ability scores than those who do not enroll. However, women who enroll have lower spatial scores than men who enroll. Similarly, women at three levels of math course work (algebra I, geometry, and algebra II) scored below men in spatial ability and women at four levels (algebra I, geometry, algebra II, and calculus) scored below men in mathematics achievement.

Hypothesis #3: Classroom Processes Related to Enrollment

Hypothesis #3 states that particular combinations of classroom processes will be related to high enrollment of women in math classes. To examine this hypothesis we correlated 34 classroom process variables with women's enrollment in advanced math classes. We focused on the relationship between classroom process variables and the continuation rate for women in the different geometry classes. Nine categories of classrooms were defined based on the percentage of women continuing from geometry into advanced math classes, ranging from 45% to 100%. Only four significant correlations were identified. They are so few that they could be spurious.

The implications of the correlations are that women continue to enroll in mathematics when they are in classrooms that are interactive and instructive. It doesn't matter whether this interaction occurs more with men or women students—just that an active instructional environment is established. The classroom with the lowest percentage of women continuing had the most discipline problems and the most social interactions. This finding indicates that more time was spent off the task of instructing mathematics than in other classrooms. Interestingly, fewer males also continued with math studies from that class. There is little in the literature from previous studies that either substantiates or conflicts with these findings.

Hyothesis #4: Differential Treatment of Men and Women

Hypothesis #4 states that differential treatment of men and women students will be observed in math classrooms and this will be related to enrollment in advanced math classes. To study this hypothesis we used observation data and statements of teachers on the teacher questionnaires.

TABLE 8.6
Mean Frequencies of Interaction Variables
For 22 Geometry Classes*

Variable		Mean
F10	All interactions/female student-teacher/verbal, math	38.69
F11	All interactions/male student-teacher/verbal, math	46.88
F15	Female student question/math	5.60
F16	Male student question/math	6.59
F18	Teacher question/female student/math	3.72
F19	Teacher question/male student/math	4.60
F34	Female volunteer responses to teacher/math	1.23
F35	Male volunteer responses to teacher/math	1.67
F40	Teacher response/female student question/math	5.49
F41	Teacher response/male student question/math	6.32
F43	Teacher instruction/female student/math	5.48
F44	Teacher instruction/male student/math	6.56
F54	Teacher social interactions/female students	0.97
F55	Teacher social interactions/male students	1.41
F62	Teacher acknowledge female students/math	2.87
F63	Teacher acknowledge male students/math	3.59
F65	Teacher praise female student/math	0.26
F66	Teacher praise male student/math	0.34
F80	Teacher encouraging female student/math	0.23
F81	Teacher encouraging male student/math	0.26
F88	Interaction teacher-female student/relevance of math	0.00
F89	Interaction teacher-male student/relevance of math	0.07
F100	All corrective feedback/female students/math	8.03
F101	All corrective feedback/male students/math	10.13
F104	Teacher positive interactions with female students	0.41
F105	Teacher positive interactions with male students	0.40
F111	Teacher negative interactions with female students	0.06
F112	Teacher negative interactions with male students	0.14

*50 percent women in classes.

Observation

Because there were approximately 50% women in the geometry classes, the number of teacher interactions with men and women should be about equal if equal treatment is being given. Table 8.6 displays the average frequency of observed interactions of teachers with male and female students during a geometry classes in the study.

Though few of the differences are statistically significant, the trend is rather clear. Men are spoken to more often than are women (F10, F11). Men ask more questions (F15, F16), and teachers ask men more questions (F18, F19). Women volunteer answers about as often as do men (F34, F35), but men are called upon to respond more frequently than are women (F40, F41). Men receive a little more individual instruction (F43, F44), social interaction (F54, F55), acknowledgement (F62, F63), praise (F65, F66), encouragement (F80, F81) and corrective feedback (F100, F101).

Overall, men students are treated somewhat differently than are women students in geometry classes. This is in agreement with Bean's finding (1976) that showed teachers initiating more contacts with men students than with women students and with Dweck and Reppucci (1973) who suggest that math teachers provide more feedback to men.

Teacher Questionnaire

To see whether teachers perceived differences in the behavior of women and men students and to see whether we could detect any sex bias on the part of teachers, we arranged the 22 geometry classes into nine categories. These categories of classrooms were based upon the percentage of women continuing from geometry into advanced math classes, ranging from 45% to 100%.

The nine geometry teachers who had 89% or more of their women students enrolled in advanced math classes reported that more women than men requested advice about continuing in math studies and that the women students' parents met more often with the teachers. The four teachers with fewer than 65% women continuing in mathematics reported that men requested such advice more often than women, and that the parents of men met more often with the teachers than did the parents of women students.

All 22 teachers felt that men and women were equally good at mathematics and that men and women did not differ in spatial ability. Most of the teachers tended to feel that family, college, or career plans had about equal influence on women's and men's decisions to take advanced mathematics.

Hypothesis #4 is thus confirmed in part by the observation data. Overall, men students are treated somewhat differently than are women students in geometry classes, though the differences were not statistically significant, and they did not relate to the enrollment of women in advanced math classes. As stated in the discussion of Hypothesis #3, women were more likely to enroll in classes where the instruction provided was actively interactive regardless of whether the interaction was with men or women.

The responses of teachers on the questionnaires did not indicate any teacher bias. They reported women to be equally as good at mathematics as were men and that women should be prepared in the same way as men for colleges and careers. This conclusion is different from Ernest's finding (1976) that 41% of math teachers felt that men did better than women, whereas none felt women did better than men.

Hypothesis #5: School Program and Counselor Advice

Hypothesis #5 states that schools in which women students are exposed to math-related programs or career education programs will have a higher enrollment of women in math classes than will schools without such intervention. To study this question we interviewed school administrators and career education personnel. Counselor questionnaires also provided information about the influence of the school environment.

All schools in our sample had some sort of career education program for their students. The degree of formality of this program varied from school to school, and primarily between urban and suburban schools. In most of the urban schools (three of the four in our sample), career education seemed to be given low priority. Career centers were given a small amount of space and were run by a technician or a counselor who also had numerous other responsibilities within the school. Those in charge of the career education programs reported that communication from the administration and the math department to the career centers is generally limited. Only one urban school reported an active recruitment for their math program. This program receives support from the business community and students are exposed to a wide range of math-related career options. The program does not necessarily encourage women to enroll in math any more than it does men, but this is the school with the highest enrollment of women students in advanced math courses.

In the suburban schools, the picture is somewhat different. Career planning was seen as more important; there was only one suburban school in our sample that stressed college attendence per se over career planning. Career planning in the suburban schools seems to receive more space, a full-time counselor, and better communication with the administration and the math department. However, none of the suburban schools reported active recruitment of women into the math program; nor did they report having programs to encourage women to increase the range of their career choices.

Because there were so few active career education or math programs in our sample of schools, we cannot confirm the hypothesis that relates high involvement of women in advanced mathematics to school career programs—except in one school. The reason for the higher involvement of women in this urban school may be that these young women, having entered the math program, continue taking mathematics because they do not have the mother role model suburban women have. In suburbia, mothers are likely to have college degrees in liberal arts or social sciences, and if young suburban women follow their mother's model, they do not need advanced mathematics. The young urban woman achieving well in mathematics can aspire to be a doctor, an architect, or physicist because she may be the first in her family to go to college—she creates her own model.

Fifty-three counselor questionnaires were returned. None of the counselors reported giving different career plan advice to men than to women. They reported that overall women sought more advice than men. They felt that previous grades in mathematics and the advice of math teachers and parents influenced men and women students the most in making decisions to continue in math studies.

The findings from the counselor questionnaires are different from those reported by Casserly (1975) and Luchins (1976). These researchers reported that some counselors admitted discouraging women students from taking advanced math courses. The counselors in our study made no such admissions. It may be that counselors' stereotyped attitudes are decreasing toward the end of this decade.

IMPLICATIONS AND RECOMMENDATIONS

Our findings indicate that the most important factors influencing women's decisions to enroll in advanced math classes are parents' encouragement and support, students' successful experiences in math classes, spatial ability, and career plans.

These data suggest that parents should be informed of the importance of their influence upon students' career choices and decisions to take advanced mathematics. This finding is somewhat surprising in that secondary students tend to try to establish their own values and life styles and many verbally reject parental influence. Nonetheless, at some crucial level parents do affect student decisions through their support and recognition that math studies are important to mental development and as an entrance to some careers.

Students' spatial ability correlated with math achievement. Women students with higher spatial ability and math achievement tended to be the ones who continued in math studies. The students who said they are good at mathematics are the same ones who tended to score high on the space relationships and math achievement tests. This relationship was similar for men and women, although men scored slightly higher than women on the space relationships test.

Teachers were found to interact somewhat more often with men students than with women students. However, this fact did not seem to influence women's decisions regarding enrollment in advanced mathematics. The classroom processes that did relate to re-enrollment concerned an active instructional involvement of teachers with students, whether they were men or women. The continuation of math studies was lowest in the classrooms in which the most disciplining occurred and in which there were more written assignments and less instruction. This finding suggests that teachers should be actively involved with students, providing instruction, questions, and feedback.

The study findings also suggest that the counseling programs and career education programs offered at these 11 schools have little influence on women's decisions to enroll in advanced math classes. Because the women taking geometry in this study appear to have already formulated their career plans, it seems that junior high schools as well as high schools should provide career education programs that expose young women to a wide range of career options. Women may too quickly choose sex-stereotyped careers if such exposure does not occur.

In one school, where women and men students are given many opportunities to see what it means to be a physicist, architect, or engineer through a math, engineering, and science association, a high percentage of women are enrolled in advanced math classes. This is the only elaborate school program, and it appears to have an effect on student enrollment in advanced mathematics. This small urban school has a greater percentage of men and women students enrolled in advanced mathematics than do the other 10 high schools in this sample.

In conclusion, this study provides evidence that enrollment in advanced math classes is related to certain student abilities. Although parents can be encouraged to support their children to take advanced mathematics and school career education programs can expose young women to a wider range of career choices, spatial ability may be sex-linked and not so amenable to change. However, the differences in the test scores of men and women were slight, and the important idea here is to make able women and men students aware of their own potential and more aware of the career doors that are open to those who achieve in advanced mathematics.

These findings should be made available to in-service secondary teachers, school counselors, and parent groups. Each of these groups can be influential, especially at the junior high school level, in encouraging young women to consider careers in math and science. Young women should be encouraged to include advanced math when they plan their high school curricula. In addition, instructors in schools of education should make pre-service teachers aware of their responsibility to be supportive of young women to select a school curricula that will permit careers in math and science.

ACKNOWLEDGMENT

This research was supported by NIE Grant No. NIE-G-78-0024 to SRI International.

Factors Related to Young Women's Persistence and Achievement in Advanced Placement Mathematics

Patricia L. Casserly and Donald Rock
Educational Testing Service

Introduction

There have long been many barriers to sexual equality of opportunity in the worlds of both work and academe. Legislation has removed some. Others have fallen before society's gradually increasing awareness of the personal and societal costs of sex-stereotyped expectations and opportunities. Yet the potential gains from these changes are still only partially realized because many young women, and those who counsel them, fail to recognize the need for equality of *preparation*.

Because mathematics is the "critical filter" to entrance and advancement in an increasing number of academic and professional fields the project at hand was designed to study factors within secondary schools that tend to affect young women's enrollment, perseverance, and achievement in extensive programs in mathematics. Identifying and publicizing the factors that tend to keep young women from pursuing rigorous mathematics programs in upper secondary school will permit educators to eliminate these barriers. Conversely, those strategies and tactics found positively related to young women's continued work in these areas can then be deliberately encouraged by schools and school systems, thus assuring considerably more college-bound young women a mathematics background that will assist them in pursuing almost *any* field of further education they may later wish to choose.

The College Board's Advanced Placement (AP) Program, with its definitions and measures of *first-year college studies done in school,* provides clear and practical examples of such "extensive" programs in mathematics, among other fields. Repeated studies, both at the Educational Testing Service (ETS) and at participating colleges, have shown that qualified candidates: (a) outperform, in advanced courses, otherwise similar students who, without advanced placement in high school, completed their first-year college work at college; and (b) have a higher tendency to persist in their fields of advanced placement study than do college freshmen in similar introductory courses.

In 1979, the national ratio of females to males taking the AP mathematics examination was one to two. Yet in some schools the ratio of females to males taking the AP mathematics examinations approached or mirrored population ratios of the sexes. What accounts for this phenomenon? An initial study (Casserly, 1975), made possible by grants from the National Science Foundation and the College Board, investigated some of the factors that influenced young women to pursue AP programs in mathematics and science. Its conclusions were as follows:

1. AP courses in mathematics, chemistry, and physics provide young women with an excellent curricular stimulus and preparation toward professional careers in these and related fields.

2. AP teachers in mathematics, chemistry, and physics are excellent agents for recruiting girls to these fields for study and later careers.

3. Much effective college and career counseling takes place in AP classes. Often AP teachers are the only good source within the school of specific information about the financial, academic, and professional opportunities now open to young women in these fields.

4. Many guidance counselors are poor sources of encouragement for girls interested in mathematics and the physical sciences.

5. Older girls are often credited by current AP girls as having encouraged their interest in science and mathematics and supported their determination to continue in the field.

The focus of that study was both broader and narrower than the one at hand. It was broader in that it was concerned not only with young women's participation in high-level mathematics but with their participation in AP chemistry and physics as well. The study was narrower in the following ways:

1. It was of 1 year's duration, with no opportunity to follow up the young women in their later education or to learn why some who had done well in AP courses chose not to take the AP examination.

2. We concentrated on AP classes only, not on females before they enrolled in these classes.

3. We interviewed only young women in these classes, and not young men. So we knew only how females perceived the attitudes of their male peers, but not whether their perceptions were valid.

The present study expands the work of the initial study and fills in some of the obvious gaps in the knowledge and insights that it produced.

Two recent studies by Haven (1972) and Fennema (1974a) have sought to answer the "Why?" of women's lack of persistence and achievement in mathematics by looking at both cognitive and affective variables. Haven (1972), identifying the characteristics of girls, teachers, schools, and communities that are associated with the selection of advanced mathematics courses in high school, found that the two most significant variables were: (a) perception of the usefulness of mathematics studied in high school to future studies and occupations; and (b) interest in natural sciences as opposed to social studies. Other significant variables were encouragement to take advanced mathematics courses by mother, father, guidance counselor, members of the mathematics department, or peers.

Fennema (1977) identified two affective variables that appeared crucial in explaining sex-related differences in mathematics study in primary and secondary schools. They are the tendency of females to stereotype mathematics as a male domain and their anxiety in learning mathematics. She also found sex-related differences in other affective variables such as achievement motivation in mathematics and perceived usefulness of mathematics in careers. Others, including Hilton and Berglund (1974) and Fox (1975c), found significant sex differences in the perceived usefulness of mathematics; Sherman and Fennema (1977) had similar results.

In the area of attitudes, Fennema (1974a) observed that girls' self-concepts tend to decrease with age, and that even when girls are achieving better than boys in mathematics, they tend to rank themselves lower in ability. Casserly (1975) and Fox (1975, 1976a, b) both observed that special programs and advanced courses are likely to be most beneficial to young women if a sufficient number of women enroll.

PROCEDURE

Design Overview

In this study we chose to observe, in depth and over time, a small number of schools and selected students in them, in order to gain a better understanding of how certain specific school-related factors serve to encourage able young women to persist and achieve in mathematics. Within eight high schools, we studied the females (and their male peers) in "5 year" Advanced Placement calculus programs because: (a) such an interscholastic, national criterion assured the study useful similarities among the students and the variables at hand; (b) females in 5 year mathematics programs were most likely to be those with interests and gifts related to the field; and (c) schools with such 5 year mathematics programs were most likely to have deliberately organized strategies and tactics to observe.

The School Sample

The eight schools included in the sample were chosen in the following manner:

1. Schools presenting at least 20 AP mathematics candidates in 1977 were identified by ETS in a statistical summary that also yielded the ratio of females to males who wrote examinations from each school. Letters to these 160 schools asked for the sex distribution of enrollment in AP mathematics classes during the current and previous 2 years and the ethnic, racial, and socioeconomic (SES) composition of each school.

Of the 145 schools that responded to the initial letter, 142 agreed to participate, if invited, in the study. Only public and parochial schools with a consistent record of comparatively large numbers of females in AP calculus classes in the immediate past were considered.

2. Each of the remaining schools was then assigned to one of four categories:

  a. High participation (approaching 50%) by females in AP mathematics classes and high proportion of females taking the AP examination.
  b. High participation by females in AP mathematics classes but low proportion of females taking the AP examination.
  c. Average (according to national AP norms for coeducational schools) female participation in AP mathematics classes but high proportion of those females enrolled taking the AP examination.
  d. Average female participation in AP mathematics classes and average or low proportion of females taking the AP examination.

3. Two schools were then picked from each of the four cells and asked to participate in the study. We tried to pick in each cell at least one school that was relatively heterogeneous in racial composition and/or socioeconomic status of the student body. We also tried for the widest possible cultural and geographic distribution. (Unfortunately, although three of the chosen schools had significant numbers of blacks enrolled, very few black students were on the accelerated mathematics track at any time in their school careers.)

In doing this, we realized that we were deliberately limiting the sorts of data analysis that could be done. But we believed it more important to investigate the variables in question over a broad variety of schools and students for the sake of maximally valid generalizations than to settle for a more "reliable" set of findings based on a more homogeneous set of schools. The schools that ultimately participated in the study are listed alphabetically below.

Burnt Hills-Ballston Lake Central
  Schools
Burnt Hills, NY 12027

Cardinal Spellman High School
  Bronx, NY 10466

John Marshall High School
  Cleveland, OH 44111

McKinley High School
Honolulu, HA

Newton North High School
  Newtonville, MA 02160

Pittsfield High School
Pittsfield, MA

Skyline High School
Salt Lake City, UT 84109

South Eugene High School
Eugene, OR 97401

In fact the schools turned out to be more similar than we had expected during the years of the study, so we could not contrast the various cells as we had expected. (In only one school did girls fail to continue with mathematics or decide not to take the AP examination for non-academic reasons. In the other seven schools those few girls and boys who chose not to continue or not to take the AP calculus examination did so after sound consideration and agreement with their mathematics teachers.)

The Schedule

During the first year of the study each of the eight schools was visited for a 3- to 4½-day period. During that time an extensive questionnaire was administered to all tenth-grade students in honors mathematics sequences and to the students (eleventh and twelfth graders) in AP calculus classes. At least five females from each AP class, chosen at random from class rolls, were interviewed individually, their questionnaire responses serving as a basis for the discussion. Additional young women were also interviewed to supplement, clarify, and expand some of the themes that developed. These interviews often took place in groups of two to five students.

TABLE 9.1
1978 Interviews by School

| | School | | | | | | | | |
	1	2	3	4	5	6	7	8	Total
AP girls chosen at random	5	5	5	5	5	5	5	5	40
Additional AP students	8	12	7	7	6	13	10	5	64
Teachers	6	5	6	4	7	8	12	7	49
Counselors	3	1	1	2	1	1	2	1	12
Other adults in school	2	1	2	1	1	2	2	2	13
Middle schools	2	2	2	2	0^a	2	0^b	0^b	12

[a] Little articulation between levels in this system; students come from scores of feeder schools.

[b] Blizzard and school closing made visits to middle schools impossible.

At least two mathematics teachers (the AP teacher and the teacher of the accelerated tenth-grade mathematics course) and one guidance counselor were also interviewed at some length. In most schools we talked with all members of the mathematics department and took advantage of the invitation to sit in on classes. We also visited the major middle schools from which the senior high schools draw, and we interviewed the teachers of algebra, and/or the head of the mathematics department and a counselor concerned with mathematics placement. A summary of the high school interviews is given in Table 9.1.

The following activities were accomplished during the second year:

1. In early spring, a roster was sent to each school to collect data on all of the students in the original tenth-grade sample. Data requested included tenth-grade mathematics grades, subsequent mathematics courses, and the mathematics course the students were intending to enter in the fall of 1979.

2. All teachers in the mathematics department were surveyed about their professional training and experience.

3. We revisited the schools for 1–3 days after the rosters were completed, intending to interview at least three young women in each of four categories: those intending to enter the AP calculus course; those taking another twelfth-grade mathematics course; those who had persisted in their study of mathematics through eleventh grade, but were not planning to take mathematics in the twelfth grade; and those who had dropped from the advanced mathematics track (or from mathematics entirely) after the tenth grade. But there were not enough young women in the latter three categories to permit us to follow that plan. It also seemed appropriate to interview males in the latter three categories. Males proved anxious to participate in the study, and their teachers were anxious to have them

TABLE 9.2
Number of Student Interviews: Year 2

Category of Student	Sex of Student	
	F	M
AP mathematics in twelfth grade	28	11
Another math course in twelfth grade	23	15
No math after eleventh grade	18	11
No math after tenth grade	8	3
Total by Sex	77	40
Grand Total	117	

do so. A summary of the numbers of male and female student interviews conducted during the second year is given in Table 9.2.

4. We also followed up, by means of a mailed questionnaire, those students, both male and female, who had been in AP calculus classes during the first year of the study. Most of these students were now in college. The numbers and percentages responding are given in Table 9.3.

The Instruments

In the first year a student questionnaire and three interview schedules were used to collect data for the study. The questionnaire was used to survey students in tenth-grade accelerated and AP mathematics classes during 1978. It was administered to a total of 360 tenth graders and 301 AP calculus students. The questionnaire was designed to elicit four types of information: first, questions on family background, number and sex of siblings, subject's placement in the family, SES characteristics, and sources of emotional support for the student's aspirations from family, peers, and others in and outside of school; second, the student's school history, including perceived attitudes of teachers and counselors, participation in and preference for various school-related activities, and perceptions about mathematics (both retrospective and concurrent). The third part contained 25 Likert-type items on perceptions about mathematics,

TABLE 9.3
Mailed Questionnaire to Graduates: Year 2

	Sex of Student	
	F	M
Number of questionnaires mailed	137	164
Number returned	98	104
Percent returned	72	63
Number included in data analysis	94	96

"proper or desirable" adult roles for men and women, and items that we hoped would relate to self-esteem and confidence. The fourth part of the questionnaire asked the student to write a description of how he or she envisioned how this same day would be 10 years hence in as much detail as possible. The questionnaire was also useful in identifying appropriate teachers and counselors for interviews, in addition to those teachers regularly assigned to AP math students, and thus allowed us to supplement the regular, structured interviews (common to all schools) with whatever special studies proved appropriate.

Interviews were held with teachers and with counselors during the first year of the study, focusing on perceptions of each school's mathematics program, counseling activities, and general social and academic "climate." Teachers and counselors were also asked about their personal mathematics histories, their perceptions of expanding opportunities for women, and their feelings concerning acceptable life styles for women today. A separate interview schedule was used with middle or junior high school personnel. It covered the same areas outlined above, but also dealt specifically with articulation of the mathematics curriculum between the middle and senior high school.

Student interviews and questionnaires were used in the second year. The interview schedule was designed for the former tenth-grade accelerated students (now near the end of the eleventh grade) and concentrated on their experiences in mathematics during the intervening year and other factors that had either strengthened or modified their immediate curricular choices (for the twelfth grade) or their more general long-range goals. The questionnaire, used to survey all former AP calculus students during the second year, concentrated on their perception of the articulation between high school and college work and on the appropriateness to their college careers of their AP calculus course and the colleges' action in regard to it.

Results and Discussion

This report will focus: (a) on short statements about the hypotheses that shaped the study; (b) on a selected number of findings that are particularly important for educational practice; and (c) on a path-analytic solution of the relative effects of peers and adults, in and out of school, on students' persistence and achievement in mathematics. Although a number of the response differences of the females and males are statistically significant, we feel there is social significance in the fact that the distributions resemble each other more than we had expected.

The following hypotheses guided the collection and analysis of data:

1. Young women in AP and other fifth-year math classes where their

proportion approaches or equals that of males will have been identified as having high mathematics ability early and put into an accelerated or enriched, homogeneously grouped mathematics program at that time.

2. AP young women took algebra I in the eighth grade almost as a matter of course; their opportunity to opt out of fast-track mathematics went unnoticed.

3. These young women will report efforts of AP mathematics teachers or their surrogates in early senior high school to inform them of the AP program and the advantages it would provide them among their senior-year electives.

4. They will have discussed with an AP teacher their plans for college, their probable major, and their possible choice of career.

5. For these females, the sex of the AP teacher and other significant teachers is less important than other characteristics. They see their AP mathematics teachers as nonsexist, positive reinforcers of their aspirations, however nontraditional these aspirations may be.

6. When young women in these advanced classes report that their male classmates are traditionally sexist in their attitudes toward the "proper" interests and careers for women, they will also report strategies for dealing with the perceived sexism.

7. Young women's appraisals of the mathematics ability of the other females in the class will be similar to their appraisals of the males' ability.

8. The young women's confidence in their own mathematical abilities will be directly proportional to the proportion of females in the AP mathematics class.

Hypothesis 1, that there would be a positive relationship between "persistence" (in the AP or fifth-year mathematics course) and early (starting in grades 4 or 5) homogeneous grouping in mathematics courses was based on an earlier study (Casserly, 1975). In the present study such grouping was common, but had not occurred as early as expected. The mean initial year of acceleration for both sexes was sixth grade, with a range of grades 1–10 for males and 1–12 for females. All the schools allow entry to the accelerated track by "late bloomers" who have high motivation by offering special courses that compress 2 years of mathematics into one, or by offering summer courses specifically for acceleration rather than remediation. Indeed, in these schools persistence in mathematics is high among students of all ability levels; 60% to 75% of all twelfth graders were enrolled in mathematics.

The second hypothesis (that most AP females, along with males, took algebra I in eighth grade as a matter of course) holds true, even though for approximately a fifth of the sample, eighth grade was the first year that their mathematics curriculum (algebra I) was clearly differentiated from "regular" mathematics. Earlier achievements, enriched courses, and teacher counseling led girls as well as boys to assume this acceleration to be part of a natural sequence. Young AP women reported, "We were already 'primed' toward challenges."

In or by ninth grade, all students in the participating schools had been informed about the requirements and advantages of the mathematics sequence leading to AP calculus in grade 12 (as well as other less demanding mathematics tracks). Seven of the eight schools provided extensive descriptions of curricular offerings in students' handbooks, supplemented by teachers' discussions. Frequently teachers used more advanced students, as well as returning graduates, to "recruit" younger students to the more demanding curriculum. (This practice confirms hypothesis three.)

Hypotheses four and five have to do with the AP or advanced teachers' interactions with students, both as sources of information on the importance of mathematics in college and careers and as champions of their students' aspirations in whatever direction they might lie. Data from the previous study suggested that often AP teachers (not necessarily the AP mathematics teachers) were the only persons in the school who supported a girl's dreams and tried to raise her aspirations. Counselors also were important, but frequently only in grade 12—too late to encourage girls to make the curricular choices that would enhance their opportunities for reaching their desired goals.

The questionnaires and interviews confirm the importance of AP and other mathematics teachers as counselors and mentors (distinct from role models) in their students' lives. When students who continue mathematics in college look back at high school, the AP mathematics teacher stands out as exemplary, even in comparison to college teachers. But while students are still in school, 55% of the girls and 47% of the boys also identify teachers encountered in much earlier school years (usually in grades 4 through 7) as being crucial, first to their sense of self-worth, then to their persistence in mathematics, and to their initial career aspirations. While visiting these close-knit departments, we were similarly impressed by the teachers' active, caring conversations about their former students.

Equal but smaller percentages of girls and boys (11%) reported experiences that tended to depress either their confidence in their mathematical ability or their interest in the subject before high school. Both females and males tended to regard discouragement as a challenge to be overcome by extra effort. However, males somewhat more than females tended to externalize, blaming the teacher for their difficulties, whereas females tended to internalize their difficulties, perceiving teachers as champions of persistence and allies in overcoming problems and attendant anxieties.

Hypothesis six focuses on strategies we had seen in the previous study adopted for dealing with the perceived sexism of peers. In the present study, we again found humor employed to this end, but the need for such a strategy in all but two of the schools seemed relatively slight. The feminist movement is seen generally as less strident than it was in 1975, and the necessity for a two-income family (at least to "get started") is more apparent than it was a few years ago. A third explanation may be offered, in some way perhaps a function of the other two: the ratio of females to males was higher in these classrooms than in the Casserly (1975) study, and hence the tendency toward defensiveness had diminished. For instance, young women in the present study apparently no longer needed to date outside the AP math class.

Hypotheses seven and eight deal with attitudes and perceptions of "girls" versus "boys" and "self" versus "others" with regard to specific mathematical ability. In only two schools were there statistically significant sex differences between the perceived mathematical ability of the students themselves and those of others of the same or other sex. These schools also had among the lowest ratios of females to males in AP calculus classes and ranked highest in sexually stereotyped behavior. There were no statistically significant differences in the relationship between students' grades in mathematics (or English) and their self-perceived abilities. This outcome is contrary to the findings of Fennema and others.

Broader Implications

> We're doing something good? That's nice to hear, but I don't think we're doing anything special.

> Well, we've always had a good strong math department. We're anxious to keep all students [in the mathematics curriculum]—not girls in particular. . . . But not boys in particular either.

> Girls are as able as boys and they need math just as much. Why wouldn't they be represented equally [in math honors courses]?

These quotations are typical opening responses of adults in the participating schools to the initial, and the central, question of this study: Why do so many girls continue through the honors mathematics sequence in this school? The hypotheses identified some factors we expected to find. And we did find common features across the heterogeneous schools in the study, but not always the ones we expected. Also, in a few schools, there were some elements that had clearly hindered a number of highly able young women.

The entire project was, after all, an attempt to answer a number of different questions related to a common central point: What makes a mathematics department or a curriculum strong? More particularly, what makes it "successful" with young women; that is, why are they persistent? One teacher explained:

> Well, we're not talking about curriculum at all in the strict sense of the word. We're not talking about textbooks. We're talking about school climate, teachers' professional backgrounds and interests, and how much and how well they relate to students and to each other. To what other teachers are doing. Articulation throughout the system is important.

Mathematics Teachers—What Are They Like?

Of the 75 teachers in the eight mathematics departments of the study, 53 had undergraduate degreees in "pure" math. The others held undergraduate degrees in physics, biology, engineering, electronics, chemistry, or business. Only six had undergraduate degrees in education. Fifty-seven of the teachers held masters degrees, of which only 19 were given by graduate departments of education; four of these 19 degrees were M.S.'s, or the teacher held an M.S. in addition to the masters in education. Five additional teachers held MAT's; one held a graduate degree in engineering; two held the Ph.D.; and two, the Ed.D. Although most of the degrees were in mathematics, computer science, or mathematics education, there was a broad range of fields of graduate study, extending from psychology and counseling to history, art, and Russian.

Almost half held or had held jobs in addition to teaching. About half of these were simply second jobs to supplement income. But the rest had or had had other deliberate, professional careers in research and development, engineering, electronics, community development (Peace Corps), surveying, stockbrokering, computer analysis, coaching, and even music. To almost all of the teachers in these schools, teaching mathematics represented a rewarding, positive career, not a refuge from the "real" world. A number of them were helping elementary teachers upgrade their mathematical skills—and therewith their sense of why high school mathematics is integral to young people's education. Students in every school remarked that such teachers' experience in the "real" world made a positive difference in the way they (the students) felt about the relationship between classroom learning and everyday life. Two or three such teachers in a school are enough to make the difference.

In five of the schools, most math teachers and mathematics department heads were men; in the other three, women were in the majority or headed the department. In three of the eight schools, the AP mathematics teachers were men; but in each of the other five, the AP mathematics teacher was a woman, or a woman taught the more advanced AP mathematics course.[1] In three of these five schools the same AP women teachers taught either the tenth- or eleventh-grade accelerated mathematics course and reported special efforts to encourage able young women who might be wavering to persist. The teachers were hesitant to say that the presence of women teachers in higher level mathematics courses was related to young women's success in mathematics. However, for many of those young women who had had or were having difficulty in mathematics, it seemed an important factor in their not giving up.

Said one young woman of her vivacious calculus BC teacher:

> It's not that she's a woman; it's the kind of woman, the kind of person she is
> . . . Do you know she had trouble in math once, too? I suppose it's a case of
> 'if she could do it, maybe I can, too.'

It became clear at all the schools in the study that the gender of the teacher per se was not enough to affect young women's persistence positively, but that gender and certain kinds of shared experiences could.

Like most people, teachers are rather cautious when asked to discuss the personal attitudes and experiences they bring to the classroom, but they are not shy about commenting on the strengths (and, occasionally the perceived deficiencies) of others. With three rather glaring exceptions, teachers perceived each other and were perceived by the students as expecting the same level of performance from females as from males, welcoming increased opportunities in the society for women, and encouraging able young women to aim high and consider the same array of careers as young men do.

But even more important to many young women (and fewer young men) was that teachers, "rigorous but never harsh," communicated the intrinsic beauty of mathematics. Moreover, a fourth of the teachers who had encountered difficulties at certain stages in their own development as mathematicians shared their remembered perplexity and frustration with their students. These teachers were careful to point out that if one goes far enough in the field, one is bound to be baffled by concepts one needs or wants to know, and that the accompanying anxiousness is a healthy response to frustration, one which can be mobilized to facilitate learning and overcome obstacles. This "math anxiousness" was not allowed to disintegrate into debilitating loss of self-esteem, nor was it magnified and distorted into a crippling, pathological affliction.

Each of these teachers employed a variety of teaching styles but also overtly recognized that "in a class of 25 there were apt to be 25 learning

---

[1]There are two AP calculus courses. Calculus AB covers a semester of precalculus and one semester of calculus. Calculus BC covers 2 semesters of calculus.

styles." So they encouraged students to help each other. Many also provided opportunities for their students to tutor younger or less advanced students. Girls took advantage of these opportunities far more frequently than boys. "Which is good?" one teacher remarked. "Girls more than boys need to put their own struggles in perspective."

These teachers had created a fostering climate for mathematics in their schools that was actually palpable: Mathematics resource centers were large, comfortable and *full*. Teachers were always available to consult with any student who needed help, and students felt free to work with teachers currently not their own. Teachers spent a good deal of time talking among themselves about students who were having problems with particular concepts, developing strategies to help these students over the hurdles. It was clear that students were passed on from teacher to teacher as individuals with particular strengths and/or weaknesses in mathematics and with particular interests and goals, with each remaining a collective, departmental responsibility.

Just as the teachers knew where their students' various abilities might lead them, so too they knew to put mathematics in a full array of contexts for all their students. Its innate beauty, its connections with artistic and aesthetic endeavors, as well as its utility in a broad array of other fields, were all brought into the classroom. This strategy was particularly beneficial to girls. For in this study girls were found to have a greater variety of reasons for and satisfactions from studying mathematics than did boys. They also seem to have broader or less channeled interests.

These mathematics teachers felt that, while girls certainly need to be as aware as boys of the utility of mathematics in other fields, to emphasize only its utility is to sell short both the students and the field.

We deliberately dwell on the teachers' backgrounds and techniques because to the students, it is these teachers and their classes that constitute the visible learning environment of the school. Paradoxically enough, this fact becomes even clearer to the students once they've left, and find themselves, at college, with teachers whose backgrounds and techniques are often very different from those they knew at school.

Path Analyses

This section supplements the previous discussion with an analysis based on a hypothetical causal model. The unique values of this sort of causal analysis are these: (a) it is a multivariate approach that controls for other possible influences on a dependent variable, thus yielding the "net" apparent influence of any given variable on another; and (b) it provides a way to estimate the indirect effect of a prior or (apparently) causal variable on another variable two or more steps down the hypothetical causal chain.

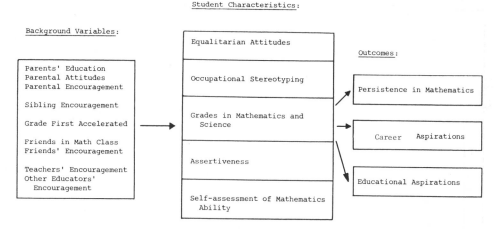

FIG. 9.1   The general causal model.

Figure 9.1 presents the traditional pictorial representation of our general causal model. This model was formulated prior to data collection to represent the relationship of variables assumed on a conceptual basis to underlie the development of young men and women in accelerated mathematics programs.

Figure 9.2 is an example of the type of diagram that can be drawn after data collection to represent the relationships that were found. Figure 9.2 presents the path analysis results for AP women (n = 134). Similar analyses were carried out for AP men and for both men and women in the 10th grade accelerated math. Because of space limitations only the diagram for AP women is presented. Here arrows are accompanied by standardized partial regression coefficients[2] (path coefficients) that indicate the relative importance of the variable at the tail of the arrow as a possible cause of the variable at the head.

The reader should note that path models are primarily generated on theoretical and/or logical grounds and thus may or may not accurately reflect the "true" cause; they do, however, provide an orderly means of presenting and statistically testing the reasonableness of a given explanation of complex behavior. We will take each of the "effects" boxes as shown on Fig. 9.1 and discuss its "causes" from our analyses. When we discuss the hypothesized effect of one variable on another the associated path coefficient will be shown in parenthesis.

---

[2]The authors recognize that comparisons of the relative size of standardized regression coefficients across populations may lead to incorrect interpretations unless the raw score coefficients reflect the same population differences. Therefore, in this study, we will only draw conclusions about a given differential effect across populations if the raw score weight was consistent with the standardized weight.

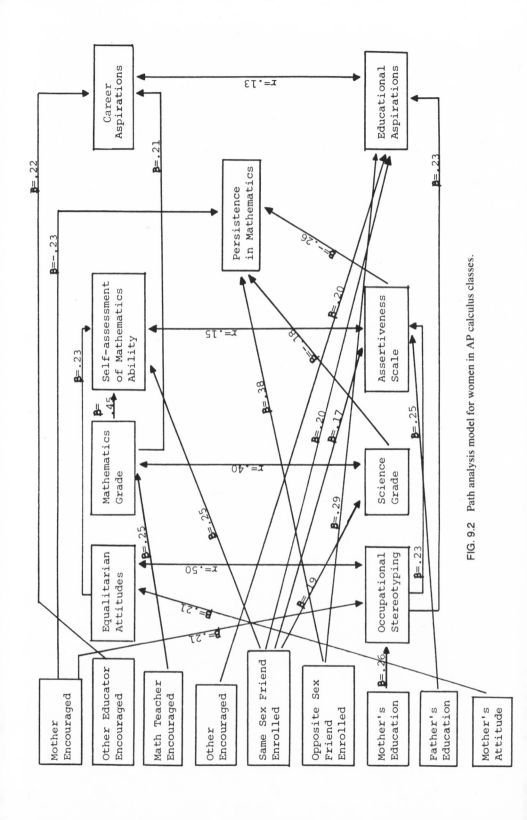

FIG. 9.2 Path analysis model for women in AP calculus classes.

Equalitarian Attitudes and Occupational Stereotyping. These scales are closely related to each other in what they measure, both conceptually and statistically (correlation coefficients ranging from .49 to .62) for tenth grade AP women and men. Equalitarian attitudes are those that permit flexibility in the personal relationships of adult men and women to each other and to offspring. Subjects who rate low on this scale believe in more rigid traditional roles of men and women within the family. Occupational stereotyping indicates the degree to which various occupations and positions within business and professional hierarchies are perceived as being more appropriate for one sex or the other.

These two scales resulted from a factor analysis of the twenty-five Likert scale items dealing with attitudes towards men's and women's roles in society. A third factor emerged which was called an assertiveness scale which had to do with one's behavior in front of one's peers.

The final selection of variables to be included in the path analytic models was primarily based on logical considerations with some data reduction help from factor analysis as described above. The posing of logical models based on theoretical notions to reduce the number of variables, was considered more likely to minimize type I error (finding significance when it doesn't exist) than an entirely exploratory approach. This is particularly critical when the ratio of variables to sample size is large.

For tenth-grade girls, views about the roles and abilities of men and women were related to the attitudes of their mothers and fathers. Girls tended to have more equalitarian attitudes when their fathers were supportive of their career goals (.18), and were less traditional in occupational stereotyping when their mothers had positive attitudes towards their career goals (.30). Particularly liberal ideals about men's and women's roles (items from both Equalitarian Attitudes and Occupational Stereotyping scales) were also predicted by mother's education (.26 and .19, respectively).

The Equalitarian Attitudes and Occupational Stereotyping of tenth-grade males were not predicted by as many family background variables. In fact, the only variable of any sort that predicted level of sex-role stereotyping was the mother's attitude toward the student's career or occupational goals (.20).

For the twelfth-grade AP women, family variables continued to predict the strength of sex-role stereotyping by their daughters. Mother's attitude was related to daughter's equalitarian attitudes (.21) and lack of traditional occupational stereotyping was predicted by mother's education (.26) and mother's encouragement in math (.21). For young men in the AP classes, friends seemed to be more important than they were earlier in relation to views of men's and women's roles. Young men who had young women friends in the AP class had more equalitarian attitudes than those who had no such friends (.17). Those young men who felt that they received encouragement from peers for participating in advanced mathematics courses tended to be more equalitarian in their attitudes (.17) and less rigid in their occupational stereotyping (.23). Father's education was also related to both stereotyping measures, Equalitarian Attitudes (.25) and Occupational Stereotyping (.18).

Grades in Mathematics and Science. Both male and female tenth graders who performed at a high level in math reported that math teachers gave them encouragement (.17 for each sex). By the twelfth grade, young men's grades were no longer related to encouragement from math teachers, but young women's grades were (.25).

The math grades of the tenth grade males were clearly positively related to their perception of mothers' attitudes toward their career goals (.38). The situation for young women was in marked contrast; there was a negative relation between math grades and mothers' approval of their career goals (− .26). It may be that the more mathematically oriented girls were encountering less enthusiasm from their mothers about their career plans than girls who were inclined toward more traditionally feminine occupations.

For tenth graders, the presence of close friends in the accelerated math classes appeared to affect grades. For boys, same sex friends were a positive influence (.22), whereas for girls it was the presence of an opposite sex friend that related to higher grades (.25). Though the presence of friends in twelfth grade accelerated math classes continued to influence self-assessment in math and persistence in taking math courses, it seemed no longer important in affecting grades.

Self-Assessment of Math Ability. In both tenth and twelfth grades, students' self-assessment of their math ability was affected by their grades in mathematics courses to a large degree, an effect far larger than that of any other variable. The importance of math grades in determining self-ratings was somewhat lower for twelfth grades, though grades were still by far the more influential single variable (.54 for males and .45 for females, as compared to .64 and .65 for tenth graders). These young women in AP courses appear to be realistic in their self-assessments of mathematical ability.

For young men, several family and peer variables also predicted math self-concept. Self-ratings in math were higher for tenth-grade males perceiving themselves as getting encouragement from their fathers (.13) and reporting favorable paternal attitudes toward their career goals (.22). By the time they reached twelfth grade, young men's perceptions of their father's support were no longer related to self-assessment in math. At this grade level, the enrollment of a same sex friend in the AP class was positively related to math grades (.21).

For girls, neither family nor peer variables affected mathematics self-concept at the tenth-grade level, but by the twelfth grade the presence of a same sex friend in the AP class had a significantly positive effect (.25), as it did with males.

Assertiveness. This variable, which was constituted of items having to do with the willingness to speak up and reveal one's intelligence in and out of class, was related to fathers' supportive attitudes towards occupational goals both for young men (.24) and for young women (.22) at the tenth-grade level. Assertiveness was also influenced by equalitarian attitudes and lack of heavy occupational stereotyping. Tenth-grade males were higher in assertiveness when they held more equalitarian attitudes (.23). Likewise, the more assertive young women were high in equalitarian attitudes (.17) and held less tradition-bound occupational stereotypes (.35).

In the twelfth grade the relationship remained between assertiveness and non-stereotyped ideas about men's and women's roles and abilities. For young men as well as young women assertiveness continued to be predicted by low occupational stereotyping (.23 for both sexes). Equalitarian attitudes were also related to assertiveness in twelfth-grade males (.23).

A particularly interesting finding was the negative path coefficient between math grades and assertiveness for female tenth graders (–.18). This result suggests that young women who achieve at a very high level in high school mathematics do not like to call attention to their gifts, whereas young men do not report feeling such hesitation.

Persistence in Mathematics. Those who continue to take math after the tenth-grade level were those who did well in it. Both young men (.27) and young women (.31) with a record of success in mathematics tended to stick with it.

The grade at which the student was first accelerated had a significant impact on persistence in math for tenth-grade girls (.19) but not for boys; this variable did not remain a significant predictor of whether students in twelfth-grade AP classes continued in mathematics the following year when most were in college.

For young men, the encouragement of math teachers was important in the decision to continue taking math both for tenth graders (.27) and twelfth graders (.31). For young women, math teachers' encouragement was influential at the tenth-grade level (.19) but not beyond. What did make a difference in the twelfth-grade females continuing on in math was the presence of an opposite sex friend in the AP math class (.38).

One interesting finding was the *lack* of relationship between young women's self-assessment in math and the decision to continue taking it. This variable played a role in persistence in math for tenth-grade males (.21); it was not measurably important for young women at any point.

Career Aspirations. Math teacher's encouragement, which had a positive impact on math performance and on continuing to take math, had little direct effect on math-related career aspirations.

The importance influences early in high school were self-assessment in math ability for the young women (.20) and fathers' attitude (.22) and persistence in math (.24) for the young men. By the time students had reached twelfth grade, their aspirations to go into math-related careers were still predicted by their persistence in taking math, significantly for the young men (.29) and positively but not quite significantly for the young women.

The significant factors for young women were the math grades they had made (.21) and the encouragement of adults in the school other than the math teacher (that is, other teachers, counselors, etc.) (.22). Because the young women were enrolled in a broader range of other AP fields than were their male counterparts in AP calculus, a sex difference in the influence of other adults in the school is not surprising.

Educational Aspirations. Because the educational aspirations referred to the highest level of educational attainment the student planned on reaching (independent of field), it was not highly related to the career aspirations variable ($-.07$ to .15) and was predicted by a different set of variables for the most part.

However, one variable that clearly influenced level of educational aspirations of young women in AP classes (.20) as well as math-relatedness of career goals was the encouragement of adults in the school other than the math teacher. For males there was some indication that fathers' supportiveness had an impact on both aspects of further plans. This factor affected math-related career goals in the tenth grade (.22) and influenced level of educational aspirations in the twelfth grade (.25).

Level of educational aspirations was heavily influenced by peer effects for young men and young women in AP classes. Females were likelier to have higher educational goals when they had friends, both same sex (.20) and opposite sex (.27), in their AP calculus class. For young men the picture was more complicated. Educational aspirations were higher when males had an opposite sex friend enrolled in AP math (.19), but lower when they perceived their peers as encouraging their participation in advanced mathematics ($-.21$).

Young women's educational goals were strongly influenced by their feelings about women's roles in the world. In formulating their ideas about how far they would go educationally, tenth grade women were influenced by their equalitarian attitudes (.40) rather than by their past performance in math or their self-assessment in mathematics ability. Their perception that traditional male occupations are appropriate choices for women was related to their educational goals in the twelfth grade (.23), whereas past performance and self-confidence in math were still unrelated to goals. Clearly, being good at mathematics is not enough to increase women's participation in the highest levels of the educational system unless their attitudes about "proper" roles for adult women are simultaneously liberalized.

SUMMARY

The role of parents was most important in developing early positive attitudes towards women's roles both in male and female students. For young women these attitudes were virtually the only significant effects (within the relationships examined in this study) that parents exerted. For young men there were stronger, more persistent, and focussed links between parental support, on the one hand, and the students' performance, self-assessment, and setting of high educational goals on the other.

It is not clear from the data what factors resulted in this sex difference in the effect of parental support. There might actually have been less support for young women to perform well in math and plan careers based on this ability. Another possibility is that young women were less affected by parental behaviors than by other environmental factors. This is a plausible possibility because for females there is likelier to be dissonance between parents' generalized encouragement and society's specific expectations about women's roles and career options. Still another hypothesis is that young women were working more consistently in accordance with their abilities than were young men: that the performance of males is more likely to be affected by non-intellectual variables.

The effect of peers within the advanced mathematics classes was generally a positive one for both sexes. For young women the presence of friends in advanced classes positively affected math grades, self-concept in mathematics, the decision to continue taking math courses, and the level of educational aspirations.

Performance for both male and female students in advanced math classes was significantly related to encouragement from math teachers. This positive effect continued beyond AP calculus for young women, whereas it became less significant for young men at this level.

Most young women in advanced secondary-school math courses enjoy strong family and teacher support for study in this field. Thus those among them who go on to pursue math-related careers and to seek higher levels of mathematics education generally do so as a result of this general support's being supplemented by specific encouragement from certain others. For it is precisely these others (A.P. teachers of other subjects, adult acquaintances, etc.) who place mathematics in the context of broader collegiate studies and of later life, and, thus, provide a catalytic spark to the kindling laid at home and in the mathematics classes.

By the time they are enrolled in AP calculus, young women make decisions about math-related careers on the basis of previous grades, whereas young men are not significantly influenced by their grades in previous math classes. It seems that for young men being in an AP calculus class is reason enough for them to feel free to plan for any career they wish. (Indeed, grades may be incidental to their career choice.) But for young women to plan on careers heavily dependent on mathematics they must feel very proficient indeed.

Path analyses indicate that family, school personnel, and peers all influence young women's performance and plans in mathematics. The family is primarily important in the early development of liberal attitudes towards women's roles. The math teacher is then in the position to provide specific knowledge, encouragement and motivation for persistence and grade performance. Finally, decisions of whether to opt for math-related careers are based on self-confidence (past math grades) and confirming encouragement from school personnel outside of mathematics.

So what? What have we found? And what is to be done?

What we have found is a range of quite various high schools—serving many different sorts of young people—all of which nevertheless foster persistence and achievement in mathematics equally among young women and young men up through Advanced Placement Calculus. All these schools share certain characteristics which can be deliberately induced by educators elsewhere. The three most important of these are:

- Organized mathematics departments with enough informed and caring teachers who see their subject—for girls and boys—both as a valuable end in itself and as a significant element of other fields.
- Enough teachers of these other fields—and certain rare guidance counselors—with a liberal, non-sexist sense of this pervasive impor-

tance of mathematics in all school studies, as in adult careers and later life in general.

- Enough such teachers—and therewith, to the students, a critical portion of the entire "teaching" school—who translate these personal attitudes and skills into classroom actions designed to encourage and help *all* students learn as much of this elegant, fundamental subject as they possibly can.

ACKNOWLEDGMENT

The research reported in this chapter was supported in part by Grant No. NIE-G-77-0064 from the National Institute of Education.

10 The Impact of Early Intervention Programs Upon Course-Taking and Attitudes in High School

Lynn H. Fox, Linda Brody, and Dianne Tobin
The Johns Hopkins University

Introduction

Concern about sex differences in mathematical achievement has become more acute in recent years as modern technology has made mathematical understanding essential for many of the high-level careers available today. Sells (1980) points out that the avoidance of high school mathematics, not ability, is the critical filter that keeps many females from pursuing mathematically oriented careers. Comprehensive reviews of the literature on sex differences in mathematics prepared for the National Institute of Education (Fennema, 1977; Fox, 1977; Sherman, 1977) support this as well. Girls who do not study mathematics on advanced levels are limiting their course-taking options in college and thus their career options as adults.

Efforts focusing on biological differences between the sexes have not shed light on why many females who do have aptitude and ability in mathematics do not take advanced mathematics or enter mathematically related fields (Ernest, 1980; Fox, 1974a, b; 1975 a, b, c; 1976 a, b, c, d; Haven, 1972; Sells, 1980). Several social and educational explanations for the differences in course-taking behavior have been postulated (Fox, 1977; Fox, Tobin, & Brody, 1979):

1. Girls receive less encouragement than boys from parents, teachers, guidance counselors, and peers to pursue advanced mathematics courses in high school;

2. Girls are less likely than boys to perceive the usefulness of high school mathematics courses to their future goals, perhaps partly because,

249

in adolescence, girls are not encouraged to aspire to and plan for professional careers;

3. Mathematics classes are commonly thought of as male domains and girls in adolescence may avoid them for this reason;

4. Girls have less self-confidence as learners of mathematics than boys.

Whereas it is serious enough that girls with average ability do not study mathematics to the same degree as do their male counterparts, it is even more alarming that girls who are highly able in mathematics and should become high-level mathematical reasoners in the future are not taking mathematics courses at the same rate and level as their male cohorts.

A longitudinal study of mathematically gifted youth initiated in the fall of 1971 by Professor Julian C. Stanley and his project associates Lynn H. Fox and Daniel P. Keating at The Johns Hopkins University provides information about sex differences. The Study of Mathematically Precocious Youth (SMPY) set as its goals the identification, description, and facilitation of highly able students. SMPY used the Scholastic Aptitude Test (SAT), a test intended for use with college bound high school students, to identify seventh grade students with exceptional ability in mathematics. A variety of programs including fast-paced mathematics courses in algebra, geometry, and precalculus were designed to enable students to learn mathematics at a higher level and at a faster rate than the regular mathematics sequence in their schools would permit. Because this was also a research study, batteries of affective and cognitive tests were given to the students identified as high mathematical reasoners in order to study why some students were more able than others to develop their mathematical talent to the fullest. The initial findings of the study have been documented in two books, *Mathematical Talent: Discovery, Description, and Development* (Stanley, Keating, & Fox, 1974) and *Intellectual Talent: Research and Development* (Keating, 1976). In brief, those findings pertinent to this study are as follows:

1. Fewer females than males are eager to accelerate their progress in mathematics; and

2. Special accelerated and enriched classes in mathematics conducted by SMPY at The Johns Hopkins University were highly effective in promoting the successful study of advanced mathematics for boys but not girls in mixed-sex classes where the numbers of girls were small.

Additional studies of high ability girls in Advanced Placement Program (APP) Calculus courses (Casserly, 1980), girls in all-girl schools (Jacobs, 1974), and adult women mathematicians (Helson, 1971; Luchins & Luchins, 1980) suggest that even girls with high potential in mathematics need special encouragement if their talent is to reach fruition. These girls and adults report a variety of things that made a difference for them. Those most often suggested were:

1. Access or exposure to female role models;
2. A "critical mass" or sizable number of females in a program;
3. All-girl classes in mathematics during early adolescence;
4. Early experiences in programs for the gifted;
5. Access to special programs within their schools or school systems as opposed to non-school based programs; and
6. Supportive attitudes of parents and teachers.

RESEARCH DESIGN

This study was designed to assess the impact of three different types of special programs at the junior high school level upon the mathematics course-taking behavior and attitudes of highly able girls. The treatments assessed included: a 1977 summer career awareness class for seventh-grade girls and a 1973 summer accelerated mathematics program for seventh-grade girls at The Johns Hopkins University campus, and four school system-based accelerated mathematics programs for seventh-grade boys and girls held in 1974–75, 1975–76, 1976–77, and 1977–78. (A detailed description of the career awareness class and the accelerated summer class for girls at The Johns Hopkins University can be found in *Women and the Mathematical Mystique* (Fox, Brody, & Tobin, 1980).) Control and comparison groups of highly able boys and girls were selected from SMPY's 1973 and 1978 Talent Searches. Assessment measures included aptitude and achievement tests, the Fennema-Sherman Mathematics Attitude Scale, and a questionnaire.

The analysis included an investigation of the impact of the programs on students' plans to take such courses as precalculus, calculus, chemistry, physics, and computer science in high school. Variables related to students' acceleration in mathematics were also studied as well as the problem of population attrition within the programs. The achievement of the students in the school system based accelerated classes was evaluated for possible sex differences.

Questionnaire responses and the Fennema-Sherman Mathematics Attitude Scales were used to measure attitudes and interests with respect to mathematics, the impact of significant others in relation to mathematics, and plans for future careers and life styles. Comparisons were also made between responses on some of the attitude measures and related factors such as acceleration, career goals, and life style plans.

It was hoped that the analysis of course-taking behavior, acceleration, achievement scores, and attitudinal data would help explain why these highly able girls do or do not continue to study advanced mathematics, as well as which types of intervention programs are most effective in encouraging such girls to continue taking courses in mathematics.

RESULTS

Analysis of Course-taking, Acceleration, and Achievement

The major focus of this study was to investigate course-taking behavior patterns with respect to mathematics, science, and the special programs. The students' plan to take mathematics and science courses in high school, their willingness to accelerate their study of mathematics, and achievement and attrition in the special classes were analyzed and are described in the following sections.

High School Mathematics and Science Courses

The results of the students' responses to the questionnaire item regarding their plans to take precalculus in high school are shown in Table 10.1. The groups with the highest percentage of students planning to take precalculus in high school are the School System boys, School System girls, and the Control boys. In comparing the sexes within groups and groups within each sex, significant differences were found

TABLE 10.1
Distribution in Percents of Students
Planning to Take Precalculus in High School By Group and Sex

Group	Sex	N	Definitely Will	Probably Will	Don't Know	Will Not
School	Boys	158	91.2	7.0	1.9	0.0
System	Girls	68	89.7	5.9	4.4	0.0
Talent	Boys	47	70.2	14.9	14.9	0.0
Search	Girls	44	72.7**	11.4	15.9	0.0
Career Class	Girls	22	77.3	4.5	18.2	0.0
Hopkins' Accel. Class	Girls	22	72.7	0.0	0.0	27.3
Control	Boys	24	95.8	0.0	0.0	4.2
Groups	Girls	24	70.8	0.0	0.0	29.2

Significant Chi-Square Comparisons

School System boys versus Talent Search boys	$x^2 = 16.97$	$p < .001$
Control boys versus Control girls	$x^2 = 5.4$	$p < .05$
Control boys versus Hopkins' Accelerated Class	$x^2 = 4.75$	$p < .05$

* Percents do not total 100 due to rounding.

** Four Talent Search girls indicated plans to take calculus but not precalculus. Since precalculus is normally a prerequisite for calculus, it was assumed that they will take precalculus as well, possibly under another name, and they are included in this percentage.

TABLE 10.2
Distribution in Percents of Students
Planning to Take Calculus in High School By Group and Sex

Group	Sex	N	Definitely Will	Probably Will	Don't Know	Will Not
School	Boys	156	77.6	14.7	1.3	6.4
System	Girls	68	75.0	14.7	4.4	5.9
Talent	Boys	47	63.9	31.9	4.3	0.0
Search	Girls	44	72.8	15.9	9.1	2.3
Career Class	Girls	22	68.2	18.2	13.6	0.0
Hopkins' Accel. Class	Girls	21	33.3	0.0	0.0	66.7
Control	Boys	22	68.2	0.0	0.0	31.8
Groups	Girls	20	40.0	0.0	0.0	60.0

Significant Chi-Square Comparisons

School System boys versus Talent Search boys $x^2 = 11.24$ $p < .05$
Control boys versus Hopkins' Accelerated Class $x^2 = 5.22$ $p < .05$

*Percents do not total 100 due to rounding.

between the School System boys and the Talent Search boys ($p < .001$), between the Control boys and the Control girls ($p < .05$) and between the Control boys and the Hopkins' Girls Accelerated Class ($p < .05$). A comparison of the School System girls with the Talent Search girls just missed significance at the $p < .05$ level.

Students' responses to the question about their plans to take calculus in high school are shown in Table 10.2. The groups with the highest percentages planning to take calculus were the School System boys and girls and the Talent Search girls. Significantly more School System boys than Talent Search boys ($p < .05$) indicated plans to take calculus. The greater percentage of Talent Search girls than Talent Search boys reporting definite plans to take calculus, though not statistically significant, was nonetheless surprising. On the other hand, only 4.3% of the Talent Search boys said they didn't know if they'd take it, whereas 11.4% of the Talent Search girls reported they didn't know or would not take calculus, so that more of the girls than boys still show signs of hesitation with regard to taking calculus. The comparison between the Control boys and the Control girls was not statistically significant, but the comparison between the Control boys and the Hopkins' Accelerated Class did reveal a significant difference in favor of the boys ($p < .05$).

There were no significant differences found in Chi-Square comparisons of plans to take chemistry in high school although the highest percentages of girls planning to take chemistry were found in the Hopkins' Accelerated Class and the Career Class, neither of which had unusually high percentages planning to take either precalculus or calculus. Even though comparisons with other groups in the study were not statistically significant, there may be some treatment effect encouraging some individual girls in those two Hopkins classes, both of which had Career Awareness components, to study chemistry.

Like mathematics, physics is often viewed as a male domain, and sex differences were expected when plans to take the course were analyzed. Chi-Square comparisons involving the School System, Talent Search, and Career Class groups, however, revealed no significant sex or group differences. Comparisons between the Control boys and Control girls and between the Control boys and the Hopkins' accelerated class were significant, however, at the .01 and .05 levels, respectively because more boys than girls took physics courses.

Significantly more School System boys than School System girls expected to take computer science in high school (p < .001). Because this course may not be available in all schools, group comparisons are difficult. Presumably, however, the School System boys and girls in the study have equal access to computer science courses because they are in the same school systems. The sex difference in course-taking with respect to computer science, therefore, may be an indication of differing attitudes and interests. There were no significant differences in other group comparisons of plans to take computer science in high school.

Acceleration

Because this study was aimed at identifying ways to encourage mathematically able girls to take more mathematics courses, it seemed valuable to study programs that led to acceleration of the study of mathematics. Presumably the girls who have successfully completed more difficult mathematics courses before the time when girls traditionally begin to drop out of mathematics in high school will be less likely to stop taking mathematics courses and, even if they should drop out of mathematics courses after tenth or eleventh grade, they may have completed calculus by that time. Bright students in most school systems normally cannot begin algebra I before the eighth grade. Thus, students who complete algebra I, algebra II, and plane geometry by the end of ninth grade can be considered to be at least 1 year accelerated in mathematics. If these accelerated students continue to take a precalculus course in tenth grade and calculus in eleventh grade, they remain at least 1 year accelerated.

The distribution in percents of students in the various groups who are

TABLE 10.3

Distribution, in Percents, of Students Who Completed Algebra I, II,
and Geometry by the End of Ninth Grade (Variable A),
Precalculus by the End of Tenth Grade (Variable B), and Calculus
by the End of Eleventh Grade (Variable C) Consolidated So That
Actual and Projected Course-taking Are Combined into the Categories
of "Yes" and "No" With Respect to Each Variable

| | | Variable A | | | | Variable B | | | | Variable C | | |
| | | | % | % | | | % | % | | | % | % |
	Group	N	Yes	No	N	Yes	No	N	Yes	No
I.	School System Boys	148	86.5	13.6*	148	83.3	16.2	148	77.7	22.3
II.	School System Girls	64	81.3	18.7	64	75.0	25.1*	64	64.0	36.0
III.	Talent Search Boys	47	59.5	40.5	47	57.5	42.6*	47	57.5	42.6*
IV.	Talent Search Girls	44	40.9	59.1	44	40.9	59.1	44	40.9	59.1
V.	Career Awareness Class	22	36.4	63.6	22	31.8	68.2	22	31.8	68.2
VI.	Hopkins' Accel. Class	26	46.2	58.3	26	46.2	53.8	26	19.2	80.7*
VII.	Control Boys	26	19.2	80.8	26	30.8	69.2	26	34.6	65.3*
VIII.	Control Girls	25	12.0	88.0	23	8.7	91.3	23	8.7	91.3

*Percents do not total 100 due to rounding.

or can be projected to be accelerated at least 1 year in mathematics, on the basis of questionnaire responses to questions about current and future course-taking plans, are shown in Table 10.3. Three variables were used: Variable A refers to the completion of algebra I, algebra II, and plane geometry by the end of ninth grade; Variable B refers to completing the precalculus sequence by the end of tenth grade; and Variable C refers to completing calculus by the eleventh grade.

Nine hypotheses with respect to acceleration were tested in this study and the results of Chi-Square Tests of significance are shown in Table 10.4 and the accompanying key.

The first hypothesis states that boys and girls differ in their enrollment in accelerated mathematics courses in high school. To test this the boys and girls in the untreated groups were compared on Variables A, B, and C. A comparison of the control boys and control girls from the 1973 Talent Search revealed no significant differences at the end of ninth or tenth grade, but there was a significant difference ($p < .05$) in the eleventh grade (Variable C) when more boys than girls took the calculus course. Thus, among those students who had no special program, the boys were more likely than the girls to accelerate their study of mathematics by taking calculus in eleventh grade. No sex difference was found, however, for the comparison of projected course-taking for boys and girls in the 1978 Talent Search. There were no significant differences between these boys and girls on any of the three variables.

Thus, the first hypothesis was supported in terms of actual course-taking outcomes for gifted students who were seventh graders in 1973 but

TABLE 10.4
Results of Chi-Square Tests of Hypotheses Relative to the Impact
of Different Treatments Upon Mathematics Course-taking

	Hypothesis	Group	Variable	Level of Significance
I.	Boys and girls differ with respect to mathematics courses taken in high school.	VII vs. VIII	A	n.s.
			B	n.s.
			C	$p < .05$
		III vs. IV	A	n.s.
			B	n.s.
			C	n.s.
II.	Girls who participate in an accelerated program will differ from girls who are not in a special program with respect to mathematics courses taken in high school.	VI vs. VIII	A	$p < .01$
			B	$p < .01$
			C	n.s.
		II vs. VIII	A	$p < .001$
			B	$p < .001$
			C	$p < .001$
		VI vs. IV	A	n.s.
			B	n.s.
			C	n.s.
		II vs. IV	A	$p < .001$
			B	$p < .001$
			C	$p < .05$
III.	Girls who participate in an accelerated mathematics program will differ from boys who were not in an accelerated program with respect to course taking in high school.	VI vs. VII	A	$p < .05$
			B	n.s.
			C	n.s.
		II vs. VII	A	$p < .001$
			B	$p < .001$
			C	$p < .05$
		VI vs. III	A	n.s.
			B	n.s.
			C	$p < .01$
		II vs. III	A	$p < .05$
			B	n.s.
			C	n.s.
IV.	Girls and boys who participate in accelerated mathematics classes will not differ with respect to mathematics courses taken in high school.	II vs. I	A	n.s.
			B	n.s.
			C	n.s.
V.	Girls who participate in a school system based accelerated program will differ from girls who participate in a special summer accelerated program with respect to course-taking in high school.	VI vs. II	A	$p < .001$
			B	$p < .01$
			C	$p < .001$
VI.	Girls who participate in a career awareness program will not differ from girls who have no program with respect to course-taking in high school.	V vs. III	A	$p < .05$
			B	n.s.
			C	n.s.
		V vs. IV	A	n.s.
			B	n.s.
			C	n.s.

TABLE 10.4 *cont'd.*

	Hypothesis	Group	Variable	Level of Significance
VII.	Girls who participate in acceler-ated class will differ from girls in a career awareness class with respect to course-taking in high school.	V vs. II	A	$p < .001$
			B	$p < .001$
			C	$p < .05$
		V vs. VI	A	n.s.
			B	n.s.
			C	n.s.
VIII.	There is no difference between mathematically gifted girls who were seventh graders in 1973 and were not in a special program, and those who were seventh graders in 1978 and were not in a special program with respect to mathematics course-taking in high school.	VIII vs. IV	A	$p < .05$
			B	$p < .01$
			C	$p < .01$
IX.	There is no difference between math-ematically gifted boys who were seventh graders in 1973 and were not in a special program, and those who were seventh graders in 1978 and were not in a special program with respect to mathematics course-taking in high school.	VII vs. III	A	$p < .001$
			B	$p < .05$
			C	n.s.

KEY

Dependent Variables

A. Number and percentage of students completing Algebra I, Algebra II, and Plane Geome-try by or before the end of the ninth grade (at least one year ahead of schedule).

B Number and percentage of students completing all pre-requisite courses for the Calculus by or before the end of the tenth grade.

C. Number and percentage of students who completed Calculus by or before the end of the eleventh grade.

Groups

I. The boys who participated in special accelerated mathematics classes in four school systems in the years 1974-75, 1975-76, 1976-77, and 1977-78 when the boys were seventh graders.

II. Girls in accelerated mathematics programs conducted by four school systems in the years 1974-75, 1975-76, 1976-77, and 1977-78 when the girls were seventh graders.

III. Boys who participated in the 1978 Talent Search and were not in an accelerated program.

IV. Girls who participated in the 1978 Talent Search and were not in an accelerated program.

V. Girls in a Career Awareness program in the summer after seventh grade in 1977.

VI. Girls in an accelerated mathematics class at the Johns Hopkins University in the summer after the seventh grade in 1973.

VII. A group of boys who were not in an accelerated mathematics program who were seventh graders in 1973 and matched with Groups VI and VIII on measures of ability and socio-economic variables.

VIII. A group of girls who were not in an accelerated program who were seventh graders in 1973 and matched with Group VI on measures of ability and socio-economic variables.

not supported in terms of the projected course-taking plans of gifted students in 1978. The most optimistic interpretation of these results would be that attitudes and behaviors of bright girls have become more like those of their male cohorts in the 5 year interval. One hopes that this is indeed the case. It is, however, possible that the eventual course-taking behavior of the 1978 students will be more like that of the 1973 group than their projections.

The second hypothesis states that girls who participate in an accelerated mathematics program will differ from girls who are not in a special program with respect to the study of mathematics in high school. To test this hypothesis, the girls in the accelerated mathematics programs were compared with the girls in the two untreated groups. A comparison of the 1973 Hopkins class with the Control girls revealed significant differences on Variables A and B, but not on C. These differences were largely a result of the fact that six girls from the accelerated class who had completed all their precalculus requirements by the end of tenth grade took college algebra instead of calculus in eleventh grade. Although their reluctance to take calculus contrasts with the behavior of the comparison group of boys, the girls are basically still more accelerated than the Control girls. A comparison between this class and the 1978 Talent Search girls, however, yielded no significant differences on any of the three variables. In fact, the percentage of girls who were accelerated (or projected to be accelerated) was slightly higher for the 1978 Talent Search group than it was for the 1973 Hopkins' class.

The School System accelerated girls were also compared with the two untreated groups and there were significant differences favoring the School System girls in both comparisons on all variables. Thus, even though some of the 1978 Talent Search girls have or are willing to accelerate, they are, as a group, less likely to have accelerated than have the girls in the School System accelerated classes. This hypothesis is then supported for comparisons of groups of girls within the same age/grade cohort.

The third hypothesis states that girls who participate in an accelerated mathematics program will differ from boys who are not in an accelerated program with respect to course-taking in high school. To test this hypothesis, the two groups of accelerated girls were compared with the two groups of untreated boys. A comparison between the 1973 Hopkins' accelerated class and the Control boys revealed a significant difference in favor of the girls at the end of the ninth grade but no difference at the end of the tenth or eleventh grades. A comparison of this class with the 1978 Talent Search boys revealed no significant differences on Variables A and B, but there was a significant difference in favor of the boys ($p < .01$) on Variable C. A comparison between the School System accelerated girls and the Control boys revealed significant differences at all levels in favor of the girls. A comparison between the School System accelerated girls and the Talent Search boys revealed a significant difference on Variable A, but not on B and C.

The results are somewhat complex, especially when viewed in conjunction with the results of the tests of the first and second hypothesis. If one compares only students within the same time period, the results are somewhat clearer. For the 1973 Hopkins Accelerated Class, special treatment for girls appeared to put them ahead of both their male and female cohorts at grade 9, but the effect was not lasting. By the end of grade 11, untreated boys were ahead of untreated girls and on a par with girls who had a special program. Thus, special treatment appears at best to have helped some gifted girls keep pace with what the boys were able to accomplish without special assistance. A similar pattern appears for the 1978 groups. Girls who have a special program (School System girls) appear on the basis of projections to be ahead of both male and female cohorts by grade 9 and maintain their lead over girls but not boys in grades 10 and 11. The difference in 1973 and 1978 results appears to be that girls in 1978 who have no special program are not projected to fall behind their male cohorts. As noted before, this must be viewed with cautious optimism.

The fourth hypothesis states that girls and boys who participate in accelerated mathematics classes will not differ with respect to mathematics courses taken in high school. A comparison of the boys and girls in the School System accelerated classes revealed no significant differences on the three variables. Thus, this hypothesis was confirmed.

The fifth hypothesis states that girls who participate in a school system based accelerated program will differ from girls who participate in a special summer accelerated program with respect to course-taking in high school. A comparison of the 1973 Hopkins' class girls revealed significant differences on Variables A, B, and C with the School System girls showing greater acceleration.

It had been assumed that this hypothesis would support the contention that access to school-based programs was critical. Given the previous findings of possible differences over time, however, this hypothesis does not lend itself to a clear interpretation. It may very well be that gifted girls in 1978 are more willing to accelerate their progress in mathematics than were girls in 1973 and the location or control of the program is irrelevant. Or, it may be that a full year program simply has a greater impact than a summer program.

The sixth hypothesis states that girls who participate in a Career Awareness program will not differ from girls who have no program with respect to course-taking in high school. The directionality of this hypothesis was due to the fact that the Career Class was not intended to change course-taking behavior. However, a comparison between the Career Class girls and the Control girls revealed that there was a significant difference favoring the Career Class girls on Variable A, though not on Variables B, and C. There were no significant differences in comparisons between the Career Class girls and the Talent Search girls. Thus, this hypothesis received some support.

The seventh hypothesis states that girls who participate in an accelerated class will differ from girls in a Career Awareness Class with respect to course-taking in high school. A comparison between the Career Class girls and the School System accelerated girls revealed significant differences in acceleration favoring the School System girls at all three grade levels, thus supporting the hypothesis. The hypothesis did not hold true, however, in a comparison of the 1973 Hopkins' class with the Career Class. There were no significant differences between these two groups. This latter result may again reflect a difference in the time of the treatments.

The eighth hypothesis was intended to compare the two untreated groups of girls in the tudy with respect to acceleration: the Control girls and the Talent Search girls. It states that there is no difference between mathematically gifted girls who were seventh graders in 1973 and were not in a special program, and those who were seventh graders in 1978 and were not in a special program with respect to mathematics course-taking in high school. Consistent differences between the two groups at all three grade levels favoring the 1978 group were revealed, thus refuting the hypothesis. Again we may be cautiously optimistic that changes over time have occurred.

The ninth hypothesis is the same as the eighth but for the two groups of untreated boys. It states that there is no difference between mathematically gifted boys who were seventh graders in 1973 and were not in a special program, and those who were seventh graders in 1978 and were not in a special program with respect to mathematics course-taking in high school. There was a significant difference between the two groups on Variables A and B favoring the 1978 Talent Search group, but this difference apparently disappeared by eleventh grade, because there was no significant difference on Variable C. The 1978 group accelerated at a younger age, but both groups appeared willing to accelerate. Because changes over the 5 year interval are not so consistent for boys, differences found for girls over this time have greater importance.

Enrollment, Attrition, and Achievement in the School System Programs

Summing across all the classes in the four school systems, there were 208 boys and 100 girls who enrolled in the special classes. Of these students, 136 boys and 55 girls completed the program through algebra I, algebra II, and plane geometry (which was the sum total of the program in some of the systems). Thus, the overall completion rates favored the boys, but the difference was not statistically significant.

Because of a high drop out rate among girls participating in accelerated classes at The Johns Hopkins University where boys greatly outnumbered girls, the ratio of boys to girls enrolled in each of the classes was compared to the attrition rate in the class to determine if the two might be related. The number enrolled in each class and the percent who completed the three courses are shown in Table 10.5. No clear pattern emerged from the analysis.

In three of the five classes in which the number of girls was equal or nearly equal to that of the boys, the attrition for girls was equal or less than that of the boys. In the eight classes in which boys clearly outnumbered girls, the attrition rate for girls was lower than that of the boys in only two classes. Thus, a reasonable ratio of females to males or a "critical mass" of girls may be a factor in preventing attrition. It is interesting that in the two classes with the fewest girls (3), all the girls completed the program. Perhaps when the number of girls is very small, they form a cohesive group and none drop out so as not to desert the others.

Although data on reasons students did not complete the programs were not available for all classes, information from some classes suggested two major reasons that some students did not complete the programs: logistics and motivation. Although the classes were run by school systems, they were systemwide and thus met in the afternoons, evenings, or on Satur-

TABLE 10.5
Number of Students Enrolled in the School System Accelerated
Classes and Number and Percent Who Successfully Completed
Algebra I, Algebra II, and Plane Geometry

System	Class	Number Enrolled		Number Completed Algebra I, II and Geometry		Percent Completed Algebra I, II and Geometry	
		Boys	Girls	Boys	Girls	Boys	Girls
A	I	19	5	10	2	52.6	40.0
	II	16	3	10	3	62.5	100
B	I	19	6	7	1	36.8	16.7
	II	17	6	6	1	35.3	16.7
	III	14	3	9	3	64.3	100
	IV	15	13	13	2	86.7	15.4
C	I	15	8	14	7	93.3	87.5
	II	14	4	11	2	73.1	50.0
	III	8	8	5	5	62.5	62.5
	IV	6	6	3	4	50.0	66.7
	V	7	6	6	3	85.7	50.0
D	I	28	21	17	14	65.5	77.8
	II	31	14	25	8	80.6	57.1

TABLE 10.6
Means and Standard Deviations on Aptitude and Achievement
Tests for Students in School System Accelerated
Mathematics Programs, by Sex

Test	Sex	Number	$\overline{X}$	s.d.
SAT-M	Girls	73	518	77
	Boys	185	556	91
SAT-V	Girls	65	436	92
	Boys	171	405	89
Algebra I*	Girls	87	168	6
	Boys	208	168	6
Algebra II*	Girls	65	165	7
	Boys	166	166	7
Geometry*	Girls	41	168	8
	Boys	114	171	8

*The converted scale scores on Cooperative Mathematics Test Series tests for Algebra I, II, and Plane Geometry are given.

days; some students had problems with transportation or conflicts with extracurricular activities. If the accelerated classes had been conducted during the regular school day within the home school, more boys and girls would have remained in the programs. Indeed some students dropped the special classes but continued to accelerate their mathematics study by taking advanced courses in a high school. So some students, male and female, failed to complete the program bacause of logistical problems rather than because they disliked the class or failed to achieve in it. Some students, male and female, dropped the courses because they were not enjoying them enough to want to work hard and do the heavy homework assignments.

In three of the four school systems the Scholastic Aptitude Test or the School and College Ability Test were used to screen participants. The mean scores of boys and girls on these measures of mathematical and verbal aptitude are expressed as SAT equivalents in Table 10.6. The results of the Cooperative Mathematics Series Test of achievement for algebra I, and algebra II, and plane geometry are also shown in Table 10.6. Boys and girls who completed the special accelerated programs scored very high on these tests. The mean score on the mathematical aptitude test was greater than 500 and verbal aptitude scores were greater than 400 for both sexes, with boys scoring somewhat higher on the former test and lower on the latter than girls scored. On the algebra I test the mean score for both sexes was at the 97th percentile on eighth grade national norms. On the test of algebra II the mean scores were at the 93rd and 95th percentiles, respectively, for girls and boys. On the test of plane geometry the girls and boys scored at the 97th and 98th percentiles, respectively. There were no significant differences in achievement on these three achievement measures as tested by analyses of covariance, using mathematical aptitude (SAT-M) as the covariate. Scores on the SAT-M correlated with scores on both measures of algebra achievement for boys and girls, but geometry scores were correlated with the aptitude and algebra scores for boys but not for girls as shown in Table 10.7.

Ability as measured by the SAT-M was not related to completion of the programs in a systematic way. The average SAT-M scores for the dropouts of the programs were sometimes higher and sometimes lower than the averages for those students who completed the courses. The differences were, however, typically less than 10 points for both sexes.

Thus, girls who persist in the programs do as well as the boys; and girls who do not persist are not less able than those who do. Factors other than ability must account for the differential completion rates in the special programs.

Analysis of Attitudes

Differences between boys and girls in mathematics achievement, particularly with respect to the study of advanced mathematics courses in high school and college, are often assumed to be outgrowths of sex differences in attitudes, interests, and aspirations. Thus, in the present study it

TABLE 10.7
Correlation Matrix of Test Scores for Students in School
System Accelerated Mathematics Programs, by Sex[1]

	SAT-M	SAT-V	Alg. 1	Alg. 2	Geom.
SAT-M	—	.26* (65)	.42** (69)	.54** (49)	.29 (26)
SAT-V	.31** (171)	—	.19 (61)	.20 (49)	-.37 (19)
Alg. 1	.59** (180)	.11 (166)	—	.46** (65)	-.14 (30)
Alg. 2	.50** (150)	.02 (150)	.69** (166)	—	.28 (30)
Geom.	.32** (97)	.08 (83)	.40** (113)	.50** (91)	—

*p < .05
**p < .001

[1] Correlations for girls are shown in the upper right diagonal of the table, and correlations for boys are shown in the lower left diagonal. The number of cases for each correlation is shown in parentheses.

seemed important to look for similarities and differences in attitudes, interests, and aspirations between mathematically talented boys and girls within and across treatment groups. Not all students who were in the treatment programs actually become accelerated and some control students accelerated themselves. It seemed desirable, therefore, to compare accelerated and non-accelerated students on measures of attitudes within and across treatments as well.

The Fennema-Sherman Mathematics Attitude Scales (F-S MAS) were mailed to 367 high scorers in the 1978 SMPY Talent Search conducted at The Johns Hopkins University by The Study of Mathematically Precocious Youth (SMPY); 337 responded (189 boys and 148 girls), a response rate of 91.8%. The students were seventh graders who had voluntarily participated in a mathematics contest, scored well and thus were presumed to have favorable attitudes towards mathematics. When compared with the high school normative population, the gifted students did indeed have favorable attitudes. This fact was particularly striking on the two scales that deal with self-confidence as a learner of mathematics and persistence and enjoyment of mathematics (the effectance motivation scale). This result was gratifying as it was consistent with the logic that gifted students who elect to participate in a talent search should perceive themselves as competent in mathematics more than would students in general as represented by the norms. Significant sex differences were found on only two of the eight scales, confidence and male domain, and these are discussed in the following sections.

A random subset of students from the 1978 Talent Search and students in the treatment groups completed a questionnaire assessing attitudes about reasons for studying mathematics, reasons to work and the importance of various factors in selecting a career. Questions about careers and lifestyle plans, educational aspirations, and remembrances of the encouragement of significant others were also asked.

Career Choice

Students were asked to list their first, second, and third choices for future careers as part of the Questionnaire sent to all participants. The answers were grouped into the six categories developed by John Holland (1958) for his vocational interest inventories, that is, investigative realistic, artistic, social, economic, and conventional. Because all of the students in the study were mathematically talented, it was expected that aspirations toward investigative careers would predominate and the results verified this expectation.

Career choices were then recategorized into investigative and non-investigative careers. As shown in Table 10.8, approximately 71% of the

TABLE 10.8
Distribution in Percents of Responses to First Career Choice
Categorized by Investigative versus Non-Investigative
by Sex and Group

Group	Sex	Total Number of Persons	Investigative	Non-Investigative
School	Girls	61	63.9	36.1
System	Boys	143	70.6	29.4
Talent	Girls	43	53.5	46.5
Search	Boys	47	70.2	29.8
Career Class	Girls	22	68.2	31.8
Total	Girls	126	61.1	38.9
	Boys	190	70.5	29.5

boys and 61% of the girls in the study had investigative career interests. Slightly more girls than boys expressed interest in careers of a social, conventional, economic, or artistic nature, but these differences were not statistically significant.

Reasons to Work

Students were asked to respond "not important," "somewhat important," or "very important," to 5 items related to reasons that they would work in the future. The five items were: (a) society and my family expect me to work; (b) it will probably be financially necessary for me to work; (c) I feel an obligation to myself to work; (d) I feel an obligation to society to work; and (e) I would be bored if I did not work. Mathematically talented girls and boys differed strikingly in this area. The response distributions for those items on which boys and girls differed significantly are shown in Table 10.9. Boys were more likely than girls to say that "society and family expect me to work" and "financially necessary" were very important reasons, whereas girls were more likely than boys to say that an "obligation to self" or an "obligation to society" were very important reasons. When asked to indicate the most important reasons for working, almost half the boys (49.3%) said "financially necessary," whereas over half the girls (56.9%) said "obligation to self."

Subgroup comparisons, however, suggest that sex differences in responses to the reasons to work were moderated by other factors. Girls and boys who had investigative career interests differed on response pat-

TABLE 10.9
Distribution in Percent of Response to Items Which Yielded
Significant Results for Questions Related to Reasons to Work

Question	Group	N	Not	Somewhat	Very	p
				Importance		
Society and my fam-	Girls	102	35.3	55.9	8.8	.01
ily expect me to work.	Boys	147	20.4	58.5	21.1	
It will probably be	Girls	102	3.9	33.3	62.7*	.05
necessary for me to work.	Boys	147	3.4	62.7*	77.6	
I feel an obligation to	Girls	102	0.0	16.7	83.3	.01
myself to work.	Boys	147	8.8	19.0	72.1*	
I feel an obligation to	Girls	102	13.7	50.0	36.3	.05
society to work.	Boys	147	27.2	46.3	26.5	

*Percents do not total 100 due to rounding.

terns to an "obligation to society," but not on the other reasons, whereas girls and boys with non-investigative career interests differed on their responses to "financially necessary" and "would be bored." Thus, one might conclude that boys and girls who have mathematical talent and congruent career interests don't differ very much except that the investigative girls feel more of a social obligation than the investigative boys. Among non-investigative boys and girls one sees a more traditional male-female difference. These boys feel a financial need to work more than the girls, where the girls see possible boredom as a more compelling reason. Boys who have not and do not expect to accelerate their mathematics education differ from their female cohorts in that they feel that society and family expecting them to work is a more compelling reason to work than do the non-accelerated girls. Accelerated boys and girls are more alike than different with respect to responses to reasons to work, but the girls are less likely than the boys to see both financial necessity and social and family expectations as important.

Factors in Job Selection

Factors that might be important to the students when they finally select a job were included as part of the questionnaire. Students were asked to respond "very important, "somewhat important," or "not important," to the following factors: (a) the amount of mathematics needed; (b) the amount of education needed; (c) cost of education needed; (d) belief that I will be able to do the job well; (e) belief that I will enjoy the job; (f) opportunity to use my special abilities to the fullest; (g) opportunity to earn a high salary; (h) having a position that is looked up to by others; (i) possibility of a flexible time schedule; (j) challenge of difficult work;

(k) many job openings in the field; (l) opportunities to be helpful to others or useful to society; and (m) chance to work with people rather than things. Table 10.10 shows those items for which significant sex differences were found. The girls seems to be more concerned than their male cohorts about their ability to "do the job well," to "use my abilities to the fullest," and, to a lesser extent, to enjoy the "challenge of difficult work." Within the groups of girls and boys who participated in a school system sponsored accelerated program, there were also differences in the value of "being helpful to others or society." More girls than boys in this group thought being helpful was "very important" and more boys than girls thought it was "not important."

Career and Life Style Plans

As a measure of career commitment, the students were asked to indicate whether they planned to work full time or part time as adults, have interrupted careers for child-rearing, or did not expect to work during most of their adult life. As part of this question, students also indicated what work pattern they would prefer for their spouses. Girls and boys in all groups differed significantly in their responses for themselves and their spouses as shown in Table 10.11. Significant differences were found between the boys' preference for their spouses and the girls' expectations for themselves, but the boys' expectations for themselves did not differ from what the girls' preferred for their spouses.

Less than half the girls (47%) but about 97% of the boys expect to have a full-time career always. Many girls (40%) want a full-time career except while raising small children and only 14% have limited career expectations. Approximately 94% of the girls expect their prospective spouses to work full time always but only 13% of the boys expect their prospective wives to have full-time careers. Over half the boys (57%) expect their

TABLE 10.10
Distribution of Significant Responses to Items Related
to Factors in Job Selection in Percents by Group and Sex

| Question | Group | N | Importance | | | p |
			Not	Somewhat	Very	
Belief that I will be able to do the job well.	Girls	102	0.0	13.7	86.3	.05
	Boys	145	4.1	20.7	75.2	
Using my abilities to the fullest.	Girls	102	0.0	21.6	78.4	.05
	Boys	146	4.8	30.1	65.1	
Challenge of difficult work.	Girls	102	1.0	44.1	54.9	.05
	Boys	146	8.2	37.0	54.8	

TABLE 10.11
Distribution in Percents of Responses to
"Career and Life Style Plans for Self and Spouse"
by Group and Sex

			Total Number of Persons	Full-Time Career Always	Full-Time & Part-Time Career Combination	Limited Career Expectations
School System	Girls	Self	35	48.6	45.7	5.7
		Spouse	33	93.9	6.1	0.0
	Boys	Self	96	95.8	4.2	0.0
		Spouse	85	9.4	34.1	56.5
Talent Search	Girls	Self	44	45.5	29.5	25.0
		Spouse	44	95.5	2.3	2.3
	Boys	Self	46	97.8	2.2	0.0
		Spouse	44	18.2	25.0	56.8
Career Class	Girls	Self	22	45.5	50.0	4.5
		Spouse	21	90.5	4.8	4.8
Total	Girls	Self	101	46.5	39.6	13.9
		Spouse	98	93.9	4.1	2.0
	Boys	Self	142	96.5	3.5	0.0
		Spouse	129	12.5	31.0	56.6

Significant Chi-Square Comparisons

Career and Life Style Choice for Self

School System girls versus boys	$x^2 = 41.37$	$p < .001$
Talent Search girls versus boys	$x^2 = 34.87$	$p < .001$
Total girls versus boys	$x^2 = 80.62$	$p < .001$

Career and Life Style Choice for Spouse

School System girls versus boys	$x^2 = 77.15$	$p < .001$
Talent Search girls versus boys	$x^2 = 53.61$	$p < .001$
Total girls versus boys	$x^2 = 151.50$	$p < .001$

Life Style Self versus Life Style Spouse

School System girls	$x^2 = 16.93$	$p < .001$
School System boys	$x^2 = 137.34$	$p < .001$
Talent Search girls	$x^2 = 30.23$	$p < .001$
Talent Search boys	$x^2 = 59.15$	$p < .001$
Career Class girls	$x^2 = 11.11$	$p < .01$
Total girls	$x^2 = 55.23$	$p < .001$
Total boys	$x^2 = 195.74$	$p < .001$

Girls' Life Style Choice for Self versus Boys' Life Style Choice for Spouse

School System	$x^2 = 34.5$	$p < .001$
Talent Search	$x^2 = 7.7$	$p < .05$
Total	$x^2 = 52.6$	$p < .001$

*Percents do not total 100 due to rounding.

prospective wives to work only until they marry and have children or not at all.

Girls who participated in either the Career Class or the School System accelerated programs were significantly less likely than the Talent Search girls, to project a limited career for themselves (around 5% of the treatment group as compared with 25% of the Talent Search group). Because self-selection played a role in participation in the special classes, one could speculate that girls with limited career expectations do not elect to participate in special programs; on the other hand, one could speculate that participation in the special programs heightened the girls' commitment to having a career. For boys there were no treatment group differences in response to career and life plans for self.

Acceleration and life style plans were related for girls but not boys. Accelerated girls were more likely to desire full-time careers always and less likely to have limited career goals than were non-accelerates.

Reasons to Study Mathematics

Previous research on sex differences in mathematics has suggested that boys and girls, even the mathematically gifted, differ with respect to the perceived usefulness of the study of mathematics, particularly with respect to its importance for their future career plans. The mathematically gifted boys and girls in the present study, however, were very similar with respect to responses to questions relating to reasons to study mathematics beyond algebra I.

Table 10.12 shows the results for the seven items on the questionnaire concerning reasons for studying mathematics. Total group comparisons are given for every item. The largest percentage (two-thirds or more) of both sexes rated "Mathematics will be important for my future career" as "very important." Slightly more than half of both boys and girls thought that "Mathematics were required to get into a good college" and "Mathematics is needed in this technological age" were very important reasons. Slightly less than half of both sexes thought that "Mathematics is interesting to study" was a very important reason. The statements "Mathematics is easy to learn" and "Many of my friends will be taking advanced mathematics courses" were not considered to be "very important" by very many of the girls and boys. Slightly more than half the boys and a little over a third of the girls rated "Mathematics teaches logical thinking" as "very important." This difference was not significant within the total group comparisons but did reach significance in comparisons between boys and girls in the accelerated school system programs and in comparisons between boys and girls who indicated investigative career choices.

TABLE 10.12

Distribution in Percents of Responses to

Questionnaire Items Related to Reasons to Study Mathematics

Question	Group	N	Not	Somewhat	Very	p
			\multicolumn{3}{c}{*Importance*}	
Math is important	Girls	102	2.9	29.4	67.6	n.s.
to my future career.	Boys	147	3.4	23.8	72.8	
My friends will be tak-	Girls	102	73.5	23.5	2.9	n.s.
ing advanced math.	Boys	146	61.0	31.5	7.5	
Advanced math is need-	Girls	102	1.0	41.2	57.8	n.s.
ed to get into a good	Boys	145	6.9	37.9	55.2	
college.						
Mathematics teaches	Girls	102	16.7	45.1	38.2	n.s.
logical thinking.	Boys	147	8.8	38.1	53.1	
Mathematics is inter-	Girls	101	11.9	40.6	47.5	n.s.
esting to study.	Boys	146	13.7	41.1	45.2	
Mathematics is neces-	Girls	102	4.9	41.2	53.9	n.s.
sary in a technological	Boys	147	4.1	41.5	54.4	
age.						
Mathematics is easy to	Girls	101	36.6	51.5	11.9	n.s
learn.	Boys	147	42.2	37.4	20.4	

Mathematics as a Male Domain

Of the students who were administered the F-S MAS, the boys were significantly more likely than the girls to respond "agree" or "undecided" to stereotyped assertions on the Mathematics as a Male Domain subscale. Yet on the questionnaire only 6% of these boys noted that people at their schools believe such stereotypes, whereas 21% of the girls felt such attitudes existed in their schools. It is girls, not boys, who tend to check "strongly agree" to the positive items and "strongly disagree" to the negative ones. On four of these items (which reflect stereotyped thinking of mathematics as a male domain), as many as a fifth to a third of the boys were undecided or accepted the stereotypic image. For example, on one item, "Females are as good as males in geometry," approximately 92% of the girls agreed, but a third of the boys were undecided or disagreed. On only one item, "It's hard to believe a female could be a genius in mathematics," did more than half of the males respond with a strong response in support of female competence. The feeling one might get from analyzing the responses is that gifted boys believe a few atypical females can achieve in mathematics, but many are not at all confident that women in general are equal to men with respect to mathematics.

Gifted and talented adolescent females have the same problems of all adolescent females with respect to developing their self-image of feminity. With respect to mathematics and feminity, two items point out the possible conflict between gifted girls and boys. On the item, "When a woman has to solve a math problem, it is feminine to ask a man for help," less than 10% of the girls were undecided or agreed, whereas more than 36% of the boys were undecided or agreed. Over 14% of the boys were also undecided about the question of female mathematicians being masculine. Only 41% strongly disagreed.

Self-Confidence

Boys in the Talent Search scored higher than the girls on the self-confidence as a learner of mathematics scale of the F-S MAS. With the exception of two items on the scale ("I think I could handle more difficult mathematics" and "I have a lot of self-confidence when it comes to math"), 95% of the boys agreed with the positive items and disagreed or strongly disagreed with the negative items. With the exception of the same two items, at least 85% of the girls agreed or strongly agreed with the positive items and disagreed or strongly disagreed with the negative items. In some cases the differences between the boys and girls was simply a matter of degree of positiveness.

When one looks at the content of the items, the response patterns make sense in relation to previous research findings on women and mathematics. The item to which the largest percentage of girls responded "strongly agree" was, "I can get good grades in mathematics." The positive items to which the largest percentage of girls responded "disagreed" or "undecided," were:

> "I have a lot of self-confidence when it comes to math,"
> "I think I could handle more difficult mathematics," and
> "I am sure I could do advanced work in mathematics."

The negative items for which the largest percentage of girls were undecided or agreed, were:

> "Math has been my worst subject,"
> "Most subjects I can handle, but I have a knack for flubbing
> up math," and
> "I'm not the type to do well in math."

Thus, some girls know they make good grades but still persist in projecting future failures or a denial of their ability—even though this is a sample of girls who are among the most mathematically talented girls in the nation (at least the top 2% on in-grade tests such as the Iowa Test of Basic Skills).

Of course, some of the highly able boys responded similarly to these items, but the difference still seems to be meaningful in practical terms. Twice the percentage of girls than boys were uncertain or negative about their ability to handle more difficult math, and well over twice the percentage of girls than boys admitted to lacking confidence when it comes to mathematics.

Support of Significant Others

When asked who or what did they feel had encouraged the development of interest and ability in mathematics, male and female students were more likely to recall a teacher than a parent. If one parent was mentioned, fathers were mentioned more frequently than mothers. This parental preference was especially true for boys. When asked at what age this encouragement had first happened, boys and girls responded similarly with the majority recalling events at ages 5 to 12.

Level of Educational Aspiration

As part of the questionnaire, students were asked to indicate the highest level of education to which they aspired. The results as shown in Table 10.13 indicated that about two-thirds of both sexes hoped to attend a gradute or professional school beyond a 4-year college program and only 2% of the boys and no girls in the School System, Talent Search, and Career Class groups expected to obtain less than a college degree. Significant sex differences were found only when girls who had participated in the special all girls' Accelerated Algebra Class or the girls' Career Class at Hopkins were compared with the total population of boys and the School System boys. These girls' classes included exposure to female role models, many of whom had attained or were working on M.D. or Ph.D. degrees. Approximately 86% of the girls' Algebra Class and 82% of the Career Class wanted a degree beyond the 4 year college level, far exceeding the boys as a whole and all other girls with respect to their level of aspiration.

CONCLUSIONS

The major finding of this study is that special programs for the mathematically gifted do have an impact on the course-taking behaviors and plans and aspirations of girls. Girls who participated in special School

TABLE 10.13
Responses in Percents to Highest Level of Education
Expected to Complete by Group and Sex

	Sex	Number	Less Than College Degree	Four Year College	Graduate or Professional School
School	Girls	68	0.0	35.3	64.7
System	Boys	158	2.5	37.3	60.1*
Talent	Girls	44	0.0	31.8	68.2
Search	Boys	47	0.0	21.3	78.7
Career Class	Girls	22	0.0	18.2	81.8
Total	Girls	134	0.0	31.3	68.7
Group	Boys	205	2.0	33.7	64.4*
Hopkins' Accelerated Class		21	4.8	9.5	85.7
Control Girls		20	5.0	25.0	70.0
Control Boys		20	0.0	20.0	80.0

Significant Chi-Square Comparisons

Girls Career Class and Hopkins Accelerated Class vs. School System girls	$\chi^2 = 4.73\ p < .05$
Girls Career Class and Hopkins Accelerated Class vs. all other girls	$\chi^2 = 4.57\ p < .05$
Girls Career Class and Hopkins Accelerated Class vs. School System boys	$\chi^2 = 7.32\ p < .01$
Girls Career Class and Hopkins Accelerated Class vs. all boys	$\chi^2 = 5.38\ p < .05$
Girls Career Class and Hopkins Accelerated Class vs. all other groups	$\chi^2 = 5.47\ p < .05$

*Percents do not total 100 due to rounding.

System accelerated mathematics classes achieved as well as the boys in these classes and had strong commitments to studying advanced mathematics courses. Girls who participated in a program that included a career awareness component and exposure to female role models had higher levels of educational aspiration than boys or girls who received no treatment or an accelerated mathematics program only. Girls who participated in any type of treatment program were less likely than girls who were not in programs to have weak career commitments for their lifestyle plans. The completion rate of boys and girls in the school system programs were, however, somewhat low and such programs would probably be more successful if they were conducted during the regular school day rather than after school hours or on weekends.

Although some sex differences were found on attitudinal and interest measures, mathematically able boys and girls, particularly seventh graders in the 1978 Talent Search, are more alike than different with respect to attitudes and interests. It appears that the younger generation of mathematically gifted girls have more positive perceptions of the importance of studying mathematics than past generations of gifted girls. This conclusion is further supported by the sex differences in course-taking found among 1973 Talent Search students who had no special program and the lack of sex differences in course plans of the 1978 group. Boys in 1973 and 1978 were similar in course-taking but girls in the 1978 Talent Search were more accelerated or expected to be more accelerated than girls from 1973.

The areas in which the boys and girls from the 1978 Talent Search differed most relate to reasons to work and career and lifestyle expectations for themselves and their future spouses. Although girls feel less pressured to work because of financial necessity or social expectations than do the boys, the majority do seem oriented towards post-secondary education and graduate school and an eventual professional career. These girls, however, may still need a great deal of support and encouragement in order to realize their potentials. It is clear that the attitudes of their male cohorts are not totally supportive. Although the percentage of boys who still stereotype mathematics as a male domain is small, the majority of the boys are not expecting their future wives to have a strong commitment to careers. Thus, programs aimed at increasing women's participation in the world of work at the professional levels should direct some attention to the attitudes of boys. Perhaps these gifted boys need exposure to professional females as role models just as much as do the gifted girls.

Even though the 1978 Talent Search participants differed little on measures of attitude and projected course-taking, the girls as a group were less self-confident than the boys with respect to mathematics—and this was within a very able group. The relationship of self-confidence to persistence in mathematics courses at the advanced levels should be studied further. Students from the 1978 Talent Search should graduate from high school in or before 1983. It will be very interesting to see how these students, male and female, develop their abilities and select their college majors and careers and to determine what factors have helped or hindered their progress.

ACKNOWLEDGEMENT

This research was supported by Grant No. NIE-G-77-0062 from the National Institute of Education.

11 Understanding Mathematics Course Enrollment and Mathematics Achievement: A Synthesis of the Research

Susan F. Chipman and Donna M. Wilson
National Institute of Education

Introduction

The educational decisions of young people limit their later occupational possibilities as adults. This seems particularly true of decisions to participate in or to avoid high school mathematics courses. Rarely is mathematical knowledge acquired anywhere else. And that knowledge is required for many of the best career opportunities in our society: the skilled trades, engineering, scientific and medical careers, and computer science. In recent years there has been particularly intense concern that young women are less likely to take the mathematics courses that lead to those career opportunities. Many are concerned, too, that relatively few students of either sex finish high school with strong preparation in mathematics. The statistics of mathematics participation were summarized in Chapter 1. In this chapter, we synthesize the results of recent research studies that were aimed at understanding why there are sex differences in mathematics course enrollment and, consequently, in achieved mathematical knowledge.

All of the studies reviewed took place within the span of a few years; indeed, most were funded in a single, special grants competition conducted by the National Institute of Education to address the concern about the participation of women in mathematics. That competition specified the following research question: What are the major positive and negative factors related to the participation and achievement of women in

The opinions expressed herein are those of the authors and do not represent the official policy or position of the National Institute of Education.

the study of mathematics and to their preferences for occupations requiring mathematical competence? The emphasis is upon understanding sex differences rather than course decisions or achievement per se. Also, the designs of the studies reflect the understanding of these problems that prevailed at the particular time they were initiated. For this reason, these studies form a relatively coherent group, a "cohort" of research studies. Although the review centers upon these studies, obviously it cannot be confined totally to them. Important background, information, concepts, and theories are reviewed as necessary to integrate these studies into a comprehensive account. On the other hand, this chapter does not purport to be a review of all research related to women and mathematics. A review of the state of research and theoretical understanding at approximately the time these studies were undertaken is provided by a set of three papers commissioned by the National Institute of Education (Fennema, 1977; Fox, 1977; Sherman, 1977).

The identities of and major sources for the studies under review are listed in Table 11.1. Because of their comprehensiveness and additional tables and appendices, the final reports submitted to the research agencies were used as the primary source of information for this review. For reasons of economy of space, these studies are referenced in this chapter by the name of the first investigator only. Not all of this information is contained in the earlier chapters or in journal publications reporting these studies. In some instances, the investigators supplied additional information not included in the final reports, valuable assistance for which we thank them.

We begin with an overall characterization of the studies. At the time these studies were initiated, general consensus had developed that sex differences in mathematics achievement are explained primarily by differences in mathematics course participation. Evidence supporting the approximate validity of that assumption was summarized in Chapter 1. Consequently, the prediction of course participation was the primary focus of these studies, although much attention was also given to achievement. Little attention was given to the development of preferences for occupations requiring mathematics, possibly because it was believed that failure to study mathematics precluded the development of such preferences or made them irrelevant. Because cognitive differences between the sexes are known to be minimal, explanations of the sex difference in mathematics participation were sought primarily in attitudinal or motivational variables such as mathematics anxiety or the sex-stereotyping of mathematics. The exception was an emphasis upon spatial abilities, attributable both to the frequent finding of sex differences on these measures and to the plausibility of a connection between spatial abilities and the learning of mathematics. We give comparable emphasis to the issue of

TABLE 11.1
Sources for the Studies Reviewed

Armstrong, J.M. *A national assessment of achievement and participation in mathematics.* Denver, Colorado: Education Commission of the States, 1979. (ERIC Document Reproduction Service, No. ED 187562) Final report on NIE-G-77-0061.

Boswell, S. *Women and mathematics: The development of stereotypic attitudes.* Institute for Research on Social Problems, Boulder, Colorado: 1980. (ERIC Document Reproduction Service No. ED 186477) Final report on NIE-G-78-0023.

Brush, L. *Why women avoid the study of mathematics: A longitudinal study.* Cambridge, Massachusetts: ABT Associates, 1979. (ERIC Document Reproduction Service No. ED 188887) Final report on NIE-C-40-77-0099.

Brush, L. *Encouraging girls in mathematics: The problem and the solution.* Cambridge, MA: ABT Books, 1980.

Casserly, P., & Rock, D. *Factors relating to young women's persistence and achievement in mathematics, with special focus on the sequence leading to and through Advanced Placement mathematics.* Princeton, New Jersey: Educational Testing Service, 1979. (ERIC Document Reproduction Service No. ED 214798) Final report on NIE-G-77-0064.

Connor, J. & Serbin, L. *Mathematics, visual-spatial ability and sex roles.* Binghamton, New York: State University of New York, 1980. (ERIC Document Reproduction Service No. ED 205385) Final report on NIE-G-77-0051.

Fennema, E. & Sherman, J. Sex-related differences in mathematics achievement, spatial visualization and affective factors. *American Educational Research Journal,* 1977, *14,* 51-71.

Fennema, E., & Sherman, J. Sex-related differences in mathematics achievement and related factors: A further study. *Journal for Research in Mathematics Education,* 1978, *9,* 189-203.

Fox, L. *Women and mathematics: The impact of early intervention programs upon course taking and attitudes in high school.* Baltimore, Maryland: Johns Hopkins University, 1979. (ERIC Document Reproduction No. ED 188886) Final report on NIE-G-77-0062.

Lantz, A. & Smith, G. *Determining the importance of factors influencing the election of mathematics courses.* Denver, Colorado: University of Denver, 1979. Final report to the National Science Foundation on grant SED-78-17103.

Lantz, A.E., & Smith, G.P. Factors influencing the choice of nonrequired mathematics courses. *Journal of Educational Psychology,* 1981, *73,* 825-837.

Parsons, J. *Self perception, task perceptions and academic choice: Origins and change.* Ann Arbor, Michigan: University of Michigan, 1980. (ERIC Document Reproduction Service No. ED 186477) Final report on NIE-G- 78-0022.

Sherman, J. *Women and mathematics: Prediction and change of behavior.* Madison, Wisconsin: Women's Research Institute of Wisconsin, Inc., 1980. (ERIC Document Reproduction Service No. ED 182162) Final report on NIE-G-77-0063.

Sherman, J. Predicting mathematics performance in high school girls and boys. *Journal of Educational Psychology,* 1979, *79,* 242-249.

Sherman, J. Mathematics, spatial visualization and related factors: Changes in girls and boys, grades 8-11. *Journal of Educational Psychology,* 1980, *72,* 476-482.

Stallings, J. *Factors influencing women's decisions to enroll in advanced mathematics courses.* Menlo Park, California: SRI International, 1979. (ERIC Document Reproduction Service No. ED 197972) Final report on NIE-G-78-0024.

Wise, L. L., Steel, L., & MacDonald, C. *Origins and career consequences of sex differences in high school mathematics achievement.* Palo Alto, California: American Institute for Research, 1979. (ERIC Document Reproduction Service No. ED 180846) Final report on NIE-G-78-0001.

spatial ability. A great many potential explanatory variables, diverse but also redundant with each other, had been mentioned in previous research and in less formal discussions of women's participation in mathematics. In order to carry out this review, it has been necessary to classify together variables that seem to be approximately the same. In the later discussions of these variables or variable classes, there is more information about the specific nature of the variables in each study.

Table 11.2 provides an overview of the characteristics of the studies reviewed in terms of the major variables included in each study. As indicated earlier, the variable labels represent our classification of the more diverse variable labels actually used in the studies. Where appropriate, the table indicates that data were collected relating to the variable. These data were not always reported. Potential dependent variables were not always treated as such. That is, the study may not contain analyses attempting the prediction of those variables. Nevertheless, interested researchers may be able to obtain these data for future analyses. Table 11.3 summarizes the information available about the characteristics of the subject samples in these studies.

ORGANIZATION OF THE REVIEW

This chapter is divided into four major sections. The first section is organized around the major predictor variables that were investigated. Each variable is discussed individually, gathering together information from the various studies. The second section discusses the relationships among the variables and the difficulty this creates in determining which are the truly important or causal variables. The third section considers the analyses that the investigators performed in order to deal with these interrelationships among variables and to characterize what is important in determining mathematics enrollment decisions and achievement. We present our view of the conclusions that can be justified on the basis of these analyses. Finally, we conclude by discussing the implications of the results for mathematics education and the apparent needs for future research.

THE MAJOR PREDICTOR VARIABLES

The review of these variables addresses three major classes of variables in succession. Cognitive variables are discussed first, followed by attitudinal or affective variables. These two major classes of variables are reasonably distinct from or independent of each other. Statistical techniques for assessing the independence of variables tend to distinguish these two classes but cast doubt upon the meaningfulness of the distinctions among the variables within these groups. Once the discussion of cognitive variables has provided the necessary background, we consider how cognitive and affective variables might be linked—because they are not truly independent. Perhaps because the variables that purport to measure the influence of other persons were generally measured by student perceptions, they tend to be strongly associated with measures of student attitudes. Nevertheless, the influence of other persons is discussed together with the effects of school, community, and other social or institutional variables, under the heading of the social environment, our third class of variables.

In each section treating a major variable, some discussion of issues of conceptualization, definition, and measurement is incorporated in the review. Evidence concerning the degree of apparent relationship between the individual variable and the outcomes of interest—math enrollment and achievement—is discussed. Then, evidence concerning sex differences with respect to the variable is discussed. This review of the individual variables may permit us to dismiss certain variables as having little potential explanatory value. However, the reader should take care not to jump to hasty conclusions about the importance of individual variables because the strong patterns of interrelations among these variables can be misleading. For the reader who prefers to skip over the details of the findings from each study, there is an overall summary of findings at the end of this section.

COGNITIVE VARIABLES

It seems obvious that the general cognitive ability or specific mathematical ability of an individual might affect the decision to study mathematics as well as the resulting level of achievement. This apparently simple statement unfolds into a number of complex research problems. The term *ability* has the connotation of referring to some intrinsic property of the individual as an information processor—such as memory capacity, the efficiency of memory processing, or the neural wiring to carry out imaginary mental rotations of objects. But the practical technology called *ability testing* has not yet been successfully linked to such fundamental theories of cognitive processes. Instead, the testing and definition of abilities is a very empirical process. Performance is sampled within a domain of tasks or situations. Statistical techniques (chiefly, factor analysis) are used to locate sets of tasks that "go together," have something in

TABLE 11.2

Characteristics of the Studies Reviewed

Study	IQ	Verbal Ability	Spatial Ability	Other	Math Utility	Math Anxiety/ Confidence	Math Liking	Stereotyping Math As Male Domain	Career and Education Plans
					Predictor Variables				
Armstrong			Paper Form Board		Yes	Yes, also general anxiety	Yes	Yes, and general stereotyping	Both
Boswell									
Grades 3-6			Hidden Patterns	Interest	Yes	Combined Attitudes	Combined Attitudes	Yes, and sex role measure	
Grades 7, 9, 11			No	Personality	Yes	Combined Attitudes Task Competence	Combined Attitudes	Yes	Occupational Interest
Brush	Yes	Yes	DAT	SES	Yes	Yes, also English	Yes	Yes	Yes
Casserly				SES	Yes, not reported	Yes		General Stereotyping	Yes
Connor	Yes	Yes	Various						
Fox						Yes, F-S	Effectance Motivation F-S	Yes, F-S	Yes
Lantz				SES	Yes	Yes	Yes	Yes, also general stereotyping	Yes
Parsons					Yes	Yes	Yes		Career
Sherman		Yes	DAT		Yes	Yes	Effectance Motivation	Yes	
Stallings			DAT			Yes	Yes	Yes	Yes
Wise		Yes	Yes	SES		No, general confidence	Interest		Both

280

TABLE 11.2 Continued

Study	Predictor Variables						Potential Dependent Variables		
	Teachers (Counselors)	Parents	Peers	School Factors	Classroom	Rating of Influences	Intent to Enroll	Math Enrollment	Math Achievement
Armstrong	Both, S.J.	S.J.	S.J.	Yes		Yes	Age 13	Grade 12 detailed	Age 13 / Grade 12
Boswell Grades 3–6			S.J.				No	No	Yes
Grades 7, 9, 11		Parent Q.					Yes	Yes	Yes
Brush	S.J.	S.J.	S.J.				Yes	Yes	Yes, not predicted
Casserly	S.J. Interviews	S.J.	S.J.	Yes		Yes, not reported		Yes	Grades
Connor									Yes
Fox	S.J., F-S	S.J., F-S			Sex ratio		Some	Some	Yes
Lantz	S.J.	S.J.	S.J. Sig. Other			Yes	Yes	Yes, 1st optional course	Previous grade
Parsons	S.J., Ques. Observation	S.J. Parent Q.			Yes	Yes	Yes		Yes, not predicted
Sherman	S.J.	S.J.	S.J.					Yes	Yes
Stallings	T. Ques. Observation C. Ques.	S.J.	S.J.	Yes	Yes	Yes, not reported	Yes		Yes, not predicted
Wise				Yes				Yes	Yes, Grades 9, 12

Codes: SES = Socioeconomic Status
S.J. = Student Judgment, as opposed to responses from the persons themselves
F-S = Fennema - Sherman scales

TABLE 11.3
Characteristics of Study Participant Samples

	Age/Grade	Sex	Size (m/f)	Location	SES	Ability/Achievement	Time
Armstrong	13 year olds and 12th graders	m,f	1,453 1,788	national probability sample	national probability sample	national probability sample	Spring, 1978
Boswell							
Study One	Ph.D.s received (1968-1978)	f	279 math 91 psychology 90 English	nationwide (42 states represented)			Spring, 1978
Study Two	Grades 3 thru 6	m,f	562	Colorado	middle class	collected, not reported	Spring, 1978
Study Three	Grades 7, 9, & 11	m,f	593 (279/314)	Colorado	middle class	65th-77th percentile	Spring, 1978
Brush	Grades 6, 9, & 12 (grades 7 & 10 follow-up) (grades 8 & 11 2nd follow-up)	m,f	514 (239/275) 3 yrs. data 302 (143/159) 12th grade 1976	New England -rural, small city, and suburb	lower-middle and working class	collected but not reported	Fall, 1976 1977 1978
Casserly	Grades 10, 11 & 12 Grades 11, 12, h.s. graduates follow-up	m,f	685 (371/314) 319 (144/174)	New York, Utah, Massachusetts, Ohio, Hawaii, and Oregon	diverse	Accelerated and Advanced Placement students	1978; 1979
Connor							
Study One	Grades 7 & 10	m,f	339 (179/160)	Suburban-Rural school district		mean IQ about 109	1978 & 1979
Study Two	Grades 7 & 10	m,f	934 (466/468)	Upstate New York and neighboring high schools			
Study Three	Grade 8	m,f	434 (231/203)	Upstate New York Suburbs			

TABLE 11.3 *cont'd.*

	Age/Grade	Sex	Size (m/f)	Location	SES	Ability/Achievement	Time
Fox	Grades 7, 8, & 9 (Various Programs)	m,f	360 (210/153)	Maryland, Midwest Nationwide		Most scored at or above 97th percentile on math concepts of I.T.B.S.	1973 1974 1976 1977
Lantz	Enrolled in last required math course	m,f	1,418	California Bay Area; Colorado; Wyoming	diverse		1978
Parsons	Grades 5 – 11 Grades 5 – 12	m,f	339 668 follow-up plus new sample	Michigan suburb		Collected but not reported Above average	Spring, 1978 1979
Sherman Study One	Grade 12 follow-up	m,f	413 (194/219) 310 (152/158)	Midwest	diverse	Above average	1975 1978
Study Two	Grade 8 Grade 11 follow-up	m,f	483 (223/260) 210 (75/135)	Midwest	diverse	Above average	1976 1979
Stallings	Grades 9, 10, 11 & 12 Primarily geometry	m,f	2,117	California Bay Area	diverse		Spring, 1978
Wise Study One	9th graders who were retested as 12th graders	m,f	7,500	National sample	National sample (in school)	National sample (in school)	1960 PROJECT TALENT
Study Two	12th graders who supplied data in all three follow-up surveys (ages: 19, 23, & 29)	m,f	12,759	National sample, as retained	National sample, as retained	National sample, as retained	1960 and later

common, and those that seem to be independent of each other. The hypothetical "something" that such a set of tasks has in common is called a factor and sometimes may be called an ability.

Every performance that can be sampled has learned, culturally influenced aspects to it—at a minimum the culturally conditioned willingness to perform in the testing situation. For this reason, calling a test an ability test rather than an achievement test, a test of learning, involves a presumption that everyone has had an equal opportunity to learn and practice the performances tested. Often this presumption is not justified. In addition, the practical constraints of testing—paper and pencil administration, limited time—frequently result in a sample of performance that is very unevenly representative of or merely similar to the domain of performance that truly interests us. It would not be surprising if the ability to do a familiar type of problem that takes less than a minute to solve had little relation to the ability to learn a new field of mathematics or to the ability to solve a problem that takes a month to solve. For this reason, it is always important to ask whether the test is a valid predictor, whether it has a strong relationship to the performance that is of genuine interest.

In the history of cognitive testing, it has been found that all intellectual performances have something in common; that is, persons who do well or poorly on one intellectual task tend also to do well or poorly on other, quite different intellectual tasks. This common factor in performance has been called "g" or general intelligence. The effort to define mathematical ability or abilities as distinct from general intelligence has had mixed success (Aiken, 1973). Children who excell in mathematics score high on tests of general intelligence (Duncan, 1961; Geng & Mehl, 1969; Kennedy & Walsh, 1965). Generally, tests of specific mathematical ability factors have not predicted success in mathematics any better than have tests of general intelligence (Aiken, 1973).

Beyond general ability, the cognitive variable that has promise for predicting future mathematics performance seems to be previous mathematics achievement. Previous grades in mathematics appear to be the best available predictor of success in college mathematics (Wick, 1975). There seems little reason to believe that one can usefully distinguish between measures of mathematical ability and achievement in mathematics when predicting future behavior.

Because of the concerns that guided the design of these studies, cognitive variables were not extremely well represented. Mathematics achievement, of course, is the most prevalent measure. Measures of general intellectual ability are scarce. In contrast, measures of spatial ability were very well represented in these studies, because of the plausibility of the relationship between spatial ability and mathematical performance and because of the reported sex differences in spatial ability.

Previous Mathematics Achievement

Past mathematics achievement, which is not really distinguished from general intelligence or general academic achievement, is the most powerful predictor to be found in the studies under review. For example, Wise reported that the correlation between ninth grade mathematics achievement and later high school math course participation in the 1960 Project TALENT sample was .62. The correlation between ninth grade and twelfth grade mathematics achievement was .78. Similarly, Sherman reported a correlation of .79 between eighth grade and eleventh grade math achievement scores, and the average math achievement scores of groups of students ultimately taking differing numbers of years of mathematics indicate a high correlation with math enrollment as well. Boswell found math achievement scores to be strongly correlated with the intention to study more mathematics: correlations of .55 (males) and .51 (females) in ninth grade and .75 (males) and .61 (females) in eleventh grade. Brush also found achievement to be strongly associated with enrollment intentions. An exception to these findings is Parson's report of a very low correlation between a composite math achievement variable (incorporating both grades and test scores) and the intention to take more mathematics. This inconsistent finding probably results from the fact that 95% of her sample continued studying mathematics as well as from the problematic quality of intentions expressed by such young students. Armstrong also reported rather low correlations between math achievement and the enrollment intentions of 13-year-old students. Fox reported that the SAT math scores of students were not particularly related to whether or not they continued in special accelerated math programs, a result that might be attributed to the high ability level of all students participating. In contrast, Casserly reported that grades in tenth grade accelerated mathematics ($r = .37$ for females, .40 for males), as well as self-assessment of mathematics ability (.28 females, .35 males), were important in determining whether students continued with the study of mathematics. In summary, mathematics achievement scores appear to be more strongly correlated with eventual, actual enrollment than with expressed intentions to enroll, and to become more strongly correlated with intentions as students become older.

Sex Differences. This topic is discussed more fully in Chapter 1. In the Project TALENT sample, as in other studies sampling the same age group, sex differences in mathematics achievement at the ninth grade level were negligible. Though earlier mathematics achievement was the strongest individual predictor of later math enrollment in that study, it contributed nothing to the explanation of sex differences in enrollment.

Spatial Ability or Skill

In recent years, there has been a tendency to regard spatial ability as a fundamental ability underlying achievements in mathematics. Intuitively, the capacity to mentally rotate, translate, and transform objects appears to be important in mathematical thinking, at least in geometry. Fennema (1977) reported on the body of mathematical opinion supporting this view. In discussions of sex differences in mathematics performance, spatial ability has been a particularly prominent topic because it has been generally believed that there are sex differences in spatial ability (Maccoby & Jacklin, 1974). An important feature of recent discussion of sex differences in spatial performance has been the hypothesis that they might result from sex-linked recessive inheritance of spatial ability (Bock, 1967). This hypothesis predicts a certain pattern of correlations among the spatial abilities of family members. It has not been supported by recent data from large familial studies (Vandenberg & Kuse, 1979) despite the use of a spatial test that produced exceptionally large sex differences in performance. In contrast, there is considerable evidence that spatial test performance is rather easily changed by training and experience (Carpenter & Just, 1981; Conner, Serbin, & Schackman, 1977).

Research evidence that spatial ability is related to mathematics performance is surprisingly scanty. Smith (1964) and Werdelin (1961) are the two most frequently cited references, but neither provides strong evidence for a relationship between spatial ability and mathematics performance. Several reviewers of the literature have concluded that no such relationship has been shown: Very (1967), Fruchter (1954), even for geometry: Werdelin (1961), Lim (1963). In some analyses, spatial abilities have been classified as a separate factor, independent from tests of more specifically mathematical performance (Aiken, 1973).

A major difficulty in this research is the fact that the concept of spatial ability is not uniformly defined nor based on a sound theory of psychological processes. Many different tasks, which can be performed with diverse mental strategies, have been called tests of spatial abilities. There are two recent reviews of this literature: McGee (1979) and Lohman (1979). Various tests of so-called spatial ability do not necessarily have high correlations with each other, as contrasted with their correlations with other kinds of tests. Thus, there is no single, unitary spatial ability that these tests are measuring. Lohman concludes that a considerable portion of performance on spatial tests—especially complex spatial tests—is explained by variation in general intelligence. Further, three classes of spatial tasks seem to be distinguished by the data: (1) spatial relations—tasks involving mental rotation; (2) spatial orientation—tasks requiring the subject to imagine how a stimulus array will appear from another perspective; and (3) visualization—tasks such as paper folding, form board, WAIS Block design, and so on. The latter are very similar in their classification of individuals to measures of "g" or general intelligence. Lohman also warns that spatial tests measure spatial problem solving skills—which may consist of verbal analytic strategies—rather than the ability to perform mental analogues of spatial operations, as is often assumed. In a report of their recent work on strategies in spatial problem solving, Carpenter and Just (1981) comment on the irony that a person who is classified by psychometric tests as high in spatial ability may simply be very good at evading spatial problems.

The same points apply to mathematics itself. Traditionally, among mathematicians, there has been a contrast between algebraists and geometers, based largely on preferences for spatial thinking. There is more than one way to do mathematics. In addition, mathematical thinking is complex, drawing upon many and diverse elemental mental processes. Therefore, it is not surprising that efforts to demonstrate relationships between spatial ability and mathematics performance have met with little success.

Present Results Relating Spatial Ability and Mathematics. A number of the present studies report data on the spatial abilities of male and female students and sometimes on the relationship to mathematical performance. These studies, together with two other recent studies, are summarized in Table 11.4

The studies summarized in Table 11.4 report a number of significant correlations between spatial tests and mathematics achievement. Where the DAT test is used, it seems that a correlation of about .50 is found between scores on this spatial test and general tests of mathematics achievement (Fennema & Sherman, 1977a, 1978; Sherman, 1980b) in a high school population enrolled in college preparatory mathematics. (The DAT Space Relations test requires the examinee to select the three-dimensional shape that would be formed by folding a two-dimensional shape on indicated fold lines.) Stallings' findings are consistent with this, but there is added interest in the variation in the size of the correlation between the DAT and tests of specific mathematical content. As one would expect, it appears that spatial performance is more strongly related to performance in geometry and analytic geometry than to performance in calculus, algebra, and arithmetic. (The result for arithmetic may be invalid because of the low ability level of this subject group.) On the other

TABLE 11.4
Results Relating to Spatial Ability

Study	Test Used	Sex Differences in Scores	Relation to Mathematics Achievement	Notes
Armstrong	15 items from Paper Form Board	Age 13: 51.5 (M) 56.6 (F) significant Grade 12: 71.3 (M) 69.4 (F) not significant	Not reported	
Brush	DAT Space Relations	Grade 9: 66.43 (M) 64.40 (F) not significant	r = .52	Modified measures of math achievement.
Connor & Serbin	ETS factor referenced: cube comparisons, hidden patterns, Gestalt completion, paper folding, card rotations, DAT-abridged	No significant sex differences in grades 7 or 9. Trend favoring males on abridged DAT.	Visualization measures sometimes showed significant correlations with math achievement (cube comparison, paper folding, card rotations, DAT)	
Fennema & Sherman 1977	DAT Space Relations	Grade — Overall Mean Score Males (n) Females (n): 9 36.38 (194) 35.46 (219); 10 40.15 (181) 37.75 (169); 11 42.87 (199) 39.31 (167); 12 44.88 (70) 44.53 (34)	Correlations Male Female; Grade 9-11 .51** .45**; Grade 12 .28* .37*	Includes only students enrolled in "on grade" math courses.

TABLE 11.4 cont'd.

Study	Test Used	Sex Differences in Scores	Relation to Mathematics Achievement	Notes
Rosser	experimental tasks measuring spatial orientation and visualization	No significant sex differences in overall performance. Females superior on "within-dimensional" tasks (e.g., 2D display, 2-D response).		Subjects aged 3, 4, 5, years; 4, 6, 8 years; grades 2 and 5 in various studies.
Sherman	DAT	Grade 8: 33.20 (M) 31.45 (F) Grade 11: 42.23 (M) 39.96 (F) "no significant sex differences"	r's Grade 8 DAT & Grade 11 Math ETS Math Concepts .50**(M) .54**(F) Mental Arithmetic Problems .62**(M) .53**(F)	
Stallings	DAT	In some subgroups males scored higher, in others no sex differences.	Calculus $r = .20$ analytic geometry $r = .68$ trigonometry $r = .38$ algebra II $r = .15$ geometry $r = .53$ algebra I $r = .49$	Course specific math tests
Wise	visualization 2-D visualization 3-D mechanical reasoning	Grade 9 12.93 (M) 11.54 (F) $p < .001$ 8.57 (M) 7.84 (F) $p < .001$ 11.72 (M) 8.65 (F) $p < .001$	Correlations with math achievement were less than .20	Data collected in 1960

hand, Connor and Serbin attempted to distinguish both types of mathematical performance and types of spatial performance, while examining their interrelations, but did not find consistent patterns of correlations across subject groups. They concluded only that tests of visualization—the modified DAT, paper folding and so on—are more likely to relate to mathematics achievement than are Gestalt completion and hidden patterns tests. There may have been problems with the modified tests that they used because the correlations between their achievement measures and both verbal and spatial ability measures are lower than others report. In Project TALENT (Wise) there were three subject variables that might be called spatial: Visualization in 2-D, Visualization in 3-D, and Mechanical Reasoning. None of these variables is listed among those having a correlation greater than .20 with mathematics achievement. Thus, the evidence concerning the relationship between spatial performance and mathematics achievement remains mixed, with some hints that both the type of spatial performance measured and the mathematical content may be critical.

The Issue of Unique Predictive Contribution.   These inconsistencies aside, there is the problem that isolated correlations between spatial tests and mathematics performance are almost meaningless. As mentioned above, Lohman (1979) reports that spatial tests are strongly correlated with tests of general intellectual ability and that this is particularly true of complex tests of visualization, such as those just reported to correlate with mathematics achievement. Thus, the correlations between spatial and mathematical tests might simply reflect the strong relationship between general intelligence and mathematics achievement. Sherman (1980b) and Fennema and Sherman (1977a, 1978) also reported that tests of vocabulary have correlations of about .50 with mathematics achievement. The critical analyses to determine whether all of these correlations are due to what spatial and vocabulary tests have in common (general intelligence) or whether the relationships are partially independent of each other were not done. The regression analyses performed in Connor and Serbin's Study 2 indicate that spatial ability measures contribute something to the prediction of mathematics achievement beyond what vocabulary measures accomplish. Though commonly used as a quick index of general intelligence, vocabulary is a less than perfect measure of general intelligence because it does not require operations of reasoning or transformations of information. In contrast, those aspects of general intelligence are well represented in spatial tests. Thus, the contribution of distinctly spatial abilities remains uncertain. Stallings' results suggest the possibility that spatial performance might have a distinct effect upon performance in geometry and analytic geometry, but unfortunately Stallings' study did not incorporate any other measures of intellectual ability so the appropriate analysis could not be done. Sherman (1980b) reported that spatial-visualization scores contributed significantly to the prediction of girls' performance but did not do so for boys. However, the meaning of this outcome is doubtful for methodological reasons (which are discussed in greater detail in a later section of this chapter). Indeed, the difference in regression coefficients for visualization for males and females was not statistically significant in Sherman's analysis.

In counterpoint to the foregoing discussion, a recent study of Rice University students (Burnett, Lane, & Dratt, 1979), found that sex differences in spatial ability scores could statistically account for differences in math SAT scores. However, in a university emphasizing engineering, it is quite possible that the study of mathematics covaries with experience in spatial thinking so that there may be no causal relation.

In summary, we do not yet have a sound estimate of the degree to which distinctly spatial abilities may contribute to mathematics performance. This contrasts with a substantial history of research showing that various spatial tests are better predictors of success in courses such as mechanical drawing and shop than are tests of general intellectual or verbal ability (McGee, 1979). Such research suggests that it might be more profitable to seek direct relationships between sex differences in spatial performance and sex differences in participation in such fields as engineering and physical science, rather than to seek indirect relationships through mathematics.

Sex Differences in Spatial Test Performance   A number of the studies summarized in Table 11.4 reported no statistically significant sex differences in spatial test performance either for the entire study or for various subgroups and tests within the study. In one large, nationally representative sample, the Armstrong Women and Mathematics sample, 13-year-old females were found to perform significantly better than males on a spatial ability measure. Nevertheless, these results are not inconsistent with reports of an advantage for males in earlier studies (Maccoby & Jacklin, 1974). Although her sample of subjects was large and representative, Armstrong's scale had a small number of items of a single type, not representative of the entire class of spatial ability measures. Average spatial performances of males and females in a population typically differ by a small amount, a fraction of a standard deviation, which will be statistically significant if the sample is very large, as for example, the Project TALENT sample. When the sample numbers in the hundreds rather than in the thousands such differences may not be found. The lesson of this is that the usual way of speaking of group differences in performance distorts reality by converting overlapping, perhaps almost identical, distributions of performance into conceptual dichotomies. Therefore, most people exaggerate the size and possible significance of sex differences in spatial performance. The possibility that sex differences may be more prominent in some tasks than in others warrants attention in any future reviews. Relatively large sex differences have been found on a test involving the rotation of objects in three dimensional space (Sanders, Soares, & D'Aquila, 1982; Vandenberg & Kuse, 1979). Because we do not have a sound estimate of the unique contribution of spatial performance to mathematics achievement, it is not possible to estimate what portion of sex differences in mathematics achievement (often also small, sometimes non-existent, see Chapter 1) might possibly be attributed to differences in spatial performance.

Linking Cognitive Ability to Motivation

The foregoing discussion of cognitive abilities has been written as if they could be cleanly distinguished from preferences, interests, attitudes, likes, and dislikes. But that is not so. Krutetskii (1976) has been studying children gifted in mathematics for many years. He characterizes such children as having a "mathematical frame of mind," a tendency to categorize things in terms of mathematics and logic, to find mathematical meaning in many aspects of reality. This sounds more like the description of an interest or of a cognitive style than of an ability.

Earlier the point was made that we cannot distinguish meaningfully between measurements of mathematical ability and mathematics achievement. Another of Krutetskii's observations seems relevant to this issue. Although mathematically gifted individuals seem to leap over the steps of reasoning through which others plod, Krutetskii says that this is not so if one observes them at an early enough age. Perhaps interest and practice produces what is later seen as exceptional ability.

Modern cognitive theory provides a way of understanding how experience and learning can result in characteristics that approximate our naive concept of ability—without implying the inherent, biological basis that is also part of our understanding of the word ability. Recent efforts to model complex cognitive functions (Newell & Simon, 1972), often mathematical thinking, have resulted in theoretical systems called production systems. These have two major aspects to them: operations that are performed, and conditions of application specifying when the operations are to be performed. Anderson (1976), especially, has extended the theory of production systems to incorporate phenomena of learning. With experience, a long sequence of operations that once occurred in a step-by-step fashion, each with its own condition of application, may be efficiently combined into a single efficient, complex operation. Similarly, with experience, the conditions of application can become much more complex pattern recognizers so that the learner can distinguish what is the appropriate complex action to take in a wide variety of particular situations. For example, expert chess players are now understood to be able to recognize many patterns of game situations (Chase & Simon, 1973). Such lightning recognition of relevant characteristics of a situation, together with rapid, complex, and appropriate action is what we tend to perceive as evidence of ability.

This new theoretical account of ability does not rule out the possibility of inherent individual differences, but it suggests a rather different conceptualization of them. They might exist in the most elemental operations or perceptual capacities—for example, to distinguish red from green—that are available to enter into the learning process. Alternatively, there might be differences in the rate at which experience results in more consolidated, complex performances or in flexibility of access to information in memory, and so on. This second kind of individual difference would affect a very broad range of performances—possibly explaining the phenomenon of general intelligence. However, the efforts to identify the cognitive process differences corresponding to the individual differences discussed in mental testing research remain largely a matter of theoretical speculation (Cooper & Regan, 1982).

If interest and involvement may create ability, it is at least equally likely that ability has an impact upon motivation: people tend to like those activities in which they do well. Consequently, it may prove impossible to fully disentangle the roles of cognition and motivation in mathematical performance. We shall be returning to this point later on.

AFFECTIVE VARIABLES

The affective or motivational variables that have been suggested as influencing the decision to study mathematics are many and diverse. It is extremely helpful to have a theoretical model of the decision process to organize the discussion of motivational and social variables affecting mathematics enrollment and achievement, providing a plausible account of the interrelations among these variables. These variables are not an unordered list of independent influences. We know that they interact in a dynamic process that accounts for many of the strong intercorrelations among them, even though the task of specifying and scientifically confirming a model of that process may exceed current technical capabilities.

Parsons and her colleagues (Meece, Parsons, Kaczala, Goff, & Futterman, 1982; Parsons, Adler, Futterman, Goff, Kaczala, Meece, & Midgley,

1983) have provided an extremely helpful organization of these variables by applying general theoretical accounts of behavioral choice to the question of women and mathematics. (Lantz and Smith and Casserly and Rock made similar formulations.) This theory links the decision to engage in an activity to two major constructs: the expectancy for success on a task and the value of the task for the individual. These two major ideas can be used to organize our understanding of the probable impact of many variables: the past history of success and failure, socialization experiences, and future goals.

Expectancies of success are clearly related to such variables as confidence in one's mathematics ability, past achievement in mathematics, and estimated difficulty of the future task. The relationships among these variables are complicated by the fact that individuals may differ in their interpretations of past success and failure—in the extent to which it affects their estimates of ability or their future expectations. In addition, expectancies of success, estimates of ability, and the interpretation of success and failure may be affected by the opinions of other persons surrounding the individual—parents, peers, and teachers.

Parsons and her colleagues suggest that the value that engagement in an activity has for an individual can be broken down usefully into several different aspects:

1. *Attainment value,* the activity's ability to confirm salient and valued characteristics of the self such as competence, intelligence, masculinity, or femininity. It is obvious that confirmation of intelligence is often an important motivating value of success in mathematics. In addition, questions of the sex role appropriateness of mathematics enter here. Parsons, however, points out that there is variation in the degree to which sex role identity is salient and central to an individual's self concept.

2. *Intrinsic value or interest.* A number of the studies reviewed here measured this sort of variable—Effectance Motivation in Mathematics, for example, described as a measure of enjoyment of mathematical problem solving. Liking for mathematics might also be classified here.

3. *Utility value.* Students' judgments of the usefulness of mathematics were investigated in these research studies. Career expectations and career goals also affect the perceived usefulness of mathematics, as may the adequacy of their information about the mathematical requirements of careers.

The other aspect of the value of an activity is its cost. The perceived cost of engaging in an activity may depend upon the judged effort that it requires, its displacement of other competing activities, as well as the psychological cost of failure if it should occur. Any negative aspects of success in mathematics—anticipated social rejection, and so on—would also be classified as a cost. Once again, the opinions of others might affect all of these aspects of the value and cost of participating in mathematics. Furthermore, social and economic constraints on the career opportunities that are realistically available to the individual would affect career plans and, indirectly, the value of mathematics.

Having outlined this general framework, we turn to the discussion of the major affective and social variables (or classes of variables) included in these research studies. For each, we will summarize the evidence linking it to mathematics enrollment and mathematics achievement as well as the available information about its relation to other major variables. First, indicators of value are discussed: the perceived utility of mathematics and then indicators of liking or intrinsic value. Next, confidence in mathematics learning and related indicators of expectancies of success are discussed. The foregoing appear to be the most powerful of the affective and social variables studied. The discussion then proceeds to social influences that may be thought of as modifying expectancy and value: the conceptualization of math as a male domain, the encouragement of parents and teachers, the classroom, school, and larger social environment.

A Methodological Concern. The interpretation of these attitudinal variables is not entirely straightforward. The questionnaires that are used to measure these variables are not infallible yardsticks. Some people will use extreme values on scales; others will not. The expression of true opinions may be tempered by the person's impression of what is a socially acceptable answer. For example, a girl might not find it acceptable to say that she is better in mathematics than all the boys in her class, even if she really thinks that she is. It is often suggested that males are less willing to admit to anxiety or other psychological distress. Although the problem of "social desirability" as an influence upon attitude responses is a familiar one, it has no simple solution. In this research, it is always possible that social desirability or other factors that affect the level of response will be acting differently for males and females. We can never be certain that the apparent sex differences in these subjective variables are genuinely differences in the characteristic the scale purports to measure.

The Perceived Utility of Mathematics

In this section, we discuss the impact of students' perception of the utility of mathematics upon their decisions to enroll in mathematics courses. Two other sets of variables are closely related and will be discussed as well: (1) actual and perceived mathematics requirements of the careers to which students aspire; and (2) educational aspirations.

Relation to Math Participation. Armstrong found that the perceived usefulness of mathematics (in both daily life and in relation to educational and career plans) was significantly (p < .001) related to the amount of mathematics taken by both males (r = .34) and females (r = .30) in the twelfth grade. The relationships between enrollment and mathematics preparation required for a job appeared stronger still (.50, .40), as did the relation to educational aspirations (.48, .45). At age 13, however, general usefulness seemed to be a better predictor of intended enrollments (.38, .26) than these other variables. Lantz found the subjective value of mathematics, an attitude scale that included questions about the general usefulness of mathematics as well as its usefulness to later educational, career and life plans, to have the greatest relationship of any attitudinal variable to the student's intention to take mathematics courses (overall r = .34, p < .001). This variable was strongly correlated with perceptions of mathematics needed in the student's planned career (r about .50), a variable that may itself have had a slightly stronger relation to course plans (r's = .30, .39, and .40). Students who carried out their intention to enroll in optional mathematics courses also rated the usefulness of mathematics to their future plans as the most important reason for deciding to enroll in mathematics. Sherman reported that the average perceived utility of mathematics was higher for students who later took more years of mathematics. Parsons found correlations of about .40 between estimates of utility and the intent to take more math in one year and about .25 the following year. Brush reported that usefulness of mathematics did not seem to be a good predictor of intentions to enroll in mathematics, but she also found that a change in the perceived usefulness of mathematics was associated with a change in preference for math courses. Wise reported that sex differences in career interests predicted enrollment, preceeded differences in achievement, and, indeed, probably can explain sex differences in enrollment and achievement in the Project TALENT sample. Fox reported that those girls who accelerated in their high school mathematics programs were more likely to plan full-time, substantial careers than were other equally able girls who did not accelerate. Stallings also reported that career plans appeared to have been formulated by the time students were in geometry and making decisions about enrollment in optional mathematics. She also reported that girls continuing the study of math were more attuned to career plans than those not continuing.

Thus, there is considerable evidence that the perceived usefulness of mathematics, especially the perceived requirement for mathematics in a planned career, is important to decisions to enroll in mathematics. Of course, students' perception of the mathematical requirements of their career choices may be inaccurate. Students generally are poorly informed about the actual uses of advanced mathematics (Brush, Stallings), and there is some evidence that girls are or have been less informed than boys. The "utility" of mathematics also seems to be strongly influenced by college requirements, especially for females (Casserly, Wise, Armstrong).

Relation to Mathematics Achievement. The perceived usefulness of mathematics may also have some relationship to mathematics achievement. Armstrong reported correlations of .30 for boys and .20 for girls at age 13, both statistically significant ($p < .001$). At this age, the judged mathematics required for a future job was not correlated with mathematics achievement but educational aspirations were (.24 and .24). In twelfth grade, educational aspirations showed the strongest relationship to math achievement (.46 and .40), followed by the amount of mathematics required by the expected job (.41 and .32) and the judged usefulness of mathematics (.29 and .26). Needless to say, these relations in a cross-sectional study provide little information about the reasons underlying the relationships. Wise reported that interest in mathematics and mathematics related careers predicted math achievement gains in high school after controlling for the level of math course participation. Similarly, Boswell reported that interest in masculine occupations was correlated with achievement greater than that expected on the basis of ability measures (r about .20). She also reported some moderate correlations between usefulness and mathematics achievement in high school (.15 and .29 at grade 9, .35 and .16 at grade 11). In eleventh grade, Boswell found a strong association between math achievement and interest in male occupations: .50 for males and .55 for females. At later ages, previous enrollment decisions may be affecting achievement, and students who are able in mathematics may be more knowledgeable about the utility of mathematics or more willing to admit its utility. The direction of causality is unclear.

Sex Differences. There may be some sex differences in the perceived utility of mathematics. It is not clear whether there is any sex difference in how useful students think mathematics is for themselves. Armstrong found no sex differences in the judged usefulness of mathematics. Lantz reported no sex difference in two of three samples, a difference favoring males in the third sample. Brush and Casserly reported the usefulness of mathematics lower for females. Several studies reported that mathematics was judged to be more useful for males than for females (Parsons, Boswell). Parsons reported that these views may have changed during the 2 years of her study. Fox reported large sex differences in reasons for working and expectations for a full-time career, which in turn was related to girls' decisions to accelerate in mathematics. Similarly, Casserly reported a large effect of females' feelings about women's role in the world upon their educational aspirations.

Another feature of students' perception of the usefulness of mathematics should be mentioned. For both males and females, the perceived usefulness of mathematics declines with age (Brush, Parsons). One factor that probably contributes to this decline is the fact that students are able to name only uses of arithmetic as uses of mathematics (Brush, Stallings). They appear to know little about the uses of advanced high school mathematics.

Relations to Other Predictor Variables. The perceived utility of mathematics has substantial relationships to the other important attitudinal variables. Lantz reports correlations with liking for mathematics in the range of .40 to .60 and with confidence in the range of .30 to .50. In close agreement, Parsons reports that the utility of advanced mathematics has a correlation of about .40 for females and .50 for males with her variable measuring interest in and liking for mathematics. The utility of advanced mathematics also had a correlation of about .30 for females and .40 for males with Parsons' measure of mathematics confidence (a combination of estimate of math ability, current and future expectations for success in math courses). Similarly, Armstrong reported that judged usefulness had correlations of about .50 with a math attitudes measure combining math confidence and liking for mathematics.

Liking for Mathematics and Other Indicators of Intrinsic Value

Liking for mathematics or interest in it appears to have a moderate relationship to enrollment in mathematics courses. In Parsons' study, a variable composed of items indicating liking for or interest in mathematics had correlations of .36 to .42 with the intent to enroll in future mathematics courses. In the Lantz study, correlations between liking for math and intention to enroll ($r = .26$) or actual participation (.36, .30) were smaller but highly significant. Armstrong reports a correlation of .38 for females and .47 for males between enjoyment of mathematics and the study of mathematics in grade 12. Sherman reports correlations of about .30 between her enjoyment variable, Effectance Motivation in Mathematics, and later indicators of mathematics achievement. Mean values of this variable were higher for students who took more years of mathematics. In students' rankings of the importance of various factors influencing their decision to study mathematics, liking for mathematics ranks rather low (Parsons, Lantz). However, Armstong's results indicate that liking for math may be more important for older students: For 13-year-olds it was ranked sixth of nine factors, but at grade 12 it was ranked third. Also, Stallings reports that 75% of the girls she interviewed who continued in mathematics, mentioned liking mathematics as a reason for continuing.

Relation to Other Predictor Variables.   Liking for mathematics appears to be strongly related to confidence in mathematics ability, to self perception of mathematics ability. Lantz reports correlations of .60 to .70 between liking and confidence in mathematics ability. Parsons reports correlations ranging from .44 to .64 between her measure of interest and liking and perceived mathematics ability. In Parsons' data the relationship of liking and interest to objective indicators of achievement appears much weaker: correlations ranging from .07 to .21. Obviously, the strong relationship between self perceptions of mathematics ability and liking for mathematics complicates the problem of determining how either might affect math enrollment decisions.

Sex Differences.   Given the close relationship between liking and confidence in mathematics ability, it is interesting that there is little evidence of a sex difference in liking for mathematics. Armstrong found no sex differences in the enjoyment of mathematics in either the 13-year-old or twelfth grade samples. Brush reports no sex difference in liking for mathematics. Parsons states that boys and girls do not differ in their enjoyment of mathematics. There was no significant difference in the Lantz study. Boswell reports little sex difference, and Sherman says the same about effectance motivation in mathematics.

Age Differences.   One of the findings of these studies that should be of greatest concern to mathematics educators is that liking for mathematics may decline severely in the high school years. Brush dramatically charts this decline over sixth through twelfth grades. Parsons and Sherman agree in reporting negative change in a variety of attitudes toward mathematics. The same trend may be evident in Armstonrg's data from a nationally representative sample through the age differences are small.

Confidence in Math Ability and Math Anxiety

Not surprisingly, it is difficult to distinguish confidence in one's mathematics ability and mathematics anxiety as separate variables. Instead, they seem to label opposite ends of the same continuum. When Fennema and Sherman (1977a) attempted to construct separate scales to measure each of these concepts, the two scales were found to have a correlation of

− .89 with each other. On the other hand, factor analyses conducted by Armstrong in developing her instruments suggested some differentiation of the concepts. Her confidence scale contains unemotional statements of poor performance and lack of understanding, whereas the anxiety scale contains items that refer to fear, dread, tension, and feelings of being at ease.

Relation to Math Achievement.   Confidence in mathematics appears to have a correlation of about .40 with mathematics achievement whether it is measured concurrently (Fennema & Sherman, 1977a) or 3 years prior to the achievement measure (Sherman). Parsons reported somewhat lower correlations (averaging about .30) between perceived math ability and a measure combining math grades with achievement test scores. Casserly found that self assessments of math ability among tenth graders in accelerated math classes and twelfth graders in AP calculus were strongly related to math grades (r's = .61, .64, .56, .47), equally so for males and females. The results of Sherman's regression analyses indicate some possibility that confidence in math ability may predict both grades in later mathematics courses and later mathematics achievement scores. However, the large simultaneous regressions and discriminant analyses that she performed do not provide a rigorous test of the extent to which the addition of the confidence variable can improve upon prediction from the most important variable predicting math achievement—earlier math achievement (r = .79). Wise reported that for females general confidence (no math confidence measure was available) had some association with mathematics achievement.

Relation to Math Participation.   Armstrong found correlations of .47 (males) and .42 (females) between math confidence and math participation among twelfth graders and correlations of .28 (males) and .19 (females) with the course plans of 13-year-olds. Math anxiety also had significant, but generally lower, correlations with course participation. Sherman's regression analyses suggested that confidence in math ability may predict enrollment more strongly than does math achievement. Both males and females who took more years of mathematics had higher math confidence scores. In discussing her interview results, Sherman states that girls continuing in math had higher math confidence scores than did girls of comparable ability who did not continue. Similarly, Stallings reported large differences in anxiety and the perceived difficulty of mathematics between girls continuing and not continuing in mathematics, but no relation between actual geometry achievement and continuing. Lantz reports that degree of math confidence differentiated students who actually enrolled in advanced mathematics from those who did not, and that it was a better predictor than previous math grades. In Brush's study confidence in math was part of a composite "feeling" variable that correlated with course plans. In Parson's study, perceived math ability had higher correlations (.24 to .42) with the intent to take more math than the objective measure of mathematics ability did ($-$.11 to .26). On the other hand, Casserly reported that self-concept of mathematics ability among twelfth grade AP math students had no relation to continuing in math in college or to aspiring to math related occupations, but the ability level of such students is so high that there is no reason to expect a strong relation. In summary, confidence in mathematics ability or mathematics anxiety is a variable that shows some promise of being able to predict both mathematics enrollments and mathematics achievement.

Sex Differences.   There is also considerable consistency in reporting sex differences in confidence in one's math ability. Armstrong reported significant and relatively large sex differences in both math confidence and math anxiety at both the age of 13 and twelfth grade. Parsons reports that boys were consistent in giving themselves higher ratings of math ability than girls did, that they considered math courses to be easier, and that they had higher expectations of success in future math courses. However, boys did not have higher expectations for success in their current math courses, and in fact their performance was no better than girls'. Lantz also reports that females consistently estimated that they had less likelihood of receiving a satisfactory grade even though there was no sex difference in previous performance. Fennema and Sherman (1977a) reported that males had more confidence in their math ability after eighth grade, whereas Boswell reports greater math anxiety for girls in all grades. Brush found that girls think math is more difficult and report more anxiety in quantitative situations, but no such sex difference in admissions of anxiety about English was found. Fox also reports that boys in the mathematics talent search had higher scores on the scale of self-confidence as a learner of math, but in this case boys also scored higher on the math SAT. Overall, the results indicate that girls have less confidence in their mathematics ability, independently of any objective difference in performance. A complication in the interpretation of these results is the suggestion in Boswell's data that self-reported grades are less related to math achievement scores for females than for males (Grade 7: .70 and .63, Grade 9: .65 and .55, Grade 11: .86 and .50). Interestingly, no one seems to have analyzed whether admissions of extreme, truly paralyzing mathematics anxiety are more frequenty found among females. The implications of such a finding would be quite different from the possible meaning of small average differences in scores. These might be explained by sex differences in socially acceptable responses. However,

Brush ruled out the possibility that her finding of higher math anxiety in females reflected higher admissions of academic anxiety in general by including measures of anxiety in English in her study.

Changes in Confidence in Math Ability.   Sherman's data indicate that confidence in math ability is a moderately stable characteristic: there was a correlation of .56 between confidence measured in eighth grade and confidence measured in eleventh grade. Confidence in mathematics learning ability seems to decline during the high school years. Armstrong found this decline to be more evident than changes in liking for mathematics, especially for girls. In Brush's data, however, the decline in confidence is less severe than the decline in liking. Parsons did a cross-lagged analysis of her data that indicated that changes in self perceptions of math ability were related to perception of other persons' estimates of ability and to beliefs about the difficulty of the current math course. Both of these were affected by estimates of performance in the current math course. This would be consistent with Casserly's report of a strong correlation between grades and self-assessment of ability.

The Stereotyping of Mathematics as a Male Domain

There are a number of different senses in which mathematics might be said to be stereotyped as a masculine domain. One might ask whether mathematical activities are usually carried out by males, or whether mathematics seems to be more used by adult males than by adult females. One can ask whether males are better, or necessarily better, than females at doing mathematics. One can ask whether females may or should do mathematics, whether it is compatible with femininity. Naturally, the typical responses one gets depend upon which of these questions, or which combination of them, is asked. Boswell found that the majority of female Ph.D.'s in mathematics believed that their field is stereotyped as masculine. In fact, of course, most Ph.D.'s in mathematics are males. She also reported that elementary school students in third through sixth grades judge that students of the same sex as their own are better in mathematics, whereas in later years girls tend to agree that boys are better at mathematics. In addition, Boswell's students tended to consider that adult males are more competent in mathematics than adult females are. Again, these opinions are in agreement with the objective facts of average achievement and performance. Parsons found that students in fifth through twelfth rated the usefulness of mathematics for males greater than the usefulness for females in one year but not the following year. She also reported that the students in her sample did not consider males to be higher in math ability.

Sex Differences. Several of the present studies used the Fennema-Sherman scale of Math as a Male Domain. (Fennema & Sherman, 1976a) Both sexes generally respond that math is a subject appropriate for everyone, but girls are more extreme in saying so (Brush). These sex differences in response to this scale seem to be found by everyone (Armstrong, Brush, Lantz, Fox, Sherman). Parsons raised the possibility that changed views of the socially desirable response may be affecting responses, especially girls' responses, to this sort of scale so that it is not really effective in measuring what one hopes to measure.

Relation to Math Participation. The sex stereotyping of mathematics is generally considered to be a variable relevant for girls, a possible barrier to their participation in mathematics. The evidence from these research studies indicates that Math as a Male Domain has little predictive value for girls' enrollment or achievement in mathematics. Brush reported that this variable was not a major predictor of course preferences for junior high school students or of course plans for high school students. Lantz also reports that it is not strongly correlated to participation in math courses: r's = .04, .00, .05 for males and .17, .12, .12 for females. Armstrong reported a correlation of similar size—.188—between this variable and the number of math courses taken by twelfth grade females, but no significant correlation with 13-year-olds' course plans. Armstrong also reported a significant correlation of the same size and direction (.179) between Math as a Male Domain and the math course plans of 13-year-old boys, pointing out the hazard of drawing hasty conclusions from occasional findings of small significant correlations. In Sherman's data, mean scores on this variable do not seem to vary systematically in relation to the number of years of math studied. Countering general expectations and these findings, Parsons reported a tendency for the stereotyping of mathematics as more useful for males to be weakly associated with greater valuing and enjoyment of math as well as with intentions to enroll in more math for both males and females.

Relation to Math Achievement. Math as a Male Domain (positive scores mean math open to all) was also reported by Armstrong to have positive correlations with math achievement for both 13-year-old (M: .267; F: .451) and twelfth grade students (M: .209; F: .313). Boswell also reports some evidence of small negative correlations between stereotyping and achievement for both males and females. These correlations may simply indicate some tendency for more able students to take more liberal views of sex roles. Brush found correlations of .25 and .35 between overall ability and the attitude that math is open to both males and females. In one of her many regression analyses, Sherman found that

Math as a Male Domain was the only non-cognitive variable that emerged as a significant predictor of female problem–solving performance. Cross-lagged correlations confirmed the possible significance of this variable in this case, but it is an isolated finding.

Summary. Overall, the stereotyping of mathematics as a male domain does not seem to show much promise as a variable predictive of either enrollment decisions or achievement. This result may be considered surprising because of the rhetorical salience of this hypothesis in discussions of the women and mathematics issue. It is, however, consistent with the indirect and personality dependent effect postulated for stereotyping variables in the Parsons model.

THE INFLUENCE OF THE SOCIAL ENVIRONMENT

It is generally assumed that many sex differences in academic and life choices are caused primarily by the influence of other persons surrounding the individual, persons who convey messages about what is expected, or what is socially acceptable. Most of the studies under review attempted to assess the impact of other persons—parents, peers, teachers, and counselors—and to determine whether these influences were different for males and females. In most instances, these influences were measured by the students' perception of the other persons' attitudes, expectations, or beliefs. Only Parsons systematically collected both attitudes expressed directly by parents and teachers and the student's perception of those attitudes, in such a way that direct comparisons of actual and perceived attitudes are possible. In addition, both Parsons and Stallings observed the classroom behavior of teachers, seeking insight into the process of teacher influence upon student performance. Casserly also interviewed teachers, counselors, and other school personnel.

Because of the nature of these measures, it may be instructive to begin the discussion of results concerning the influence of other persons by summarizing Parsons' findings. Not surprisingly, teachers' estimates of students' ability were strongly related to the objective index combining grades and achievement scores, $r = .50$ for females and .57 for males. Parents' estimates may have been somewhat more strongly tied to objective indicators for girls ($r = .49, .51$) than for boys ($r = .36, .42$). This relationship to the objective indicators was stronger than that found for the child's own estimate of his or her own math ability (r's .16 to .39). The child's perception of others' estimates of the child's ability was strongly related to the child's own ability estimate (r's $= .70$ to .80). This may mean that the young child's perception of others' opinions almost totally determines the opinion about the self, but it also suggests that young students simply may not differentiate between their own opinions and the opinions of other persons around them. The relationship between the child's ability estimate and the parents' actual estimates of the child's ability was very weak (r = .16 to .30), whereas the relationship to the teacher's estimate may have been somewhat stronger (.36, .47). Parsons' longitudinal analysis suggested that perceptions of others' estimates of one's ability might be causally related to changes in one's own ability estimate, but the results also suggest that these are really two different measures of the same thing. The most important message of these results may be that the individual's perceptions of other people's attitudes and beliefs are very unreliable measures of those attitudes and beliefs.

Parents

In Parsons' study the actual responses of parents indicated that they considered boys and girls to be equal in math ability. However, they also held the somewhat contradictory view that math is more difficult for the girls. Parents also considered math to be less important for girls than it is for boys. Fathers considered themselves better in mathematics than mothers considered themselves to be, although mothers rated themselves higher in overall high school performance. No significant relationship could be found between parents' conception of their own math ability and the child's self–concept of math ability. That is, there was no evidence of a role model effect.

Relation to Math Participation. In Parsons' study parents' actual estimates of the student's ability had little relation to the student's intention to enroll in mathematics courses (r's = .06 to .24), and the relation of teachers' estimates of ability to enrollment intentions was also weak (r = .20). The student's perception of parents' and teachers' ability estimate was marginally more related to enrollment intentions (r's = .14 to .35). Despite the strong relationship between this perception of others' opinions and the student's own ability estimate, the latter seems to have been more strongly related to enrollment intentions (r's = .24 to .42). The student's perception of parental encouragement—the variable most often found in the other studies—had a very weak relation to enrollment intentions (r's = .08 to .19).

Other studies also reported similar statistically significant but small correlations between perceived parental encouragement and math study. Lantz found a correlation of about .24 with actual math course participation. Armstrong found correlations of .13 to .28 with the enrollment intentions of 13–year–olds and correlations of about .30 with the actual math course enrollments of twelfth graders. Sherman also reported that the parents of students who eventually took more math courses had been perceived as somewhat more encouraging when the students were in eighth or ninth grade. Similarly, Stallings reported that parental expectations and support frequently differentiated students who continue in math from those who did not.

Relation to Math Achievement.   In Armstrong's study, perceived parental encouragement was not related to math achievement at age 13 but for twelfth graders the correlation between encouragement and math achievement was also about .30. Sherman also reported significant correlations of .30 or above between parental encouragement and measures of math achievement for females but not for males.

Sex Differences.   In general, there seem to have been few sex differences in the degree to which parents were perceived as encouraging students to study mathematics.

Relation to Other Predictor Variables.   Students' perceptions of mother's and father's attitudes are strongly correlated: Lantz reported r = .60. In addition, there are indications that mothers may have the stronger effect. Parsons' analyses indicated no independent effect of fathers beyond that shared with mothers. Lantz found that students rated mothers more important than fathers as influences upon their enrollment decisions. Perceptions of parental encouragement seem to be more strongly related to judgments of the utility of mathematics and to math confidence than they are to enrollment.

Teachers

Teachers appear to be at least as important as parents in encouraging students to study mathematics. As mentioned earlier, Parsons found the teacher's actual estimate of the student's ability to be much more strongly related to the student's own estimate than was the parents' actual estimate. Parsons found strong relationships between teacher expectancies and student expectancies of success in math and estimates of math ability (r's = .34 to .67). Similarly, Sherman found student's confidence as math learners to be quite strongly related to earlier perceptions of teacher encouragement (r = .41 for boys, .47 for girls).

Relation to Math Participation.   Lantz found that teachers were rated as the second most important influence on enrollment decisions, after the usefulness of mathematics for students who actually enrolled and after the mother for students who did not enroll. Stallings (personal communication) found that career plans and parents were rated as more important influences on math enrollment than were teachers. Armstrong found that teachers were ranked just above parents as an influence by twelfth graders and just below parents by 13–year–olds. In this study perceived teacher encouragement had a somewhat stronger relationship (r = .42) with actual course enrollment of twelfth graders than did perceived parents' encouragement, but the relation to the plans of 13–year–olds was weak (.24, .16) though statistically significant. About half of the advanced placement students Casserly interviewed—both males and females—indicated that teachers had been crucial to their self-confidence, their continuation in math study, and their career direction.

Sex Differences. In her nationally representative sample, Armstrong found no sex difference in teacher encouragement for students in twelfth grade and a small, statistically significant difference in favor of females at age 13. Similarly, there was no sex difference in teacher encouragement for the tenth graders in accelerated mathematics in Casserly's study.

Effects of Classroom Interaction. Despite strong evidence that teacher expectations and perceived teacher encouragement may have important effects upon math enrollment, neither Parsons nor Stallings was able to link classroom interaction variables with student behavior. After extensive analytic efforts, Parsons was able to show that in the classrooms where bright girls had lower expectancies, they received less praise and less interaction. Stallings reported that girls appear to be more likely to continue studying math when their math classes are interactive and instructive, but that it does not seem to matter if the interaction is with male or female students. All teachers in Stallings' study reported that they considered males and females to be equally good at mathematics. This result differs from some earlier reports (Ernest, 1976), and may reflect changes in socially acceptable views.

Counselors

These studies provide relatively little information about counselors. Student reports consistently rate counselors to be unimportant as an influence upon their enrollment decisions (Lantz, Armstrong, Stallings). In Armstrong's study, perceived counselor encouragement had weak relationships with both enrollment and achievement (r's of about .20 to .25). Both Wise and Lantz reported that counselors seemed to have a negative impact on math course enrollment for both males and females. Obviously, this might reflect the self-selection of students who choose to consult counselors.

Peers

Student ratings of the influences on math enrollment decisions (Armstrong, Lantz) indicate that peers are the least important of all influences on their decision. Again, Armstrong reported correlations of .20 to .25 between perceived peer attitudes and course enrollment and achievement. Parsons reported that peers were not seen as discouraging enrollment in math, but 95% of her sample intended to continue in math. Lantz speculated that students may underestimate the influence of peers because students who actually enrolled in math were much more likely to report that their friends would be taking math than were students who did not enroll. Asking students about the opinion of the single person who was most important to them—friend, parent, teacher, whomever—she found this to be one of the single best predictors of enrollment intentions (r's = .38, .26, .42). Obviously, students may select who is important to them on the basis of shared values and attitudes or may have distorted perceptions of the attitudes of these important persons. It is likely, too, that the influence of the social environment acts through the values and expectations of the individual and that these are the determinants of decisions that are perceived by the individual.

Social Status

Brush found that socioeconomic status was a significant predictor of math enrollment for girls but not for boys. Armstrong also found somewhat larger correlations between socioeconomic background variables and either math course enrollment or math achievement for females than for males. Sherman's interviews of girls continuing in math and those not continuing, matched for ability, indicated the more favorable situation, greater frequency of intact families, and so on, among those continuing in math. These results undoubtedly relate, also, to Wise's report that for girls discontinuing the study of math was related to expectations of working after high school, interest in office work, and so on. These effects might be associated with social class variation in sex role expectations and with strong effect that social class had upon the likelihood of college attendance for females at the time of Project TALENT sample. College entrance requirements remain an important determinant of the "utility" of high school mathematics courses, especially for females.

School Effects

The most obvious way in which the characteristics of schools can affect mathematics participation and achievement is through the availability of math courses. Many high schools do not offer advanced math courses. Armstrong's study, in which this variable was considered, does not indicate that course offerings explain much variance in math course participation; that is, her regression analyses indicate that the combination of math course offerings, school size, and SES can account for at most 3% to 7% of the variance in math course enrollment. Casserly, who was explicitly interested in understanding what school characteristics were associated with high rates of participation of females in advanced placement mathematics, reported that early identification of mathematically able students and academic tracking are favorable conditions for female students. This seems consistent with Wise's report that schools with accelerated science curricula showed unexpected math achievement gains in female students. Although Casserly's sample of schools was selected to contrast schools with high and average participation of females in Advanced Placement math, these differences in participation were not substantial during the period of the study. Stallings found high female mathematics enrollment in schools that had high black student enrollment and career education programs. In part, this probably reflects cultural differences in expectations for women. Fox was not able to find support for the hypothesis that the proportion of girls in an accelerated mathematics program would affect the probability that girls would persist in the program. Whatever the explanation, a recent report from Sells (personal communication), as well as Casserly's data, indicates that the proportion of girls enrolled in advanced mathematics varies greatly from school to school even today.

SUMMARY OF PREDICTOR VARIABLE RESULTS

Predictive Potential

Cognitive Variables. The variable most strongly associated with continued enrollment in mathematics and with future mathematics achievement is previous mathematics achievement (or general scholastic achievement or general intellectual ability). The association of this cognitive variable with the expressed enrollment intentions of younger students may not be as strong. Neither these studies nor the previous literature provide much evidence of a relationship between spatial abilities and mathematics achievement or enrollment beyond that accounted for by their common relation to general intellectual ability. Like other measures of intellectual ability, measures of spatial ability do have a substantial relation to mathematics achievement and enrollment.

Affective Variables. In most studies, the perceived utility of mathematics was found to have a moderately strong association with continued enrollment; students rank the usefulness of mathematics as one of the most important influences on their decision to study math. For older students, the more specific relation of mathematics to their later educational and occupational plans is more strongly associated with enrollment.

Liking for mathematics also has a moderately strong relation to enrollment and to the intention to enroll, as does confidence in one's mathematical ability. The stereotyping of mathematics as a male domain has only a weak negative relation to mathematics achievement and enrollment, evidently about as much for boys as for girls. It may be that more able students tend to have more liberal attitudes.

Social Influences.   There seems to be a weak positive relationship between parental encouragement and continued enrollment in mathematics. Evidence of an association between teacher encouragement and continued enrollment is somewhat stronger, especially for older students. Evidence about peer influence is mixed: students rate it as very unimportant but tend to report that their friends have the same attitudes and plans for math study that they do. Little evidence was found for role model effects of any kind; neither the mother's attitude towards math nor achievement in mathematics, nor the sex of teachers nor the proportion of female students seemed to have much relation to continued enrollment. For females only, there seems to be a weak association between socioeconomic status and continued enrollment, beyond that expected because of the general relation between achievement and socioeconomic status. Schools with ability tracking and accelerated math and science programs may favor the persistence of females in the study of mathematics.

Sex Differences

Sex differences in the cognitive variables are negligible at the beginning of high school, prior to the enrollment differences that produce differences in mathematics achievement. Sometimes there are sex differences in the perceived general utility of mathematics, and math may be seen as somewhat more useful for males. Sex differences in aspirations to a life or career in which math is seen to be useful are more substantial. Sex differences in confidence in one's math ability are consistently found, but there is no sex difference in liking for or interest in mathematics. More strongly than males, females express the view that mathematics is a field open to both females and males. There seems to be no sex difference in the extent to which parents or teachers encourage students in mathematics.

THE CHALLENGE OF ANALYSIS: INTERRELATED VARIABLES

Until this point, discussion has been largely confined to relationships between individual variables and mathematics enrollment or achievement. Unfortunately, the whole of our understanding of the determination of these outcomes amounts to considerably less than the sum of these parts. Not surprisingly, earlier mathematics achievement, confidence in oneself as a learner of mathematics, and liking for mathematics—for example—are all related to each other. Therefore, it is difficult to say which of these variables should be regarded as more basic, more "causal," to which should be attributed the effects of whatever these variables have in common. This intuitively obvious dilemma has a technical description. Regression analysis—the primary method of analysis (with some variants and elaboration) used in the studies discussed here—assumes that the explanatory variables being used are independent, unrelated to each other. When this assumption is violated, the analysis can still be done, and the results can still be used for practical prediction. However, the theoretical meaning of the regression weights—which tell us about the relative importance of variables when the variables are uncorrelated—is vitiated. To understand why, consider the case of two differently named variables that are almost perfectly correlated. In this body of research mathematics anxiety and confidence in oneself as a learner of mathematics are two such variables. One of these variables can substitute for the other; they really measure the same thing. So one could assign all of the weight to one and none to the other, or vice versa, or anything in between without affecting the quality of the prediction that one can make. The higher the correlation between two variables, the more closely one approaches this situation. To be more precise, the effect that variables have in common can be attributed to one or the other or divided in any way between them. What actually happens is a matter of chance depending upon the particular sample of data: The prediction might be very nearly as good with a very different regression equation. Obviously, when you have a large number of interrelated variables, the possibilities multiply and the situation becomes more confusing.

In the studies under discussion, the problem of interrelations among the variables was very severe. Table 11.5 summarizes some of the reported relationships among the major variables. One common approach to this problem is to perform a factor analysis in order to create new variables that capture the common features of the original variables and that are uncorrelated. Several of these researchers performed factor analyses. Fennema and Sherman (1977a) found that their three cognitive variables—a vocabulary test, mathematics achievement, and spatial ability—formed a single factor, whereas affective variables including the perceived encouragement from other persons, formed a second factor. For females only, there was a third factor formed by the two sex role related variables—Mathematics as a Male Domain and Attitude Toward Success in Mathematics. The outcome of the factor analyses performed by Brush was similar. She combined all indices of ability into a single variable. Several different affective scales were combined into a single

TABLE 11.5

Intercorrelations of Predictor Variables

Cognitive Variables	Verbal	Spatial	IQ	Math Achievement	Utility	Liking[1]	Confidence	Math Open (+) or Male Domain	Parents	Teachers	SES
Verbal		.55 B .41 S	.80+ B	.60 .70 B .50 S	.08 S	.03 S	.22 S	.13 S	.07-15 S	.13 S	
Spatial	.48		.60 B	.53 S .50-60 B	.25 S	.21 S	.26 S	.03 S	.02-07 S	.23 S	
IQ	.80+	.60		.70+ B	.14 B	(.10B)[2]	(.10B)[2]	.35 B		.20 B	.40+ B
Math Ach.	.60	.54	.70+		.32 S	.31 S	.44 S	.18 S	.19-24 S	.34 S	
Affective Variables											
Utility						.57 S .35+ B .40-60 P .40-60 L	.30-50 L .30-50 P .45 B .56 S	.25 B .10-.25 L .37 S	.45 A .48 B .30-48 L .50-58 S	.40 A .41 B .60 S	.00 B
Liking					.49		.63 F-S .64 B .65 S .65-70 L	(.10B)[2] .35 S	.45 B .40 A .34-43 S	.66 S	(.00B)[2]
Confidence					.44	.65		(.10B)[2] .34 S	.55-60 B .25 L .36-46 S	.50 B .63 F-S .65 S	(.00B)[2]
Male Domain					.24	.22	.22		.37-39 S		.13-24B
Parents					.47	.41	.44	.38		.28 B .38 S .48-.59 S	
Teachers					.47	.66	.59	.33	.54		

Codes indicate source of correlations: A = Armstrong; B = Brush; F-S = Fennema & Sherman (1977); S = Sherman, personal communication, Grade 8 data; L = Lantz. Upper half matrix contains all data located; lower half matrix contains the mean of those values.

[1] For Sherman data, the variable was Effectance Motivation in Mathematics.

[2] Correlations for Brush's combination of Confidence, Enjoyment, etc. variables.

"Feelings" variable. Usefulness and an index of support from teachers were retained as separate variables although these last three have inter-correlations of about .40. Again, the attitude that math is open to all emerged as a genuinely independent potential predictor variable. Another of Brush's variables—socioeconomic status—was uncorrelated with everything except the ability measure with which it had a correlation of about .40. Armstrong also found that all of her attitude items factored together, with such variables as the encouragement of teachers and sex stereotyping appearing to be separate factors. However, she judged her effort to construct new uncorrelated variables based on the factor analysis to be only partially successful: diffuse intercorrelations (ranging from .05 to .58) remained. Similarly, Lantz' factor analysis yielded moderate cor-relations—.30 to .50—among confidence, utility, liking, and perceived parental encouragement. Only sex role stereotyping (incorporating math as a male domain) was uncorrelated except for a moderate negative corre-lation (− .29) with the perceived utility of mathematics.

In summary, efforts to find or construct truly independent sets of pre-dictor variables were less than successful. Constructed variables some-times lose the intuitive meaningfulness of the originals, as well. This is certainly a problem when one wants to use the results as a guide to practical action to change the values of the predictor variables. There are other ways to deal with the problem posed by correlated predictor vari-ables. Most of these require the taking—implicitly or explicitly—of some theoretical position about how the data should be interpreted, about which variables should be regarded as primary or basic. The choice may be made according to which single variable appears to have the most explanatory power, especially if no others are comparable to it. This notion is embodied in stepwise regression procedures, where the theoret-ical import of what is being done is not made explicit. It is possible that the most powerful variable really summarizes the impact of a set of other, more fundamental variables that are causally related to it. Such notions are incorporated in another approach, used by several of these research-ers, which is called path analysis. In path analysis (Blalock, 1971; Dun-can, 1975; Joreskog, Sorbom, & Magidson, 1979) the researcher specifies a theoretical model of the interrelationships among all the variables. One can specify a complex, interacting system of variables. It can be hy-pothesized, for example, that sex role stereotyping affects career aspira-tions which in turn affect the perceived usefulness of mathematics and thus ultimately influence the decision to enroll instead of simply assuming that sex role sterotyping directly affects the decision to enroll in mathe-matics. Similarly, perceived encouragement from other persons might act through influences upon both the perceived utility of mathematics and the individual's self–confidence as a learner of mathematics. Such a complex, dynamic model does seem more appropriate to this problem than the idea of independent, additive influences that is the theory underlying regression analysis. Once a model has been specified, the path analytic procedure can determine whether the pattern of correlations in the data is consistent with the model. Unfortunately, it is quite possible that several different models could be equally consistent with the data. Consequently, reported conclusions from the path analyses are partially due to the assumptions specified prior to the analysis. We know only that the data are "not inconsistent with" the specified model. For example, Casserly and Rock specified a model in which the possible causal effect of math study in high school upon career aspirations was explored. However, we have seen from longitudinal data that there is reason to believe that career aspirations are more appropriately seen as a causal determinant of math study. Only for males was the causal path between persistence in math study and math related occupational aspirations found to be significant. Although it is not customary to test alternative path models, in this instance it would have been useful to know if the data were also consistent with the opposite causal hypothesis, or if the opposite causal relationship were significant for females.

The interlocking relationships among the variables that people have considered important to understanding women's participation in mathematics test the technical limits of our analytic methods. For this reason, it is all the more important to seek consistency in the results of different methods rather than to rely upon the conclusions of a single study. Table 11.2 displayed the variables incorporated in the studies under review. Note that there were three different major dependent variables that these studies attempted to predict: the intention to enroll in mathematics, actual math course enrollment, and mathematics achievement. In the next section, we integrate the analyses predicting course enrollment and enrollment intentions. Results relating to math achievement are discussed in Chapter 1.

PREDICTING MATH COURSE ENROLLMENT AND INTENTIONS TO ENROLL

A glance at the table characterizing these studies reveals some of the complexity involved in attempting to integrate the analyses performed in the studies under review. Three of these studies have good information about the actual course participation of students: Armstrong, Wise, and Sherman. The first two were nationally representative samples. The last two were longitudinal studies that permitted examination of the effect of variables over time. Boswell sampled a single school district and had a relatively low rate of voluntary participation, especially in the eleventh-grade group. Armstrong, Brush, Parsons, and Stallings had information about intentions to enroll in mathematics courses. Lantz had both intentions to enroll in the next math course and information about whether these intentions were realized in the following year. Some of the other studies would contain such information, but it was not explicitly analyzed. Only Sherman and Brush had a good representation of both cognitive—including non-mathematical cognitive measures—and affective variables. Wise's data set, though strong in many ways, was not collected for this purpose and does not have the affective variables specific to mathematics. In addition to this variation in the study variables, there are differences in the methods of analysis used to investigate the relationships of those variables.

Two of the analyses used relatively conventional regression analyses. After using factor analysis to arrive at relatively independent variables, as described earlier, Brush entered variables into a simultaneous regression. In her regression analyses, Brush found that her combined measure of cognitive ability (I.Q., math achievement, spatial ability) and socioeconomic status were the only significant predictors of plans to study mathematics in high school, and socioeconomic status was significant only for girls. In only one analysis, for boys only, was the affective composite variable, "Feelings," a significant predictor. These results seem quite consistent with Wise's results from a longitudinal analysis involving more genuine prediction. He performed his analyses by entering the variable with the largest correlation first and then examining the partial correlations with the remaining variables. Ninth grade math achievement was the best single predictor ($r = .62$) of math course enrollment during high school (although a measure of general academic aptitude was almost equally good—$r = .60$). In addition, for individuals of equal ninth grade achievement, expected educational attainment was the most significant additional predictor, having a partial correlation of .39 with math course enrollment. An associated variable, enrollment in a college preparatory curriculum, as well as the math level of the expected occupation, interest in math, interest in office work (a negative factor) were also significant predictors, resulting in a multiple correlation of .73. These additional variables could be considered indicators of the utility of mathematics for the individual. Numerous small but statistically significant partial correlations remained after these. For girls, these related to the characteristics of the girl's father and to her interests and plans. For boys, they related to interests and abilities. These findings seem consistent with Brush's finding of SES as a significant predictor for girls. Both a larger sample size and the "harder" dependent variable of actual enrollments seem to have permitted Wise to detect additional small effects. Although her analyses included the variable, Brush was not able to demonstrate an effect of the perceived utility of mathematics.

Armstrong took a rather unusual approach to a conventional regression analysis. First, she regressed the mathematics course participation of twelfth graders on a set of variables including socioeconomic status and school characteristics such as course offerings. Then, she entered either all of variables reflecting the influence of other persons or all of the variables reflecting the individual's attitudes and values into a stepwise regression as the second step. The most important other person variables were parental educational expectations and parental, teacher, or counselor encouragement. The most important individual attitude variables were educational aspirations, mathematics preparation required for expected job, and attitudes towards mathematics (confidence, anxiety, enjoyment, usefulness). The chief conclusions that can be drawn from this are: (1) that all of the other person variables taken together can account for about 20% of the variance in course taking for females and 25% for males; and (2) that all the individual attitudinal variables taken together can account for about 30% of the variance for females and about 35% for males. The primary difference seems to be that socioeconomic status, among the variables taken into account first, had a bigger effect for females than for males. These figures can be compared to the approximate 36% of the variance that Wise could account for with the single achievement variable at the beginning of high school. Although Armstrong also found a correlation of .55 to .60 between course taking and achievement, measures of achievement taken after differences in enrollment cannot be considered as predictors of enrollment. No general ability measure was included in the study. Perhaps grades in mathematics, having a correlation of .45 with course taking, could be considered as a cognitive variable. It alone would then account for 20% of the variance. Unfortunately, there is no way to determine how much these accounted for proportions of variance would overlap with each other.

Parsons' analyses of the determinants of enrollment intentions were path analyses expressing her theory of cognitive mediation of decision processes. All variables were considered to have their effect through their impact upon either the student's expectancy of success in mathematics or the student's perception of the value of mathematics. For the most part, the outcome of the path analyses seems consistent with the notion that the intent to enroll can be predicted as well by indices of the perceived value of mathematics and expectancies for success in mathematics as it can with models incorporating many additional variables that presumably have their effects mediated by these two major variables. These two major factors appear to be about equally important in determining enrollment intentions. In some analyses, a surprising additional negative effect of the student's perception of socializers' opinion of the student's ability appeared. This probably indicates only that the composite index of the student's expectations and self-estimated ability was not optimally constructed. From the analyses, it appears that the addition of an objective composite index of ability and achievement cannot improve upon the prediction of intention to enroll that is possible from subjective variables. Direct correlations between the objective indicator and intentions were exceptionally low ($-.11$ to $.26$) in Parsons' study as compared with other results, whereas correlations with self-perceived ability and future expectations of success were higher. This may reflect the low meaningfulness of intentions to study mathematics that are expressed in seventh through ninth grades (the status of most of Parsons' subjects), the above average ability level of her subject sample, and the fact that school grades (included in Parsons' objective index) are less effective predictors than achievement test scores. The total variance accounted for achieved in Parsons' analyses is typically $.35$, whereas Wise's analysis of actual enrollment achieved about $.50$.

Lantz applied a model very similar to that of Parsons. In a study without any cognitive variables other than the previous math grade, the subjective value of mathematics, math confidence, the attitude of the student's self-selected significant other person, and socioeconomic status were the strongest predictors of math course participation. About 33% of the variance was accounted for by this model. The subjective value of mathematics, in turn, was affected by the mathematics needed for the planned career, by parental encouragement, by liking for mathematics, and by the attitude of the significant other person. Later path analyses of these data (Smith, 1983) indicated that future aspirations (career expectations and the amount of math required by the expected career) were the most important direct influence on participation, followed by liking for mathematics and its perceived utility. Separate models fitted for males and females indicated that liking may be relatively more important for females whereas utility may be more important for males. Mathematics confidence did not make a useful predictive contribution.

For students in accelerated math programs leading to Advanced Placement calculus, Casserly found math achievement as indicated by grades to be the best predictor of persistence in the study of math. The grade level at which acceleration occurred and perceived teacher and father encouragement also contributed significantly to prediction for females, whereas self-assessment of math ability was a significant predictor for males. The multiple correlations for the prediction of persistence were about $.50$ in both cases, thus accounting for about 25% of the variance in this highly selected population for which prediction should be more difficult. In the Casserly path analyses, the variables available to measure the possible utility of mathematics—educational and career aspirations— were placed subsequent to persistence in math study in the hypothesized causal path so that no clearcut measure of their possible contribution to continued enrollment in mathematics was available. It might be that the encouragement variables are effectively standing in for utility variables because they are related. Compared to other variables, for girls educational aspirations had a relatively high correlation with continued enrollment ($r = .27$) but math related occupational aspirations did not ($r = .06$). For boys, those occupational aspirations seemed relatively more important ($r = .26$) than educational aspirations ($r = .14$). Variables such as liking for mathematics were not included in the analysis although the self-assessment of math ability would be considered a measure of confidence. For females, it was the objective measure, not the subjective measure that was placed later in the hypothesized causal path, that was important.

In the remaining studies that attempted to predict math enrollments, large numbers of highly intercorrelated variables were entered simultaneously into multiple regression or discriminant analyses. Thus, the resulting regression weights must be interpreted with great caution.

Sherman's (1980b) results seem consistent with this general picture that has emerged above. Examination of the mean eighth grade scores for groups of students differing in the years of math ultimately studied suggests that the cognitive variables—vocabulary, spatial–visualization, and mathematics achievement—are all strongly and about equally associated with enrollment in advanced mathematics. Confidence in oneself as a learner of mathematics seems to have a somewhat weaker, but still substantial, association with advanced enrollment. Enjoyment of mathematics (possibly more so for females than for males), perceived encouragement from teachers and parents, and the perceived usefulness of mathematics were moderately associated with advanced enrollment. In contrast, attitudes toward success in mathematics and—at least in one subject sample—the stereotyping of mathematics as a male domain appeared to have no relation to enrollment status. Discriminant analyses in which all of these variables were considered simultaneously were as inconsistent with each other as one might expect but seem to indicate the importance of the cognitive variables as determinants of enrollment. In addition, confidence in oneself as a learner of mathematics always appeared as a significant predictor, suggesting that it may have an effect independent of the cognitive variables.

An exception to these findings is Fox's report that math SAT scores were not particularly related to continuing in special accelerated math programs. However, the extreme ability level of the students, the special nature of the programs, and the small sample mean that there is no real contradiction in these results.

SUMMARY OF ANALYTIC FINDINGS

It is evident that the cognitive status of the student at the beginning of high school is the most powerful predictor of later math course participation that was located in these studies. Of course, the substantial correlations (around .30 to .40) between the cognitive and affective measures imply that much of this predictive power cannot be uniquely attributed to the cognitive variables. To a considerable extent, intellectual ability, confidence in oneself as a learner of mathematics, enjoyment of mathematics, judgments of the value of mathematics, and so on, form an inseparable complex. In particular, subjective estimates of ability or measures of confidence might be expected to be closely tied to objective measures of ability, even though it is their departure from objectivity that makes them interesting. It appears probable that confidence in one's mathematical ability does have some independent predictive value.

The cognitive variables may have their effect upon intentions through their impact upon the student's subjective estimate of his or her ability in mathematics. In predicting intentions, there is a possibility that subjective perceptions of ability may be as good as objective indicators in predicting the intention to enroll. Parsons' results suggest this, but Brush's do not—perhaps because the composite "Feeling" variable obscures the effect of confidence and expectation for success in math. Also, Casserly's path analyses clearly show that it was the objective measure—math grades—that made the significant contribution to predicting future enrollment for females. Grades were also necessary predictors for males, in addition to subjective assessment of ability.

More predictive power was achieved in the predictions of actual enrollments than in the prediction of enrollment intentions. It is quite possible that young students' expressions of enrollment intentions are just unreliable, that another answer would be given on another day. But there are also obvious differences between intentions and actions that may be associated with different relations to the predictor variables. There are a number of reasons why one might expect the objective measures to appear more effective in predicting actual enrollment. Although the student's subjective ability estimate may be what influences momentary intentions, actual ability is likely to affect success in courses and to modify the student's confidence. Parsons found confidence to be modified by perceived course difficulty. Objective test scores may influence counselors' advice—recall that visits to counselors were associated with decisions not to take mathematics. Obviously, ability tracking policies enhance the importance of cognitive variables as predictors of enrollments. Finally, there is the methodological point that yardsticks of confidence or of self-assessed ability are rather rubbery compared to yardsticks of ability.

Ideally, then, one would like to know how to partition the predictable variance in math course enrollment into: (1) that which is predicted in common by both objective indicators of cognitive ability and subjective measures of confidence; (2) that which is independently predicted by objective indicators; and (3) that which is independently predicted by confidence. The contrast between such analyses for intentions and actual enrollments would also be illuminating. Although we do not have such a clearcut partition, there are a number of indications that student confidence has some independent predictive value: Sherman, Stallings, and Lantz all report that girls who drop mathematics differ in mathematics confidence from girls of equal objective performance who continue.

In Wise's analysis, variables related to the potential utility of mathematics were shown to add to the prediction possible from cognitive variables. In the studies confined to affective variables and in student ratings of factors influencing their decisions, the perceived utility of mathematics emerges as very important. Lantz' results suggest that the perceived utility of mathematics might be more important in determining the intention to enroll, whereas confidence or actual ability may be more important in determining whether that intention is fulfilled. It is unfortunate that so few of the studies included both cognitive and affective variables. Because the cognitive variables seem to be so powerful, the outcomes of predictive analyses that omit them are likely to be misleading. It is possible that the relative importance and interrelations of the affective variables would emerge much more clearly if cognitive ability were first statistically controlled.

EXPLAINING SEX DIFFERENCES IN MATH ENROLLMENT

Despite its great importance to understanding individual differences in math course enrollment, cognitive status at the beginning of high school contributes virtually nothing to the explanation of sex differences in math course enrollment. As reviewed in Chapter 1, sex differences in mathematics achievement, and of course in other cognitive measures, are negligible at that time. Using their regression analysis for predicting enrollment, Wise, Steel, & MacDonald (1979) could attribute only 4% of actual sex differences in enrollment to ninth-grade achievement differences, whereas 79% could be attributed to the interest and educational expectation variables. The data set did not include measures of confidence in oneself as a learner of mathematics, and no comparable analysis is available that incorporates such a variable. However, it is evident that these interest and utility related variables approximately suffice to explain sex differences in enrollment. Furthermore, in the years since these data were collected in the early 1960s, the obvious changes in the educational and career expectations of young women have been accompanied by a great reduction in the sex difference in math course enrollment. So the perceived utility of mathematics probably was an important source of the sex difference in enrollments, and smaller sex differences in the perceived utility of mathematics still persist today. Although the Wise et al. results explain nearly all of the sex difference in enrollments without considering math confidence, the intercorrelations of these variables mean that confidence, if examined alone, might also appear quite important. There does not seem to be any way to determine whether women's confidence in their mathematics ability has changed as much as their career interests have in the last 20 years. Sex differences in math confidence were consistently found in these recent studies: they may explain much of the continuing difference in enrollments. However, Casserly's analyses do not suggest that this was true for her high ability female students. Her results also suggest the possibility of an independent effect of encouragement by teachers and parents for girls, although this could have been a manifestation of the general effect of perceived utility.

In subjective discussion of the women and mathematics issue, people appear to have considered what influences behavior when ability is held constant, just as students neglect abililty in subjective reports of influences upon their enrollment decisions. In this research, acknowledgement of the importance of ability (or prior achievement) and its statistical control probably would have yielded a much more definitive picture of the influence of affective variables and good quantitative accounting for sex differences in enrollment. In the general case, one might object to giving such implicit priority to the cognitive variables when analyzing group differences in performance because the affective variables might have influenced cognitive growth at an earlier time. In a previous section of this chapter, we discussed how affective differences might generate apparent ability differences. For the case of women and mathematics, however, there seem to be no important cognitive differences between the groups at the time the critical decisions are being made, and the problem is therefore simplified.

IMPLICATIONS

The primary purpose for doing this type of research is to improve educational practice through the improved understanding of educational problems. Therefore, we wish to consider what implications these results have for efforts to improve the participation of women in mathematics, how these might generalize to the situation of underrepresented minorities, and also what implications the results may have for mathematics education in general.

The Women and Math Question

We have learned that enrollment in mathematics courses really is the critical issue in eliminating sex differences in mathematical knowledge and skill. When females do enroll in mathematics courses, their grades are as high as those of males and differences in other measures of achievement are small or non-existent. There is little evidence either that spatial ability is important to mathematics achievement or that it contributes anything to the explanation of sex differences in mathematics achievement. In general, mathematics enrollment decisions seem to be determined primarily by earlier mathematics achievement, but this is not the explanation of sex differences. Two other influences upon enrollment decisions seem most likely to be the source of sex differences in enrollments. One is the perceived utility of advanced mathematics for the student's intended future life and career. Students seem to know very little about the actual use of advanced mathematics (Brush, Stallings) so that this is an area in which education could be improved (cf. *Scientific American*, 1964). For girls, the expectations of the educational system itself seem to be relatively more important in supporting continued enrollment. Sex differences in interest in the careers that require mathematics have diminished: for example, the percentage increase in female engineering students has been spectacular. It seems likely, however, that such differences in interest will persist for a long time and will result in continued differences in mathematics enrollment. There are sex differences in the very fundamental interest patterns that predict college major and occupational selections among males who have not experienced arbitrary restrictions of opportunities (Dunteman, Wisenbaker, & Taylor, 1979). Nevertheless, schools might act to encourge girls' interest in non-traditional and mathematics-related careers.

A second likely source of sex differences in math course enrollment is self-confidence as a learner of mathematics. Females are somewhat less confident, especially with respect to expectations of success in future mathematics courses. There is no evidence, however, that females are particularly subject to paralyzing anxiety in mathematics. It may be that sex differences in math confidence simply reflect lingering stereotypes about women and mathematics that are very pervasive. As long as every report of somewhat better performance by a group of males is greeted by headlines like, "Do males have a math gene?" (Williams, 1980), it may be difficult to eliminate the sex difference in math confidence. Undoubtedly, all discussions of the women and mathematics issue, regardless of their intent, help to maintain the life of these stereotypes. The research indicates that teachers can be an important influence on student confidence, that the student's self-assessment of ability, for example, is more closely related to the teacher's opinion than to the parent's (Parsons). Unfortunately, the specifics of how teacher influence on confidence comes about have not been identified. Teachers should certainly attempt to give girls appropriate assurance about their mathematical ability and should not attribute girls' success in mathematics only to hard work overcoming difficulty. Perhaps the most effective approach to the problem of confidence would be to reduce the possible influence of confidence upon enrollment decisions. Mathematics requirements and academic tracking policies greatly reduce the possible influence of student confidence, and these have been found to favor the participation of females in advanced mathematics (Casserly). Casserly's analyses suggest that the encouragement of mathematics teachers can have a direct effect upon the continued mathematics enrollment of female students with high ability. Such factors may help explain why some schools have much better participation than others do.

Generalization to Other Underrepresented Populations

Various groups of minority students are more severely underrepresented in advanced high school mathematics courses than female students are today (Morning, Mullins, & Penick, 1980). For example, a survey of high school students who were seniors in 1980 (National Center for Education Statistics, 1980) indicates that black, Hispanic, and Native American students were only about half as likely to have taken advanced math courses as white students, whereas Asian American students were about twice as likely to have done so. (Data for males and females within each ethnic group were not provided.) To what extent can the results of the research on women and mathematics illuminate this problem? It is most likely that the overall structure of the problem is similar, but that the specifics of what is important are different. Therefore, the most justifiable generalization from the research is probably in the form of suggestions for effective research design and data analysis. Nevertheless, some extrapolations can probably be made with assurance.

Certainly we can expect that math achievement will retain its importance as a predictor of mathematics enrollments within any group. Anyone who neglects the importance of mathematics achievement in attacking these problems is unlikely to succeed. Sketchy as the available data are, the underrepresentation of these groups in advanced mathematics is known to be accompanied by group differences in average achievement that are evident from an early age. The first priority in assisting these groups should be to overcome these early differences in achievement. There may be cultural values and social circumstances that influence career interests and opportunities and thus influence the perceived utility of mathematics study, as sex roles and sex stereotypes have influenced it for women. Some previous research (Dunteman et al., 1979) indicates that lack of interest in scientific and technical occupations is probably not the issue for black students, in contrast to its importance for women. A recent study (MacCorquodale, 1980) indicates that minority students may have even poorer information about the actual relation between mathematics and particular occupations than students do in general. There are some indications that affective variables, rather than perceived utility, may be relatively more important for minority students (Lantz). However, little positive result can be expected from programs directed solely at attitudinal change, without attention to math achievement. If comparable research were done for these groups (and some relevant projects are underway), it is likely that socioeconomic status would emerge as a more important variable, if only as a variable influencing early achievement and educational and career expectations. It may well be that both students and teachers have less confidence in minority students' ability to learn mathematics. As for female students, though, the best solution to problems of confidence may be a structure of requirements and curricular expectations that diminish the effects of confidence.

The experience with research on women and mathematics may also suggest a different definition of the problem of primary interest. Whereas many believe that sound mathematical education is important for all, the chief reason for concern about underrepresentation in the study of advanced mathematics is its implications for later participation in the elite scientific and technical careers requiring mathematical preparation. This may suggest that both research and practical efforts should be focused on those individuals who seem to have the potential for high levels of achievement. Even though those individuals may seem relatively priviledged, their fate may be most important to the attainment of these equalitarian goals. In order to help these students, we need better information about the implications of differing levels of mathematics achievement for career potential: the follow-ups of the Project TALENT sample (Wise) suggest that very high levels of math achievement may be essential for persistence in math-related careers.

General Implications for Mathematics Education

The research reviewed here has pointed out some rather serious problems affecting mathematics education for all students. The review of enrollment data in Chapter 1 emphasized the fact that few students of either sex are studying advanced mathematics. Poor preparation in mathematics is not just a problem of women; many believe that it is a very general problem in the United States today. Although college entrance requirements or a personal liking for the subject may cause individuals to continue studying mathematics, advanced mathematics in high school tends to be seen as important only for those who intend to enter what are considered to be math-related careers. Yet, the newspapers are full of stories of general public and political importance that require knowledge of rather advanced mathematical concepts for full comprehension (Czepiel & Esty, 1980). Late decisions to enter mathematics-related careers seem to be rare events (Wise), even for those with strong mathematics preparation, but there are reasons to think that the general population requires a better understanding of mathematical ideas than is common in the U.S. today. Several of these studies found a decline in attitudes toward mathematics during the high school years, a decline not shared by other subjects (Brush). In part, this may happen because almost no one knows what the mathematics studied in high school is really used for. Students' ideas about the uses of mathematics concern applications of arithmetic. Most students know only that mathematics is required to enter the career they desire, not why it is required or how it will be used. Therefore, it seems likely that increased emphasis upon the uses and applications of mathematics—rather than the exclusive presentation of "pure" mathematics—would benefit all students. There are indications that something about the style of teaching or classroom interaction in high school mathematics may be unattractive to students. Lecturing, with low student involvement, appears to be more common in mathematics classes (Fey, 1969). In addition, student confidence in ability to learn mathematics declines in high school. Thus, many of the changes that seem to be needed to improve opportunities for female students actually seem to be needed for all students.

Needs for Future Research

The review of these research studies suggests that additional useful information about the women and mathematics question might be obtained through additional analyses of existing data to clarify questions about the magnitude of the predictive contributions of spatial visualization, math confidence, and so on. Theoretically determined orders of consideration of variables, with appropriate consideration of theoretically interesting alternatives, would have been preferable to the atheoretical approaches to analysis that were often used. It would be interesting to know to what extent the subjective variable of confidence can replace math achievement in predicting enrollment. Reanalysis of data sets with better definitions of the utility of mathematics—definitions related to the individual's career aspirations—and of confidence—emphasizing expectations for future success in math—might yield better evidence for the importance of these affective variables and better quantitative measures of that importance. Perhaps liking for and interest in mathematics should be given this kind of closer examination because it is so frequently mentioned in interviews as a reason for continuing to study mathematics.

Obviously, we now know how to design a better study of this type. The exercise of thinking through how one expects the vast list of potentially relevant variables to have their effects and to interact with each other—as path models require—seems to have been worthwhile, whether or not one actually uses path analysis. We now have better information about which variables should figure prominently in such a model. The expressed math enrollment intentions of young students proved to be a less predictable variable than actual enrollments, though interesting to consider in addition to actual enrollment data. Cognitive variables, especially measures of general ability, should have been better represented than they were. We know more about the meaning or lack of meaning of students' statements about the attitudes and behavior of other persons in their lives. Although the remaining uncertainty is intellectually dissatisfying, it is not obvious that the outcome of a new study would change our understanding sufficiently to have practical importance. In contrast, the research reviewed here did yield a significant correction of earlier views of the determinants of math course enrollment. The importance of earlier achievement had been slighted. Whereas some hypothesized influences—perceived utility and confidence—were confirmed as important, others—the sex-stereotyping of mathematics, the influence of role models—were found to be unimportant. Investigations of influences upon key variables such as perceived utility may be worthwhile in their own right because they are the points of leverage for intervention efforts. There seems to be an important lesson for future research in the fact that the intense focus on sex differences (that is, group differences) led to the neglect of major variables influencing individual behavior and thus weakened the investigation of the issues and variables of central concern.

Perhaps more research on the determinants of early career directions is needed: that question, though repeatedly mentioned in the grants announcement that resulted in most of these studies, was given little attention, only enough to show that it indeed was an important question. Whereas the sex–stereotyping of mathematics as a subject seems to have been irrelevant to girls' enrollment, the sex typing of expected life roles and eventual occupations remains important. A number of on-going research studies attempt to investigate the nature of women's decisions to enter non-traditional careers in math, science, and technology. The review of research on career decisions is beyond the scope of the present chapter. There is a recent meta-analysis of studies of women's choice of science careers (Lantz, Carlberg, & Eaton, 1981) that provides information comparable to our review of results concerning individual variables. Women choosing science were differentiated from other women by their high ability, strong career commitment, and general patterns of interests, particularly their interest in mathematics. Again, this in an indication that interest in mathematics should be investigated more thoroughly even though the present studies did not indicate that there is a sex difference in liking for or interest in mathematics.

More research attention should be given to the talented, to those girls and women who are actually likely to enter mathematical and scientific careers. Maines (1980) is investigating women students of mathematics in college and graduate school. In a sense, the fate of these women always was the central concern, and they probably should have been given more attention from the outset. Equally, there is a need for special attention to talented minority students. Research on samples of the general population tells us little about such individuals because they are rare: for example, very few students in Brush's study expressed any interest in mathematics-related careers. Whereas Casserly's results indicate that ability and achievement remain important determinants of persistence even within highly talented groups, the investigation of attitudes, values, and environmental encouragement is most germane for those students who are clearly capable of pursuing advanced mathematics. The effects of such variables may be much larger for students in the higher ranges of ability than for those in the lower ranges. Perhaps Parsons' continuing follow-ups and analyses will provide more insights as more of the students discontinue the study of mathematics.

There are some important research questions of broader significance. The research indicates that teachers are important, perhaps especially as an influence on student confidence. Yet, the efforts to identify the ways in which that influence was realized in classroom interaction were rather unsuccessful. The means by which teacher expectations are communicated to students is a question of significance far beyond women and mathematics, or mathematics instruction. So are other aspects of students' confidence in their ability to learn. Evidently—because schools with similar student populations differ greatly in mathematics enrollment patterns—there are important characteristics of school environments still to be discovered. These challenges remain for researchers.

Obviously, we need a better understanding of what is wrong and what is right with mathematics instruction in the high schools. We need to understand what causes the decline in attitudes toward mathematics during the high school years, and to develop approaches to instruction that will be more successful. Because of the cumulative nature of mathematical knowledge, it is likely that some absolute level of mastery is necessary in order to continue successfully. Therefore, it is not surprising that achievement is an important predictor of continued enrollment. Research into the fundamental nature of mathematics learning is just beginning. We need to go beyond predictive correlations with socioeconomic status, spatial ability, gender, or ethnicity. More useful than proof that spatial ability helps predict mathematics performance would be information about how spatial thinking is actually used in solving mathematical problems. We need better descriptions of what successful students are learning, and we need to develop ways teaching so that their accomplishment will be more widely shared.

12 Strategies to Increase Mathematics Enrollments

Alma Lantz
Eclectic Systems Research

Introduction

With increased awareness of the potential contribution of women to a technological society, there has been an increasing concern that women participate in technical occupations and have the prerequisite skills to enter the field of their choice. Further, science and mathematics education in the United States is falling behind that of the Soviet Union, Japan, Western Germany, and France (Manpower Comments, 1980). Therefore, mathematics education is not only a concern to those committed to equal opportunities for women, but must be a concern to all sectors of our society. Increasing enrollments in mathematics is important to insure equality, strength, and prosperity in the future. The purpose of this chapter is to assess the effectiveness of various strategies to increase female enrollment in mathematics and to summarize what has been learned that might be applicable to students of both sexes. The chapter draws some conclusions about the success of both prevention and intervention efforts, and suggests that more attention should be paid to the implications of communication theory for such programs and to the style and content of mathematics instruction.

Informational Base. The chapter draws on three major sources of information. The first is the recent proliferation of studies of women and mathematics, many of which are discussed in this volume. The second is evaluations of the programs designed to increase mathematics enrollments. The third is the fact that female enrollments have increased during recent years; determining the reasons for the increase may provide information on ways to sustain or enhance this trend.

None of these sources of information is conclusive. The studies can only provide hypotheses to be tested; the determination of correlates of math avoidance does not necessarily provide appropriate mitigation strategies. Even if causation were determined by the theoretical studies, this would only provide partial information for the design of intervention strategies. That is, the "cause" may not easily lend itself to change. Consequently, the most effective method of producing long range change may not involve rooting out the cause, but rather treating the symptoms. Nevertheless, the research studies included in this volume provide an empirical foundation for a tentative theory of math avoidance. Taken collectively, they indicate the most promising paths to pursue in ameliorating the problem. Therefore, the more robust conclusions from these studies will be used to surmise those strategies that *should* produce effective interventions.

Hypothetically, the success of already implemented interventions could provide the best information concerning promising strategies to eliminate math avoidance. For several reasons current mitigation projects are also a less than perfect basis for drawing conclusions. The first reason is the context in which the intervention strategies have been initiated; they have been undertaken by educators who are not primarily interested in research, who want to do something about a problem rather than study it. Moreover, many of the projects have been implemented on small or nonexistent budgets. Consequently few, if any, have been subjected to the rigorous evaluations (which might cost much more than the project itself) necessary to isolate successful and replicable procedures. Attribution of changes in attitudes, feelings, or behaviors to a project set in a complicated human environment is virtually impossible with current measurement techniques. Determining which aspects of an intricate, multicomponent project are responsible for the observed changes is an even more difficult problem. Additionally, measuring instruments may fail to capture real changes that occur at the time of measurement or in subsequent years or may indicate spurious changes. If changes are observed, the meaning and consequences of the changes may be vague or unclear. Because of these problems and the idiosyncratic elements that seem frequently responsible for a successful program, the information from the evaluations will be discussed vis–a–vis general strategies rather than specific projects.

Finally, recent data seem to indicate encouraging trends in female enrollment in mathematics (see for example, Armstrong, 1979; Lantz & Smith, 1979). If we could understand what brought about this (unexpected) change, we would know how to capitalize on it, nourish and sustain it, and make it permanent. Because the changes are not limited to communities where special interventions have been initiated, they are explained by vague statements about women's changing self concept, view of occupational options, and the environment produced by the women's movement. To make our understanding even more unclear, however, interventions related to career education and sex role stereotyping do not seem to have produced changes in enrollment when introduced into controlled situations.

Although the purpose of the chapter is to discuss the efficacy of various strategies, the state of knowledge provides basis for little more than guesses and surmise. More than anything else, the chapter may point out procedures that do not appear to have produced measurable gains and may result in experimentation with different approaches.

Outline of the Chapter. As shown in Figure 12.1, it is assumed that three groups of variables directly influence course taking. The first is labeled *cognitive beliefs.* This encompasses various beliefs about the usefulness or utility of mathematics for the individual's educational and career aspirations. The second group of variables is labeled *affect* and includes confidence, anxiety, affectance, liking, and so on. The third category is the *ability* or *achievement* dimension, including spatial and verbal ability, math achievement, grades, and so on. The individual variables included in the cognitive, affective and ability/achievement categories have been observed to have consistently high intercorrelations, as has been noted elsewhere in this volume. From the point of view of intervention strategies, this suggests that change in one area may produce change in the other areas, either directly or as a consequence of additional course taking.

Interventions vary in the directness of their impact on student course taking. For example, as also seen in Fig. 12.1, some of the instructional variations directly affect both the achievement/ability and the affective dimensions. Other interventions are less direct; teacher training presumably affects instructional techniques, which in turn may alter student achievement/ability. The more direct interventions will be discussed first.

Intervention strategies also vary in being preventative or remedial. The prevention strategy emphasizes the importance of taking nonrequired mathematics courses to students, parents, and teachers. It relies on the assumption that providing rational reasons to take mathematics is sufficient to make students do so. As with all prevention programs, conclusions about long–term effects are nebulous. Remedial programs are designed for students who did not complete the entire mathematics sequence during their high school years. If one makes the assumption that these students would not have taken additional mathematics without the

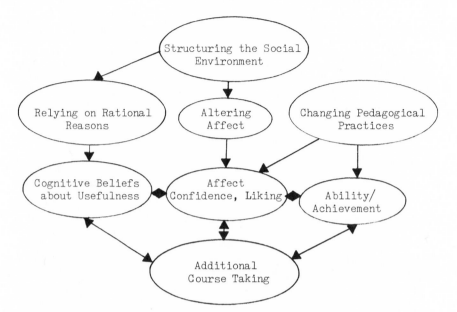

FIG. 12.1   Influences upon course taking behavior.

interventions, the evaluations should be straightforward. Nonetheless, evaluations are complicated by programs that combine affective components designed to cleanse the unconscious of debilitating associations with pedagogical components designed to enhance achievement. The discussion of the effectiveness of these strategies follows.

Ideal Conditions for Learning or Attitude Change.   As background for this discussion, it seems useful to review what social psychology and learning theory suggest about the conditions most likely to produce permanent changes in attitudes or behavior. It seems likely that the beliefs and attitudes leading to math avoidance are learned. Behaviors and attitudes are learned or maintained by following conditions:

- receiving past, present, or anticipated rewards (chocolate, good grades, approval, getting into college)
- receiving past, present or anticipated punishment (not having dates, being made to feel stupid, boredom, not getting into college)
- imitating others who are rewarded
- associating certain events with reward or punishment

Several variables influence the strength of the learned behavior. Many of these are obvious, such as the strength of the reward or punishment. Of particular relevance, however, is the difference between current and future rewards and punishments; there is every reason to expect that future or anticipated rewards have less influence on behavior than current or even past ones, because there is no certainty that the rewards or punishments will be administered. Additionally, the extent to which the future reward is valued or the intensity with which the goal is coveted is an important variable, as is one's subjective estimate of being able to achieve that goal.

The literature on attitude change and persuasion offers detailed guidance in producing or sustaining change. For example, Jones and Gerard (1967) outline some critical factors that include:

- the greater the credibility or expertness of the communicator, the greater the likelihood of a change in beliefs.
- the change in beliefs produced by a low credibility communicator may increase over subsequent time periods, whereas the change in beliefs produced by a high credibility communicator may diminish (the sleeper effect)
- the more a communicator is perceived to share the values with the audience, the greater the likelihood of a change in values
- a change in beliefs will not necessarily produce a change in values
- the more sincere the perceived intent of the communicator, the greater the likelihood of a change in beliefs
- a communication that presents both sides of an argument may produce more sustained attitude change
- attitude change may be most effective if it is associated with existing values
- fear appeals may produce a boomerang effect and be rejected by the audience
- active participation or public commitment is the most potent way of producing sustained attitude change

RELYING ON RATIONAL REASONS

Results from the Studies.   Almost all of the recent studies have shown highly consistent correlations between a cognitive belief in the perceived usefulness of utility of mathematics and the intention to elect nonrequired courses. In fact, most of the studies indicate that this is among the primary reasons for a student's plans (e.g., Lantz & Smith, 1979; Perle, 1979). In other words, students who believe mathematics is necessary, intend to take it. Moreover, significant others appear to be important in the development of the perception of the usefulness of mathematics, suggesting that beliefs about usefulness are susceptible to intervention. Beliefs about usefulness are not stable over time; they are susceptible to change in the negative as well as the positive direction (Sherman, 1979). Perceived usefulness is almost always related to personal educational and career aspirations such that election of mathematics is instrumental to achieving these ends. Perceived usefulness then represents a means to obtain a future reward, and does not necessarily reflect perceptions of current pleasure or reinforcement.

Despite a seemingly ubiquitous correlation with intentions, perceived usefulness does not appear to strongly discriminate or predict enrollment in nonrequired mathematics. For example, Lantz and Smith (1979) found no significant differences in perceived usefulness between students who stated the intention to enroll in mathematics and did, and those who stated the intention to enroll and did not (a substantial proportion), that is, usefulness made a difference in intentions but many students with good intentions did not take mathematics. Similarly, Sherman (1979) did not find usefulness to be a consistently discriminating factor in predicting enrollment. The failure of "usefulness of mathematics" to accurately predict course taking is tied to the uncertain value of the future rewards mathematics is instrumental in obtaining. Specifically, one may know that mathematics is a prerequisite for becoming a chemist. But if one is not dedicated to becoming a chemist, the knowledge will have little impact on course taking. Consequently, altering educational and occupational aspirations—which do seem more strongly predictive of enrollment (Smith, 1983)—and the intensity with which they are pursued is paramount to efforts to increase mathematics enrollment.

Interventions.   Based on the rather tenuous assumption that humans make rational decisions, the most popular intervention strategies have focused on providing factual information regarding the importance of mathematics to various educational and occupational aspirations. There are several reasons for this strategy: it is logical, it is noncontroversial, it is straightforward, and young people are suprisingly ignorant about careers. It is based on the thoughts of many adult females who now say "If I had only known."

Almost all of the interventions based on these assumptions, regardless of the age group of the audience, are one or two day "career fairs." Included in this category are the National Science Foundation's Career Workshops (at 46 schools); The Visiting Women in Science Projects for high school students, also sponsored by the National Science Foundation (at 130 schools); the Women and Mathematics project sponsored by IBM, provided by the Mathematics Association of America; and the conferences sponsored by the Bay Area Math/Science Network, funded in part by the Carnegie Corporation. Most of the conferences use "role models" to present career relevant information, which may be followed by some kind of small group discussions with the "role models". A few of the conferences incorporate various kinds of "hand–on" activities. In general, there are two distinct components of most career conferences: their informational value and the impact of the role models.

Although few of the conferences have been rigorously evaluated, several parallel lines of evidence may be used to draw tentative conclusions. First, the conferences probably result in increased information regarding career opportunities and their concommitant mathematical requirements (e.g., Denby, Devlin, & Poiani, 1977; Poiani, 1980). In other words, they increase awareness of the *potential* usefulness of mathematics. Secondly, the conferences may result in some slight decrement of sex role stereotyping. Wirtenberg (1978) noted that changes in sex role stereotyping may occur in a high school population with minimum contact and/or media presentations, such as reading materials; although as much as one third "slippage" in altered sex role stereotyping has been observed in a 9 month period (Elias, 1980). Thirdly, the presentations may stimulate additional career explorations, as was demonstrated in the Visiting Women in Science Program (Weiss, Place, & Conway, 1978) and the Women Moving Up conference (Humphreys, 1979). Fourth, the conferences may produce changes in plans or intentions (Cronkite & Perle, 1979).

The conferences may change beliefs, but there is little evidence that they have a long range impact on values or behavior. Even the most sustained career education courses do not appear to have an observable impact on course taking. A semester course in New York, sponsored by the National Science Foundation, designed to encourage high school girls to consider math or science as a career, not only did not have a positive impact on career plans, but may have had a depressant effect (Lantz, West, & Elliot, 1976). An absence of an effect of prolonged career education on enrollment in mathematics was also noted by Stallings (1979) and Fox (1979). It is not surprising, then, that single day conferences, media presentations, or published information apparently do not have much impact on career plans or behavior.

There are a multitude of reasons that the typical conference format fails to produce visible results. Specifically, the conference incorporates none of the conditions conducive to attitude change. For example, it aims only to increase information regarding the instrumental character of mathematics; it does not attempt to alter occupational values and aspirations. The conference is usually passive in nature and often requires neither commitment or active participation by the audience. It almost always presents a fear message (like math or you cannot make money). Finally, the conference rarely incorporates a two sided argument, addressing the reasons not to take math.

Experience derived from other prevention efforts is applicable. The evaluations of drug and alcohol programs aimed at high school students have indicated that addressing substance abuse directly is not effective. But approaches emphasizing values clarification and decision making skills, which focus on one's individual responsibility for one's future well being, have shown promising results. Utilizing "role playing" of future consequences and "hands–on" activities may also be productive approaches. Moreover, the results may be multiplied when they capitalize on existing naturally occurring peer groups, such as Scouts or Camp Fire Girls (Health, Education and Welfare, 1979). These tactics are part of successful conference formats. The possible role of the communicator in further decreasing the potential effectiveness of the conference is discussed below.

Role Models.   The women presenting career relevant information provide a source of information and/or inspiration, but do not act as role models in the original usage of the word. This may stem from the differences in the ages of and the rewards desired by the role models and the students. Specifically, Bandura and Walters (1963) suggested that one mechanism of learning is imitation; role models may lead to imitation by the observers if either the observer is rewarded for the imitative behavior, or the role model is rewarded, such that the observer anticipates a similar reward. In the crush to present extensive "hard" information, a role model may avoid elaborating on the rather intangible and personal rewards of her career. Also, differences in effective reinforcers for the two age groups may be a problem for women acting as role models in the conference. Young women are likely to consider a reward to be a handsome male companion, pretty clothes, and other adolescent desires. Hence, a woman describing the intrinsic satisfaction of a particular endeavor may have minimal impact on adolescent girls.

In fact, the literature does not suggest a strong effect of modeling from either teachers or parents on course taking behavior. For example, there is considerable evidence that the sex of a classroom teacher or mentor is not an important influence on many observable behaviors (Safilios–Rothschild, 1979). Parsons (1980) observed no significant relationship between parents' attitudes for themselves and children's math behaviors, although parents' beliefs about their child's ability did predict the child's course taking. Hendel (1977) found little relationship between the attitudes of math anxious parents and their perceptions of the attitudes of their offspring. Similarly, Nolen, Archambault, and Green (1977) found no relationship between teacher and student attitudes.

In general, choice of the female speaker has typically been based on one of two notions: the presumed identification of the audience with the speaker (her age) or her accomplishments as a professional. Probably neither is terribly important for young girls; for example, neither Weiss, et al. (1978) nor Poiani (1980) found any background or demographic characteristics that differentiated well received speakers from those who were less effective. Perhaps it would be better to assess speakers in terms of credibility, attractiveness, and amount of reward as perceived by themselves and as perceived by the audience. Hence, the most important variable may be the speaker's enthusiasm for her life (her perceived rewards), and the elements perceived by adolescents to be desirable and within their value system.

The most effective choice of speakers may not be female role models if the aim is to sell mathematics and to change values related to occupational aspirations. A male spouse or companion appears to be paramount in the occupational choices and aspirations of women of all ages and ability levels (e.g., Safilios-Rothschild, 1979). In fact, the best way to alleviate sex role/occupational conflict may be a stable relationship with a man who is supportive of the occupational aspirations of the woman. One method of conveying the desired information, then, would be to have an attractive male explain the desirability of women having adequate mathematical backgrounds. Using attractive males to state they enjoy nontraditional women has not been explored, but could potentially be very effective. In fact, the success of one experimental project to encourage women to choose math and science courses was attributed largely to the convictions, commitment and attractiveness of the male project director (Lantz & West, 1977).

In sum, career workshops conveying information about the importance of mathematics to future vocational options probably do that, but little more; that is, they do not alter the prerequisite career values or occupational aspirations. They may provide a basis for young students to make initial plans or explore different careers but they do not provide sufficient motivation to alter already-made plans or career decisions. Career and vocational information is a necessary component of prevention strategies, but it is not a sufficient one. Prevention efforts should focus on increasing and equalizing educational and career aspirations and the dedication with which they are pursued.

In addition to increasing the value of these future rewards, prevention efforts must increase present rewards. The next section addresses some of the punishments frequently associated with taking mathematics courses.

ALTERING AFFECT

Results from the Studies. Another major cluster of variables consistently shown to correlate with enrollment in nonrequired mathematics is those reflecting the emotional aspects and/or self assessment of mathematics ability (e.g., Armstrong, 1979; Wise, Steel, & MacDonald, 1979). These interrelated components are variously labeled confidence in mathematics ability, math anxiety, liking for mathematics, and viewing mathematics as interesting and creative. More important than the correlation of affect with enrollment is its discriminatory power in distinguishing between intention and behavior (Lantz & Smith, 1979), changes in intentions (Brush, 1979), or in predicting course taking behavior (Sherman, 1979). Males score higher than females on this dimension; they are more confident of their abilities in mathematics.

It is not surprising that enjoyment, confidence, and related affective factors are consistently and significantly related to course taking and may represent the largest "risk" factor associated with avoidance. After all, this is the dimension which reflects current rewards and punishments. For example, one may wish to pursue a career for which a math course is a requirement, but not be confident of one's ability to successfully complete it. Actual failure, or the anticipation of failure, certainly is one form of punishment, as are poor grades, boredom, or confusion. Although all of the variables are interrelated, the relative importance of the factors comprising the affective component of liking may be very different for males and females. Further, liking for mathematics may be more important to the decisions of females (Smith, 1983).

There is preliminary evidence that different events influence liking for and confidence in mathematics in males and females. Some of the recent studies illuminate these different mechanisms of self assessment of abilities and confidence. Lantz and Smith (1979) asked students to rate their comparative ability in mathematics vis–a–vis other subjects, and to compare their own abilities in mathematics with the abilities of other students. Several interesting findings emerged. First, those electing nonrequired math felt their mathematics ability was about the same as their ability in other subjects but nonelectors felt their mathematics ability was less than their ability in other subjects. Electors felt their ability in mathematics compared favorably with the mathematical ability of other students. Nobody seemed to think their ability in mathematics was greater than in other subjects. The reason for the absence of perceived mathematical superiority may be found in grading practices. Among college bound seniors, the reported grades in mathematics were the lowest of any subject (Educational Testing Service, 1979). Because this represents the majority of the population taking optional mathematics, it seems likely that mathematics teachers are less lenient in grading practices than are teachers in other subjects.

Females electing nonrequired mathematics consistently and significantly estimated their chances of future success in mathematics lower than that of male electors (Lantz & Smith, 1979). However, the sexes did not differ on their past grades in mathematics, on comparisons of individual relative abilities, nor on abilities relative to other students. These differences in the development of anxiety/confidence may be largely explained by attribution theory. In an attempt to describe the perceived causes of success and failure, Weiner and Kukla (1970) suggested that success or failure may be attributed to any combination of four causes: ability, luck, task difficulty, and effort. Reliable and consistent sex differences in attribution have been noted in a wide variety of experimental and naturalistic tasks. Women almost always will attribute success to luck or effort, whereas males typically attribute success to ability. Conversely, women often attribute failure to the lack of ability, whereas men attribute it to bad luck or insufficient effort. This pattern was recently confirmed regarding success in mathematics by Parsons (1980). If success is ascribed to luck and failure to absence of ability, a pattern of underestimation of abilities is a logical result.

Interventions.   Two strategies have been employed to enhance the affective variables related to mathematics. One attempts to deal with the psychological aspects of "math anxiety" directly, while the other attempts to alter the instructional approach in order to enhance liking, enjoyment, confidence, and achievement. Although the two strategies overlap considerably in practice, they are distinct in theory. The math anxiety strategies are based on the assumption that mathematics cannot be learned until the emotional blocks are directly addressed, whereas the instructional approaches are based on the belief that the best way to learn mathematics is to become immersed in mathematical problems, concepts, and exercises.

The approaches taken by mathematics educators to combat math anxiety have taken a variety of forms. Tobias (1978), the popularizer of the movement, states that the objective is for the student to take control over mathematical events by learning coping skills, willingness to take risks, perserverance, altering problem solving strategies, and learning from mistakes. She maintains that a critical process is understanding the factors that make mathematics difficult; this can be followed by realizing what can make it less difficult.

To accomplish "control over mathematics" any one or combination of psychological exercises may be employed. Group desensitization is used in any one of several ways: by having the students write "math autobiographies" of past experiences with math, talking about their anxiety in doing mathematics, or assertiveness training. Tobias (1978) even describes a "guerilla theater" where an "instructor" marches into the classroom and starts scribbling a lot of formulas on the blackborad. Typically, math anxiety clinics run at least 6 weeks and are jointly conducted by a math instructor and a psychologist. The heart of the "therapy" is to talk about the problem of math anxiety, to share one's feelings, and to realize that many others have a similar affliction. These experiences are usually accompanied by mathematics instruction, remedial, or otherwise. The instruction is carried out within a nonthreatening, noncompetitive environment. Democracy and an attitude of questioning often pervade the classroom. Tobias and Weissbrod (1980) stated: ". . . there is a common goal, namely to change the classroom atmosphere from one of tension and competition, to one of trust . . . One way this is done is to replace the conventional hierarchical student-teacher relationships with that of relative equality among leaders and participants (p. 67)".

This approach has not been with critics. Hendel (1977) observed that math anxiety was closely related to test anxiety and fear of negative evaluation, and may, therefore, be a broader personality attribute (cf. Mallow, 1978). Blum and Givant (1978) commented that the approach implicitly suggests that the individual math avoider has psychological problems, rather than placing the blame for math avoidance on social factors. They also pointed out that the implied solution of counseling and therapy, rather than substantive mathematics, often results in goals that are far too low for the ability of the students. Others have criticized the approach on the basis that the psychological exercises may conjure up past negative experiences. Finally, some have observed that it has provided a new excuse for students not to take mathematics.

Tobias (1980) maintained that math anxiety programs should be judged by whether they resulted in increased enrollment in more advanced mathematics. A few of the approximately 100 programs have tracked their students. For example, Tobias and Rosebaum (1978) reported that about 25% of students who would have otherwise not enrolled in more advanced mathematics did so after completion of math anxiety clinics. Most of the evaluations, however, have been designed to measure decreases in self–reported math anxiety, usually by means of a pre–post administration of the Math Anxiety Rating Scale. In general, a reduction in anxiety and/or an improvement in attitudes to mathematics has been noted (e.g., Auslander, 1979; Tobias, 1980), but there are indications that the decrease in self–reported anxiety may be an artifact of test retest–procedures with that rating instrument: Hendel (1977) demonstrated that reductions in measured math anxiety were found even in groups not participating in any kind of mathematics intervention. A few investigators have not found differences in either anxiety or achievement (e.g., Simons, 1979).

Most of the evaluations of math anxiety programs confound the effectiveness of the therapeutic component with the altered instructional setting. Hendel (1977) found some evidence that lowering of math anxiety scores was a function of the degree of involvement with the program; those who participated most and had the longest duration of exposure to either the academic or nonacademic components experienced the largest decrease in anxiety. On the other hand, he found no evidence that participation in the nonacademic components had any impact on achievement; that is, the nonacademic components may influence anxiety but not achievement and the academic component may influence both. Therefore, anxiety may have decreased as a result of the experience with mathematics and the altered classroom setting.

Several characteristics of the math anxiety movement are thought–provoking. First, the concept struck a responsive chord among mathematics educators and students alike. This is shown by the proliferation of clinics primarily housed in mathematics departments (cf. Tobias & Melmed, 1980). It must be noted that the popularization of the "disease" model of math anxiety occurred concommitantly with trends toward increased enrollment in mathematics by females, and the movement may have influenced the increase. At the very least, it has made math anxiety a respectable and prestigious neurosis. The other approach to tackling the same problems is illustrated by the innovative instructional methods used to teach mathematics described below.

CHANGING PEDAGOGICAL PRACTICES

Results from the Studies.   Several lines of evidence merge in suggesting that current procedures for teaching math are deficient—or at any rate, do not result in appreciation of the subject for many students. Prime among these is the fact that both males and females enjoy mathematics less over the high school years. A National Assessment of educational progress showed a decline from almost 50% choosing math as a favorite subject at age 9 to less than 20% at age 17 (Brush, 1979). Further, in a study of college bound seniors, the Educational Testing Service (1979) reported a decreasing interest in mathematics as a college major. Finally, the National Science Foundation and the Department of Education (1980) described some severe problems in mathematics instruction and estimated at least 100 unfilled positions for mathematics teachers; that is, substandard teachers may be currently employed in the filled positions.

The decrement in enjoyment in mathematics over the high school years may be due to the techniques used to convey mathematics concepts and to individual learning styles, that is, to a negative interaction between instructional and learner variables. Specifically, there is considerable debate both in regard to the differences in spatial ability of males and females, and the origin and implications of the differences (if any). Many have suggested that boys' preferred style utilizes spatial skills, whereas girls' preferred style utilizes verbal skills (e.g., Maccoby & Jacklin, 1974).

Interventions. The proposed solutions to instructional problems are as varied as are the conceptions of the problem; most of the proposed solutions differ primarily in emphasis and could potentially be integrated into a single class. Only two strategies—increasing the spatial–visualization skills of females or teaching "verbal" math—seem mutually exclusive.

Increasing the spatial–visualization skills of females is one instructional strategy proposed by a variety of mathematics educators, that has been tried in several situations. Spatial skills have been developed via graphs, games, and exercises and have become course components for females in elementary to post secondary levels of education (e.g., Blum & Givant, 1978; Kreinberg, 1980). Preliminary experimental evidence indicates that training on spatial skills may improve the scores of girls but not of boys (Connor, Schackman, & Serbin, 1978). Thus, initial evidence suggests that the approach is viable, but the results have not yet been related directly to course taking or achievement. Although there have been suggestions of "verbalizing" mathematics, most educators seem explicitly opposed to approach, arguing that it is imperative to develop the spatial skills, rather than to rely on existing verbal strengths (e.g., Sherman, 1979).

A second approach emphasizes the problem solving aspects of mathematics. Several mathematics courses focusing on problem solving approaches have been reported, but few have received any in–depth evaluation. The discovery or socratic method of instruction is thought to discourage the memorization of formulae, which in turn is thought to be detrimental to concept understanding. For example, Wellesley mathematics classes have utilized an approach in which students work together to solve problems: they propose a problem and test solutions to the problem logically and without numbers; they develop a theory for each solution, and the instructor makes formal ties between their discoveries and traditional theorems. The problems are first presented as logic problems rather than numeric ones. Another example is a math for girls program at Lawrence Hall of Science. The course emphasizes hands–on experience, puzzles, and computers. This course is at least in part responsible for the doubling of the total number of girls enrolled in other math courses at the Hall. The discovery approach has been suggested by Casserly and Rock (1979), Parsons, Heller, and Kaczala (1979), and Stallings (1979).

A pedagogical technique related to and often concomitant with the "discovery" style of teaching is the utilization of real–world problems as vehicles to teach math concepts. These sophisticated "word problems" serve to illustrate the value of mathematics in solving social dilemmas, thus lending a broader, and more humanitarian value to its study. For example, the Wellesley course examines such topics as the place of symmetries in art and music, planning postal routes, projecting population growth, and others. Brush (1979) discusses one course where the students in a high school geometry class designed a five room house on a specific amount of acreage using a certain amount of lumber, and so on. The students worked in groups. At the end of the project, a contractor and an architect talked about the importance of geometry to their work. The teacher then summarized the principles the students had been using intuitively by translating them into mathematical terms. An extension of these ideas is used at Mills College. The women in science courses at Mills offer a curriculum designed to get students in substantive math quickly. It features interdisciplinary courses such as modeling techniques for the social sciences, an intern program with industry, and a computer literacy program.

Evaluations of these two courses at Mills and at Wellesley are extremely encouraging. Mills showed a tripling of enrollments in regular math and computer science courses over years when the size of the student body did not increase (from 331 to 948 students). The evaluation of the Wellesley program reported that the course has had a positive effective on encouraging students to enroll in other courses, in changing their attitudes about the creative nature of mathematics, in developing confidence in their mathematical ability, and in providing them with an enjoyable classroom experience (Tobias & Melmed, 1980).

Several other features are often offered in conjunction with these experimental courses such as peer teaching or tutorial assistance, a high teacher–student ratio, and a predominantly or exclusively female environment. Additionally, almost all of the classrooms are informal, highly interactive, and democratic. The extent to which these factors influence student outcomes has not been evaluated. However, one of the earliest post–secondary interventions, started in 1974 at the University of Missouri–Kansas City, was comprised mostly of such changes. The evaluation of the course showed it to be highly effective; the percentage of women enrolling in advanced math was greater than in a comparable control group, and was greater than the enrollment of either men or women in previous years (Lantz & West, 1977). These variations, however, are extremely costly, and difficult to implement on a large scale. Thus, it would be advantageous to isolate the conditions responsible for the increasing enrollments.

Helping students "learn to learn" by supplementing their study skills has been joined with the aforementioned approaches. For example, study skills may be enhanced by realizing that words are used differently in language of mathematics than in common English, emphasizing "translation" to symbols and notation, and allocating appropriate amounts of time to read mathematics texts. Among the most interesting of these approaches has been used by Dr. Gloria Hewitt, a mathematics professor at the University of Montana. Dr. Hewitt worked individually with students who had failed their first exam in calculus. Not only did she share her own occasional anxiety, she analyzed their behavior while attempting to solve a problem. She noticed that most students equated working with sitting with pencil in hand and observed that their "work" generally consisted of contemplating the difficulty of the problem in front of them. She attempted to assist students in concentrating on the math problem, to find individual mathematical strengths, to try out intuitive ideas, and to have patience and appreciation for their incorrect efforts. Dr. Hewitt claimed that nearly all of the individuals she worked with made an A or B in the calculus course.

In sum, there is a cluster of pedagogical variables that have been used to encourage students to take additional mathematics. Most of the instructional innovations have been offered at the post–secondary level for students who have not recently taken mathematics, and they are designed to get students who are weak in skills or in confidence to get back into and/or prepare for college calculus. Some are remedial in the respect that they cover old material such as algebra or computations, whereas others offer only new material essential to learning calculus. Almost all are additions to offerings of the department; they do not substitute for calculus or any other existing course. Hence, they provide something otherwise not available. The courses are often preceded or accompanied by an examination of feelings toward math, either in individual or group settings. The clinics often contain several unique features: they use a problem solving/ discovery approach to solve concrete, humanistic problems. they may emphasize the development of visual skills and/or the translation between mathematic and verbal concepts. They are typically taught in smaller–than–unusual classes, with peer or tutorial assistance, within supportive and predominantly female environments. Most report success. Because of the many components, however, it is nearly impossible to know which of the variables is responsible for the increased enrollment, confidence, and/or enjoyment.

All of the alterations in instructional methods are based on the logical, but unproven, assumption that more positive attitudes result in increased achievement, either as a direct result of increased effort or mediated by enrollment in additional mathematics courses. In fact, these assumptions have not been adequately tested, and there is substantial evidence to the contrary, especially at lower levels of education. Specifically, the teacher effectiveness literature contends that teachers who produce high achievement in their pupils may do so at the risk of promoting unfavorable attitudes or, conversely, that teachers who produce favorable attitudes in their pupils may do so at the risk of declining achievement (see Bennett, 1976; Good, Biddle, & Brophy, 1975; Sullivan & Skanes, 1974). Promoting academic skills, according to this view, entails adherence to a well–organized curriculum and the exertion of pressure on students to apply themselves continually during class periods to relevant tasks leading to content mastery; it does *not* entail commensurate concern for the pupils' enjoyment of classroom activities and intrinsic interest in learning, or for the pupils' feelings of self–esteem and emotional adjustment. For example, Bennett (1976) investigated the relationship between teaching style and pupil achievement, and found that formal teaching was associated with significantly higher pupil achievement in the basic skills whereas informal teaching was associated with comparatively lower achievement but a significant increase in motivation (or favorable attitudes toward school and school work).

Before we leap into redesigning class procedures, we should consider the chicken and egg question: Does liking precede (cause) achievement or visa versa? It is just as plausible to hypothesize that achievement causes liking—surely it is more rewarding to do activities at which one is competent. If this is the case, the classroom should be engineered for maximum achievement, not enjoyment.

The commonly assumed link between teachers' mathematics achievement and pupils' mathematics achievement has more support. For example, Norris (1969) found that the pupils of teachers exposed to a teacher inservice program on mathematics concepts exhibited greater mathematics achievement than the pupils of teachers not so exposed; Hunkler (1968) found that the number of college mathematics courses and college preparatory mathematics courses completed by teachers was positively related to sixth grade pupils' mathematics concepts achievement. Casserley's research (this volume) also suggests the importance of well–prepared high school teachers. However, a study with third grade children yielded substantially null results (Hurst, 1967).

On the other hand, the assumption that teachers who like the subject will stimulate favorable attitudes in their pupils, whereas teachers who dislike the subject are likely to infect their pupils with similar feelings or dislike, appears to be an eminently plausible view with little empirical evidence to endorse its scientific validity (e.g., Banks, 1964). Aiken (1976) noted that several studies at the elementary school level had failed to find statistically significant relationships between teacher attitudes and either the attitudes or changes of attitude of their pupils. Nolen et al. (1977) found that while teachers' scores on "the enjoyment of mathematics" attitude dimension were not significantly related to their pupils *attitude* toward mathematics, scores on this dimension were significantly and positively related to their pupils' mathematics *achievement*. Finally, Gilbert and Cooper (1976) found a significant negative correlation between the rank order of teachers' scores on attitude towards teaching mathematics and the rank order of classroom mean scores of pupils' attitudes toward mathematics.

The other assumption embedded in the origin of innovative courses is that mathematics confidence and achievement may be related to individual preferred learning styles. However logical these assumptions, they are not warranted by the current state of knowledge. For example, Simons (1979) found no relationship between preferred learning styles and mathematical achievement or anxiety/confidence. Further, he found no relationship between teaching style and achievement or confidence/anxiety. Specifically, peer group learning and availability of tutors had no direct correlation with either affective or achievement outcomes. In fact, he concluded that altering teaching strategies alone is not enough to help math anxious students.

In summary, evaluation results suggest that altering instructional approaches is the most promising strategy. Because we cannot be sure exactly which elements are producing the encouraging results, we should carefully examine the relationship between learning and teaching styles, and between enjoyment and achievement. Further, all of the existing evidence is derived from a "special" course and a "special" population. The impact of such strategies on regular mathematics courses and regular students should be studied to see if alterations in these courses produce similar effects and, consequently, serve a prevention function, perhaps eliminating the need for the special interventions.

STRUCTURING THE SOCIAL ENVIRONMENT

The more indirect efforts to increase mathematics enrollment consist of attempts to change the characteristics of the immediate social environment surrounding and influencing the individual student. A large number of variables relevant to personal decisions may be considered as a function of the reward and punishment for certain behaviors supplied by the people in the environment (the social environment), and as a function of the programs, class size, composition, and so on, of the environment (the structural environment). Of course, these environments are interdependent: the type, numbers, or beliefs of people will reflect as well as influence the structure of the setting. Each participant/program is transactional with the environment: it both influences the environment and is influenced by it. The young women taking elective math may influence her peers and teachers while being influenced by them.

Many investigators have been fascinated by the possible influence of the male–female ratio in the classroom/work setting/school (e.g., Kantor, 1977; Fox, this volume; Lantz, Elliot, & Fox, 1979; Tidball & Kistiakowsky, 1976). Although this is a fuzzy empirical issue, utilizing sex segregated or sheltered classrooms to teach mathematics to women is a hotly debated issue. Many of the existing special programs utilize a predominately, if not exclusively, female environment. And some evaluations have concluded that this environment is typically preferred by the women, who find it one of the most rewarding aspects of the program (e.g., Lantz, 1980).

Despite the oft–stated preference for an all female environment, there is scanty evidence on the effect of the male–female ratio on attrition or achievement. For example, Fox (1979) concluded that the ratio of boys and girls in accelerated mathematics classes was not related to attrition, and Lantz et al. (1979) found no difference in attrition as a function of the percentage of women in engineering school. Therefore, the effect of the male–female ratio on attrition remains unproven.

Despite the absence of influence of "critical mass" on attrition, some evidence exists that the male–female ratio may influence affect and performance. For example, Casserly and Rock (1979) suggested that female confidence in mathematics may be proportional to the number of females in the class. Wirtenburg (1978), in a review of the educational literature, suggested that in elementary grades, same sex classes may result in girls being more active, aggressive, and less stereotyped. However, by eighth grades, the studies suggest that girls tend to perform better and to be more task oriented in mixed sex classes. On the other hand, Spangler, Gorden and Pipkin (1978), in a study of women in law school, found their performance to be better when the male–female ratios were more nearly equal. Hence, at the present time there seems to be no strong reason to exclude males from regular or special mathematics classes.

Another aspect of the social environment that might influence mathematics enrollment is school policy, politics, and programs. Lantz and Smith (1979) noted great disparity among individual schools in the same geographical area in the percentage of students enrolled in non-required mathematics, varying between 45% and 92% of the students. This difference was not accounted for by the socioeconomic status of the school. Several tantalizing possible explanations have been suggested. Fox (1979) found that girls in an accelerated program within a school district were more accelerated than girls of comparable ability whose district did not have such a program. Stallings (1979) and Wise et al. (1979) found that the availability of an accelerated science program was related to math achievement, as was the frequency of standardized testing. Programs designed for students truly talented and gifted in mathematics are less frequent. Although the effect of such activities on course taking has not been evaluated, most of the programs are experiencing an increase in applications after a few years of existence. Stallings (this volume) noted that the highest mathematics enrollment she found was in a minority urban school with active community and business support. Still unexamined are variables such as formal and informal school policies, fiscal allocations, teacher or counselor training, or organizational structure.

Social Environment. The most important element in the social environment is the people with whom the student interacts, often referred to as significant others. In theory, these significant others are presumed to be important influences on the enrollment choices of girls and boys alike. Almost every report on mathematics achievement and enrollment has highlighted the influence of significant others. However, there is absolutely no consensus, much less a majority vote, on which of the significant others are the most potent in swaying enrollment decisions, nor is there consensus on the mechanism of influence utilized by the significant others. Despite this ambiguity, several interventions have been designed and implemented to alter the reinforcement patterns provided by significant others.

If only reward or anticipated reward were present for mathematics enrollment, it would be predictable. Likewise, if only punishment or anticipated punishment were present, mathematics enrollment would also be predictable. However, for most students, some combination of both current and anticipated reward and punishment is operating. One issue, then, is to examine the relative importance of each of the rewards or punishments supplied by the groups of significant others. Interestingly, the importance of the rewards/punishment may vary for different groups of females. There has been a rather consistent suggestion that career oriented girls of high ability may be less sensitive to punishment (Safilios-Rothschild, 1979), less concerned about approval, and less influenced by significant others (Lantz, Elliot, & Fox, 1979; Vetter & Lewis, 1964). A related issue is the students' perceptions of anticipated rewards and punishments since there is considerable evidence that these perceptions may not be accurate (e.g., Hawley, 1971). A discussion of these issues for the major groupings of significant others—parents, peers, and school personnel—follows.

On the assumption that parents often do not provide sufficient incentives for their daughters to elect mathematics, and that they are in a position to offer a potent and sustained influence, several attempts have been made to contact parents directly to insure that they are well in-formed regarding the importance of mathematics to their daughters' fu-tures. In 1974, in an experiment at Michigan Tech to increase interest in science, brochures on such careers were sent directly to parents. No significant differences between the experimental and the control group of daughters were noted (Lantz & West, 1977). Within the same year, the University of Kansas invited the parents of high ability young women to attend a workshop on careers with their daughters. The same format is used in the workshops designed for women sponsored by the Bay Area Math/Science Network and by the Women and Math Project. The impact of attendance has not been measured by either project. One high school in Denver, Colorado sponsored father–daughter breakfasts where the im-portance of mathematics was discussed. This program was not evaluated. To date then, there is little evidence that approaching parents, especially for such short periods, has any substantial impact.

In most of the studies of high school students, the student respondents have reported that peers do not significantly influence their behaviors (cf., Casserly & Rock, 1979). This same result was found by Lantz and Smith (1979)—students in their sample ranked peers as thirteenth in a list of 14 potential influences. However, the students were asked to name their most important significant other, and almost half of them named a peer. The students were then asked whether this significant other would ap-prove of taking nonrequired math. The answer to that question was one of the items most highly correlated with enrollment behavior, belying the suggestion that peers do not influence teenage behavior.

There is some dispute regarding the availability and importance of the reinforcement provided by female peers for nonconforming behavior (e.g., Casserly & Rock, 1979; Lantz et al., 1979; Safilios-Rothschild, 1979), but there is overwhelming evidence that male peers are more im-portant to girls and exercise the greatest influence on the educational and occupational aspirations (Ellis & Bentler, 1973; Farmer & Bohn, 1970; Hawley, 1971; Lantz et al., 1979; Wirtenberg, 1978). Women tend to be less conservative in sex–role stereotyping than men, and women often perceive that men are more conservative than many are (Safilios-Rothschild, 1979). This suggests that many women may anticipate punish-ment for nonconventional behavior. In fact, Sherman (1979) noted that young women taking 4 years of mathematics had greater sex role strain than their nonelecting counterparts. This may be because they are in a position to experience it.

By and large, few interventions have addressed the real or perceived views of adolescent males, although a few have included them in career activities designed specifically or females. The Visiting Women Scientist program used this procedure and found that boys (not surprisingly) were not as enthusiastic about the program as the girls (Weiss et al., 1978). Wirtenberg (1978) concluded from a review of interventions designed to alter sex role stereotypes that it was usually easier to change the attitudes of women than those men. She noted that although females may have something to gain in this process, males may feel they have something to lose—especially at that age. Consequently, strategies to alter the existing views of males should be approached cautiously and carefully.

The most frequent target of efforts to alter attitudes and stereotypes other than students has been school personnel. This is, in part, because they comprise a more accessible population and represent a direct link to the students. Nonetheless, the extent of their potential impact is debatable; some studies ascribe considerable power to them, especially for students continuing to take mathematics (e.g., Lantz & Smith, 1979). There appears to be a consensus indicating that mathematics teachers have more influence than vocational counselors, if for no other reason than the greater duration of their contact with the students. Further, it appears to be easier to alter the perceptions of teachers (Poiani, 1980). By and large, however, the majority of the programs designed to alter attitudes for teachers include or are potentially applicable to counselors.

Two examples of this approach are noteworthy. Michigan Tech offered a two week workshop to science, math teachers, and counselors during the summer. The workshop included presentations, group projects, evaluations of existing materials, and generation of new career education materials. At the end of the two weeks, the participants designed their own evaluation form to be completed at the end of the following year. Although they did not measure the direct impact on the students, the teachers reported increased contact with the students, other teachers, and parents encouraging enrollment in math and science options (Lantz & West, 1977). A similar program, EQUALS, is an activity of Bay Area Math/Science Network, cosponsored by the Office of Education and Carnegie Foundation. EQUALS brings educators and educational administrators together to examine skills training and nonsexist career activities. Each teacher assesses and analyzes the problems and needs of his/her school's mathematics program. This program has had somewhat mixed results in increasing the enrollments of females in the schools of participating teachers, but is in extremely high demand. Pulos, Kreinberg, and Stage (1979) concluded that the program influenced the student's attitudes toward mathematics, but was less effective in the area of career awareness.

An expanded conglomerate of activities for adults working in education is represented by the Bay Area Math/Science Network (Stage, 1979). The network serves as an umbrella and a focus for many diverse activities relating to mathematics. The network is extremely active and popular, directing a lot of enthusiasm, referrals and information. Despite this sustained level of activity, no data is currently available regarding its impact on enrollments or achievement of the Bay Area students.

In sum, the evaluations of the strategies involving parents have not showed notable changes, whereas strategies to involve opposite sex peers have not been attempted. The most common of the interventions involving significant others have focused on school personnel, such as math and science teachers and guidance counselors. The evaluations of those programs are not conclusive, but tentative evidence indicates that the programs may be productive. The best program formats concentrate on the active problem assessment and materials development, and active participation of the school personnel.

MAINTAINING OR INCREASING
PROGRAMMATIC EFFORTS

There is a substantial literature, derived from both research and evaluation, which describes the factors that facilitate the initiation, implementation, and institutionalization of programs similar to the innovations in mathematics instruction and may be used to predict the future of programs to increase participation in mathematics. The essential steps in adoption of mathematics programs are knowledge of the innovative procedure, a positive attitude toward the procedure, evaluation, trial, and adoption of the innovation. The characteristics of the innovation influence all of these stages. The relative advantages of the innovation in comparison to current practices, its compatability with the current system, its perceived complexity, and its triability—the possibility of utilization on a limited basis—all affect its adoption (Rogers & Shoemaker, 1971). Moreover, the availability of credible, quantitative information (e.g., evaluations) about the strategy is critical (Yin, 1973). Berman and McLaughlin (1975) noted that innovations that were to replace existing practice, which emphasized training rather than technology, which focused on practical rather than theoretical issues, and which developed materials locally, had the best chance of being successfully implemented. Similarly, Orlich (1979) concluded that curriculum innovations are easier to implement than those requiring organization change.

Berman and McLaughlin (1975) commented that the innovative procedures, initiated as part of a problem solving effect and designed to meet local needs, were most likely to be successful than efforts initiated because of opportunistic motives. (Notice that the more successful programs discussed in this chapter typically require active participation and some sort of public commitment to the issues, for example, the needs assessment conducted by EQUALS teachers.) Berman and McLaughlin (1975) hypothesized that the motivational stance of the implementor is important because it tends to lead to mutual modification of the innovation and the setting. Nonetheless, the innovative procedure must be central to and consonant with the perceived priorities of the institution. In addition, the adequacy of the administrative and technical arrangements, available skills, training, communication channels, and of the organization affect the implementation process (Williams, 1975).

The political processes involved in program implementation are critical, because Berman and McLaughlin (1975) concluded that outcomes are primarily, if not solely, dependent on such internal factors and local decisions. They observed that the implementation strategy is crucial, and found that adaptive on–line planning, staff training keyed to the local setting, and local materials development were typically part of a successful strategy. They also noticed that successful strategies took advantage of institutional support; they had a "critical mass" of advocates who were willing to work overtime for the implementation effort, and had the explicit support of supervisory personnel, especially the relevant supervisor.

Much less has been written about the factors influencing continuation or institutionalization of innovative programs. Berman and McLaughlin (1975) concluded that continuation is dependent on four factors as perceived by the educational administrators: whether the innovation was successful (typically decided prior to any evaluation), whether it is affordable, whether it is feasible, and whether it is politically acceptable. They noted that this stage is not frequently influenced by Federal policy, although there is evidence to the contrary (cf., Lantz, 1980). They concluded that failure to institutionalize may be traced to three general sources: unrealistic expectations (the innovative strategy did not produce the desired results within the allocated time periods), incorrect assumptions about the institution, and poor implementation strategies.

In general, then, the factors involved in strategies to increase mathematics enrollments indicate that many stand a good chance of being institutionalized and adopted elsewhere. There is fairly widespread awareness of the problem and almost all of the efforts have been initiated to address a recognized local need. By and large, the interventions have been locally developed and materials locally modified and have included staff training. Most are curriculum based, not technology based, changes and most are led by dynamic and energetic people. Additionally, very few are dependent on Federal funding sources that may be expected to terminate. The only factor in the programs that make them a high risk for termination is their add–on character; that is, they do not substitute for existing procedures. If this situation can be corrected, their low cost and ease of implementation should assure their propagation. This is another argument for programs that focus on changing and improving mathematics instruction itself.

If the current cohort of girls taking an additional mathematics courses continue with their sequence, and are followed by several more years of nonrequired course taking by subsequent cohorts, we may all begin to believe the current trend represents a permanent change. To insure this change, a redoubled effort should be expended for existing interventions and in new approaches for the next few years.

SUMMARY AND CONCLUSIONS

In general, prevention efforts to alter cognitive beliefs about the usefulness of mathematics are often at least temporarily successful, but there is no current evidence that changed beliefs necessarily lead to changes in behavior. Information about the mathematics requirements for careers does not have substantial or direct impact on enrollment or achievement. The absence of impact on enrollment may be attributed to the failure of career information to alter career values or aspirations. Therefore, changing or maintaining the career aspirations and values of young women is necessary to the perception that mathematics is instrumental for their lives. The increasing value of various occupational choices made by young women may account for the observed increase in math enrollment.

Changing or maintaining values related to math is possible but has not been seriously attempted; that is, the manner in which the information is usually presented in career workshops and conferences does not accomplish this end. Specifically, the math related career information is almost always presented as a fear message—you can't be a doctor if you don't take math. While the presenter of the information is nearly always an expert who may be presumed to alter beliefs, the presenter probably does not represent (or is not perceived to represent) the values of the target audience, and thus is likely to have little impact on values. A communicator should relate math taking to present rewards of the adolescents to produce value change. In addition, the presentations do not often incorporate a two sided argument addressing all of the objections to taking mathematics—the problems of getting a "B" in math versus an "A" in English, the additional study time, boredom, and so on. The two–sided argument is important to innoculate the new attitude and values against reversal. Finally, those conferences focusing on "hands–on" activities are more likely to stimulate interest in mathematics. Additions to career workshops such as male presenters, role playing, or simulation, and the encouragement of active commitment might be effective.

The approaches attempting to alter the affective and achievement components associated with mathematics are probably better long range strategies, because these components are more stable over time and changes are more permanent. To date, it is difficult to distinguish among these approaches. Most of the successful remedial programs offer some combination of the following: anxiety reduction, exercises to increase spatial skills, "verbalizing" mathematical concepts, a discovery or socratic method of teaching, use of humanistic, real–world problems, assistance in developing study skills, tutorial assistance, low teacher to pupil ratios, and a nonthreatening classroom. Most importantly, most of the programs use teachers dedicated to conveying the subject matter. In fact, it is possible that the special programs are set apart more by the awareness and attitude of the instructor than by the content. Because of this and the indications from research, increasing the instructor's mathematical and pedagogical skills seems an important strategy to increase mathematics enrollment. However, neither the male–female ratio of the classroom nor the sex of the instructor is important.

ACKNOWLEDGMENT

The preparation of this paper was supported by the National Institute of Education.

References

Admissions Testing Program of the College Entrance Examination Board. *National report on college-bound seniors*. Princeton, N.J.: College Entrance Exam Board, 1974–1981.

Aiken, L. Intellectual variables and mathematics achievement: Directions for research. *Journal of School Psychology*, 1971, *9*, 201–209.

Aiken, L. Biodata correlates of attitudes toward mathematics in three age and two sex groups. *School Science and Mathematics*, 1972, *72*, 386–395. (a)

Aiken, L. Verbal factors and mathematics learning: A review of research. *Journal for Research in Mathematics Education*, 1972, *2*, 304–313. (b)

Aiken, L. Ability and creativity in math. *Review of Educational Research*, 1973, *43*, 405–432.

Aiken, L. Two scales of attitudes toward mathematics. *Journal for Research in Mathematics Education*, 1974, *5*, 67–71.

Aiken, L. Update on attitudes and other affective variables in learning mathematics. *Review of Educational Research*, 1976, *46*(2), 293–311.

American Mathematical Society. *Notices of the American Mathematical Society*, 1975, *22*, 303–308.

Anderson, J. *Language, memory, and thought*. Hillsdale, N.J.: Lawrence Erlbaum Associates, 1976.

Armstrong, J. *A national assessment of achievement and participation of women in mathematics*. Denver, CO: Education Commission of the States, 1979 (ERIC Document Reproduction Service No. ED 187562).

Armstrong, J., & Kahl, S. *A national assessment of participation and performance of women in mathematics*. Paper presented at the meeting of the Society for Research in Child Development, San Francisco, March 1979.

Astin, H. S. Overview of the findings. In H. Astin, H. Suniewick, & C. Dweck (Eds.), *Women: A bibliography on their education and careers*. New York: Behavioral Publications Incorporated, 1974. (a)

Astin, H. S. Sex differences in mathematical and scientific precocity. In J. C. Stanley, D. P. Keating, & L. H. Fox (Eds.), *Mathematical talent: Discovery, description, and development*. Baltimore: Johns Hopkins University Press 1974. (b)

Astin, H. S., Harway, M., & McNamara, P. *Sex discrimination in education: Access to postsecondary education.* Washington, D.C.: National Center for Education Statistics, U.S. Department of Health, Education and Welfare, February 1976.

Atkinson, J. W. *An introduction to motivation.* Princeton, N.J.: Van Nostrand, 1964.

Auslander, S. B. Minimizing math anxiety: Help for the sciences. *Journal of College Science Teaching,* 1979, 9(1), 17–21.

Bakan, P. *The duality of human existence.* Boston: Beacon Press, 1966.

Bakan, P. The eyes have it. *Psychology Today,* 1971, 4, 64–67.

Bandura, A., & Walters, R. *Social learning and personality development.* New York: Holt, Rinehart, & Winston, 1963.

Banks, J. H. *Learning and teaching arithmetic* (2nd ed.). Boston: Allyn & Bacon, 1964.

Bean, J. P. *What's happening in mathematics and science classrooms: Student teacher interactions.* Paper presented at the annual meeting of the American Educational Research Association, San Francisco, 1976.

Beardslee, D. C., & O'Dowd, D. D. The college student image of the scientist. *Science,* 1961, *133,* 997–1001.

Bem, S. L. The measurement of psychological androgyny. *Journal of Consulting and Clinical Psychology,* 1974, *42,* 155–162.

Bem, S. L., & Lenney, E. Sex typing and the avoidance of cross sex behavior. *Journal of Personality and Social Psychology,* 1976, *33,* 48–54.

Benbow, C. P., & Stanley, J. C. Sex differences in mathematical ability: Fact or artifact. *Science,* 1980, *210,* 1262–1264.

Bennett, G. K., Seashore, H. G., & Wesman, A. G. *Differential aptitude tests, Forms S & T* (4th ed.). New York: Psychological Corporation, 1966.

Bennett, G. K., Seashore, H. G., & Wesman, A. G. *Differential aptitude tests, manual* (5th ed.). New York: Psychological Corporation, 1973.

Bennett, N. *Teaching styles and pupil progress.* Cambridge: Harvard University Press, 1976.

Berman, P., & McLaughlin, W. M. *Federal Programs Supporting Educational Change.* (Vol. I, IV, VIII). Washington, D.C.: Department of Health, Education, and Welfare, 1975.

Blade, M. F., & Watson, W. S. Increase in spatial visualization test scores during engineering study. *Psychological Monographs,* 1955, 69(12), 1–13.

Blalock, H. M., Jr. (Ed.) *Causal models in the social sciences.* Chicago: Aldine Press, 1971.

Block, J. Conceptions of sex role: Some cross-cultural and longitudinal perspectives. *American Psychologist,* 1973, *28*(6), 512–526.

Blum, L., & Givant, S. *Increasing the participation of college women in mathematics-related fields.* Paper presented at MAA-NCTM conference, San Diego, April 1978.

Bock, R. D. A family study of spatial visualizing ability. *American Psychologist,* 1967, *22,* 571.

Boswell, S. L. *Women and mathematics: The development of stereotypic attitudes.* Boulder, CO: Institute for Research on Social Problems, 1980 (ERIC Document Reproduction Service No. ED 186477).

Brinkmann, E. H. Programmed instruction as a technique for improving visualization. *Journal of Applied Psychology,* 1966, *50*(2), 179–184.

Brophy, J. E., & Good, T. *Teacher-student relationships: Causes and consequences.* New York: Holt, Rinehart & Winston, 1974.

Brush, L. *Why women avoid the study of mathematics: A longitudinal study.* Cambridge, MA: ABT Associates, 1979 (ERIC Document Reproduction Service No. ED 188 887).

Brush, L. *Encouraging girls in mathematics: The problem and the solution.* Cambridge, MA: ABT Books, 1980.

Burbank, I. K. *Relationships between parental attitude toward mathematics and between student attitude toward mathematics and student achievement in mathematics.* Unpublished doctoral dissertation, Utah State University, 1968.

Burnett, S. A., Lane, D. M., & Dratt, L. M. Spatial visualization and sex differences in quantitative ability. *Intelligence,* 1979, *3,* 345–354.

Carey, G. L. Sex differences in problem-solving performances as a function of attitude differences. *Journal of Abnormal and Social Psychology,* 1958, *56,* 256–260.

Carpenter, P., & Just, M. *Spatial ability: An information processing approach to psychometrics.* Unpublished manuscript, Carnegie-Mellon University, January 5, 1981.

Casserly, P. L. *An assessment of factors affecting female participation in advanced placement programs in mathematics, chemistry and physics.* Unpublished manuscript, Educational Testing Service, 1975.

Casserly, P. L. *The advanced placement teacher as the critical factor in high school women's decision to persist in the study of mathematics.* Paper presented at the annual meeting of the American Educational Research Association, San Francisco, 1979.

Casserly, P. L. Factors affecting female participation in advanced placement programs in mathematics, chemistry and physics. In L. Fox, L. Brody, & D. Tobin (Eds.), *Women and the mathematical mystique.* Baltimore: Johns Hopkins University Press, 1980.

Casserly, P. L., & Flaugher, R. *An evaluation of minority student data from the 1975–76 GRE background questionnaire.* Unpublished manuscript, Educational Testing Service, 1977.

Casserly, P. L., & Rock, D. *Factors related to young women's persistence and achievement in mathematics, with special focus on the sequence leading to and through advanced placement mathematics.* Princeton, N.J.: Educational Testing Service, 1979.

Centra, J. A. *Women, men, and the doctorate.* Princeton, N.J.: Educational Testing Service, 1974.

Chase, W. G., & Simon, H. A. Perception in chess. *Cognitive Psychology,* 1973, *4,* 55–81.

Ciganko, R. A. The effect of spatial information training and drawing practice upon spatial visualization ability and representational drawings of 9th-grade students. *Dissertation Abstracts International,* 1973, *34,* 3131-3132.

Coleman, J. *The adolescent society, the social life of the teenager and its impact on education.* New York: The Free Press of Glencoe, 1961.

College Entrance Examination Board. *National report on college-bound seniors.* Princeton, N.J.: College Entrance Exam Board, 1974–1981.

Committee on the Undergraduate Program in Mathematics. *Report on a mathematical sciences program.* Washington, D.C.: Mathematical Association of America, 1981.

Connor, J. M., Schackman, M., & Serbin, L. A. Sex-related differences in response to practice on a visual-spatial test and generalization to a related test. *Child Development,* 1978, *49,* 24–29.

Connor, J. M., & Serbin, L. A. *Mathematics, visual-spatial ability, and sex roles.* State University of New York at Binghamton, 1980. ERIC Document Reproduction Service No. ED 214798.

Connor, J. M., Serbin, L. A., & Freeman, M. Training visual-spatial ability in EMR children. *American Journal of Mental Deficiency,* 1978, *83*(2), 116–121.

Connor, J. M., Serbin, L. A., & Schackman, M. Sex differences in response to training on a visual-spatial test. *Developmental Psychology,* 1977, *13,* 293–295.

Constantinople, A. Masculinity-femininity: An exception to the famous dictum? In A. Kaplan & J. Bean (Eds.), *Beyond sex role stereotypes: Readings toward a psychology of androgeny.* Boston: Little Brown & Co., 1976.

Cooper, L. A., & Regan, D. T. Attention, perception, and intelligence. In R. J. Sternberg (Ed.), *Handbook of human intelligence.* Cambridge: Cambridge University Press, 1982.

Cronkite, R., & Perle, T. *Evaluating the impact of an intervention program: Math-science career conferences for young women.* Unpublished manuscript, Mills College, 1979.

Cusick, P. A. *Inside high school.* New York: Holt, Rinehart & Winston, 1973.

Czepiel, J., & Esty, E. Mathematics in the newspaper. *Mathematics Teacher,* 1980, *73*(8), 582–586.

Denby, L., Devlin, S. J., & Poiani, E. L. The women and mathematics program: A preliminary statistical evaluation, *Proceedings of Social Statistics Section: American Statistical Association,* 1977.

Donady, B., & Tobias, S. Math anxiety. *Teacher,* 1977, *75,* 71–74.

Donlon, T. F. Content factors in sex differences in test questions. *Educational Testing Service Research Monograph,* 1973.

Donlon, T. F., Ekstrom, R. B., & Lockhead, M. *Comparing the sexes on achievement items of varying content.* Paper presented at the annual meeting of the American Psychological Association, Washington, D.C., September 1976.

Dougherty, K., Herbert, M., Edenhurt-Pape, M., & Small, A. *Sex-related differences in several aspects of mathematics achievement: Grades 2–5.* Unpublished manuscript, CEMREL, St. Louis, 1980.

Duncan, E. R. Identification and education of the gifted in mathematics. In G. Z. Beneday & J. A. Lawenys (Eds.), *The year book of education.* New York: Harcourt, Brace & World, 1961.

Duncan, O. D. *Introduction to structural equation models.* New York: Academic Press, 1975.

Dunteman, G. H., Wisenbaker, J., & Taylor, M.E. *Race and sex differences in college science program participation.* Report submitted to the National Science Foundation under contract No. SED77-18728, 1979.

Dweck, C. S., Davidson, W., Nelson, S., & Enna, B. Sex differences in learned helplessness II, The contingencies of evaluative feedback in the classroom and III, An experimental analysis. *Developmental Psychology,* 1978, *14,* 268–276.

Dweck, C. S., & Reppucci, N. D. Learned helplessness and reinforcement responsibility in children. *Journal of Personality and Social Psychology,* 1973, *25,* 109–116.

Eccles, J. S., Adler, T. F., & Meece, J. L. Sex differences in achievement: A test of alternate theories. *Journal of Personality and Social Psychology,* 1984, *46,* 26–43.

Eccles-Parsons, J., Adler, T. F. Futterman, R., Goff, S., Kaczala, C., Meece, J. L., & Midgley, C. Expectancies, values, and academic choice. In J. Spence (Ed.) *Achievement and achievement motivation.* San Francisco: W. H. Freeman and Co., 1983.

Eccles-Parsons, J., Adler T. F., & Kaczala, C. M. Socialization of achievement attitudes and beliefs: Parental influences. *Child Development,* 1982, *53,* 301–321.

Eccles-Parsons, J., Kaczala, C. M., & Meece, J. L. Socialization and achievement attitudes and beliefs: Classroom influences. *Child Development,* 1982, *53,* 322–339.

Eccles-Parsons, J., Meece, J. L., Adler, T. F., & Kaczala, C. M. Sex differences in attributions and learned helplessness? *Sex Roles,* 1982, *8,* 421–432.

Educational Testing Service, *National college-bound seniors.* College Entrance Examination Board, 1979.

Edwards, W. The theory of decision making. *Psychological Bulletin,* 1954, *51,* 380–417.

Ekstrom, R. B., French, J. W., Harman, H. H., & Dermen, D. *Manual for kit of factor-referenced cognitive tests.* Princeton, N.J.: Educational Testing Service, 1976.

Elias, M. Sexists attitudes yield to tv's series power. *The Denver Post,* August 17, 1980.

Ellis, L. J. & Bentler, P. M. Traditional sex-determined role standards and sex stereotypes. *Journal of Personality and Social Psychology,* 1973, *25*(1), 28–34.

Elton, C. F., & Rose, H. A. Traditional sex attitudes and discrepant ability measures in college women. *Journal of Counseling Psychology,* 1967, *14,* 538–543.

Englehard, P., Jones, K., & Stiggens, R. Trends in counselor attitudes about women's roles. *Journal of Counseling Psychology,* 1976, *23,* 365–372.

Ernest, J. *Mathematics and sex.* Santa Barbara: University of California, 1976.

Ernest, J. Is mathematics a sexist discipline? In L. H. Fox, L. Brody, & D. Tobin (Eds.), *Women and the mathematical mystique.* Baltimore: Johns Hopkins University Press, 1980.

Farmer, H. S., & Bohn, M. J. Home-career conflict reduction and the level of career interest in women. *Journal of Counseling Psychology,* 1970, *17,* 228–232.

Fey, J. T. *Patterns of verbal communications in mathematics classes.* (Doctoral dissertation, Columbia University) Ann Arbor, Michigan, University Microfilm, 1969, No. 69-3063.

Fennema, E. Mathematics learning and the sexes: A review. *Journal for Research in Mathematics Education,* 1974, *5,* 126–139. (a)

Fennema, E. Sex differences in mathematics learning: Why??? *The Elementary School Journal,* 1974, 183–190. (b)

Fennema, E. Influences of selected cognitive, affective, and educational variables on sex-related differences in mathematics learning and studying. In: *Women and Mathematics: Research perspectives for change.* Washington, D.C.: The National Institute of Education, 1977.

Fennema, E., & Sherman, J. Fennema-Sherman mathematics attitude scales. JSAS *Catalog of Selected Documents in Psychology,* 1976, *631.* (a)

Fennema, E., & Sherman, J. *Sex-related differences in mathematics learning: Myths, realities and related factors.* Paper presented at the annual meeting of the American Association for the Advancement of Science, Boston, February 1976. (b)

Fennema, E., & Sherman, J. Sex-related differences in mathematics achievement, spatial visualization and affective factors. *American Educational Research Journal,* 1977, *14,* 51–71. (a)

Fennema, E., & Sherman, J. Sexual stereotyping and mathematics learning. *The Arithmetic Teacher,* 1977, *24*(5), 369–372. (b)

Fennema, E., & Sherman, J. Sex-related differences in mathematics achievement and related factors: A further study. *Journal for Research in Mathematical Education,* 1978, *9,* 189–203.

Flanagan, J. Changes in school levels of achievement: Project TALENT ten and fifteen year retests. *Educational Researcher,* 1976, *5,* (8), 9–12.

Fox, L. H. A mathematics program for fostering precocious achievement. In J. C. Stanley, D. P. Keating, & L. H. Fox (Eds.), *Mathematical talent: Discovery, description and development.* Baltimore: Johns Hopkins University Press, 1974. (a)

Fox, L. H. Facilitating the development of mathematical talent in young women. (Doctoral dissertation, The Johns Hopkins University, 1974). *Dissertation Abstracts International,* (University Microfilms No. 74-29027). (b)

Fox, L. H. *Career interests and mathematical acceleration for girls.* Paper presented at the annual meeting of the American Psychological Association, Chicago, IL, August 1975. (a)

Fox, L. H. Mathematically precocious: Male or female? In E. Fennema (Ed.), *Mathematics learning: What research says about sex differences.* Columbus, OH: ERIC Center for Science, Mathematics, and Environmental Education, The Ohio State University, 1975. (b)

Fox, L. H. *Sex differences: Implications for program planning for the academically gifted.* Paper presented at the Lewis M. Terman Memorial Symposium on Intellectual Talent held at the Johns Hopkins University, Baltimore, November 1975. (c)

Fox, L. H. *Changing behaviors and attitudes of gifted girls.* Paper presented at the annual meeting of the American Psychological Association, Washington, D.C., September 1976. (a)

Fox, L. H. Sex differences in mathematical precocity: Bridging the gap. In D. P. Keating (Ed.), *Intellectual talent: Research and development.* Baltimore: Johns Hopkins University Press, 1976. (b)

Fox, L. H. The values of gifted youth. In D. P. Keating (Ed.), *Intellectual talent: Research and development.* Baltimore: Johns Hopkins University Press, 1976. (c)

Fox, L. H. Women and the career relevance of mathematics and science. *School Science and Mathematics,* 1976, *26*(4), 347–353. (d)

Fox, L. H. The effects of sex-role socialization on mathematics participation and achievement. In *Women and mathematics: Research perspectives for change.* Washington, D.C.: The National Institute of Education, 1977.

Fox, L. H. *Women and mathematics: The impact of early intervention programs upon course taking and attitudes in high school.* Baltimore: Johns Hopkins University, 1979 (ERIC Document Reproduction Service No. ED 188 886).

Fox, L. H., Brody, L., & Tobin, D. *Women and the mathematical mystique.* Baltimore: Johns Hopkins University Press, 1980.

Fox, L. H., Tobin, D., & Brody, L. Sex-role socialization and achievement in mathematics. In: M. Wittig & A. Peterson (Eds.), *Sex-related differences in cognitive functioning: Developmental issues.* New York: Academic Press, 1979.

French, J. W., Ekstrom, R. B., & Price, L. A. *Manual for kit of reference tests for cognitive factors.* Princeton, N.J.: Educational Testing Service, 1963.

Fruchter, B. Measurement of spatial abilities: History and background. *Educational and Psychological Measurement,* 1954, *14,* 387–395.

Fuchs, M., Weissbrod, C., & Yates, B. T. *Math anxiety: Not for women only.* Paper presented at the Eastern American Psychological Association, Washington, D.C., 1978.

Gage, N. *Handbook of research on teaching.* Chicago: Rand McNally and Co., 1963.

Geng, U. & Mehl, J. Uber die Beziehungen zwischen intelligenz und special befahigungen. *Zeitschrift fur Psychologie,* 1969, *176*(1–2), 103–128.

Gilbert, C. D. & Cooper, D. The relationship between teacher/student attitudes and the competency levels of sixth grade students. *School Science and Mathematics,* 1976, *76,* 469–476.

Goldstein, A. G., & Chance, J. E. Effects of practice on sex-related differences in performance on embedded figures. *Psychonomic Science,* 1965, *3,* 361–362.

Good, T. L., Biddle, B. J., & Brophy, J. E. *Teachers make a difference.* New York: Holt, Rinehart & Winston, 1975.

Good, T. L., Sikes, J. N., & Brophy, J. E. Effects of teacher sex and student sex in classroom interaction. *Journal of Educational Psychology,* 1973, *65,* 74–87.

Graf, G., & Ruddell, J. Sex differences in problem solving as a function of problem content. *Journal of Educational Research,* 1972, *65*(10), 451–452.

Harvey, O. J., Hunt, D. E., & Schroder, H. M. *Conceptual systems and personality organization.* New York: Wiley, 1961.

Harway, M., Astin, H., Suhr, J., & Whiteley, J. *Sex discrimination in guidance and counseling.* Washington, D.C.: National Center for Educational Statistics, U.S. Department of Health, Education and Welfare, February 1976.

Hauser, R., Sewell, W., & Alwyn, O. High school effects on achievement. In W. Sewell, R. Hauser, & D. Featherman (Eds.), *Schooling and achievement in American society.* New York: Academic Press, 1976.

Haven, E. Factors associated with the selection of advanced academic mathematics courses by girls in high school. (Doctoral dissertation, University of Pennsylvania, 1971). *Dissertation Abstracts International, 1971, 32,* 1741A.

Haven, E. *Factors associated with the selection of advanced academic mathematics courses by girls in high school.* Princeton, N.J.: Educational Testing Services, 1972.

Hawley, P. What women think men think: Does it affect their career choice? *Journal of Counseling Psychology, 1971, 18*(3), 193–199.

Hawley, P. Perceptions of male models of femininity related to career choice. *Journal of Counseling Psychology, 1972, 19,* 308–313.

Health, Education and Welfare. *Healthy people: The surgeon general's report on health promotion and disease prevention, 1979.*

Heilbrun, A. Parent identification and filial sex role behavior: The importance of biological context. In J. Cole & R. Dienstbier (Eds.), *Nebraska symposium on motivation.* Lincoln: University of Nebraska Press, 1974.

Heller, K. A., & Parsons, J. E. Teacher influences on students' expectancies for success in mathematics. *Child Development, 1981, 52,* 1015–1019.

Helson, R. Women mathematicians and the creative personality. *Journal of Consulting and Clinical Psychology, 1971, 36*(2), 210–220.

Hendel, D. D. *The math anxiety program: Its genesis and evaluation in continuing education for women.* Unpublished manuscript, University of Minnesota, 1977.

Hill, J. P. Similiarity and accordance between parents and sons in attitudes toward mathematics, *Child Development, 1967, 38,* 777–791.

Hilton, T. L., & Berglund, G. W. Sex differences in mathematics achievement: A longitudinal study. *Journal of Educational Research, 1974, 67,* 231–237.

Holland, J. L. A personality inventory employing occupational titles. *Journal of Applied Psychology, 1958, 42,* 336–342.

Horner, M. The motive to avoid success and changing aspirations of college women. In J. Bardwick (Ed.), *Readings in the psychology of women,* New York: Harper & Row, 1972.

Humphreys, S. *Conference evaluation: Women moving up.* Berkeley, CA.: University of California Press, 1979.

Hunkler, R. F. Achievement of sixth-grade pupils in modern mathematics as related to their teacher's mathematics preparation (Doctoral dissertation, Texas A & M University, 1968). *Dissertation Abstracts, 1968, 29,* 3897A.

Hurst, D. The relationship between certain teacher-related variables and student achievement in third grade arithmetic. (Doctoral dissertation, Oklahoma State University, 1967) *Dissertation Abstracts International, 28,* 4935A.

Husen, T. (Ed.) *International study of achievement in mathematics: A comparison of twelve countries.* Vol. I & II. New York: Wiley, 1967.

Jacobs, J. E. A comparison of the relationships between the level of acceptance of sex role stereotyping and achievement and attitudes towards mathematics of seventh and eleventh graders in a suburban metropolitan New York community (Doctoral dissertation, New York University, 1974). *Dissertation Abstracts International, 1974, 34,* 7585A (University Microfilms No. 74-12844).

Jones, M. A., & Gerard, F. *Foundations of social psychology.* New York: John Wiley, 1967.

Joreskog, K. G., Sorbom, D., & Magidson, J. (Eds.). *Advances in factor analysis and structural equation models.* Cambridge, MA.: ABT Books, 1979.

Kagan, J. Acquisition and significance of sex typing and sex-role identity. In M. L. Hoffman & L. Hoffman (Eds.), *Review of child development research.* New York: Russell Sage Foundation, 1964.

Kaminski, D. M., Erickson, E. L., Ross, M., & Bradfield, L. *Why females don't like mathematics: The effect of parental expectations.* Paper presented at the meeting of the American Sociological Association, New York, 1976.

Kantor, R. *Men and women of the corporation.* New York: Basic Books, 1977.

Keating, D. P. (Ed.) *Intellectual talent: Research and development.* Baltimore: Johns Hopkins University Press, 1976.

Kennedy, W. A., & Walsh, J. A factor analysis of mathematics giftedness. *Psychological Reports,* 1965, *17,* 115–119.

Komarovsky, M. Cultural contradictions and sex roles. *American Journal of Sociology,* 1946, *52*(3), 184–189.

Kreinberg, N. Personal communication, 1979.

Kreinberg, N. The equals program: Helping teachers to become researchers and problem solvers. *The Journal of Staff Development,* 1980, *1*(1), 19–30.

Krutetskii, V. A. *The psychology of mathematical abilities in school children.* Chicago: The University of Chicago Press, 1976.

Lambert, P. Mathematical ability and masculinity. *Arithmetic Teacher,* 1960, *7,* 19–21.

Lantz, A. E. *Programs for reentry women scientists.* New York: Praeger, 1980.

Lantz, A. E., Carlberg, C., & Eaton, V. *Women's choice of science as a career.* Denver: E.S.R. Associates, 1981.

Lantz, A. E., Elliot, L. A., & Fox, L. *Critical mass and social support for women choosing nontraditional careers.* Denver: Denver Research Institute, University of Denver, 1979.

Lantz, A. E., & Smith, G. P. *Determining the importance of factors influencing the election of mathematics courses.* Denver: University of Denver, 1979. Final report to the National Science Foundation on grant SED-78-17103.

Lantz, A. E., & Smith, G. P. Factors influencing the choice of nonrequired mathematics courses. *Journal of Educational Psychology,* 1981, *73,* 825–837.

Lantz, A. E., & West, A. S. *An impact analysis of sponsored programs to increase the participation of women in science related careers.* Denver: Denver Research Institute, University of Denver, 1977.

Lantz, A., West, A., & Elliot, L. A. *An impact analysis of sponsored projects to increase the participation of women in careers in science and technology.* Denver: Denver Research Institute, University of Denver, 1976.

Lavach, J. F., & Lanier, H. B. The motive to avoid success in 7th, 8th, 9th, and 10th grade high achieving girls. *Journal of Educational Research,* 1975, *68,* 216–218.

Levine, M. *Identification of reasons why qualified women do not pursue mathematical careers.* Washington, D.C.: National Science Foundation, August 1976.

Lim, H. *Geometry and the space factors.* Unpublished paper for the School Mathematics Study group, 1963.

Locksley, A., & Colten, M. E. Psychological androgyny: A case of mistaken identity? *Journal of Personality and Social Psychology,* 1979, *37,* 1017–1031.

Lohman, D. F. *Spatial ability: A review and reanalysis of the correlational literature.* (Technical Report No. 8). Palo Alto: Aptitude Research Project, School of Education, Stanford University, 1979.

Luchins, E. H. *Women mathematicians: A contemporary appraisal.* Paper presented at the meeting of the American Association for the Advancement of Science, Boston, February 1976.

Luchins, E. H., & Luchins, A. S. Women mathematicians: A contemporary appraisal. In L. H. Fox, L. Brody, & D. Tobin (Eds.), *Women and the mathematical mystique.* Baltimore: Johns Hopkins University Press, 1980.

Maccoby, E., & Jacklin, C. *The psychology of sex differences.* Palo Alto: Stanford University Press, 1974.

MacCorquodale, P. *Social influences on the participation of Mexican American women in science.* Unpublished manuscript, University of Arizona, 1980.

MacDonald, C. Personal communication, 1978.

Maines, D. *Role modeling processes and educational inequity for graduate and under-graduate students in mathematics.* Unpublished manuscript, Northwestern University, 1980.

Maines, D. R., Sugrue, N. M., & Hardesty, M. J. Social processes of sex differentiation in mathematics. Unpublished manuscript, Northwestern University, report on NIE-G-79-0114, 1981.

Mallow, J. A science anxiety program. *American Journal of Physics,* 1978, *41*(8), 862.

Manpower Comments, 17(7). September 1980.

Marshall, S. P. *Sex differences in solving story problems: A study of strategies and cognitive processes.* Final report on NIE-G-80-0095, University of California at Santa Barbara, December 1982.

Marshall, S. P. Sex differences in mathematical errors: An analysis of distractor choices. *Journal for Research in Mathematics Learning,* 1983, in press.

Matthews, E., & Tiedeman, D. Attitudes toward career and marriage in the development of life styles of young women. *Journal of Counseling Psychology,* 1964, *11*, 375–384.

McCarthy, J. L., & Wolfe, D. Doctorates granted to women and minority group members. *Science,* 1975, *189*, 856–859.

McGee, M. G. Human spatial abilities: Psychometric studies and environmental, genetic, hormonal and neurological influences. *Psychological Bulletin, 86,* 1979, 889–918.

Meece, J. L., Parsons, J. E., Kaczala, C., Goff, S. B., & Futterman, R. Sex differences in math achievement: Toward a model of academic choice. *Psychological Bulletin,* 1982, *91,* 324–348.

Mientka, W. Personal communication, 1980.

Morning, C., Mullins, R., & Penick, B. *Factors affecting the participation and performance of minorities in mathematics.* New York: Ford Foundation, 1980.

Mullis, I. V. S. *Educational achievement and sex discrimination.* Denver, CO: National Assessment of Educational Progress, 1975.

Myers, C. T. A note on spatial relations pretest and posttest. *Educatioonal and Psychological Measurement,* 1953, *13*, 596–600.

Nash, S. C. Sex role as a mediator of intellectual functioning. In M. A. Wittig & A. C. Petersen (Eds.), *Sex-related differences in cognitive functioning: Developmental issues.* New York: Academic Press, 1979.

National Academy of Sciences. *The role of applications in the undergraduate mathematics curriculum,* 1979.

National Assessment of Educational Progress. *The first national assessment of mathematics: An overview, 1972–1973 Assessment,* 1975.

National Assessment of Educational Progress. *Mathematical applications, 1977–78 Assessment,* 1979. (a)

National Assessment of Educational Progress. *Mathematical knowledge and skills: Selected results from the second assessment of mathematics,* August 1979. (b)

National Center for Education Statistics. *The condition of education: 1979 edition.* Washington, D.C.: U.S. Department of Health, Education, and Welfare.

National Center for Education Statistics. *High School and Beyond Survey,* 1980.

National Council of Teachers of Mathematics. *An agenda for action: Recommendations for school mathematics of the 1980's,* 1980.

National Institute of Education (NIE). *Grants for research on education and work.* Washington, D.C.: National Institute of Education, 1977.

National Research Council. *Ph.D's in business and industry: Survey of doctorate recipients.* Washington, D.C.: National Research Council, 1979.

National Science Foundation. *Science data book,* 1980.

National Science Foundation & the Department of Education. *Science and engineering education for the 1980's and beyond,* October 1980.

Nesselroade, J. R., & Baltes, P. B. Adolescent personality and historical change: 1970–1972. *Monographs of the Society for Research in Child Development,* 1974, *39.*

Newell, A., & Simon, H. A. *Human problem solving.* Englewood Cliffs, N.J.: Prentice-Hall, 1972.

Nolen, W. F., Archambault, F. X., & Green, J. F. *Teachers' mathematics attitudes as a mediator of students' attitudes and achievement.* Paper presented at the annual meeting of the American Educational Research Association, New York, April 1977.

Norris, F. R. Pupil achievement as a function of an inservice training program on mathematics concepts for sixth grade teachers (Doctoral dissertation, George Peabody College for Teachers, 1968). *Dissertation Abstracts International,* 1969, *30,* 1054A.

Orlich, D. C. Federal educational policy: The paradox of innovation and centralization. *Educational Researcher,* 1979, *8*(7).

Ory, J., & Helfrich, L. *A study of individual characteristics and career aspirations.* Paper presented at the annual meeting of the American Educational Research Association, San Francisco, April 1976.

Paige, J. M., & Simon, H. A. Cognitive processes in solving algebra word problems. In B. Kleinmuntz (Ed.), *Problem solving: Research, method and theory,* New York: John Wiley, 1966.

Pandey, T. N. *Sex-related differences in mathematics achievement.* Paper presented at the annual meeting of American Educational Research Association, 1980.

Parelius, A. P. Emerging sex-role attitudes, expectations, and strains among college women. *Journal of Marriage and the Family,* 1975, *37,* 146–153.

Parsons, J. E. *Self perceptions, task perceptions and academic choice: Origins and change.* Ann Arbor, MI: University of Michigan, 1980. (ERIC Document Reproduction Service No. 186 477)

Parsons, J. E., Adler, T. F., Futterman, R., Goff, S. B., Kaczala, C. M., Meece, J. L., & Midgley, C. Expectations, values and academic behaviors. In J. T. Spence (Ed.), *Perspectives on achievement and achievement motivation.* San Francisco: W. H. Freeman, 1983.

Parsons, J. E., Adler, T. F., & Kaczala, C. Socialization of achievement attitudes and beliefs: Parental influences. *Child Development,* 1982, *53,* 310–321.

Parsons, J. E., Futterman, R., Kaczala, C., & Meece, J. *Developmental shifts in expectancies and attributions for performance in mathematics.* Symposium presented at the meeting of the Society for Research in Child Development, San Francisco, March 1979.

Parsons, J. E., Heller, K., & Kaczala, C. *The effects of teachers' expectancies and attributions on students' expectancies for success in mathematics.* Paper presented at the annual meeting of the American Educational Research Association, San Francisco, 1979.

Parsons, J. E., Kaczala, C., & Meece, J. Socialization of achievement attitudes and beliefs: Classroom influences. *Child Development,* 1982, *53,* 322–339.

Pederson, D. M., Shihedling, M. M. & Johnson, D. L. Effects of sex of examiner and subject on children's quantitative test performance. In R. K. Unger and F. L. Denmark (Eds.), *Woman: Dependent or independent variable.* New York: Psychological Dimensions, 1975.

Perle, T. *Discriminating factors and sex differences in electing mathematics.* Unpublished doctoral dissertation, Stanford University, 1979.

Pines, S. A. *Procedures for predicting underachievement in mathematics among female college students.* Unpublished doctoral dissertation, Hofstra University, 1980.

Plank, E., & Plank, R. Emotional components in arithmetical learning as seen through autobiographies. *Psychoanalytical Studies of the Child*, 1954, *9*, 274–296.

Poffenberger, T. M., & Norton, D. A. Factors determining attitudes toward arithmetic and mathematics. *The Arithmetic Teacher*, 1956, 113–116.

Poffenberger, T. M., & Norton, D. A. Factors in the formation of attitudes toward mathematics. *Journal of Educational Research*, 1959, *52*, (5), 171–176.

Poiani, E. Personal communication, July 1980.

Prediger, D., McLure, G., & Noeth, R. *Promoting the exploration of personally relevant career options in science and technology*. Washington, D.C.: The National Science Foundation, October 1976.

Pulos, S., Kreinberg, N., & Stage, E. *Improving attitudes of young women in math: A successful classroom intervention*. Unpublished manuscript, Lawrence Hall of Science, University of California, Berkeley, CA., 1979.

Rennels, M. The effects of instructional methodology in art education upon achievement on spatial tasks by disadvantaged Negro youths. *Journal of Negro Education*, 1970, *39*(2), 116–123.

Richardson, F. C., & Suinn, R. M. The mathematics anxiety rating scale: Psychometric data. *Journal of Counseling Psychology*, 1972, *19*, 551–554.

Rigsby, L. C., & McDill, E. Adolescent peer influence processes: Conceptualization and measurement. *Social Science Research*, 1972, *1*, 305–321.

Robitaille, D. A comparison of boys' and girls' feelings of self-confidence in arithmetic computation. *Canadian Journal of Education*, 1977, *2*, 15–22.

Rogers, E. M., & Shoemaker, F. *Fluid communication of innovations: A cross-cultural approach*. New York: Free Press, 1971.

Rosenberg, B. G., & Sutton-Smith, B. The measurement of masculinity and femininity in children: An extension and revalidation. *Journal of Genetic Psychology*, 1964, *104*, 259–264.

Rosenthal, R., & Jacobson, L. *Pygmalion in the classroom*. New York: Holt, Rinehart and Winston, Inc., 1968.

Rosser, R. A. *Acquisition of spatial concepts in relation to age and sex*. Tucson: University of Arizona, 1980 (ERIC Document Reproduction Service No. ED 195 356).

Rossi, A. S. Barriers to the career choice of engineering, medicine or science among American women. In J. Mattfeld & C. Van Aken (Eds.), *Women and the scientific professions*. Cambridge, MA: MIT Press, 1965. (a)

Rossi, A. S. Women in science: Why so few? *Science*, 1965, *148*, 1196–1202. (b)

Sanders, B., Soares, M. P., & D'Aquila, J. M. The sex difference on one test of spatial visualization: A Nontrivial difference. *Child Development*, 1982, *53*, 1106–1110.

Safilios-Rothschild, C. *Sex role socialization and sex discrimination: A synthesis and critique of the literature*. Washington, D.C.: National Institute of Education, 1979.

Schaie, K. W. A general model for the study of developmental problems. *Psychological Bulletin*, 1965, *64*, 92–107.

Schlossberg, N., & Pietrofessa, J. Perspectives on counselors' bias: Implications for counselor education. *The Counseling Psychologist*, 1973, *4*(1), 44–45.

Schonberger, A. K. *The interrelationship of sex, visual spatial abilities, and mathematical problem solving ability in grade seven*. Unpublished doctoral dissertation, University of Wisconsin, 1976.

Scientific American. Mathematics in the modern world, 1964, *211*(3), 40–216.

Sears, P., & Feldman, D. Teacher interaction with boys and girls. *National Elementary Principal*, 1966, *46*(2), 45–48.

Sells, L. *High school mathematics as the critical filter in the job market.* Developing Opportunities for Minorities in Graduate Education, 47–39. Proceedings of the Conference on Minority Graduate Education at the University of California, Berkeley, May 1973.

Sells, L. *Fact sheet on women in higher education.* Unpublished manuscript, University of California, Berkeley, 1974.

Sells, L. Mathematics—A critical filter. *The Science Teacher,* 1978, *45,* 28–29.

Sells, L. The mathematics filter and the education of women and minorities. In L. H. Fox, L. Brody, & D. Tobin, (Eds.), *Women and the mathematical mystique.* Baltimore: Johns Hopkins University Press, 1980.

Sells, L. Personal communication, January 6, 1981.

Shaycoft, M. F. *The high school years: Growth in cognitive skills.* Palo Alto: American Institutes for Research, 1967.

Sherman, J. Effects of biological factors on sex-related differences in mathematics achievement. In:*Women and mathematics: Research perspectives for change.* Washington, D.C.: The National Institute of Education, 1977.

Sherman, J. Predicting mathematics performance in high school girls and boys. *Journal of Educational Psychology,* 1979, *79,* 242–249.

Sherman, J. Mathematics, spatial visualization and related factors: Changes in girls and boys, grades 8–11. *Journal of Educational Psychology,* 1980, *72*(4), 476–482. (a)

Sherman, J. *Women and mathematics. Prediction and change of behavior.* Madison, WI: Women's Research Institute of Wisconsin, Inc., 1980 (ERIC Document Reproduction Service No. ED 182 162). (b)

Sherman, J., & Fennema, E. The study of mathematics by high school girls and boys: Related variables. *American Educational Research Journal,* 1977, *14,* 159–168.

Silvern, L. E. Children's sex-role preferences: Stronger among girls than boys. *Sex Roles: A Journal of Research,* 1977, *3,* 159–171.

Simons, R. A. *Resolving math anxiety.* Unpublished manuscript, University of Wisconsin at Green Bay, 1979.

Smith, G. P. *On the decision to enroll in optional high school mathematics courses.* Unpublished doctoral dissertation, University of Denver, 1983.

Smith, I. *Spatial ability: Its educational and social significance.* San Diego: Robert Knapp, 1964.

Smith, W. *Science education in the affective domain: The effect of a self-awareness treatment on career choice of talented high school women.* Paper presented at the national convention of the National Association for Research in Science Teaching, San Francisco, April 1976.

Solano, C. H. *Teacher and pupil stereotypes of gifted boys and girls.* Paper presented at the meeting of the American Psychological Association, Washington, D.C., September 1976.

Spangler, E., Gorden, M., & Pipkin, R. *Token women: The effects of sex ratio on women's achievement in law school.* Paper presented at the Eastern Sociological Society Meeting, April 1978.

Spence, J. T., & Helmreich, R. The many faces of androgyny: A reply to Locksley and Colten. *Journal of Personality and Social Psychology,* 1979, *37,* 1032–1046.

Spence, J. T., Helmreich, R., & Stapp, J. The personal attributes questionnaire: A measure of sex-role stereotypes and masculinity-femininity. JSAS *Catalog of Selected Documents in Psychology,* 1974, *4,* 127.

Spence, J. T., Helmreich, R., & Stapp, J. Ratings of self and peers on sex-role attributes and their relation to self-esteem and conception of masculinity and femininity. *Journal of Personality and Social Psychology,* 1975, *32,* 29–39.

Stafford, R. E. Hereditary and environmental components of quantitative reasoning. *Review of Educational Research,* 1972, *42,* 183–201.

Stage, E. *Math/science network evaluation report.* Unpublished manuscript, Lawrence Hall of Science, University of California, Berkeley, CA, 1979.

Stallings, J. *Factors influencing women's decisions to enroll in advanced mathematics courses.* Menlo Park, CA: SRI International, 1979 (ERIC Document Reproduction Service No. ED 197 972).

Stallings, J. Personal communication, 1981.

Stanley, J. C., Keating, D. P., & Fox, L. H. (Eds.) *Mathematical talent: Discovery, description and development.* Baltimore: Johns Hopkins University Press, 1974.

Stein, A. H., & Smithells, T. Age and sex differences in children's sex role standards about achievement. *Developmental Psychology,* 1969, *1,* 252–259.

Stroup, K., & Jasnoski, M. *Do talented women fear math?* Unpublished manuscript, Emporia State University, 1979.

Suinn, R. M., Edie, C. A., Nicoletti, J., & Spinelli, P. R. The MARS, a measure of mathematics anxiety: Psychometric data. *Journal of Clinical Psychology,* 1972, *28,* 373–375.

Sullivan, A. M., & Skanes, G. R. Validity of student evaluations of teaching and the characteristics of successful instructors. *Journal of Educational Psychology,* 1974, *66,* 584–590.

Thomas, A., & Stewart, N. Counselor response to female clients with deviate and conforming career goals. *Journal of Counseling Psychology,* 1971, *18,* 352–357.

Tidball, M. E., & Kistiakowsky, V. Baccalaureate origins of American scientists and scholars. *Science,* 1976, *193,* 646–652.

Tobias, S. Math anxiety. *MS,* September 1976, 56–59; 80.

Tobias, S. *Overcoming math anxiety.* New York: Norton, 1978.

Tobias, S., & Donady, B. Counseling the math anxious. *Journal of National Association of Women Deans and Counselors,* Fall 1977, 13–16.

Tobias, S., & Melmed, E. C. (Eds.) *Paths to programs for interventions: Math anxiety, math avoidance and reentry mathematics.* Washington, D.C.: The Institute for Study of Anxiety in Learning, 1980.

Tobias, S., & Rosebaum, R. *Wesleyan math anxiety project.* Unpublished manuscript, Wesleyan University, 1978.

Tobias, S., & Weissbrod, C. Anxiety and mathematics: An update. *Harvard Educational Review,* 1980, *50*(1), 63–70.

Travers, R. M. W. (Ed.) *Second handbook of research on teaching.* Chicago: The Rand McNally College Publishing Co., 1973.

U.S. Department of Labor. *The earnings gap between women and men.* Washington, D.C.: U.S. Government Printing Office, 1976.

U.S. Department of Labor. *Employment and unemployment trends during 1977,* Bureau of Labor Statistics, 1977.

U.S. Office of Education. *Office of Education series of earned degrees conferred,* 1950–1976.

Vandenberg, S. G., & Kuse, A. R. Spatial ability: A critical review of the sex-linked major gene hypothesis. In M. Witting & A. Peterson (Eds.), *Sex-related differences in cognitive functioning: Developmental issues.* New York: Academic Press, 1979.

Veroff, J., McClelland, L., & Ruhland, D. Varieties of achievement motivation. In M. T. S. Mednick, S. S. Tangri, & L. W. Hoffman (Eds.), *Women and achievement.* New York: Wiley, 1975.

Very, P. S. Differential factor structures in mathematical ability. *Genetic Psychology Monographs,* 1967, *75,* 169–207.

Vetter, L., & Lewis, E. C. Some correlates of homemaking versus career preference among college home economics students. *Personnel and Guidance Journal,* 1964, *42*(6), 593–598.

Weiner, B. (Ed.) *Achievement motivation and attribution theory*. Morristown, N.J.: General Learning Press, 1974.

Weiner, B., & Kukla, A. An attributional analysis of achievement motivation. *Journal of Personality and Social Psychology*, 1970, *15*, 1–20.

Weiss, I., Place, C., & Conway, L. *The visiting women scientist pilot program*. Research Triangle Park, N.C.: Research Triangle Institute, 1978.

Werdelin, I. *The mathematical ability: Experimental and factorial studies*. Lund, Sweden: C. Wk. Gleevup, 1958.

Werdelin, I. *The geometrical ability and space factor analysis in boys and girls*. Lund, Sweden: University of Lund, 1961.

Wick, M. E. Study of the factors associated with success in first year college mathematics. *Mathematics Teacher*, 1975, *58*, 642–648.

Williams, D. A. Do males have a math gene? *Newsweek*, December 15, 1980, p. 73.

Williams, W. *Social policy research and analysis*. New York: Elsevier Press, 1975.

Williams, J. E., & Bennett, S. M. The definition of sex stereotypes via the adjective check list. *Sex Roles: A Journal of Research*, 1975, *1*, 327–337.

Wilson, J. W. Patterns of mathematics achievement in grade 11: Z population. *National longitudinal study of mathematical abilities*. Palo Alto, CA: Stanford University Press, 1972.

Wirtenberg, J. *Improving women's occupational potential: A review of the literature*. Washington, D.C.: Department of Health, Education, and Welfare, 1978.

Wise, L. L. *The fight against attrition in longitudinal research*. Paper presented at the Annual Meeting of the American Educational Research Association, 1977.

Wise, L. L. *The role of mathematics in women's career development*. Paper presented at the annual meeting of the American Psychological Association, August 1978.

Wise, L. L. Personal communication, 1981.

Wise, L. L., McLaughlin, D. H., & Steel, L. *The Project TALENT data bank handbook*. Palo Alto, CA: American Institutes for Research, 1979.

Wise, L., Steel, L., & MacDonald, C. *Origins and career consequences of sex differences in high school mathematics achievement*. Palo Alto, CA: American Institutes for Research, 1979 (ERIC Document Reproduction Service No. ED 180 846).

Wittig, M. A., & Petersen, A. C. (Eds.). *Sex-related differences in cognitive functioning: Developmental issues*. New York: Academic Press, 1979.

Women's Bureau. *1975 Handbook on Women Workers*. Washington, D.C.: U.S. Department of Labor, 1975.

Yin, R. *Cable television*. Santa Monica, CA: The Rand Corporation, 1973.

Author Index

Subject Index